Altered and Unfinished Lives

Eleonora Kimmel

Copyright 2006 by Eleonora Kimmel

All rights reserved.

No part of this book may be reproduced or transmitted in any form or by any means, electronic or mechanical, including photocopying or recording, or by any information storage and retrieval system, without written permission from the author and publisher. Requests and inquiries may be mailed to: American Federation of Astrologers, 6535 S. Rural Road, Tempe AZ 85283.

ISBN: 978-0-86690-568-8

First Printing: 2006

Cover Design: Jack Cipolla

Published by:
American Federation of Astrologers, Inc.
6535 S. Rural Road
Tempe AZ 85283.

Printed in the United States of America

Dedication

Dedicated to my children,
Manfred, Robert, Keith, Gerald and Karin,
for their guidance and love through all the years.

Acknowledgments

Writing this book has been an inevitable process through many steps of prescribed procedures resulting in a satisfactory completion. With each step of my research a continual addition of components based on tragic events from my own life have contributed a wealth of assistance in comprehending and articulating the experiences described within this book.

Numerous individuals contributed to this work: my family, friends, clients, public figures, newspapers and the Internet, all of which supplied birth data and critical information.

My special thanks go to Greg Reese of Boulder, Colorado, who so patiently edited my English and grammar without interfering or disturbing my original thoughts. Thank you again Greg for a job well done.

A special thank you to Kris Brandt Riske and Robert Cooper for their patience and suggestions.

Contents

Introduction	vii
The 90-Degree Circle	1
Midpoints	7
The 45-Degree Ephemeris	13
Abduction, Rape and Suicide	25
Mary Jo Kopechne	39
Bruno Hauptmann	45
Charles Stuart	51
Brandon	57
Wolfgang Amadeus Mozart	65
Robert	71
Ronald Goldman	79
John P.	85
Jayne Mansfield	89
Evelyn	95
JFK Jr.	99
Accidental Drowning	105
John Ritter	115
Highway Inferno	121
JonBenet Ramsey	137
Jimmy	143
Laci Peterson	149
Larry	155
Marilyn Monroe	159
Jet Crash	167
Nicole Simpson	175
Princess Diana	181
Natalie	187
Mario Lanza	191
Rachel Joy Scott	197
Bibliography	202
Anatomical Degrees	203

Introduction

Eleonora Kimmel is a unique and rare individual that speaks exact to the point making a point. She is an adventurous intuitive visionary, critical, confrontational and confident. Her noble nature and dignified aura give her a natural command of authority that welcomes the curious with good cheer and optimism that is quickly contagious.

Eleonora's astrological research is driven by an obsession and desire to know. It is with an unflinching passion that she delivers into the study of astrology in order to ferret out the hidden secrets to the cause of things. Eleonora has spent her life in finding the right answer and getting to know what is really going on, she is steeped in the classic delineation of planetary combinations inspired by Reinhold Ebertin. A true pioneer Eleonora sets out shouldering her way into awakening the forces of life that mold and shape every event. Throughout this book Eleonora assumes its readers are acquainted with astrology and Cosmobiology and the technique of using midpoints. This book is intended for the experienced astrologer, though it is perfect reference for all levels of experience. For example, Eleonora doesn't describe the retrograde phenomena though the course of delineation yet it is clear in that she notes the presence of retrograde as it occurs that she is paying attention and aware of it. It leads the reader an opportunity to recognize that retrograde presence is not arbitrary. Though she is deeply technical in her midpoint calculations, her work is stripped down to candid and accurate planetary definition. There is refreshing absence of house systems, psychological language, mythology or other bugaboo perspectives. Her work is brass tacks nuts and bolts astrology. There are no half-baked leaps, no stretching of orbs. No flights into fantasy as she looks reality in the eye. Most of the stories within this book tell of great hardship, grief and tragic ending. Through these circumstances of darkness we are brought to a threshold to feel, empathize and ponder life and happenstance. Our future is often determined by our own choices but sometimes there seems to be something larger than us directing our actions and activities. The written astrological symbolism in this book may have a subtle undercurrent effect upon its deader as the pages are lined with generous, crystalline and substantiated perceptions that access the unspoken and concealed. Each story of tragic "unreal" experience leaves us with a crystal clear lucid certainty of an indissoluble pact or karmic connection that can only assist us on our individual paths. Thank you, Eleonora Kimmel.

Greg Reese

The 90-Degree Circle

Everyone is familiar with the horoscope, which is the measuring device used to establish the degree positions of the zodiac, from which follows the placement of the various planets within the signs. Traditionally, horoscopes have been divided into one of several "house" systems, which offer further interpretations for the inquiring astrologer.

Cosmobiology does not recognize any house system because Reinhold Ebertin did not recognize the use of any house system. However, in the past 28 years of teaching, I have discovered that new students of cosmobiology are very reluctant to forego the houses. Since most astrologers have used at least one house system in their work and study, discontinuing active use of a house system will take time and discipline. My suggestion is to perform your own research and prove the validity of the houses to yourself.

Conversely, investigate interpretation without a house system and discover the power of planetary influence alone. Once you have seen for yourself the incredible validity and precision possible without the use of houses, it will be easier for you to abandon the use of houses.

In the past five years I have researched this by entering the degree of the house cusps in the 90-degree circle in order to observe the progressions and transits throughout the year and record the findings.

The cosmogram, composed of two circles, is the basic form used for interpretation in cosmobiology. One circle is the standard 360-degree circle for the regular planetary distribution; the other is the 90-degree circle.

Note: Accuracy in the calculation of all planetary positions will insure successful results as you proceed.

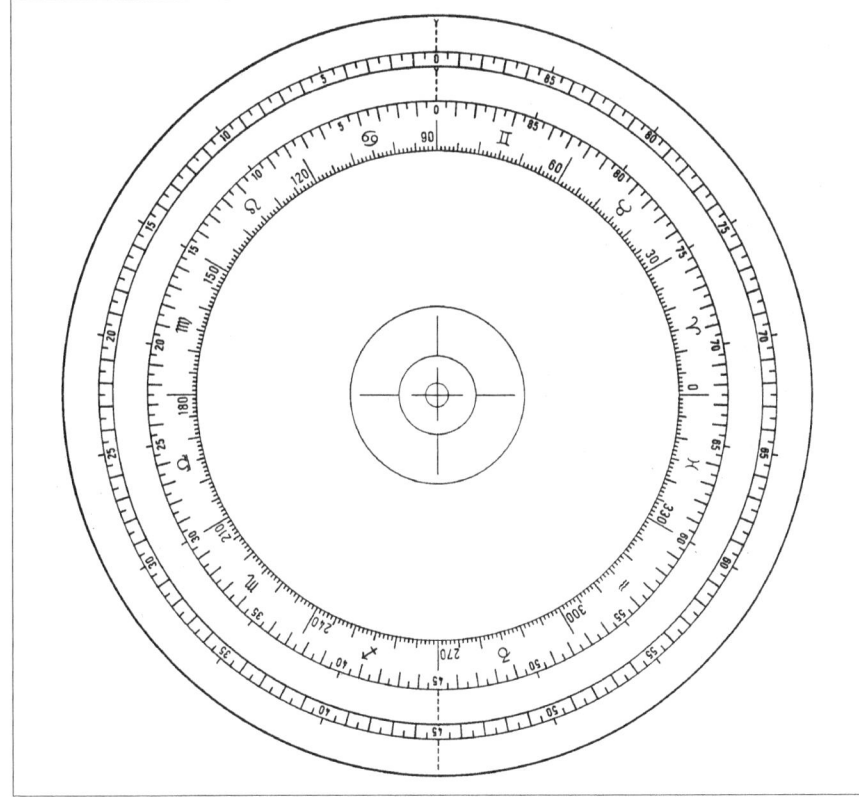

360-Degree Circle

1

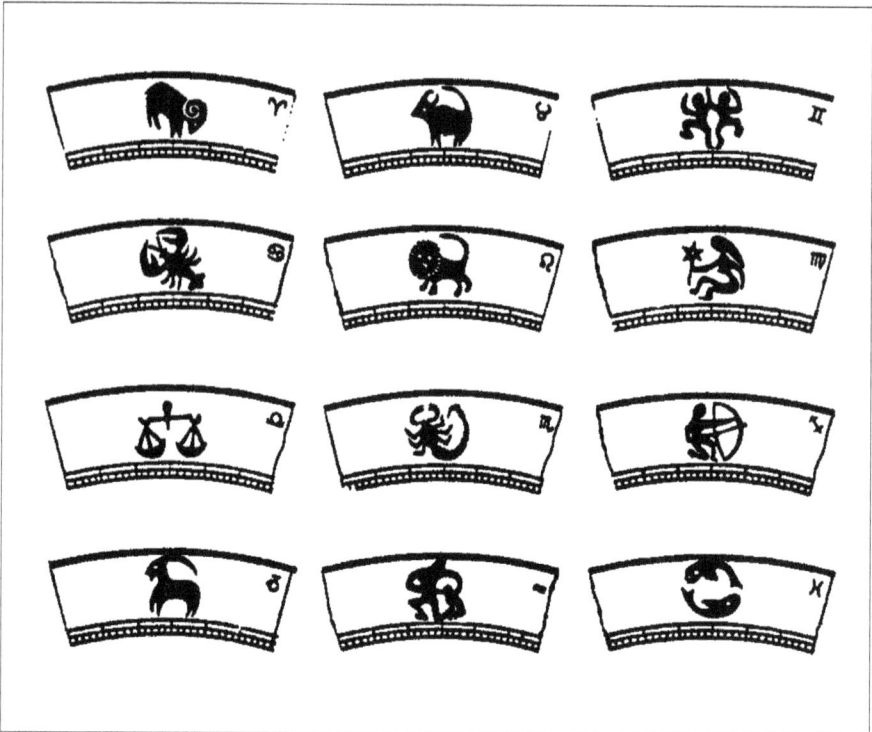
Cardinal, Fixed and Mutable Quqadruplicities

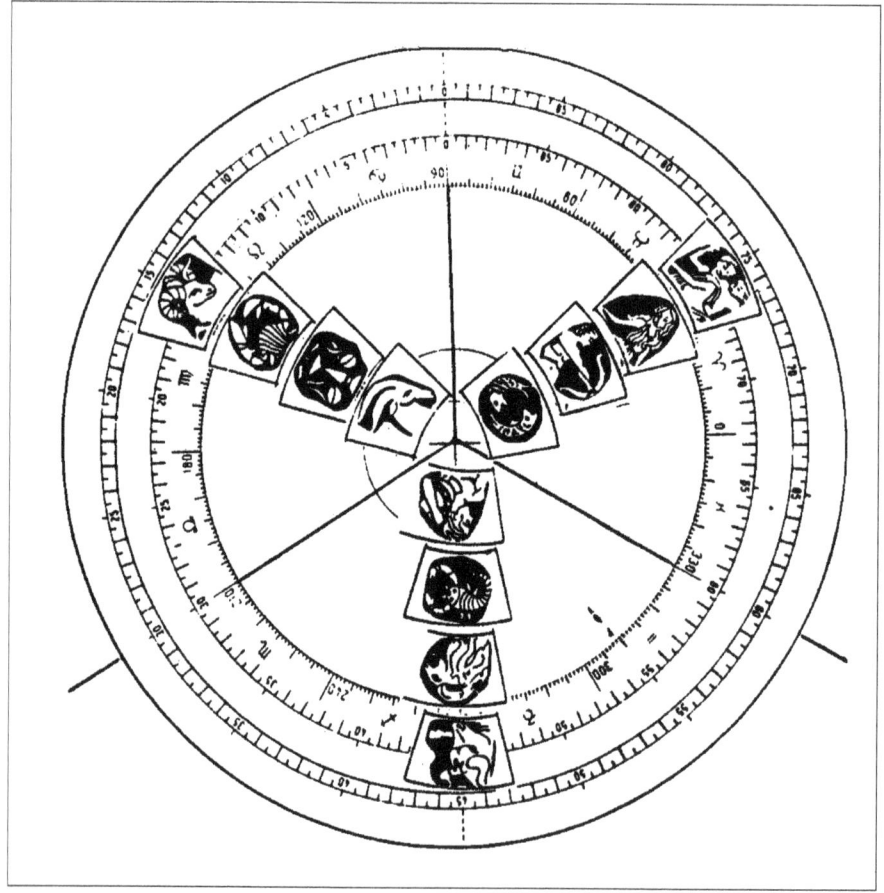
90-Degree Circle

The 360-degree circle is a recognized measuring device for investigation. To simplify the process we reduce the 360-degree circle to a fourth; i.e., the regular 360-degree has been quartered, divided in four equal parts, to provide a unique structure for discerning angular distribution of the planets. As a result, the members of the cardinal, fixed and mutable quadruplicities are grouped together with each quadruplicity occupying 30 degrees of the 90-degree circle. Not only is this method of organization more convenient, but also it makes possible interpretations, which are unprecedented.

Prior to constructing a cosmogram one must have a chart of the location of the planets. This can be derived from standard chart erection methods, so it is suggested that the student construct a horoscope as he is accustomed to, then transcribe the planets to the cosmogram in their proper places. This method will prove very helpful in making the transition from traditional astrology to cosmobiology.

Cosmobiology uses much smaller orbs to ascertain aspects than those used in standard methods. A traditional table of aspects will be of value later on. The following orbs have been adopted for use in cosmobiology, the 90-degree circle.

- Between personal points (Sun, Moon, MC,

Ascendant)—an orb of 5 degrees on each side
- Between fast moving planets (Mercury, Venus, Mars)—an orb of 4 degrees on each side
- Between slower moving planets (Jupiter, Saturn, Uranus, Neptune, Pluto)—an orb of 3 degrees on each side

The *inner* circle of the cosmogram is for placements of planetary positions as would be found in a traditional horoscope; however, since we are not using any type of house system, the Ascendant (ASC) and Midheaven (MC) positions will not be located in the usual places. The ASC and MC are treated in the same fashion as a planet and are placed according to sign position.

Cosmobiology gives attention to the Moon's Node (Dragon's Head) in interpretations; its accurate calculation is therefore essential. In the 90-degree circle there is no distinction between the North and South Node, as they are posited in the same place. In the 90-degree circle oppositions are conjunct.

The *outer* circle of the cosmogram consists of 90 degrees and is also for the placement of the planets, but they must be distributed according to their own position within the quadruplicities.

The 90-degree (outer) circle begins with 0 degrees (located at the top of the chart) and ends at the same spot with 90 degrees. Each 30-degree sector of the 90-degree circle is occupied by one of the three quadruplicities and will contain only those stellar bodies which correspond to the zodiac signs of that particular quadruplicity. All planets are to be entered in a counterclockwise manner, beginning from point zero (0 degrees).

A boundary line between each 30-degree segment of the 90-degree circle will aid accuracy as one inserts each planet on the cosmogram. If the position of the Sun, for instance, were 15 Libra, one would locate the 15-degree mark in the cardinal sector of the cosmogram (0-30 degrees) and draw in the appropriate symbol. If the Moon were posited at 27 Scorpio, one would locate the 27-degree mark of the fixed sector of the cosmogram (30-60 degrees) or, when considering the whole circle, 57 degrees and draw in the appropriate symbol. If Venus is in 12 Virgo it will be entered at the 12-degree mark of the mutable sector of the cosmogram (60-90 degrees) or, when considering the whole circle, at 72 degrees.

All symbols should be entered vertical to the center of the circle so that when the sheet is turned the symbol will always be in an upright position. One should take care to be very precise, as great precision will greatly reduce errors and make the interpretative work easier.

Mercury, Venus, Jupiter, Saturn, Neptune and Pluto have a vertical line in their symbol that can be used directly to indicate the degree-mark on the cosmogram. The symbols of the Moon, Sun, Mars, Uranus, Node, ASC and MC can be written above a small mark. In this manner, all entries can be exact to a fourth of a degree.

To further illustrate the rules and procedures one must follow to set up a cosmogram, we will use a sample chart using only the positions of planets and proceed step by step to enter them in the 90-degree circle.

Beginning with the planets in cardinal signs, for instance, the Moon is at 10 Cancer 21, so it is placed at the 10-degree 21-minute mark of the cardinal sector (0-30 degrees) of the 90-degree circle. Mars at 15 Aries 07 is also in the cardinal sign and is placed in the cardinal sector of the 90-degree circle.

Next are the planets located in fixed signs. Venus at 0 Aquarius 18 will be placed at the 18-minute mark in the second 30-degree sector (30-60 degrees). Venus is followed by Pluto, which lies at 5 Leo 36. Locate the 5½-degree mark of the fixed sector (35½ degrees) and place the symbol for Pluto just after this mark. Next comes Saturn, which lies at 23 Taurus 36. Saturn will be placed at 53 degrees 36 minutes on the cosmogram. Uranus, in 27 Taurus 42 belongs at the 57-degree 42-minute mark and is the last of the planets in the fixed signs.

Planets belonging to the mutable quadruplicity are next and will all be placed in the third sector of the 90-degree circle (60-90 degrees). Mercury located at 5 Sagittarius 07 will be entered at the 65-degree 7-minute mark. The Sun, at 13 Sagittarius 47 will be entered at the 73-degree 47-minute mark. Jupiter at 16 Gemini 43 is also a mutable sign and will be placed at the 76-degree 43-minute mark. The Moon's North Node at 18 Virgo 12 will be placed at

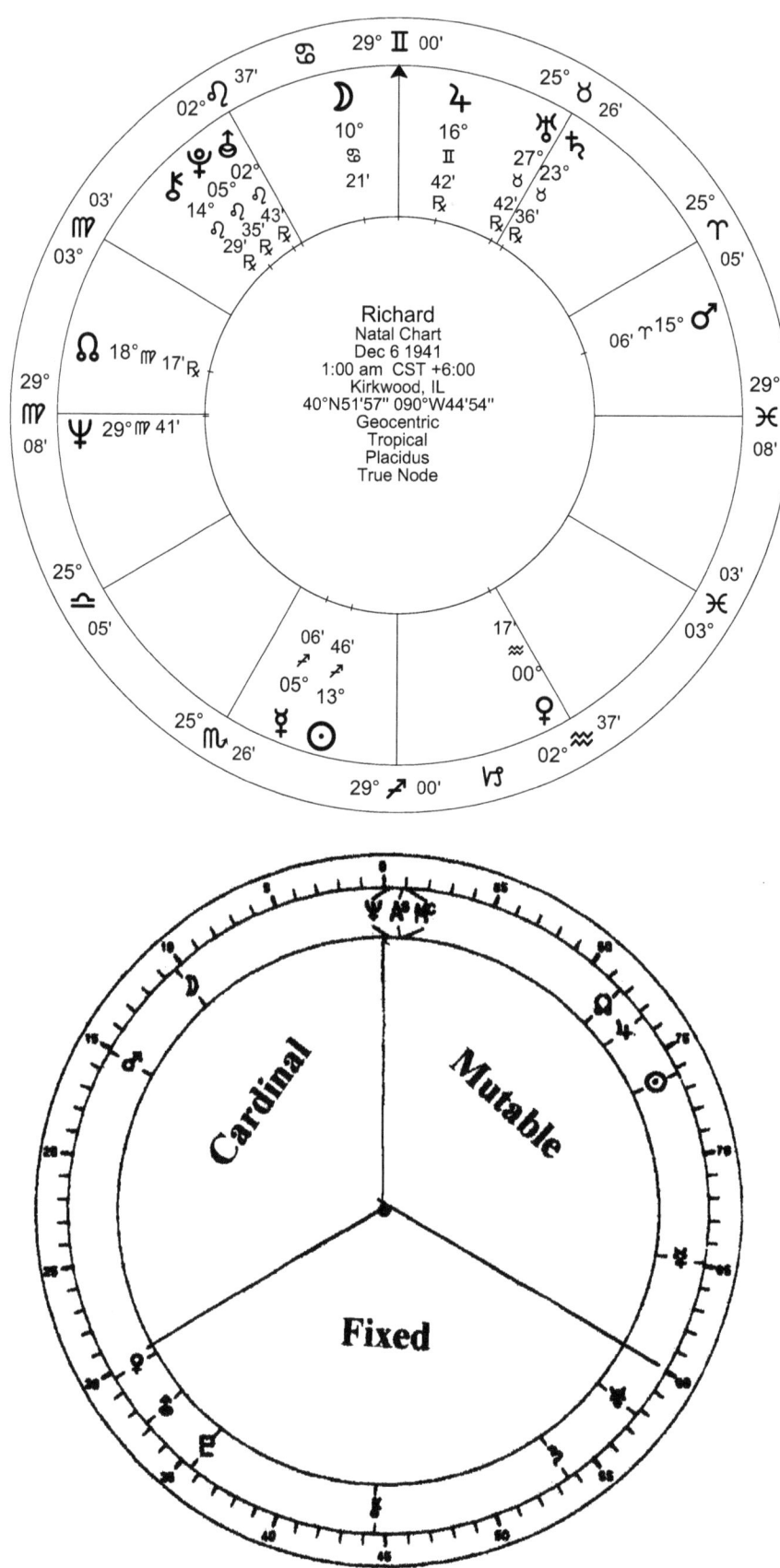

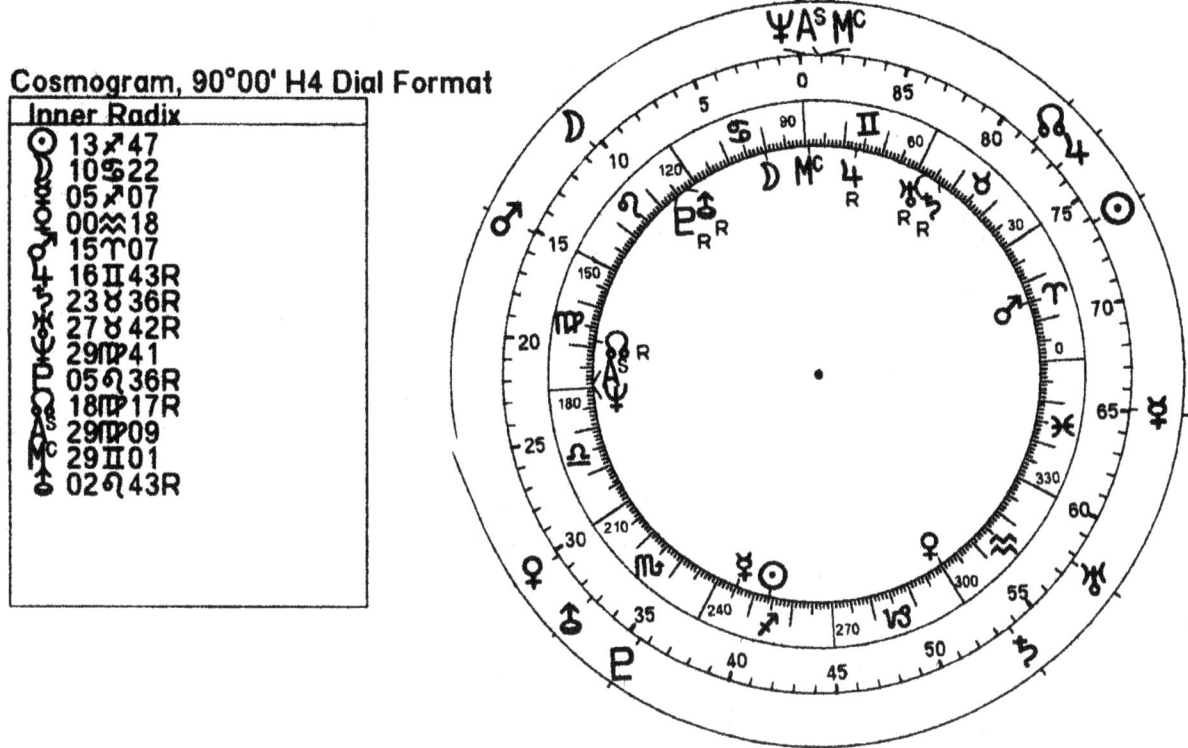

Richard's Cosmogram

the 78-degree 12-minute mark. There is no need to place the South Node because its position (18 Pisces 12) will fall at the same degree as the North Node. The ASC, MC and Neptune, whose positions are, respectively, 29 Virgo 09, 29 Gemini 01 and 29 Virgo 41—all in mutable signs—will be placed in the third sector of the 90-degree circle. Since all three planets are within one degree of each other, slanting the symbols slightly will aid accuracy. Care must be taken with "clusters" of planets like this to avoid errors.

After all the planets have been entered on the cosmogram, be sure to count them; there must always be thirteen. Double-checking for errors should precede advancing to the next phase, which is the calculation of midpoints.

Important: DO NOT ATTEMPT TO COMPARE THE PLANETARY POSITIONS IN THE 360-DEGREE CIRCLE WITH THE POSITIONS IN THE 90-DEGREE CIRCLE IN ANY WAY. THEY WILL NOT WORK TOGETHER. From this point on, the 360-degree circle will be used only for purposes of verification.

Note: In astrological manner of speech, the Sun and Moon are termed as luminaries. For the purpose of semantics, however, they shall be referred to as planets.

Midpoints

Before discussing midpoints, a review of aspects in general will be helpful. According to Nicholas deVore's *Encyclopedia of Astrology*, aspects were long ago defined as: "Familiarities or Configurations. Certain angular relationships between the rays which reach the earth from two celestial bodies, or between one ray and a given point, such as: the horizon; the degree that was on the horizon at a given moment; the point on which an Eclipse or other celestial phenomenon occurred; the place of the Moon's Nodes; or the cusps of the houses, particularly the first and tenth, etc."

Much has been written about aspects and special aspect combinations in rare birth charts within the various house systems. Cosmobiology takes a drastic step and eliminates much tradition for more realistic and scientific views. Through years of teaching the author has observed that new students immediately form opinions about aspects (good or bad). They hang onto trine aspects for dear life, and build up a fear of squares and oppositions that is very difficult to eliminate. Too much emphasis has been placed on the *type* of aspect, instead of the *planets* which are involved in the aspect.

In cosmobiology, trines and other so-called "harmonious" aspects are classified as merely conditions in an individual's environment, and not as "good fortune" to be realized at some point in the future. Trine aspects are an inherent component of an individual's character, personality, and ego; they are not guarantees of certain glamour spots in one's life.

The square aspects, also present at birth, are, on the other hand, generally considered to be the misfortunes we must all confront as we live. It seems as though some astrologers have invented a "game" in which the winner has an abundance of trines and the loser has a quagmire of squares!

The square aspects represent the conditions which are seemingly thrust in our path as we live life. These conditions can be mapped and their severity calculated, but they are by no means instruments of fate or bad luck. In cosmobiology, the degree of difficulty presented by hard aspects is determined by the definitions of the planets involved; but the means by which the influences are manifested depends upon several factors, including the environment; genetic make-up; sociological-political conditions; and the reaction of the individual in a positive or negative manner.

So a square aspect is not intrinsically "bad"; it is only the reaction of the individual to the influence that causes so much turmoil in the interpretation. The continuing improvement of traditional methods has also led to this line of thinking, so it should not be difficult for the student to see how all angular relationships between the planets are interpreted. For those of you who severely question this proposition, think back and recall an obstacle in your life or a difficult situation or time and ask yourself whether it was the aspect alone that made it so.

The cosmogram (90-degree circle) does not technically allow trines, sextiles or semisextiles, and since research has shown that their meanings are not greatly valuable in interpreting a person's reaction to the planets they are not included in cosmobiological texts.

While many textbooks available to students of astrology emphasize the "type" of aspect, cosmobiology does not. For instance, in traditional astrology,

Mars square Uranus is "unfortunate," while Mars trine Uranus is "fortunate," etc. This type of classification can be misleading, because it disregards four important properties of aspects, which are taken into consideration in cosmobiology:

1. The combination of the unique characteristic of each planet involved.

2. The role a particular aspect plays in relation to the entire chart as a unit.

3. How the individual chooses to react in given circumstances (positively or negatively).

4. Environmental conditions.

The possible reaction is always more pertinent to a given case than whether there is a trine or square aspect involved. For instance, Jupiter square Saturn is usually considered negative. In analyzing the nature of the planets involved, Saturn stands for separation, restriction, etc. and Jupiter for luck and abundance. Together the planets (even though in a square aspect) could produce an influence indicating a lucky separation—and all of us have experienced these fortunate separations in our lives.

When considering the aspects in the 90-degree circle you will also notice that there are no angular relationships which are multiples of 30 degrees; i.e., there are only squares, semi-squares, sesquisquares, oppositions, and conjunctions—all multiples of 45 degrees.

When several planets are grouped together in the 90-degree circle, they will be oppositions, squares or conjunctions in the traditional chart.

When two planets are in opposition in the 90-degree circle, they are either 45 degrees or 135 degrees apart in the 360-degree horoscope. All of this has the effect of placing more interpretative emphasis on the 45-degree-divisible-aspects of an individual's chart. Although they have been neglected in the past, semi-squares and sesquisquares receive special significance. Reinhold Ebertin, however, did place emphasis on the 150-degree angle (quincunx), especially when two of these angles are tied with a sextile.

In cosmobiology, not only are the so-called "hard" aspects given more attention, but a unique angular/distance relationship between the planets is utilized. The relationship is commonly known as the *midpoint*.

The midpoint theory was founded centuries ago and has fluctuated from prominence to obscurity in its use by astrologers. Alfred Witte, the founder of the Hamburg School of Astrology, is credited with the introduction of the midpoint system to modern astrology. Midpoints became the object of intense research by Reinhold Ebertin and were later incorporated by him into a system which presently dominates the astrological world.

Although midpoints are the major tools of cosmobiological interpretations, they are not the exclusive property of cosmobiology. Uranian astrology uses a midpoint theory, but in conjunction with a system of hypothetical planets and houses which leaves its validity in a dubious position. Midpoints have been shown to make much of traditional interpretation vague and even obsolete.

The midpoint theory, as the name implies, in-

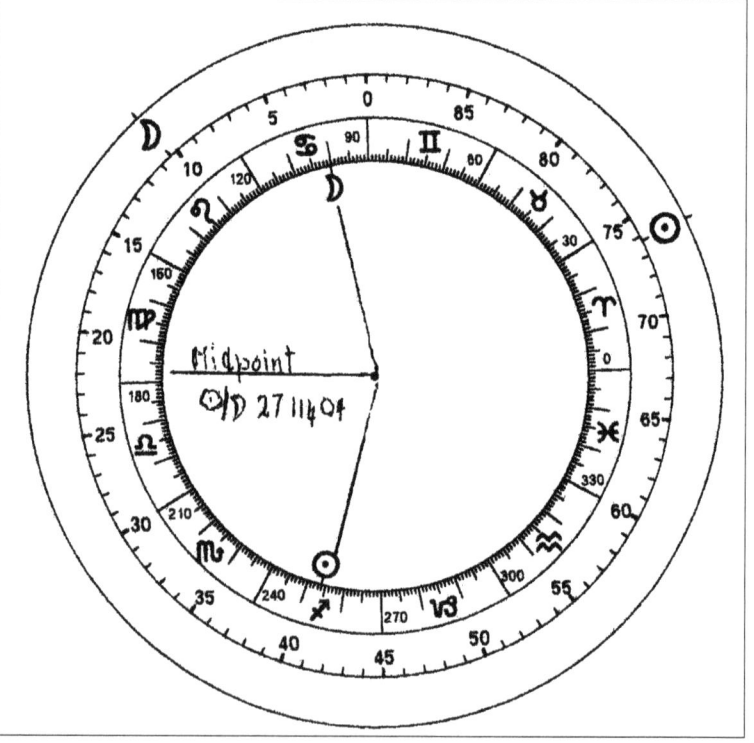

Midpoints

volves the zodiacal calculated halfway point between two planets. Midpoints are calculated using the standard mathematical midpoint formula, as follows:

1. Add together the distance (in degrees and minutes) of one planet (A) from 0 degrees Aries to the position of a second planet (B). The location (degrees and minutes) of the second planet (B) has been calculated in the same way as (A).

2. Divide the total sum by two. The resulting quotient is the midpoint (C) of the two planets in question (A and B above).

3. The formula for calculating the midpoint of two planets is: A+B divided by 2 = C. (A = degree and minute position of one planet, B = degree and minute position of a second planet. C = midpoint.

4. Example

Sun at 13 Sagittarius 47 = 253 deg. 47 min.
Moon at 10 Cancer 21 = 100 deg. 21 min.
Sum total of Sun and Moon = 353 deg 68 min.
Sum total of Sun and Moon divided by 2 = 177 deg. 04 min.

Converted into sign position, 177 degrees 4 minutes = 27 degrees 4 minutes Virgo. Therefore, the midpoint between the Sun and Moon in this example is located at 27 Virgo 04. The Sun/Moon midpoint is expressed as ☉/☽.

The natal midpoints are calculated from the position of the planets recorded at birth, and are activated when other planets "contact" them through transit or progression. Contact is made when a planet comes to the same degree as the midpoint. When this happens, an activation of the other planets involved occurs along the midpoint axis.

There are 78 natal midpoints. These are determined by using the 10 planets plus the Ascendant, MC and the Node for the calculations. These 78 midpoints are, so far, only points in the cosmogram with activating points on both ends: 27 Virgo 04 and 27 Pisces 04. Using both ends, there are a total of 156 activation points.

It will aid the student if he can picture a mobile and, using the previous example, place Jupiter at the top, with the Sun and Moon balanced on each side. If a planet contacts the same degree as Jupiter, the entire mobile of Jupiter-Sun/Moon will be activated.

The large number of activation (contact) points does not necessarily imply that each of the points in the total 156 will be activated at any given time. Although it is possible to have transit configurations involving all natal planet positions at the same time, it is usually not the case. It is rare to have more than a few midpoint axes activated at any one time by transiting planets.

Since the planets are fixed at birth it is impossible to have each one directly involved with another; therefore, we must make a distinction between the midpoint involved with a planet and a midpoint not involved with a planet.

Note: Many authors who, since the inception of cosmobiology in the U.S. in 1970, have written about midpoint axes calculate the short arc and the long (farther) arc. They insist that the shorter arc is more powerful then the longer arc, seemingly without any reference to any statistics or research. This is, in my opinion, purely theoretic because only if one has the same cases of events against shorter and longer arcs can one make a statement of the shorter or longer arc being more powerful. In 30 years of research and observation I have not found this to be the case.

A midpoint with an actual contact of a planet (that is, with a planet located at the midpoint), is a *direct* midpoint. In cosmobiology, a direct midpoint is an important configuration. For illustration purposes we shall calculate the midpoint between Moon and

Table of Permanent Value

Sign	Degrees	Sign	Degrees
Aries	0-30 = 0-30	Libra	0-30 = 180-210
Taurus	0-30 = 30-60	Scorpio	0-30 = 210-240
Gemini	0-30 = 60-90	Sagittarius	0-30 = 240-270
Cancer	0-30 = 90-120	Capricorn	0-30 = 270-300
Leo	0-30 = 120-150	Aquarius	0-30 = 300-330
Virgo	0-30 = 150-180	Pisces	0-30 = 330-360

Saturn. The Moon is located in 10 Cancer 21 and Saturn in 23 Taurus 36. We must now convert these positions to the distance from 0 Aries in order to derive a divisible value for our formula:

Moon 10 Cancer 21 = 100° 21'
Saturn 23 Taurus 36 = 53° 36'
Sum total: Moon + Saturn = 153° 57'
Sum divided by 2 = 76° 59'
(midpoint Moon/Saturn) = 76° 59'
Converted into sign = 16° ♊ 59'

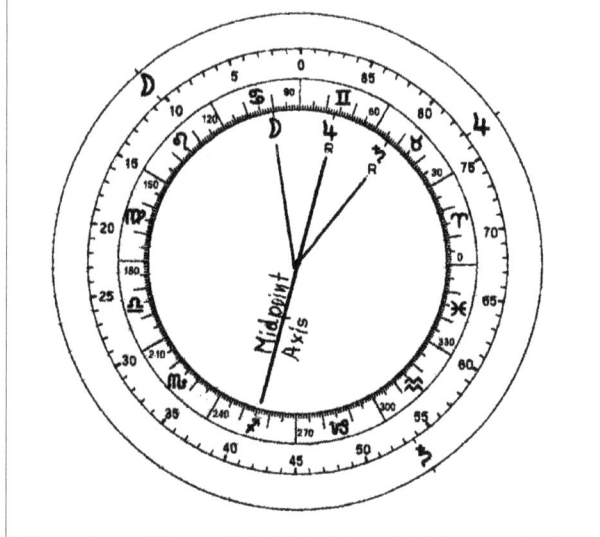

In the above example the midpoint is within 16' of exact orb of Jupiter at 16 Gemini 43. (Since Jupiter is in retrograde motion it would be a separating conjunction.)

The following illustration shows:

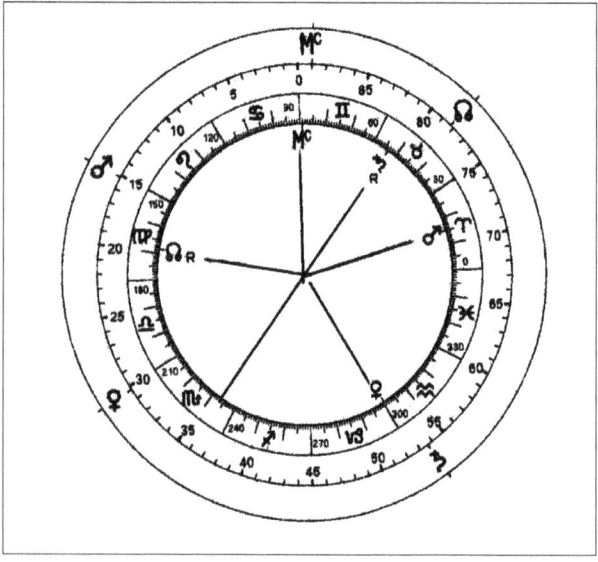

MC 29 ♊ 01 = 89° 01'
Mars 15 ♈ 07 = 15° 07'
Sum total = 104° 08'
Divided by 2 = 52° 04'
Converted into sign = ♂/MC 22 ♉ 04

Venus 0 ♒ 18 = 300° 18'
N. Node 18 ♍ 13 = 168° 13'
Sum total = 468° 31'
Divided by 2 = 234° 16'
Converted into sign = ♀/☊ 24 ♏ 16

Saturn at 23 Taurus 36 retrograde is making an applying conjunction with an orb of 1 degree 32 minutes to the midpoint of ♂/MC 22 ♉ 04, and to the ♀/☊ midpoint Saturn is forming an applying opposition to the midpoint with a 40 minute orb.

A midpoint without an actual contact of a planet (that is, with a planet making an aspect, square, semi-square, sesquisquare, to the midpoint location), is an *indirect midpoint*. The aspect made is a multiple of 45 degrees.

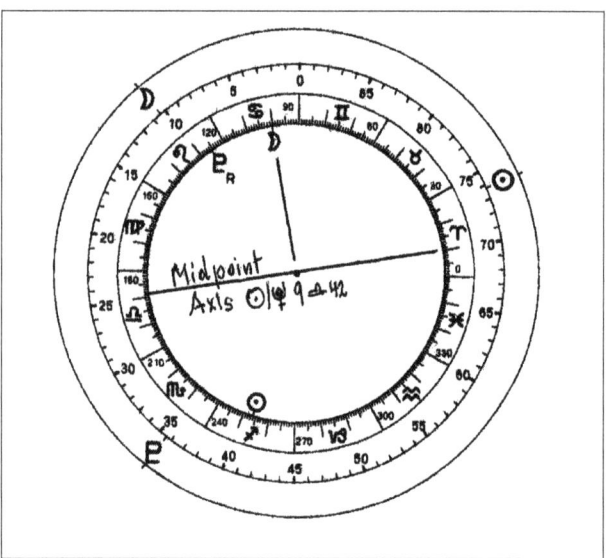

Sun 13 ♐ 47 = 253° 47'
Pluto 5 ♌ 36 = 125° 36'
Total sum = 378° 83'
Divided by 2 = 189° 42'
Converted: ☉/♇ 9 ♎ 42

The Moon at 10 Cancer 21 is forming a separating square to the midpoint of ☉/♇ in 9 Cancer 42 with a 39' orb.

An indirect midpoint is formed by a point (Moon) making an aspect based on a 45-degree angle (semi-square, square, sesquisquare) to the midpoint between two planets (Sun/Pluto) and is expressed as ☽-☉/♇.

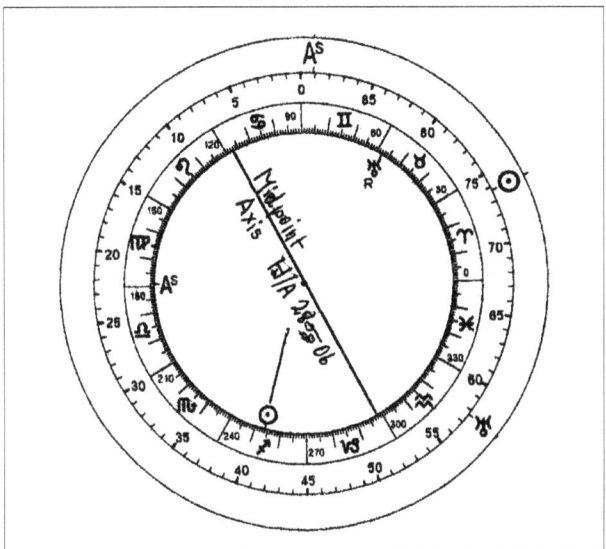

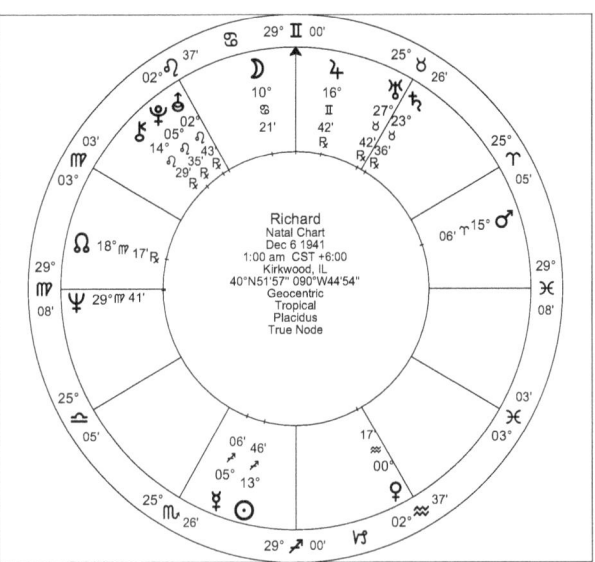

Uranus 27 ♉ 42 = 57° 42'
ASC 29 ♍ 09 = 179° 09'
Total Sum = 236° 51'
Divided by 2 = 118° 26'
Converted into sign ♅/A = 28 ♋ 26

The Sun in this example is making a separating inconjunct aspect (135 degrees) to the midpoint of ♅/A 28 ♋ 26.

Chart for Principle Subject

We know by experience that when planets are mapped on a 360-degree circle the planets are scattered in seemingly random fashion about the circle (chart). This everyday occurrence reduces the possibility of a large number of direct midpoints and consequently increases the number of indirect midpoints.

Direct midpoints are, of course, more powerful aspect relationships, but more often than not there are comparatively few to be considered.

The indirect midpoints therefore carry the bulk of a chart's interpretative value. The ability to judge the importance of particularly significant indirect midpoints and then combine them into a comprehensive cosmobiological pattern of midpoint structure is an art that will require much practice by the serious student.

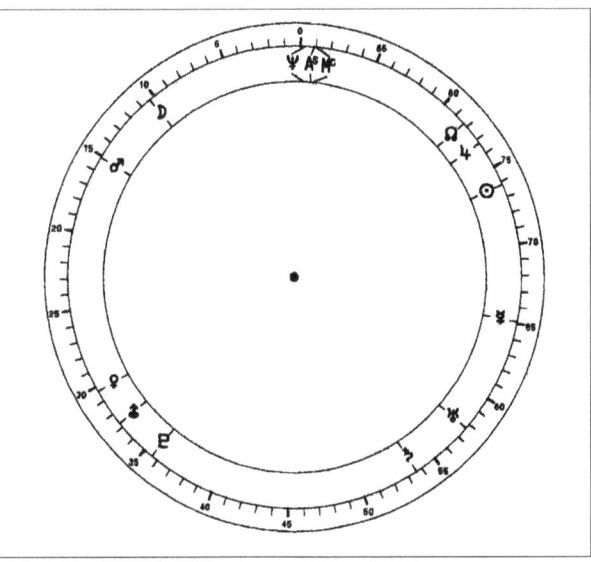

As the research of computer program software progressed big changes took place throughout the years.

The first sorting of midpoints was made by Burt Howe of San Francisco who conferred with me over the telephone to learn about cosmobiology. The first calculated charts with the sorted midpoints were introduced in 1971. This was indeed a blessing for struggling students to free them from the arduous task of calculating by hand. The early accidental death of Dr. Howe stifled his expansion of computer calculations for only a while, as Robert Hand and Neil F. Michelsen continued the research and expanded the computer programming beyond our wildest dreams. Now of course others all over the world have joined to continuously augment in the research.

Midpoints are now included in every software program, sorted by sign, degree, by planets and by cardinal, fixed and mutable sign position. They are also sorted in the 90 degrees, 45 degrees, 22.5 degrees and 11.25 degrees, which of course would be the 4th, 8th 16th and 32nd harmonic, and many more different divisions.

The most commonly used sorts are the 45-degree and 90-degree. In later demonstrations you will be introduced to how to apply the midpoints in delineating a chart. In addition, if you work with Asteroids, Vertex, Eastpoint and Transneptunian planets, be aware of the magnitute of midpoints to work with.

The 45-Degree Ephemeris

Since we now have a simple method to record celestial events with the cosmogram and the midpoint structure pattern we can begin to examine the most exciting of astrological events—the transits.

Transits are primarily responsible for the activation of the midpoint structures in cosmobiology. Traditional astrology also considers transits an important source of cosmic information.

In traditional methods, keeping in time with the important activating transits is an awkward chore which requires an ephemeris in tabular form and much patience with the many calculations involved.

Reinhold Ebertin developed a GRAPHIC EPHEMERIS on which the daily positions of the planets have been plotted on a graph. This technique not only immensely reduces the amount of time spent in calculations, but it makes possible a vivid picture of where a particular planet is (or will be) at a given time.

The graph designed by Reinhold Ebertin (the first attempts were made in 1963, and improved as time went on) describes *time* against the relative positions of the (vertically) planets, and *space,* (horizontally). The illustration on the next page shows the same graph generated by computer software.

Note: Mercury and Venus are not plotted in this graph.

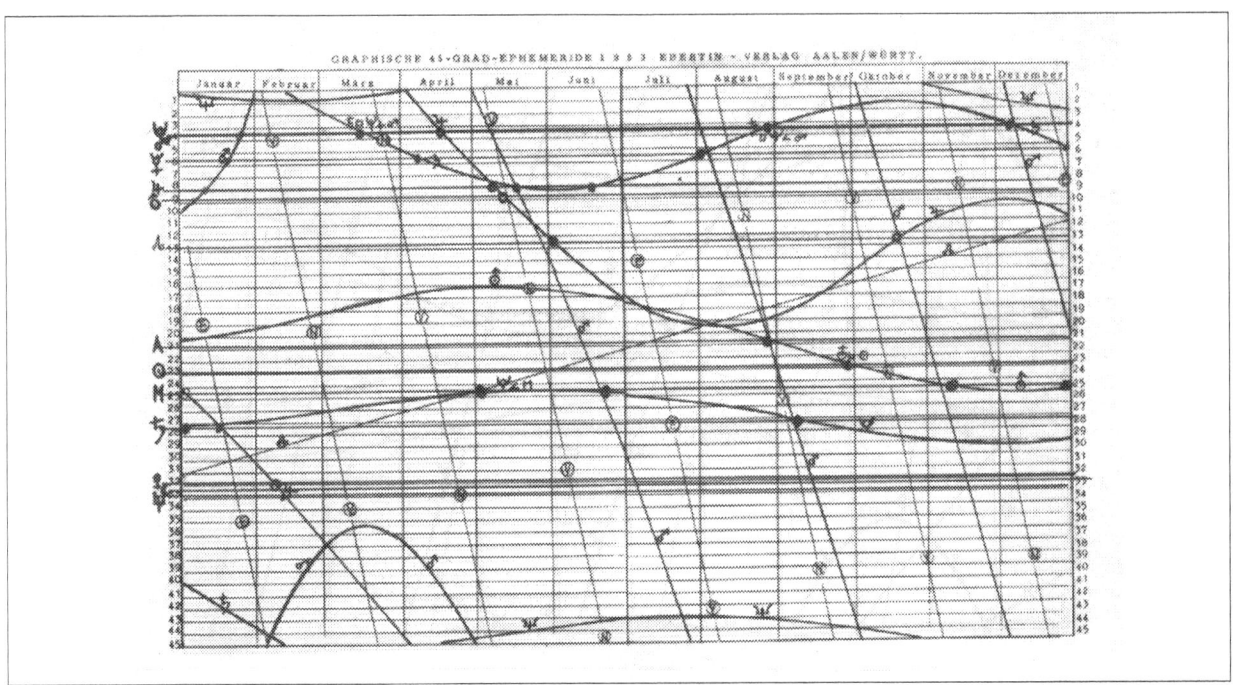

Graphic Ephemeris

13

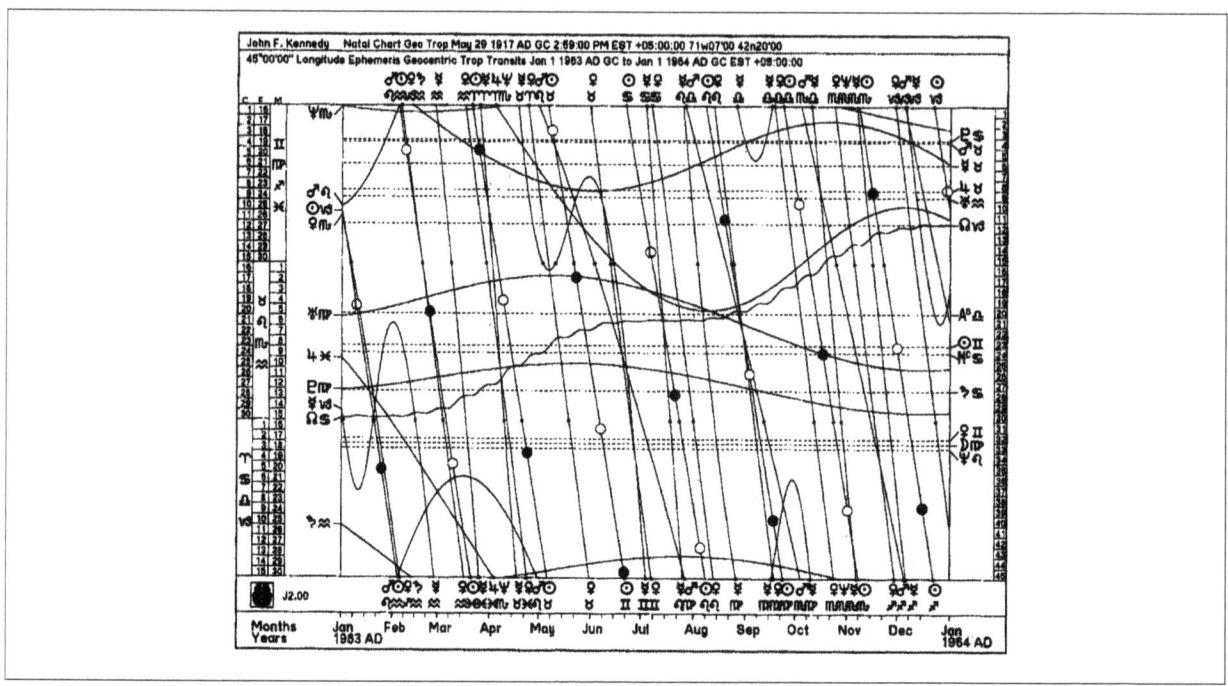

Computer-generated Graphic Ephemeris

The column on the extreme left-hand side of the page displays the linear expression of the 90-degree circle. This column, like the 90-degree circle, shows only those angular relationships between planets which are a multiple of 45 degrees, and eliminates the ambiguous trines and sextiles.

It might be easier for you to picture it in the following way, as illustrated in the diagram to the right: The left section of the form has three vertical columns. The far left represents the "C" (cardinal sign degrees). The middle "F" the degrees of the fixed signs, and the third column the "M" mutable signs. Each column represents 45 degrees. The far right side vertical column shows the degree marks from one to 45 to be of help when you draw in the lines for the planets.

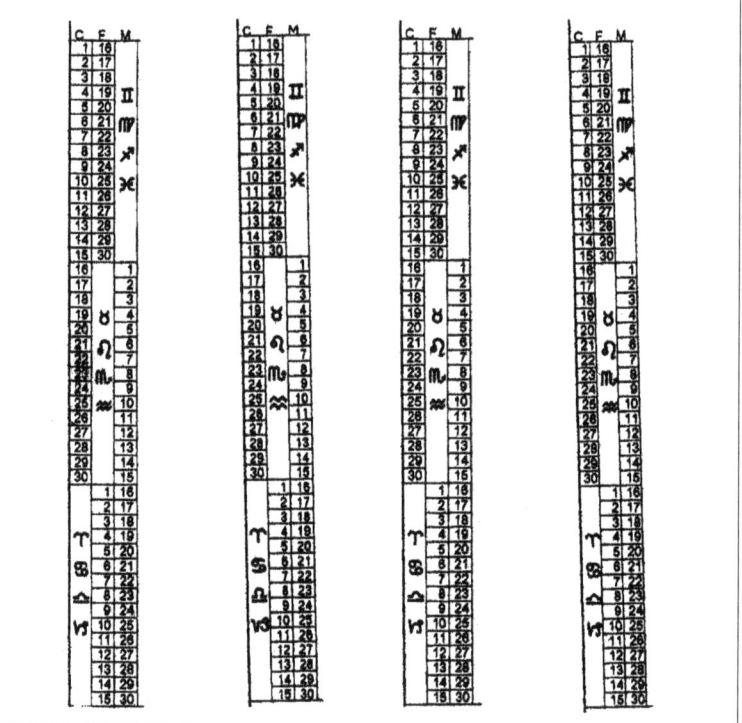

At first glance, the 45-degree ephemeris may seem to be a hopeless array of jumbled lines but after understanding what the lines represent the student will see that the graph is very simple. The lines curving or oscillating across the page represent the actual movement of the planets. When a planet changes signs during the course of its travel, this is noted by a small circle on the line representing the planet.

The faster planets (Mercury, Venus, Mars) are shown by diagonal lines running parallel from the top of the graph to the bottom.

International Nomenclature

German	English	French	Latin	Abbreviation
Sonne	*Sun*	*Soleil*	*Sol*	*SO*
Mond	Moon	Lune	Luna	MO
Merkur	Mercury	Mercure	Mercurius	ME
Venus	Venus	Venus	Venus	VE
Erde	Earth	Terre	Terra	TE
Mars	Mars	Mars	Mars	MA
Jupiter	Jupiter	Jupiter	Jupiter	JU
Saturn	Saturn	Saturne	Saturnus	SA
Uranus	Uranus	Uranus	Uranus	UR
Neptun	Neptune	Neptune	Neptunus	NE
Pluto	Pluto	Pluto	Pluto	PL
Drachenkopf	Dragon's Head	Tetede	Caput	DR
(Mondknoten)		Dragon	Oraconis	
Aszendent	Ascendant	Ascendant	Ascendium	AS
Deszendent	Descendant	Descendant	Oescendium	OE
Medium coeli	Medium coeli	Medium coeli	Medium coeli	MC
Irnum coeli	Imum coeli	Imum coeli	Imum coeli	IC
Widder	Aries	Belier	Aries	ar
Stier	Taurus	Taureau	Taurus	ta
Zwillinge	Gemeni	Gemeaux	Gemini	ge
Krebs	Cancer	Cancer	Cancer	ca
Löwe	Leo	Lion	Leo	le
Jungfrau	Virgo	Vierge	Virgo	vi
Waage	Libra	Balance	Libra	li
Skorpion	Scorpio	Scorpion	Scorpio	sc
Schutze	Sagittarius	Sagittaire	Sagittarius	sa
Steinbeck	Capricorn	Capricorne	Capriornus	cp
Wssermann	Aquarius	Verseau	Aquarius	aq
Fische	Pisces	Poissons	Pisces	pi
Transit	Transit	Transit	Transitus	t
transitiv	transitive	transitif		
Progression	Progression	Progression	Progressus	p
progressiv	progressive	progressif		
			Radix	r

The Moon is not shown on the graph because of its extremely fast movement (if the Moon were plotted on a yearly graph, the lines representing it would completely obscure the remaining planets). However the Full Moon is indicated on the Sun's line on the graph by an F enclosed in a circle. The New Moon is indicated by an N enclosed in a circle on the Sun's line. This is also explained on the bottom of the graph on the earlier issues. (A graph with the transiting Moon will be shown at a later chapter.)

Each of the planets is designated by a line marked with the appropriate symbol. The symbols used on these graphs and throughout cosmobiology are taken from the list of International Nomenclature devised by Reinhold Ebertin and his associates.

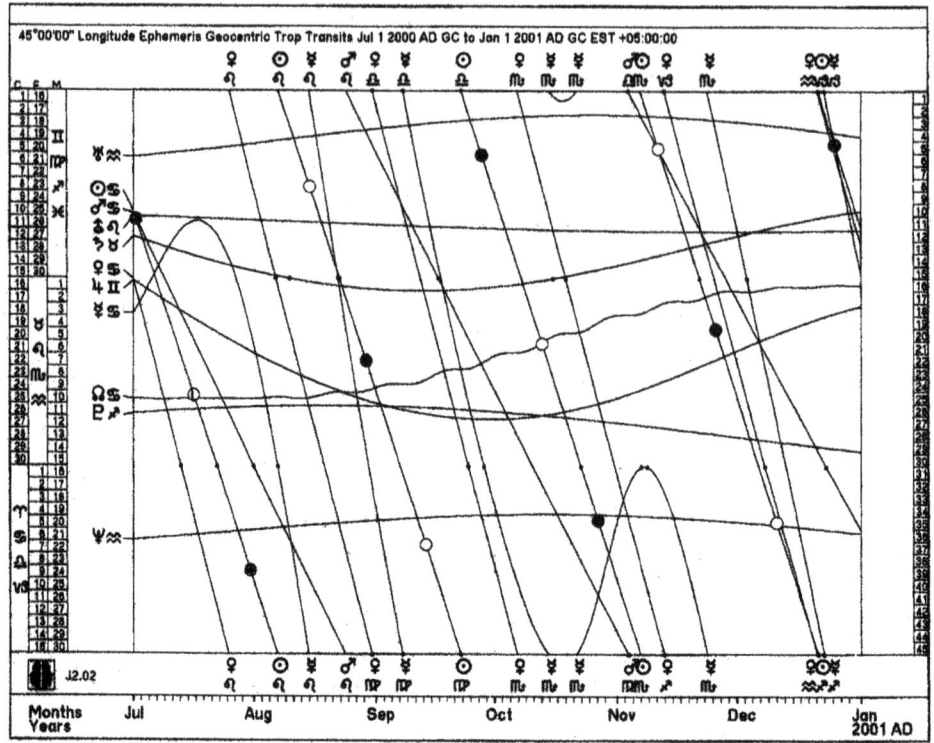

When a line runs off the page at the bottom, the same line will continue at the same place at the top of the page. The same applies to the planet lines running off the page at the top—the line will continue from the same place at the bottom of the page. It will be helpful to the student to use a regular ephemeris to check out the various planetary positions on the 45-degree ephemeris. This will increase the understanding of the 45-degree ephemeris and its construction.

The example on this page is calculated for the second half of the year 2000 for the Eastern Time Zone.

When a planet is in *direct motion,* its lines will always "move" toward the bottom of the graph. When a planet is in *retrograde motion,* its lines "move up," toward the top of the graph.

The Moon's Node is expressed by a wavering line always moving toward the top of the page.

Now that we have seen how the 45-degree rphemeris is constructed, we will proceed to learn how it works.

Since the natal planetary positions remain constant throughout the life of an individual, a line on the graph representing a natal planet cannot curve or oscillate. Therefore, all natal planetary positions are plotted as straight lines extending horizontally across the graph. The points of activation occur when a transiting planet contacts the line representing the natal planet. The points of contact can be circled in pen or pencil for a quick and easy reference.

The method for correctly placing an individual's planetary positions on the graph is similar to the method used for constructing the cosmogram. The planets are grouped according to which quadruplicity they belong. The three columns at the left of the graph represent each of the quadruplicities. Each column contains the signs of a particular quadruplicity, plus degree marks for positioning of the natal planets. In order to establish all the contacts possible for a given day, a line drawn vertically down the page at the proper date mark will serve as a visual guide for picking out the active transits.

IMPORTANT: The columns are to be read vertically. If a mistake resulting from improper use of the columns occurs it will radically change the position of a planet.

The following guides will assist the student in

placing natal planetary positions on the graph.

a. To enter a planet in a *cardinal sign,* locate the column on the graph which represents the cardinal quadruplicity.

b. Make a small mark at the degree position in the column corresponding to the degree position of the natal planet. (For counting the degrees, always use the line *under* the number.)

c. Make a similar small mark in the same degree in the column on the right-hand side of the graph.

d. Draw a straight line connecting the degree marks made in step in b and c above.

e. To enter a planet in a *fixed sign:* Locate the column in the graph which represents the fixed quadruplicity.

f. Proceed through steps b and c above in the same manner, locating the degree mark in the column designated for fixed signs.

g. To enter a planet in a *mutable sign.* follow the instructions given above for cardinal and fixed signs using the third column at the left side.

When all lines have been drawn in (using the 10 planets, ASC, MC and Node, the student will have the entire transit picture for one year on a single page!

More clarity will be realized if colored pens or pencils are used when drawing in the natal configurations. The use of the colored pens or pencils will also help the student make the transition from traditional astrology to cosmobiology more easily. (For example, for fixed signs, use red; for cardinal signs, use blue; and for mutable signs, use green.)

Examples of how to place the lines:

a. In the diagram on this page, line 1 indicates the placement of the Sun in degree of Aries, Libra, Cancer, or Capricorn (all cardinal signs). Line 1 could also indicate the position of the Sun at 16 Taurus, Leo, Scorpio, or Aquarius (all fixed signs).

b. Line 2 in our example case shows that the Moon could be at 5 degrees of any cardinal sign, or at 20 degrees of any fixed sign.

c. Line 3 indicates Mercury is at 15 degrees of any cardinal sign, or 0 degrees of any mutable sign (Gemini, Virgo, Sagittarius or Pisces).

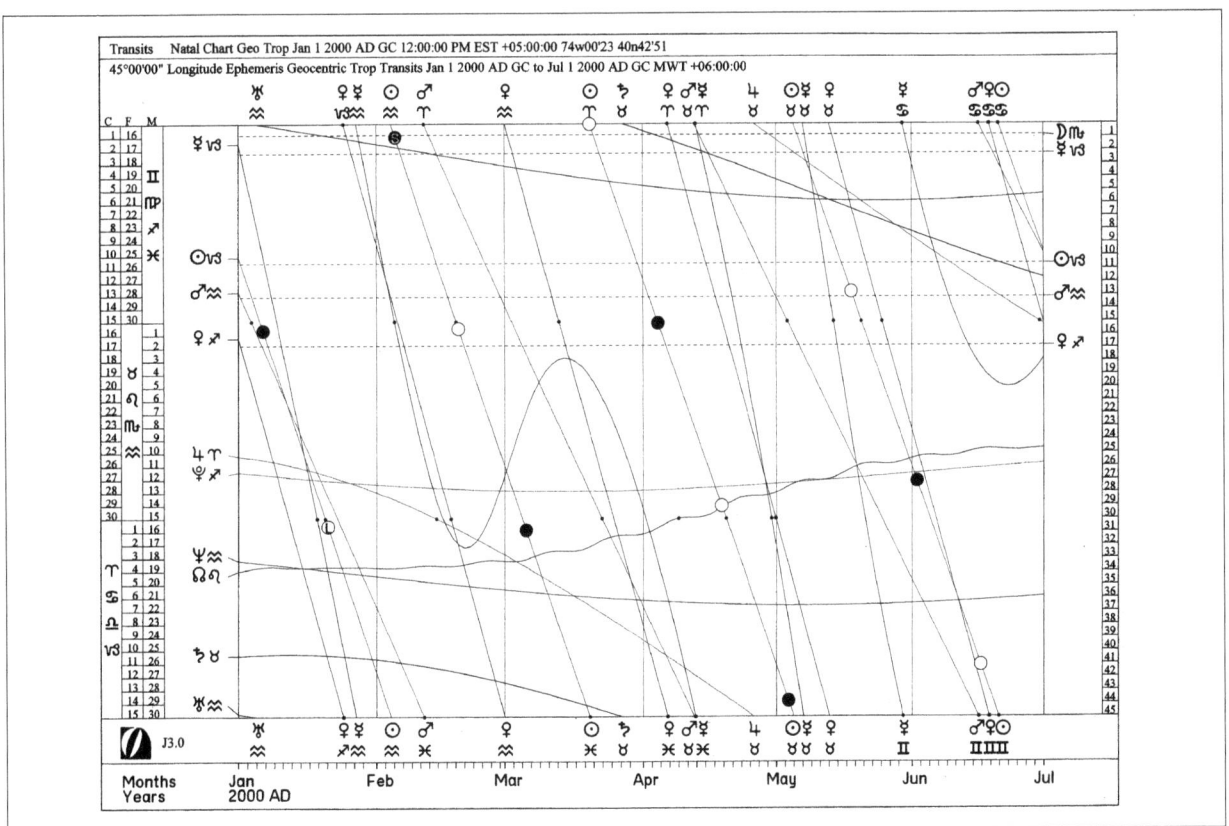

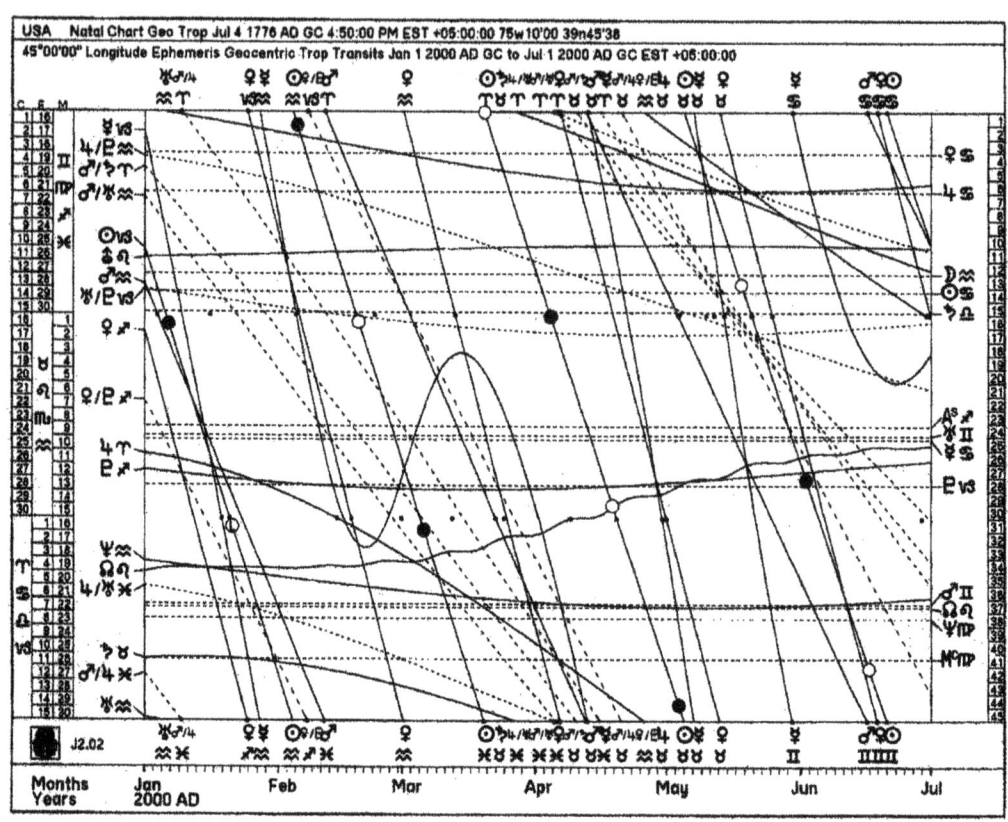

45-Degree Midpoint Ephemeris, January-June 2000

d. Line 4 indicates Venus could be 25 degrees of any cardinal sign, or 10 degrees of a mutable sign.

e. Line 5 indicates Mars is either at one degree of a fixed sign, or 16 degrees of a mutable sign.

f. To be complete, 13 lines must be entered on the graph (10 planets, plus ASC, MC and Node).

NOTE: If the student is concerned by not being able to discern (on the graph) which sign a given planet is in, the sign and degree may be written next to the symbol. However, it is strongly recommended that the graph be used with the least amount of cluttering possible.

The 45-Degree Midpoint Ephemeris

As the name implies, the midpoint ephemeris does not plot only the movement of the actual planets, but also the transiting midpoints. Not all possible midpoints are shown however, since here again the midpoints of the fast-moving planets would form so many lines that the rest of the planets would be obscured.

The application of the stellar influences here is transposed; that is, instead of the transiting planets touching off the natal midpoints, the transiting midpoints are activating the natal planets. The results of interpretation of these transits are astounding.

The midpoint ephemeris can, to say the least, provide the student with many more correspondences and much clearer and more detailed interpretations.

The 45-degree midpoint ephemeris is calculated for the first six months of the year 2000 Eastern Standard Time, with the natal components of the USA chart. In addition to the planets, seven midpoints are added by little lines as they travel. The slow-moving planets are immediately noticeable. Pluto emerges at almost 12 Sagittarius at the beginning of the year, moving forward very slowly to be at a stationary position clear through the middle of March when he turns retrograde and all that time in a 45-degree aspect to natal Pluto into the middle of May. For almost five months this force will linger on the whole structure of Pluto in the natal chart, meaning an intensifying of what Pluto stands for.

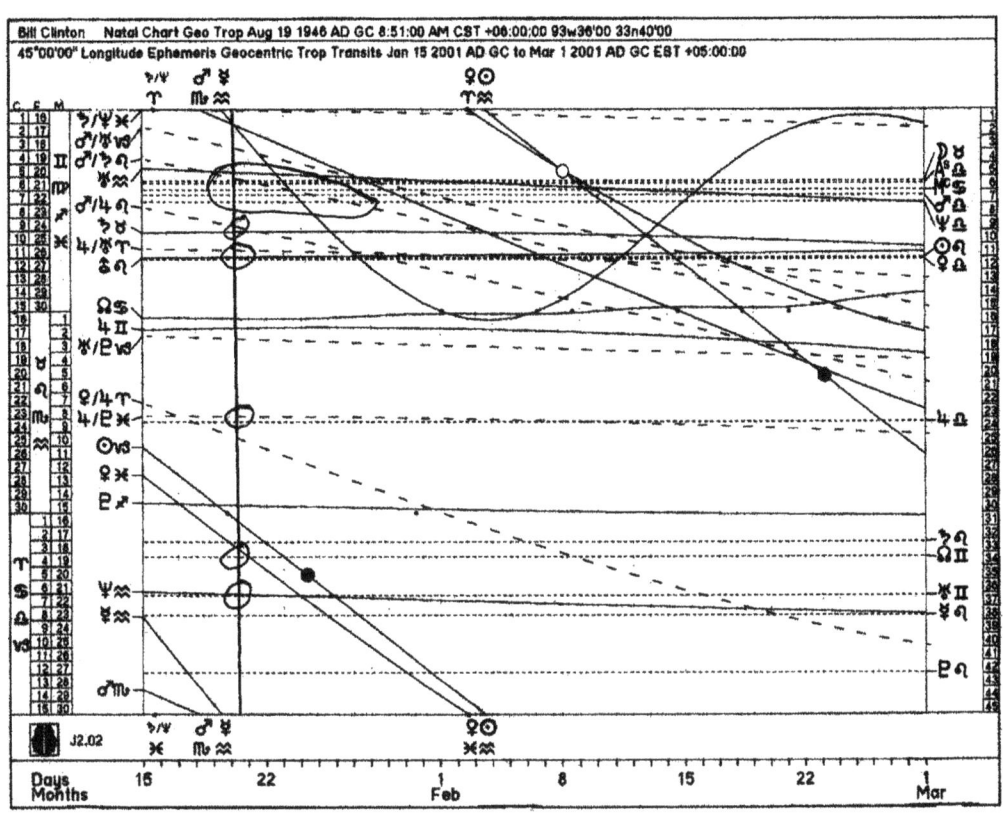

Bill Clinton, January 15-March 1, 2001

Jupiter emerges at approximately 25 degrees of a cardinal sign (Aries), connecting with natal and transit Pluto along with the faster moving planets (135 and 45 degree aspects) later in January. Both planets have an important impact for power just prior to the New Hampshire election, Jupiter does change into the sign of Taurus in mid-February.

Observe Neptune in Aquarius about three degrees at the beginning of the year, like Pluto, moving toward the stationary position on natal Mars and Node, lasting from the middle of March into early July. Quite remarkable will be the period culminating in late March and April as Uranus, Saturn, Jupiter, and four midpoints consecutively converge on natal Jupiter and Saturn. Notice that Uranus will be stationary for more then two months during the same time.

Another very interesting combination of planets is seen in the chart of Bill Clinton who left the presidency January 20, 2001. The 45-degree ephemeris is calculated for a six-week period, January 15 through March 1, 2001 EST.

Some of the most prominent contacts are: Uranus in about 19 Aquarius 30 square his Moon and sesquisquare his Ascendant, MC, Mars and Neptune: change of residence, occupation, activity, excitement, also notice the midpoint of Mars/Saturn passing over this cluster of planets. (Ebertin referred to this midpoint as the death axis). Mars/Jupiter, the "Thank the Lord" combination and Saturn in transit would mean a lucky separation. Transpluto and Jupiter/Uranus contacting his natal Sun and Venus perhaps indicates a great relief since the expression of "Lame Duck President" usually is applied to every president in his last year of office.

The 45-degree ephemeris on the next page is calculated for the month of November with the USA natal positions and the same midpoints. A vertical line is drawn for November 7, Election Day. There were indeed some interesting combinations present at that time. Note transiting Saturn at 29 Taurus 25 retrograde within five minutes of exact aspect (45 degrees) and the "Thank the Lord" midpoint in Aries close by. The Uranus/Pluto midpoint square to natal

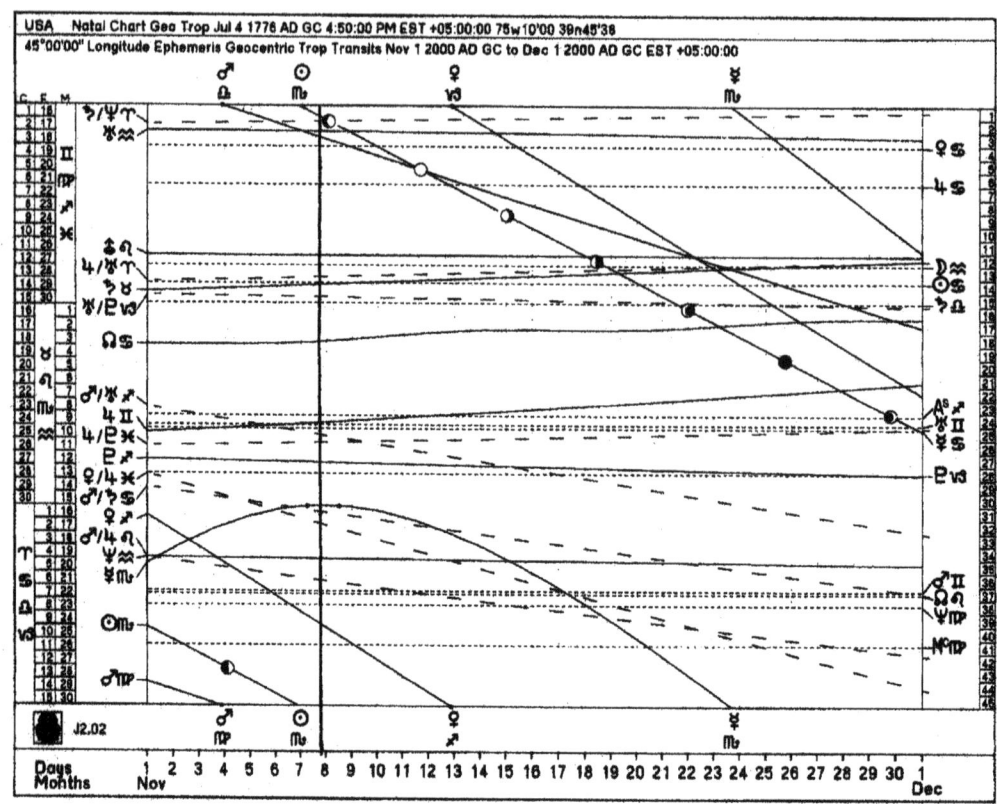

Election Day, November 7, 2000

Saturn became quite significant as the new administration unfolded. Mercury was stationary and resumed forward motion at 7:00 p.m. when the polls closed in the Eastern Time Zone. The Moon also was acting up in a void-of-course position changing into Aries at midnight.

The Transit Moon Graph

Late in the 1970s I was curious whether it would be possible to put the transiting Moon in a 45-degree form. I was able to put the planets on the graph so my research led me to experiment with the Moon since it is such an essential timing device. The secondary progressed Moon in projections indicates the month and, for the transiting Moon the hour.

Continuing with our case study of Richard we will illustrate the use of this form showing the Moon transits for the week of July 10-17, 1966. The procedure is the same as that used in the Life Diagram.

The transiting Moon on the graph is entered after the natal planets have been drawn in. At the same time this can be an aid in checking for correctness.

You need a regular ephemeris for 1966 *(Raphael's Ephemeris* for noon). Starting with the period in question, we find the transiting Moon on July 10, 1966 is at 13 Aries 17.

Note: The location in the ephemeris is for noon Greenwich Time, which is 5:00 a.m. Chicago Time (CDT). When using a midnight ephemeris, the appropriate conversion has to be made.

Since the motion of the Moon is approximately 12 degrees per day, allow two centimeters on the form for a 24-hour period; therefore have 20 millimeters available for the approximate 12 degrees the Moon transits in one day.

On July 11, the Moon is at 25 Aries 22; on the 12th at 7 Taurus 42. Connect these dots and continue in the same slant to the bottom of the page, which is 15 Taurus 00. Continue at the same place at the top (15 Taurus 00) and mark 20 Taurus 20 on July 13. On July 14 the Moon is at 3 Gemini 22; on the 15th at 16 Gemini 49; and on the 17th at 0 Cancer 44.

Identify which signs the Moon is in (on the

graph), and mark with a tiny circle the point at which the Moon changes into another sign. The vertical line drawn in between July 13 and 14 highlights the time in question.

The Moon in 29 Taurus 00 activated natal Mars (which in turn was also activated by powerful progressions). By tracing the movement of the Moon from 7:00 a.m. July 13 through 24 hours, you will notice that it contacted natal Saturn, Moon, Uranus and Mars within that period.

Not only can this form be used for transits, it can also be used for progressions. For instance the author used it for a period in life which was and perhaps will be very eventful showing monthly influences. The results were astounding! It is with transits of the Moon that we have "mind-blowing" revelations. You can observe the graph for a period of two and a half days (as long as it takes for the Moon to travel through one sign) and make note of the events that happen as the Moon transits over all the natal planets.

This whole procedure is not recommended for general practice since constructing the graph is very time consuming. However, for periods of time that seem important and/or to prove the accuracy of

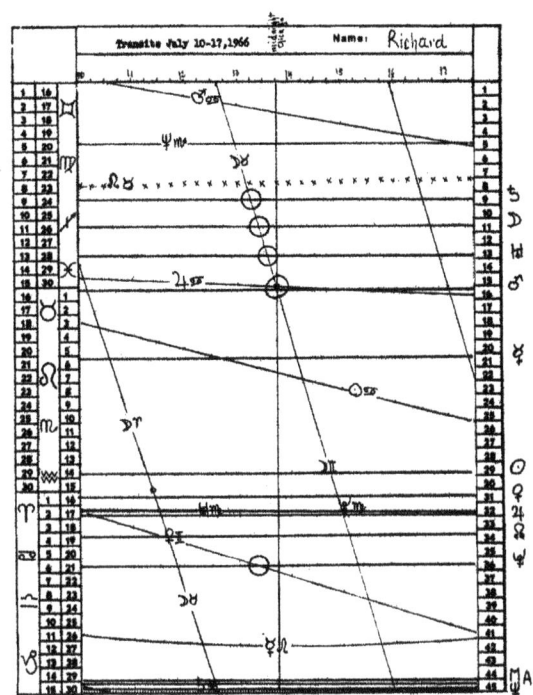

Richard's Transit Moon Graph

cosmobiology to yourself, the effort is worthwhile.

Below is the same graph, calculated for Chicago, July 10-17, 1966.

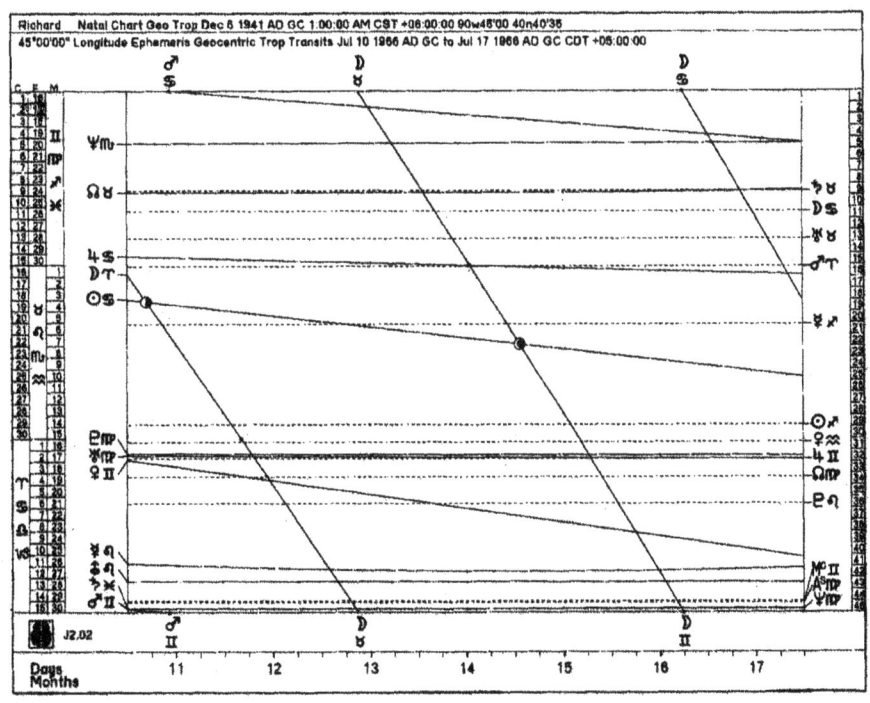

Richard, July 10-17, 1966, Chicago

21

Transit Ascendant and Midheaven

To produce a graph showing the moving Ascendant and MC before the evolution of software could not have been imagined. Of course the time span has to be shortened considerably. The best way to demonstrate this would be a graph for an actual scheduled future event to take place.

The graphs on the following two pages are for George W. Bush and Al Gore for November 7, 2000 EST from 6:00 p.m. to November 8 at midnight, and the day, of course is Election Day.

Keyword interpretations for the midpoints are:

♃/MC: Consciousness of aim

♃/♅: Lucky chance

♅/♀: Transformation

♃/♀: Desire for power

☽/♃: Happiness

♂/♄: Destructive energy

♂/♃: Success

ASC/MC: Here and now

Now you can enter the candidate's natal chart and observe how the planets and midpoints move forward throughout the day for every 15-minute time span. (The calibration is for 15 minutes each on the bottom of the page.)

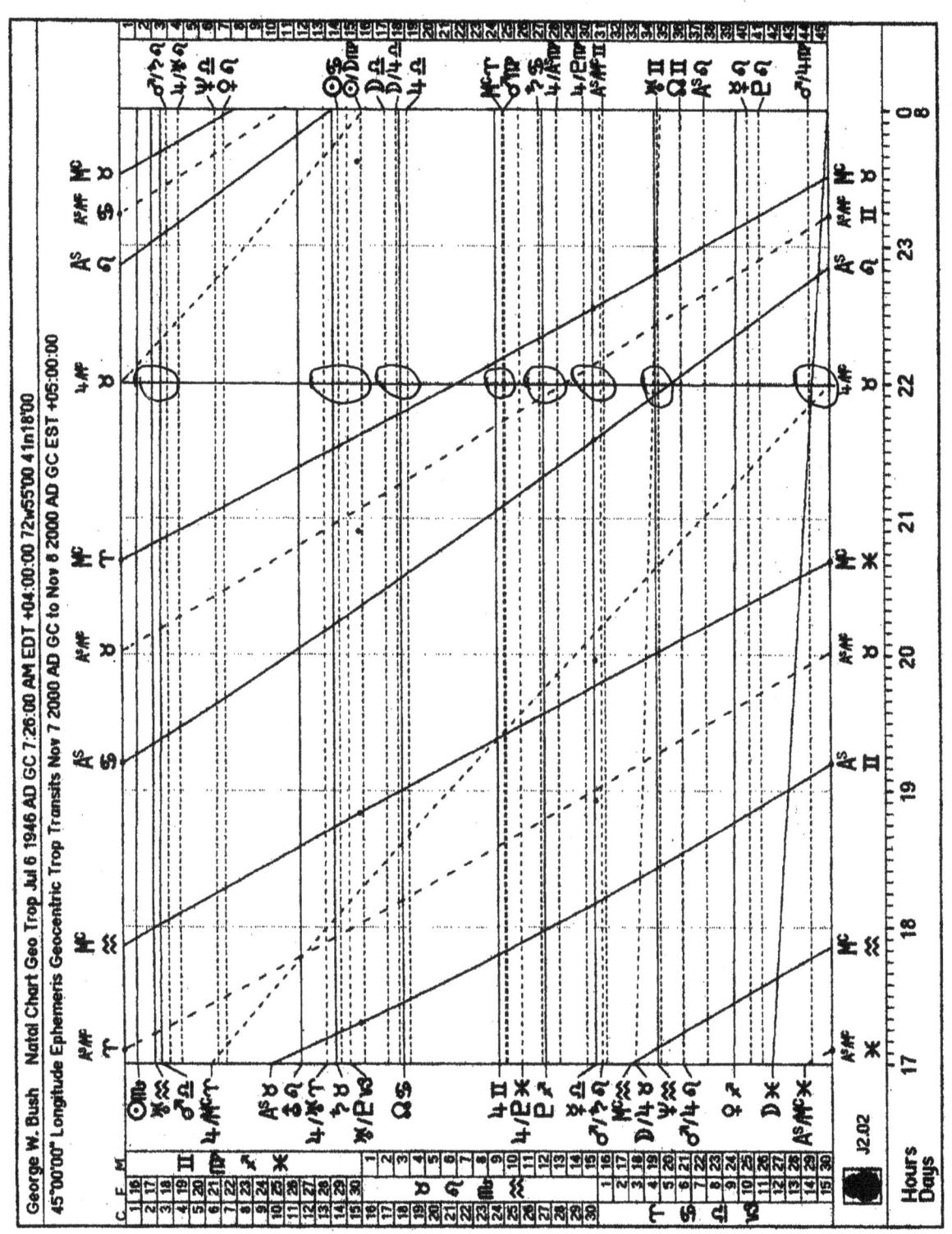

George W. Bush, Election Day

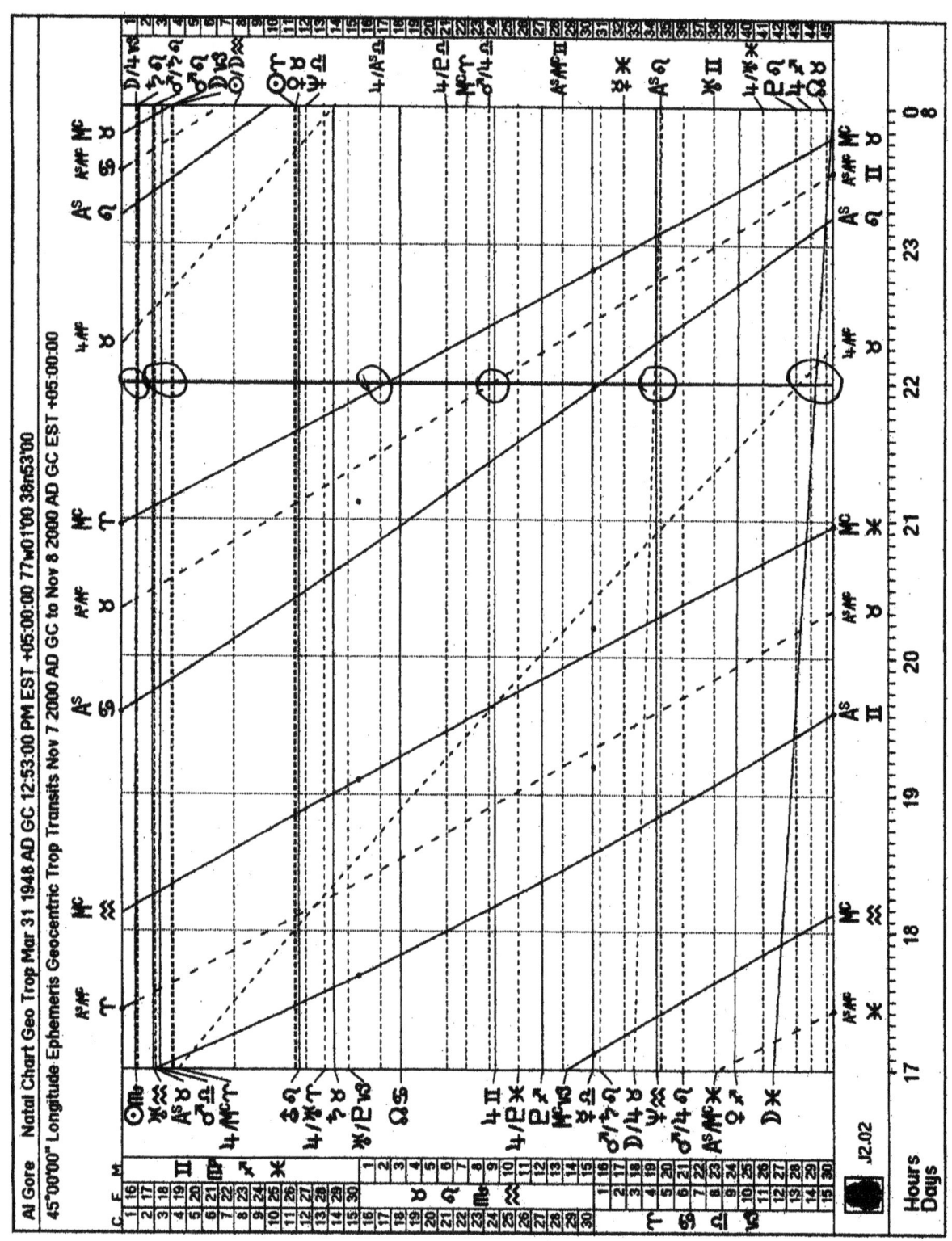

Al Gore, Election Day

Abduction, Rape and Suicide

In September 1973, Rebecca, age 18, and Amy, her 11-year-old sister, were abducted by two hoodlums who deliberately slashed a tire on Rebecca's car at a convenience store in Casper, Wyoming and then offered the girls a ride home.

However, the two men drove to a very remote area where the older girl was raped and savagely beaten and then both girls were thrown off a bridge into a very deep and narrow canyon.

Amy died instantly after hitting a rock near the riverbank. Rebecca's fall was interrupted when her hips slammed into a ledge and hurled her body further out into deeper water. With massive injuries and a broken body she managed to swim to land. Hiding half naked in the bushes until daylight, a passing motorist and his wife rescued her.

This ordeal became a nightmare for Rebecca. Suffering severe injuries, she spent many months recuperating. Rebecca coped with the death of her sister as well as her own rape. Whether she received professional help is not known but doubtful since a period of drug and alcohol abuse followed the recuperation period, providing only a temporary relief from her pain. As the years passed she overcame the alcohol and drug abuse and worked on straightening out her life.

The two criminals were eventually convicted and sent to prison.

Amy

The natal chart for Amy shows the possibility for attracting violence in her lifetime. The Sun at 24 Scorpio 08 and some of the attached midpoints point toward violence.

The Ascendant at 11 Capricorn 21 at the midpoint of Sun/Uranus represents upsetting experiences, sudden adjustments to new conditions, connections with accidents and catastrophes.

The prominent square of Mars at 2 Sagittarius and Uranus at 0 Virgo 22 and their structures show immense propensities of violence. Natal Saturn at 25 Capricorn at the midpoint of Moon/Pluto, ASC/MC indicates that Amy would be likely to attract emotional shocks or upheavals in her life that could inflict depression, emotional and mental suffering. Natal Mars/Saturn midpoint, generally present at time of death, is located at 28 Sagittarius 38.

Solar Arc

The solar arc for the abduction and death of Amy is 11 degrees, 58 minutes. Saturn at the Moon/Pluto axis at 7 Aquarius reached her natal MC at 7 Scorpio 51, Mercury at 8 Scorpio and Venus at 6 Scorpio 59 may indicate hindered growth and the necessity to struggle against difficulties or odds and separation.

Neptune at 23 Scorpio 31 was conjunct natal Sun at 24 Scorpio 08, square natal Node at 22 Leo 34 retrograde and semi-square natal Ascendant at 11 Capricorn 21 shows disadvantages through others and separation. The Node also identifies the relative, her sister.

The midpoint of Mars/Saturn at 10 Capricorn 37 is conjunct natal Ascendant at 11 Capricorn 21 and its structure represents separation and cases of death.

Transits

By adding the transits on the 90-degree dial for September 24, 1973, 9:10 p.m. MDT, Casper, Wyo-

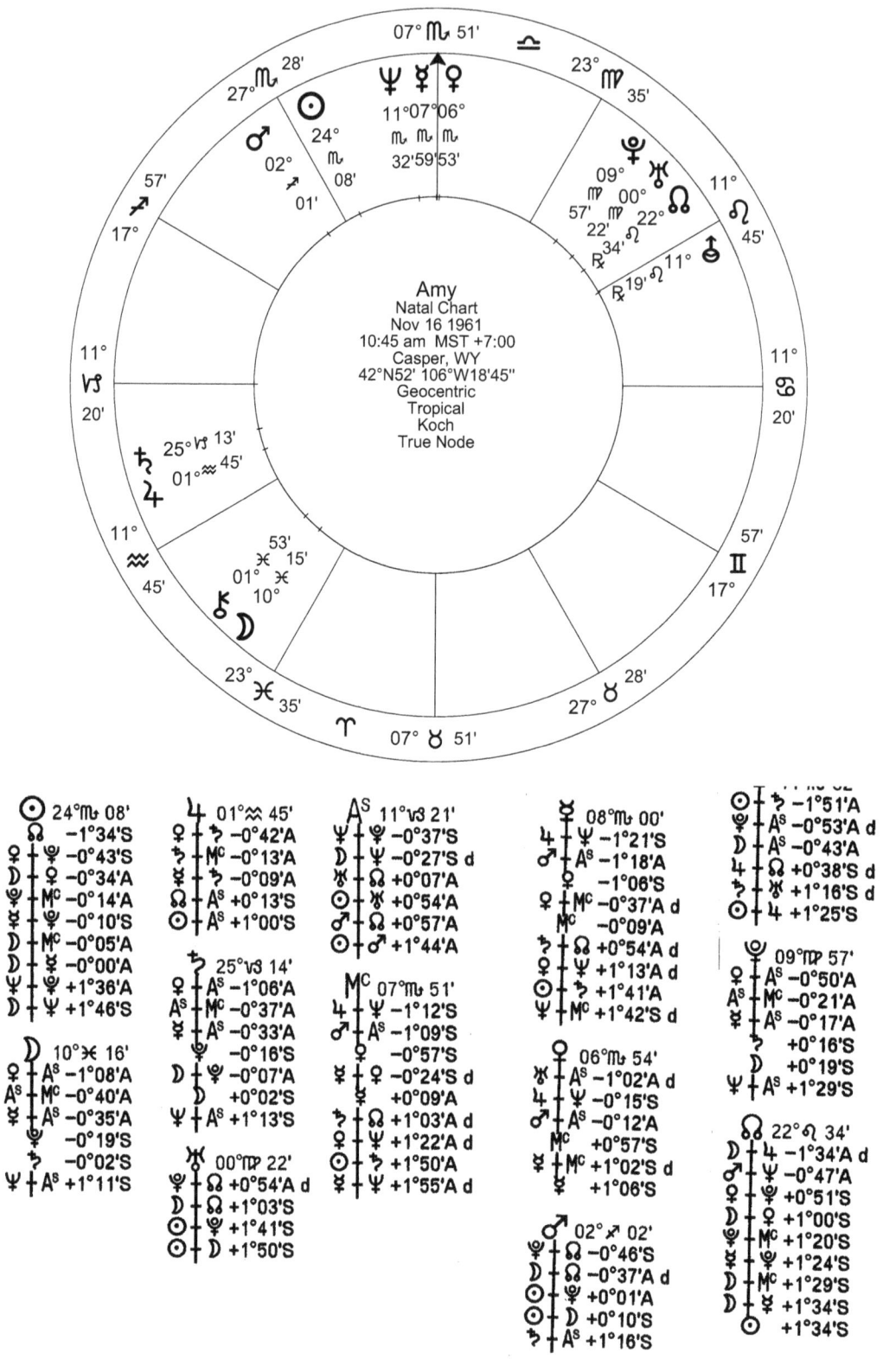

Amy's Midpoints

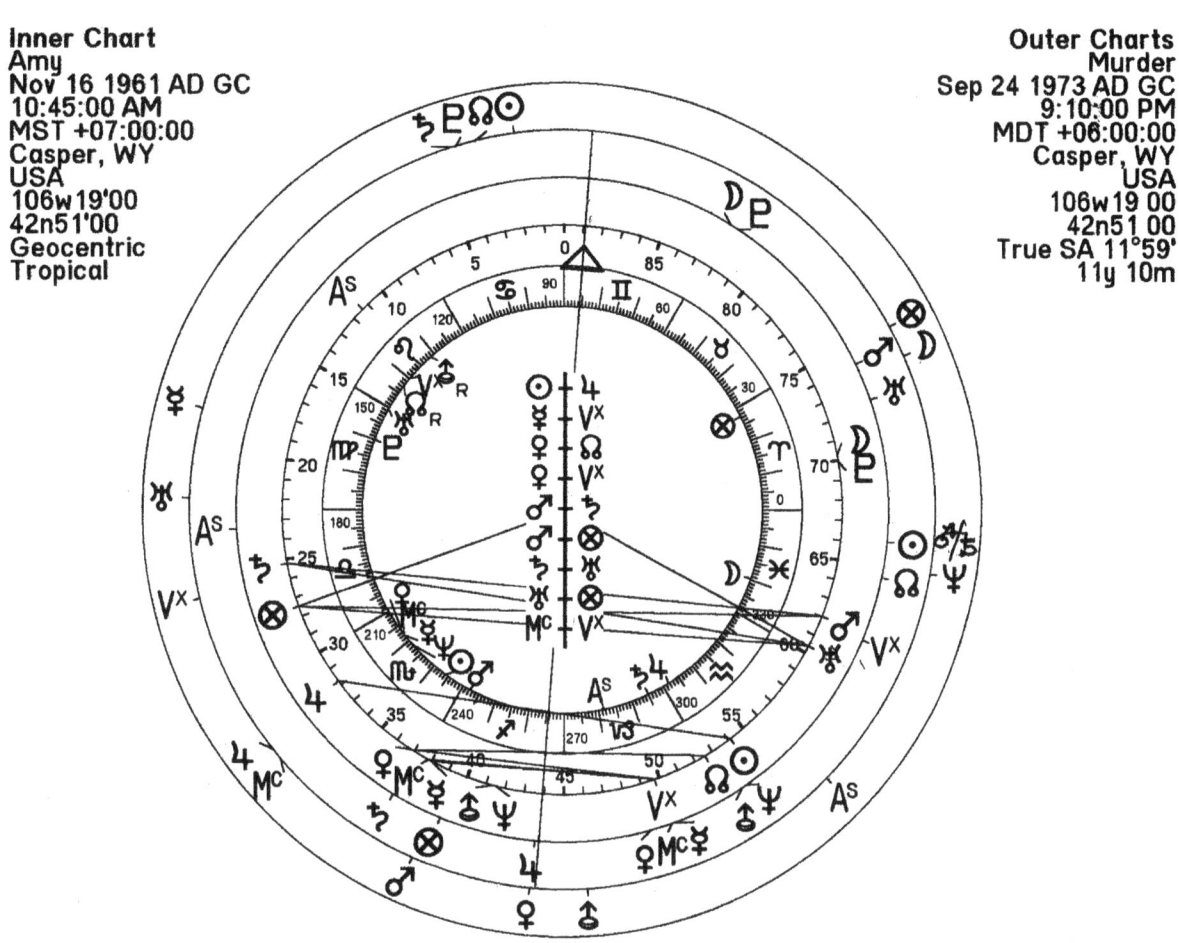

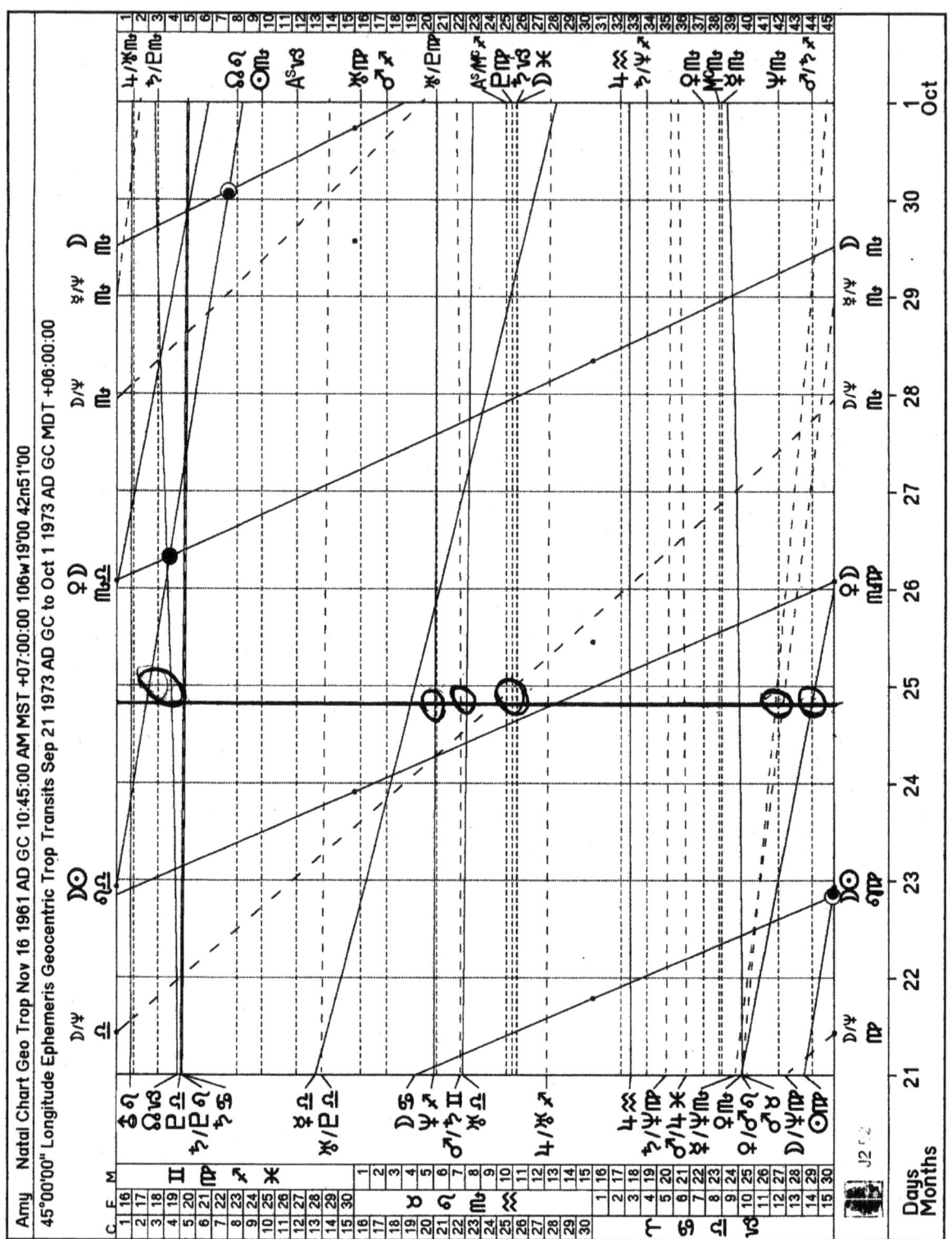

ming, at little more than an hour after the abduction, indicates a clear picture of this tragic event.

Venus at 13 Scorpio 42 semi-square the natal Mars/Saturn midpoint at 28 Sagittarius 38 indicates separation and death of a female.

Mars/Saturn midpoint at 6 Gemini 41 is within one degree of solar arc Sun at 6 Sagittarius 07.

Moon at 13 Virgo 29 semi-square solar arc Mars/Uranus midpoint at 28 Libra 11 may manifest as accidents or injuries happening to girls and women.

The transiting complex of Saturn at 4 Cancer 18, Pluto at 4 Libra, Node at 3 Capricorn 26 and Sun at 1 Libra 55 forming a grand cross in the midpoint of natal Saturn/Pluto is many times associated with kidnapping, compulsion and destructive energy.

The exact time of death is not known; however, by sheer deduction it could easily have been around 9:10 p.m. for which these calculations are used. The transiting Ascendant at 26 Taurus 17 is in opposition to natal Sun at 24 Scorpio 08, Node at 22 Leo 34 sesquisquare natal Ascendant at 11 Capricorn 21 and solar arc midpoint Mars/Saturn at 10 Scorpio 37 providing vulnerability to obstacles and inhibitions caused by others, being with negative people, harming and destroying energy.

A vertical line is drawn in the 45-degree ephemeris for the last 10 days of September 1973 to see contacts to planets and appropriate transiting midpoints.

Sun at 1 Libra 55 and Node at 3 Capricorn 26 retrograde is moving semi-square toward natal midpoint of Saturn/Pluto at 17 Scorpio 36, referring to physical separation, application of force and compulsion, common suffering shared with others.

Neptune at 5 Sagittarius 05 is square natal midpoint Uranus/Pluto at 5 Virgo 10 and equates to acts of violence.

Moon/Neptune at 24 Libra 17 square natal Saturn at 25 Capricorn 14 and semi-square natal midpoint Ascendant/MC at 9 Sagittarius represents the experience of being absorbed by foreboding.

Rebecca

In the spring of 1989, I met Rebecca at a cosmobiology workshop where her natal chart was being discussed regarding the rape and brutal assault she experienced in 1973. She was a lovely and pretty woman who talked freely about the horrendous event that happened. Married just about a year before, she worked as a sales account executive for a radio station. She also seemed happy and at that time was looking forward to having a child, which she so desperately wanted.

Later that year she did get pregnant and on July 3, 1990 her daughter Vail was born. It seems however that her happiness was not complete with the birth of her child. During the following two years she divorced her husband and it seems that she could not cope with the circumstances which surrounded her. This threw her again into periods of mood-swings, guilt and shame. Problems that seemed to have been completely cured the years following the tragedy came back in full force. She began drinking again and had bouts with depression, a condition that only asks for tragedy to strike, and strike it did.

In analyzing Rebecca's chart we need to establish whether the natal chart indicates constants that could attract the rape and violence that she experienced in 1973. Those configurations as a matter of fact do exist.

Natal

The following is a short analysis of her personal planetary points.

The Sun at 27 Gemini 42 is conjunct the Moon and Mercury, producing good intellectual powers, realistic thinking and contact with the public. The opposition and parallel to the Node is a desire to exchange thoughts and ideas with others. The midpoint of Jupiter/Pluto directs one toward leadership, and the midpoint of Venus/Mars brings strong physical love experiences, marriage and desire to have children.

The Moon at 22 Gemini 07 is parallel Mars and shows impulsiveness and involvement in quarrels, and the opposition and parallel to the Node offers cooperation with others, with the Midheaven conjunct and parallel representing the development of the ego-consciousness. The Moon is also contacting some very critical midpoints like Mars/Pluto, symbolizing audacity, daring and ambition in the personality, and the Saturn/Uranus midpoint, representing

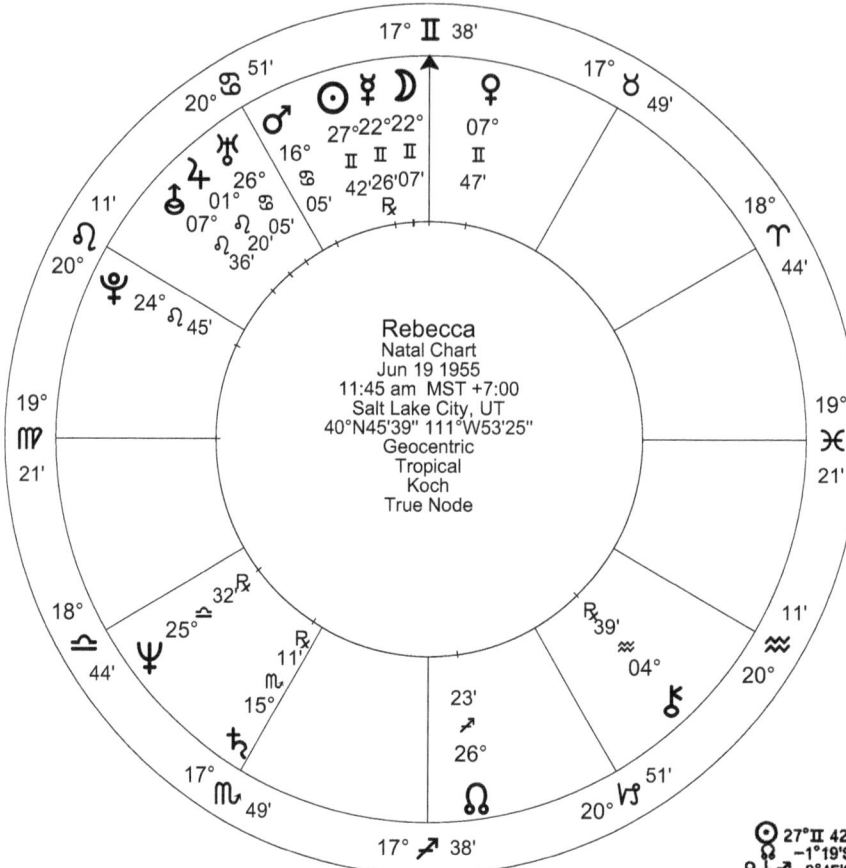

strong emotional tension and strains and separation from females. The Moon also contacts the Saturn/Neptune midpoint, manifesting emotional depression, pessimism and illness through emotional suffering.

The Midheaven at 17 Gemini 39 is conjunct and parallel to all the same planets, showing independent thinking and seeking of soul contacts.

The Ascendant at 19 Virgo 22 squares the Moon, Mercury and Node and represents a personality with a tendency toward an active exchange of thoughts and processes of getting acquainted with females. This Ascendant is a prominent focus as it contacts the following midpoints at 19 Gemini 22: Moon/MC, Mercury/MC, Mars/Pluto, Saturn/Neptune and Saturn/Uranus. The Jupiter/Transpluto midpoint indicates a joyful magical personality enjoying festive and social occasions.

There are several midpoint structures that are applicable to rape or forcible sexual attacks, such as Uranus at Venus/Mars, Mars at Venus/Pluto and Venus at Mars/Pluto. Most interesting is the structure of Mars in the natal chart contacting the Venus/Pluto midpoint, which is a configuration representing rape.

Solar Arc

The solar arc for the time of the rape is 17 degrees 25 minutes. Following are some important solar arc directions pertaining to Rebecca's experiences.

Pluto at 12 Virgo 02 is semi-square natal Uranus at 26 Cancer 06, bringing the possibility of acts of violence and subversive activities and natal Neptune at 25 Li-

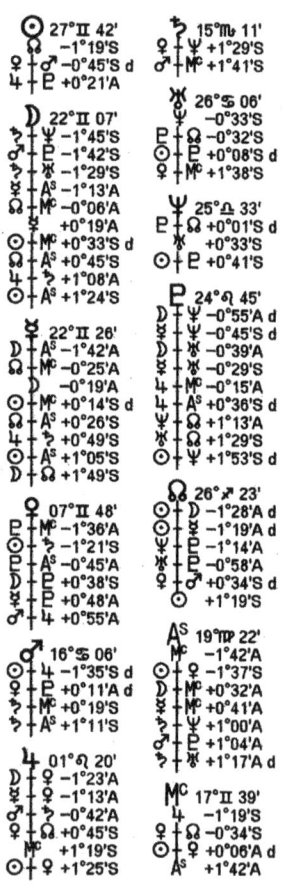

Rebecca's Midpoints

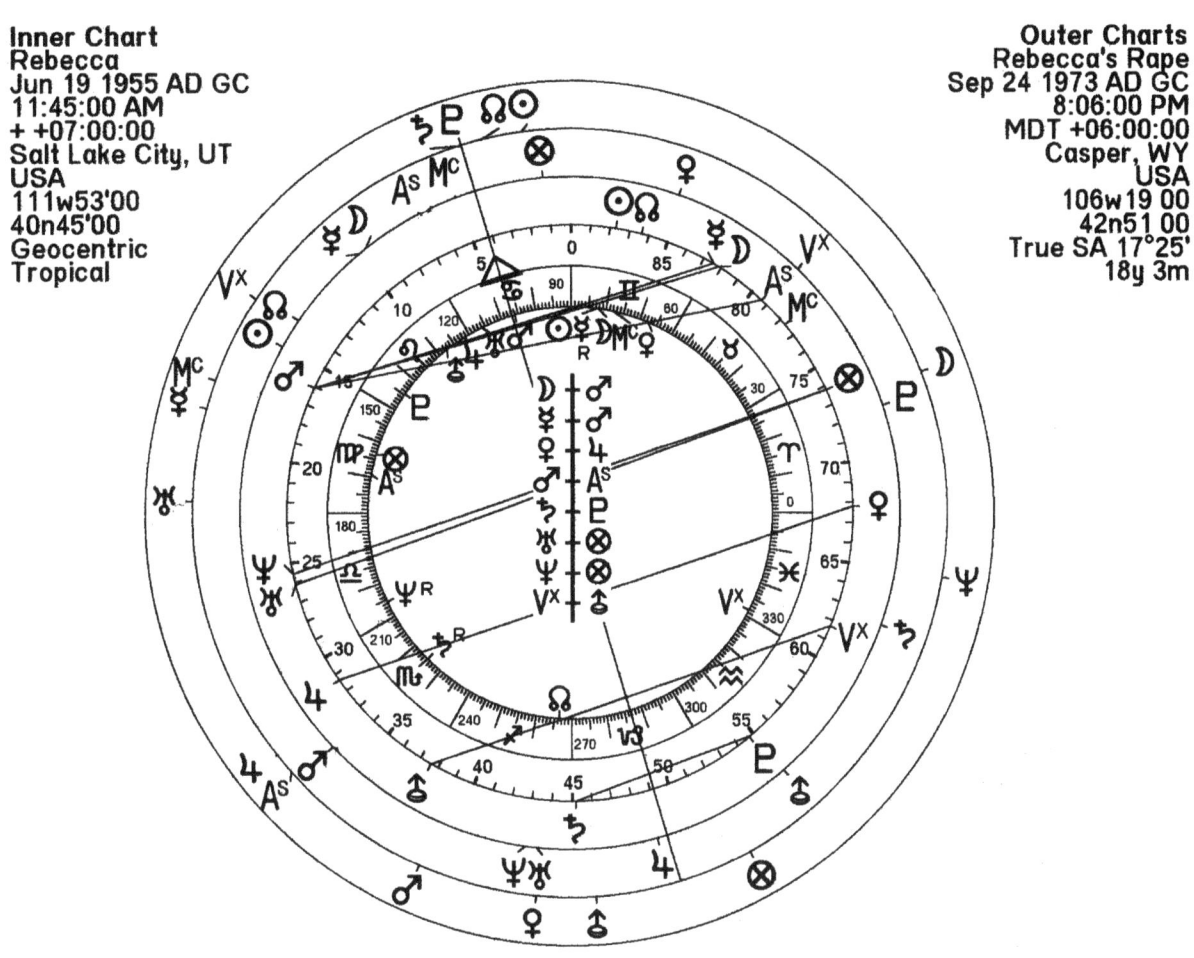

Inner Chart
Rebecca
Jun 19 1955 AD GC
11:45:00 AM
+ +07:00:00
Salt Lake City, UT
USA
111w53'00
40n45'00
Geocentric
Tropical

Outer Charts
Rebecca's Rape
Sep 24 1973 AD GC
8:06:00 PM
MDT +06:00:00
Casper, WY
USA
106w19 00
42n51 00
True SA 17°25'
18y 3m

Cosmogram, 90°00' H4 Dial Format

Inner Radix	Middle Directed	Outer Transits
☉ 27♊42	☉ 15♋07	☉ 01♎52
☽ 22♊07	☽ 09♋32	☽ 12♍52
☿ 22♊26R	☿ 09♋51	☿ 18♎34
♀ 07♊48	♀ 25♊13	♀ 13♏39
♂ 16♋06	♂ 03♌31	♂ 09♉05R
♃ 01♌20	♃ 18♌45	♃ 02♒19R
♄ 15♏11R	♄ 02♐36	♄ 04♋18
♅ 26♋06	♅ 13♌31	♅ 22♎05
♆ 25♎33R	♆ 12♏58	♆ 05♐05
♇ 24♌45	♇ 12♍10	♇ 04♎11
☊ 26♐23	☊ 13♑48	☊ 03♑26R
As 19♍22	As 06♎47	As 03♉03
Mc 17♊39	Mc 05♋04	Mc 17♑29
Vx 01♓41	Vx 19♓06	Vx 14♎03
⊕ 07♌37	⊕ 25♌02	⊕ 15♌54
⊗ 13♍47	⊗ 01♎12	⊗ 22♉03

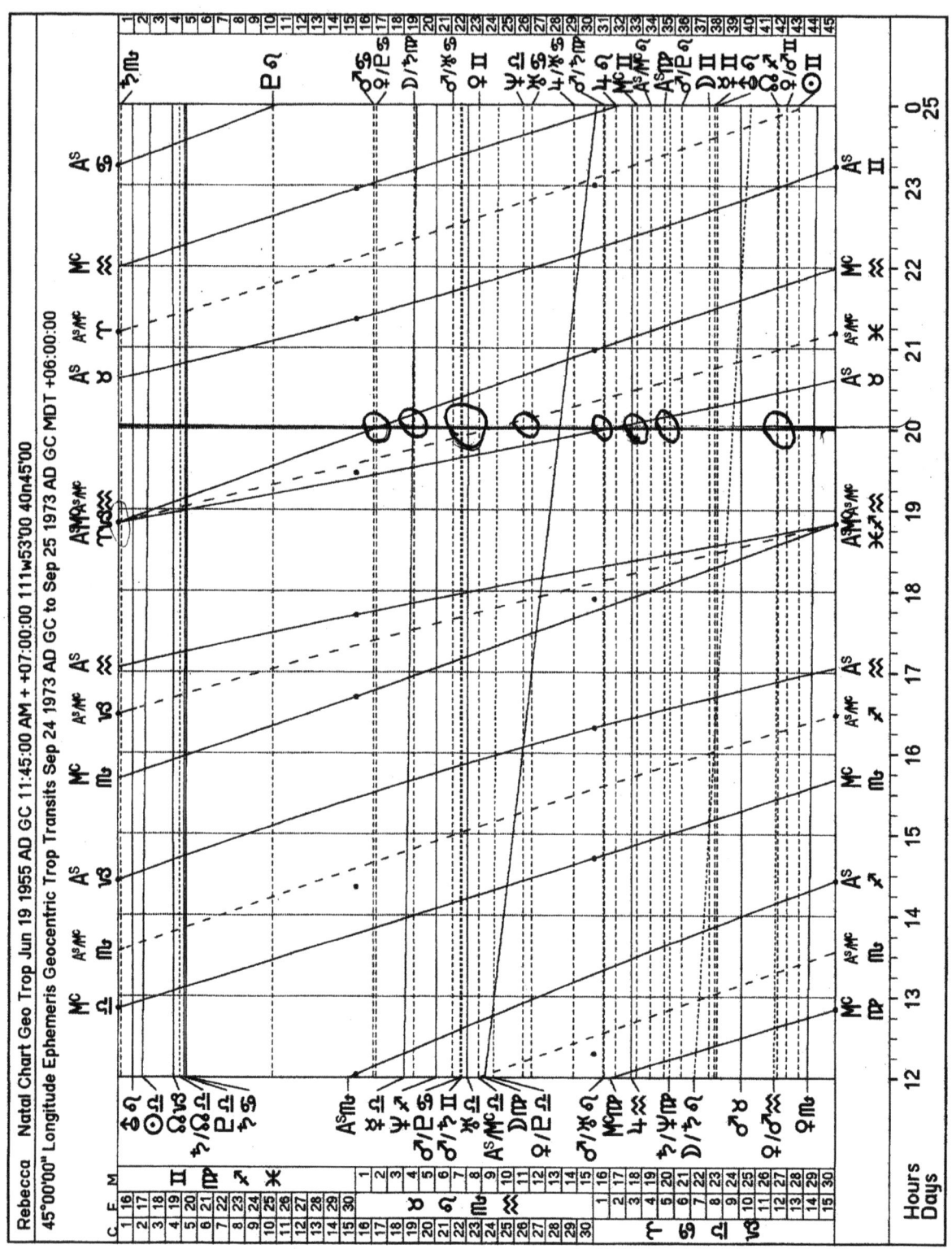

bra 33 retrograde brings peculiar soul-experiences or a grievous loss.

Mars at 3 Leo 31 is exactly conjunct the very vulnerable natal ASC/MC midpoint at 3 Leo 31 that brings violence in an important period in life.

The Midheaven at 5 Cancer 04 moved to the natal midpoint of Saturn/Pluto at 4 Libra 58 and is a very significant combination for enduring the application of force and becoming a sacrifice.

Since Rebecca survived the rape and being thrown off the bridge there would have to be a combination that would also show up in solar arc contacts. If you enter the natal Mars/Saturn midpoint located at 15 Virgo 39 and the natal Jupiter/Uranus midpoint at 28 Cancer 43 there is the "death" axis and the "Thank the Lord" axis in the inner wheel and the solar arc Ascendant at 6 Libra 47 on the outer wheel. This is a 45-degree angle to the just mentioned midpoints, which saved her life.

Transits

Pluto is at 4 Libra 11, Node at 3 Capricorn 26 retrograde and Saturn at 4 Cancer 18 moving very slowly toward the solar arc MC at 5 Cancer 04 and the midpoint of solar arc Mars/Saturn at 3 Libra 04, which is the death configuration. However, solar arc Jupiter is at 18 Leo 45 on the same axis, which may be responsible for her eventual survival.

The Sun at 1 Libra 52, always a pertinent influence, is in very close semi-square to natal Saturn at 15 Scorpio 11 retrograde. This shows the possibility of misfortunes and separation.

The Moon symbolizing the hour at 12 Virgo 52 had just passed the solar arc Pluto at 12 Virgo 10, natal Uranus at 26 Cancer 06 and Neptune at 25 Libra 33 retrograde, creating a combined potential for an extremely emotional experience, sudden fear and anxiety and emotional tensions and being exposed to or being the victim of strange influences or exploits by others and crisis in life.

The Ascendant at 3 Taurus 03, representing the minute and place, reached natal Mars/Saturn midpoint at 15 Virgo 38 by sesquisquare, creating an environment vulnerable to inhibitions caused by other people, separation, mourning and bereavement and harming or destroying energy.

The MC at 17 Capricorn 29 had just passed the opposition to solar arc Sun at 15 Cancer 07 and natal Mars at 16 Cancer 06 and opposition to natal Venus/Pluto midpoint at 16 Cancer 16, setting off the natal rape configuration within minutes of orb. These are but a few of pertinent factors to indicate the planetary components for this frightful event.

"Murdered in 1973, died in 1992…"

Natrona County Sheriff Dave Dovala reported that the body of a 37-year-old woman was recovered from the Platte River near Casper, Wyoming after she plunged to her death the night of July 31, 1992. When I heard of the tragic conclusion to Rebecca's life I was stunned. What was it that compelled her to drive to the location of the murderous event that occurred 19 years earlier? Was it fate or destiny for Rebecca to survive and suffer for 19 years only to destroy herself in the end? Was it marriage, motherhood or her own sexuality she could not cope with?

Her body may have healed and she may have pretended everything was well with her, but the fact is that the suffering continued from that very day in 1973 when the tragedy took place. It does seem that the problems were not completely resolved the years following that horrendous event.

On August 2, 1992, according to Sheriff Dave Dovala and reported by Julia Podis several days later, the following reflects the week prior to the tragedy.

"Rebecca, 37, had ignored her boyfriend's pleading and drove along the winding hilly country roads to the Fremont Canyon Bridge near Casper, Wyoming. The sky was clear and the Sun was setting, casting long shadows across the rocky hillside above and darkening the shallow, slow moving river below. Standing perilously above the narrow gorge—its red rock walls ribbed with the green and grays of life and death—she plunged to her death. The weather changed after she went off the bridge, said Dovala, who had given Becky away at her wedding three years ago. It started thundering and lightning and the wind shifted twice. It was eerie. It was like somebody was telling us something."

Rebecca's boyfriend and her two-year-old daughter from the previous marriage were with her the night she died. She just insisted to go back there.

Inner Chart
Rebecca
Jun 19 1955 AD GC
11:45:00 AM
+ +07:00:00
Salt Lake City, UT
USA
111w53'00
40n45'00
Geocentric
Tropical

Outer Charts
Death
Jul 31 1992 AD GC
8:06:00 PM
MDT +06:00:00
Casper, WY
USA
106w19 00
42n51 00
True SA 35°25'
37y 1m

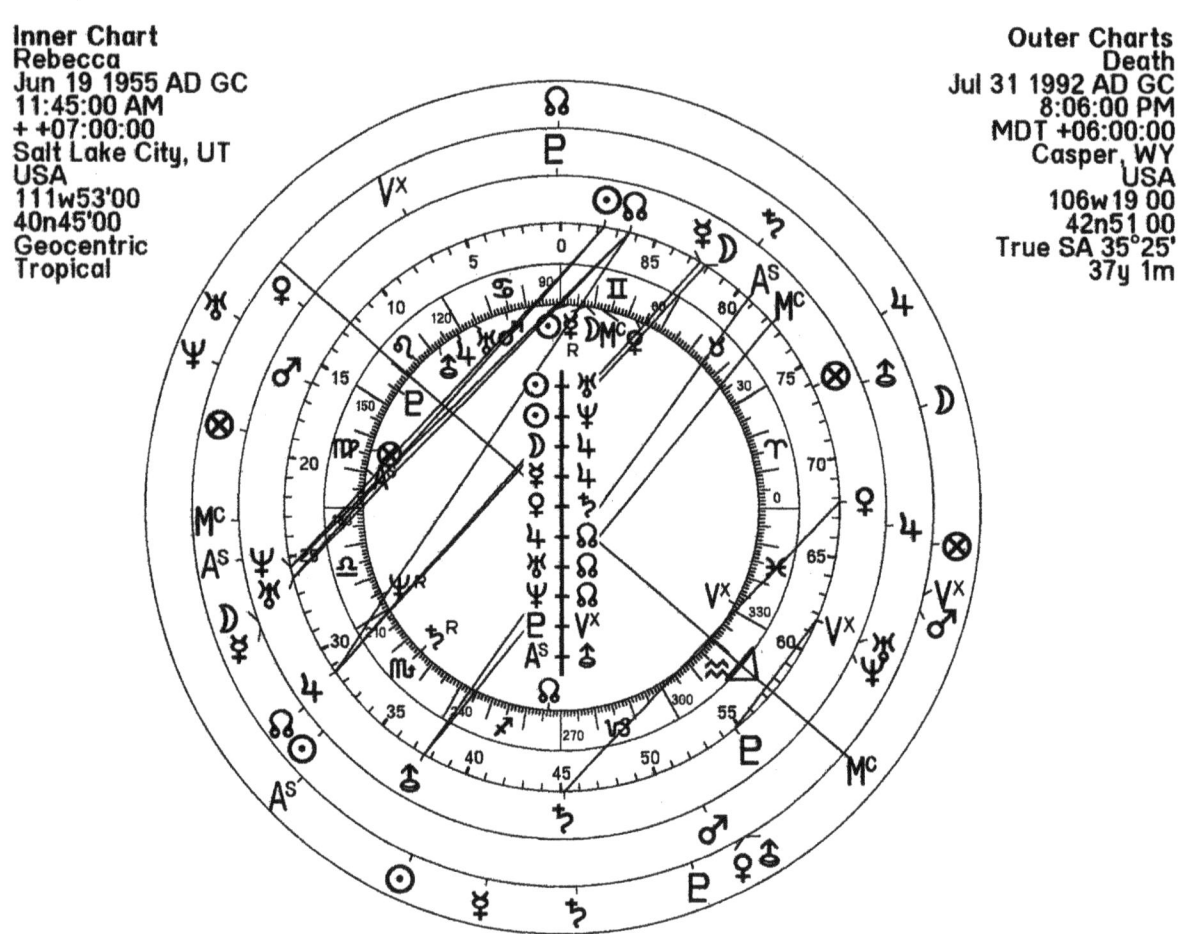

Cosmogram, 90°00' H4 Dial Format

Inner Radix	Middle Directed	Outer Transits
☉ 27Ⅱ42	☉ 03♌07	☉ 09♌05
☽ 22Ⅱ07	☽ 27♋32	☽ 11♍22
☿ 22Ⅱ26R	☿ 27♋51	☿ 12♌07R
♀ 07Ⅱ48	♀ 13♋13	♀ 22♌24
♂ 16♋06	♂ 21♌31	♂ 03Ⅱ35
♃ 01♌20	♃ 06♍45	♃ 15♍09
♄ 15♏11R	♄ 20♐36	♄ 15♒36R
♅ 26♋06	♅ 01♍31	♅ 15♑06R
♆ 25♎33R	♆ 00♍58	♆ 16♑59R
♇ 24♌45	♇ 00♎10	♇ 20♏09
☊ 26♐23	☊ 01♒48	☊ 00♑04R
As 19♍22	As 24♎47	As 03♒52
Mc 17Ⅱ39	Mc 23♋04	Mc 27♏24
Vx 01♓41	Vx 07♈06	Vx 04♍10
⊕ 07♌37	⊕ 13♍02	⊕ 22♌27
⊗ 13♍47	⊗ 19♎12	⊗ 06♓09

34

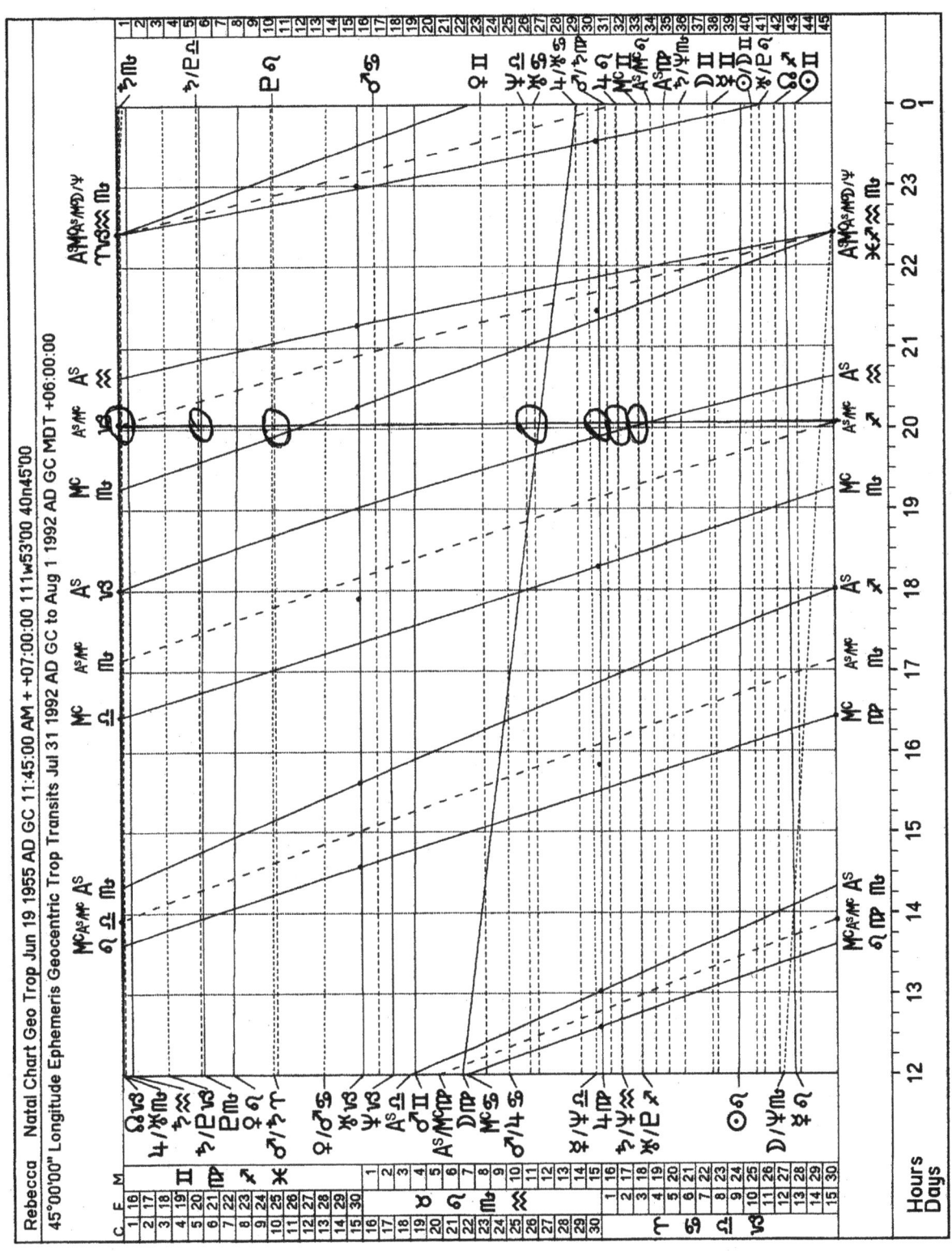

"The more I told her not to go there the faster she drove the car, he said, "When she hit 70 mph, that's when I shut up." She relived the whole ordeal from nineteen years earlier and started to cry uncontrollable. The boyfriend took the baby back to the car. It was then that he heard the unbearable sound of her body hitting the water.

The week before her death she watched the movie "Ode to Billie Joel" four times. The movie details the life of a boy who could not cope with his budding sexuality. As the story goes, he jumps off Mississippi's Tallahatchie Bridge. What impact did this movie have on Rebecca? Did she in some way identify this boy's sexual problems with her own?

According to reports from family and friends, Rebecca was terribly disturbed due to the fact that one of the connected criminals was appealing the murder case in court. She was very troubled and lived in fear of the possibility that he might be released from prison.

On July 28, 1992, three days before the fatal plunge, the U.S. Tenth Circuit Court of Appeals upheld the denial of a petition for a writ of habeas corpus filed by one of the killers. The attorney who prosecuted the case said, "I was going to call her and tell her it's all over, this was Friday afternoon. I looked for her phone number and could not find it. I thought I would call her Monday. By then it was too late."

Solar Arc

The solar arc for the time of Rebecca's death was 35 degrees 25 minutes.

Pluto at 0 Libra 10 is semi-square natal Saturn at 15 Scorpio 11 retrograde and may be misused as a self-destroying energy.

Saturn at 20 Sagittarius 36 is at the natal midpoint of Mars/Pluto at 5 Leo 25, representing an intensity of desire to forcibly overcome obstacles at any cost.

Mars at 21 Leo 30 reaches the conjunction of natal midpoint of Neptune/MC at 21 Leo 36 and brings ideas into realization; also the tendency to succumb to strange and unusual influences.

Sun at 3 Leo 07 conjunct the natal all-important ASC/MC midpoint at 3 Leo 31, indicating the close relationship of body and soul.

Uranus at 1 Virgo 30 and Neptune at 0 Sagittarius 58 retrograde are within orb to natal Mars at 16 Cancer 06 semi-square and sesquisquare, describing the quick action and self-destroying forces.

The Moon at 27 Cancer 32, Mercury at 27 Cancer 51 retrograde, Tranpluto at 13 Virgo 02 axis was slowly moving toward natal Jupiter/Uranus midpoint at 28 Cancer 43, creating an emotional pain (Moon) and the realization (Mercury) of choices to make escaped her logical thinking.

The midpoint of Sun/Moon at 0 Leo 19 was right on natal Mars/Saturn midpoint at 15 Virgo 39, symbolizing the death of a female.

The compulsive self-destructive midpoint of Saturn/Pluto at 10 Scorpio 23 makes a powerful contact to natal Sun/Moon midpoint at 24 Gemini 55 and the Uranus/Pluto midpoint at 10 Leo 25 with only a two-minute orb, bringing self-destruction directed toward the body, soul and spirit in a most brutal manner.

It is amazing that solar arc directions are so overpowering in so many ways. Most of the combinations listed were already forming early in the year. My speculation is that the birth of her daughter in 1990 and subsequent divorce may have had a significant impact on Rebecca.

Transits

We know that for any event progressions and directions only set the stage. The transits and the circumstances have to present themselves for an actual event to happen. The year heading up to this devastating tragedy was already colored by the transiting Neptune moving back and forth over her natal Mars, which shows a lack of stamina, misdirected energy, lack of emotional balance and confused psychic states.

The slow-moving Pluto at 20 Scorpio 10 was emphasizing the natal Saturn/Pluto of self-destroying energy.

Uranus and Neptune conjunct their midpoint at 16 Capricorn 05 touched off the solar arc Uranus-Neptune Square at 16 Libra 14 that represents eliminating waking consciousness.

Mars at 3 Gemini 35 moved to the natal midpoint of Moon/Saturn at 3 Virgo 39 and brings feelings of inferiority and soul conflict. Mars also touches the natal midpoint of Saturn/Pluto at 4 Libra 58 and ASC/MC at 3 Leo 30, which are the most murderous suicidal midpoint and most personal point.

The conjunction of Venus and Transpluto is also outstanding since they contact the natal Venus/Transpluto midpoint at 7 Cancer 42, emphasizing the emotional fulfillment that eluded Rebecca.

Mercury at 12 Leo 07 retrograde moved over Rebecca's natal Saturn at 15 Scorpio 11 retrograde and indicates the negative state of mind and depression. According to the report Rebecca had not had a drink of alcohol for years. She started drinking again and she and her boyfriend had two pitchers of beer prior to the ride to the bridge. Venus at 22 Leo 24 is also sextile natal Sun at 27 Gemini 42, showing a lack of clarity and aimlessness. It is located at the midpoint of natal Uranus/Pluto at 10 Leo 26 and natal Saturn at 15 Scorpio 11 retrograde, pointing toward the thought activity of only one thing—the elimination of the constant pain.

The Sun-Mars/Uranus axis at 9 Leo 05-24 Pisces 20 set off a tremendous amount of natal and directed midpoints and provoked the quick action she took.

Moon at 11 Virgo 22, indicating the hour, at the natal Uranus/Neptune midpoint at 10 Virgo 49 shows the thoughts and feelings clinging to her sister who had died nearly 20 years before.

The MC-Mars/Pluto axis at 27 Scorpio 24, the moment in time, visualizes the overwhelming power of what transpired. Then across the dial you can note the contact to solar arc Venus at 13 Cancer 12 and solar arc Mars/Neptune at 11 Libra 14 midpoint, revealing a sudden deliberate deathly action-prone combination.

Police, who have ruled out foul play, pulled Rebecca's body out of the water about an hour later. She had landed near the bank in about three feet of water—exactly where her sister was found. Like her sister 19 years prior, she had a broken neck and massive head injuries.

Mary Jo Kopechne

The following biography of Mary Jo Kopechne is a combination of excerpts from an article by Wil Haygood, a member of the *Golden Globe* staff of the *Boston Globe*, July 18, 1989 Edition Third Section: Living Page 49; and *Teddy Bare*, published by Western Islands 1971, Belmont MA 02178 and written by Zad Rust, which also includes Senator Edward Kennedy's TV speech on July 25, 1969, 7:00 p.m.

Mary Jo was born in Pennsylvania, the only child of Joe and Gwen Kopechne. They lived in a housing project, but this was before housing projects took on the negative connotation they now have.

Forty years ago almost everyone in the region worked in the coal mines. Joe Kopechne wanted something other than coal mine work, so they left for New Jersey and he worked in insurance. "Gwen and Joe had the courage to go to a new place. So they were role models," says Georgetta Potoski. She is Mary Jo's first cousin. They grew up together and spent summers together. Georgetta Potoski is sitting in her kitchen with the screen door halfway open, held open by the humid night air. She raised eight children of her own. "Mary Jo," she says, "was quiet and introverted and had a lot of self-discipline. Her family was very important to her. She was ladylike and she liked feminine things and good perfume." Potoski says Mary Jo rarely dated "until her late teens." She and Mary Jo spent hours reading. They both liked books, such as Anne Marrow Lindbergh's *A Gift From the Sea*. One summer, she says, a friend gave her and Mary Jo a box of books and they spent the whole summer reading them. Mary Jo laughed, but no one mistook her laughter for giddiness and "you didn't tell Mary Jo dirty jokes," says Potoski. "I don't mean to sound like she was prudish."

Mary Jo Kopechne had moved away from this area with her parents but she came back every summer to visit family. Mary Jo went to Caldwell College for Women in New Jersey and graduated in 1962. She had done some canvassing for Senator John Kennedy's presidential campaign in 1960. Shortly after college she headed for Alabama to teach poor children. A year later Mary Jo returned north. The 1960s were coming on, and you could feel them. It was like something glorious and also angry. Eisenhower's Washington was now President Kennedy's Washington.

Lots of young women were going to Washington and Georgetta Potoski recalls of Mary Jo, "She always had a strong determination or drive to be part of what was happening in Washington. There was magic in Washington. Kennedy had the Peace Corps, Space Program and Civil Rights." Mary Jo got herself a job with Florida Senator George Smathers. "We always felt Mary Jo would go to Washington and do great things," says Potoski. Moving through that world of the Kennedys in Washington in those early years when new ideas were born almost daily charmed Mary Jo Kopechne. She wrote letters home and shared her adventures with Potoski and family. Mary Jo never married, "I could never picture Mary Jo married with a family," Potoski says.

For a long while, politics was enough for Mary Jo Kopechne. She had taken a job traveling with Robert F. Kennedy's presidential campaign. It was a group of young women and they were called "Boiler Room Girls." If everything had turned out right many of them would have gotten jobs working in the White House. It ended with Robert F. Kennedy's assassination.

The weekend of July 8, 1969 at Chappaquiddick a party was planned to celebrate what once was, to remember and to chat about life. Around midnight Ted Kennedy and Mary Jo left the party. Ted was trying to get her to the last ferry. This all came out in the reams of testimony later. Then the car went off the bridge. Kennedy did not report the incident until 10 hours later. He has said very little of the incident. "I can live with myself," he once said of Chappaquiddick. "I feel the tragedy of the girl's death. That's on my mind. That's what I will always have to live with, but what I didn't have to live with are the whispers and innuendos and falsehoods because these have no basis in fact."

It was a Sunday when Georgetta Potoski got the phone call that her cousin was dead. Her husband answered the phone, turned to her and said, "Mary Jo just died in a drowning accident off Chappaquiddick," and before it really sank in, Georgetta said, "That's strange. Mary Jo is an excellent swimmer." "No one in the family," Georgetta says, "holds Kennedy directly responsible for Mary Jo's death. I think what the family is upset about are the circumstances."

On July 19, 1969, a nation awoke to astronauts headed for the Moon and another Kennedy tragically in the news.

Mary Jo Kopechne, from a little hard-to-find town up the road called Kingston, was found dead at the bottom of waters off a place in Massachusetts with the windswept name of Chappaquiddick. She had been in a car with Senator Ted Kennedy. They had left the party, which began in the evening of July 18 and were trying to get to the last ferry off of the island. The car went off the bridge. Ted swam to safety and by the time he returned with help, hours later, it was too late. This is the Kennedy version. There are those who believe it and there are those who don't.

Natal

Miss Kopechne's chart is very interesting indeed. The planets are all contained within six houses and the temperament distribution is very unbalanced, having 10 positions in fixed signs.

The Sun at 03 Leo 17 in very close conjunction to Pluto at 02 Leo 30 portrays a very determined woman, self-assured with a wealth of ideas and the power of attainment, as well as the desire to exercise that power. However, the negative inclinations could easily include martyrdom, danger to life and separation by Providence. The close square to the Midheaven at 06 Taurus 43 is focused on the goals and objectives in life, no matter the obstacles lurking in the future.

The conjunction and parallel to Transpluto at 01 Leo 37 helps to establish firm foundations and enhance the individual with charisma. All the foregoing contacts include Mercury 26 Cancer 30 retrograde, indicating that communication would be very much a source to have an outlet for those talents.

The structure pattern of the Sun is enormous, to say the least. To add at least one midpoint, Mercury/Jupiter, to this short analysis of the Sun, would provide the individual with a good intellect, a wealth of ideas and capacity as an orator with expressive gestures.

The Moon at 22 Aries 10 is not particularly comfortable in this sign, causing the will to be influenced by feelings, and consequently producing an impulsive nature and acting without thinking. The 150-degree aspect to Neptune at 23 Virgo 27 provides a sympathetic understanding of other people but also the danger of being exposed to strange influences as well as being exploited by others. The trine to the Ascendant at 16 Leo 25 suggests making easy contact, especially with women.

The Ascendant at 16 Leo 25 displays an impressive personality and self-confidence in a dignified manner. Also, she has a tendency to force her will upon others and is prone to accidents or operations, which is shown by the close conjunction to Mars. The square to Jupiter can be helpful in entering profitable associations or partnerships and for teamwork. In contrast the square to Saturn inclines one to prefer the association with people considerably older and inhibitions of suffering caused through the environment. The Ascendant in the midpoint of Uranus/Midheaven can bring about sudden events that would require adjustment to new circumstances.

The Midheaven at 06 Taurus 43 with its many contacts creates a persistent pursuit of Mary Jo's aim. The square to Mars is always ready for action and organizing. The conjunction and parallel to Jupiter is clearly the formula for success. In addition the

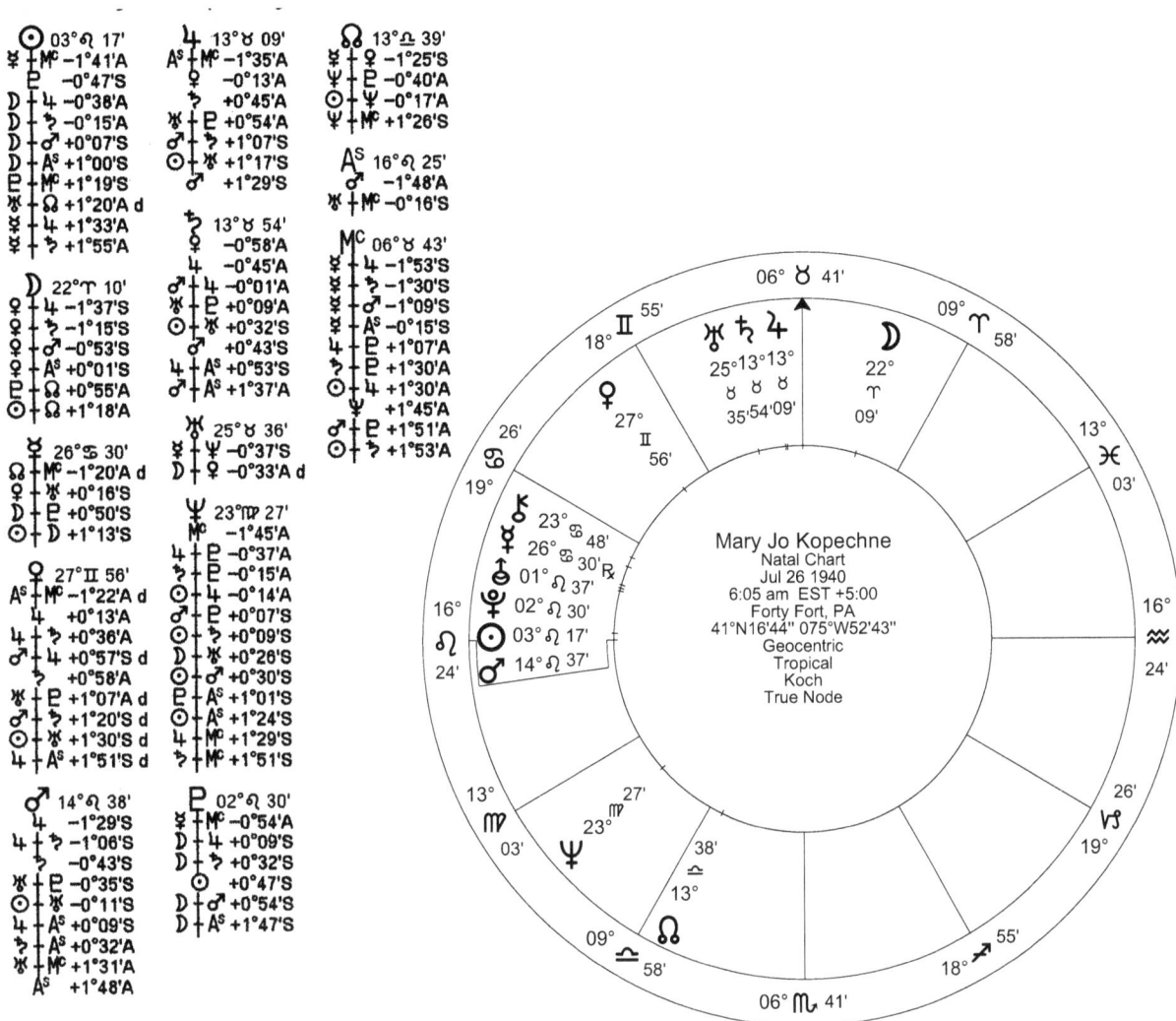

contacts imply a happy physical love life and gaining the love of another by effort. The conjunction and parallel to Saturn, however, can indicate enforced separations, mourning and bereavement. The sesquisquare to Neptune at times might produce insecurity, suffering from the consequences of wrong actions and proneness to deception. The square to Pluto can bring about recognition and power, readjustment to circumstances, but at the same time this contact is significant of a turn in destiny brought about by Providence.

Solar Arc Directions

The year 1969 indicated a variety of contacts, especially midpoints, pointing toward an eventful year ahead. The arc was 27 degrees and 48 minutes at the time of Mary Jo's death. She was also experiencing the completion of her first Saturn cycle.

Neptune was approaching the natal Moon, reinforcing the natal 150-degree aspect. Venus was still in orb of a conjunction to Mercury that put thoughts of love into perspective.

Uranus is involved through many midpoints that influence activities for that year. The connection with the midpoints of Sun/Mars, Sun/Jupiter and Sun/Saturn indicate premature action or hastiness, overtaxing one's strength and sudden events, the expectation of good fortune and sudden turns in life, emotional tension, unusual circumstances, crisis and possible mourning and seclusion.

Uranus contacting the midpoint of Mars/Pluto is a most devastating combination and represents violence and sudden calamities with great consequences, while the Jupiter/Pluto midpoint can mean fanatical striving for improvement, a quick development and adjustment to new conditions. Contacting

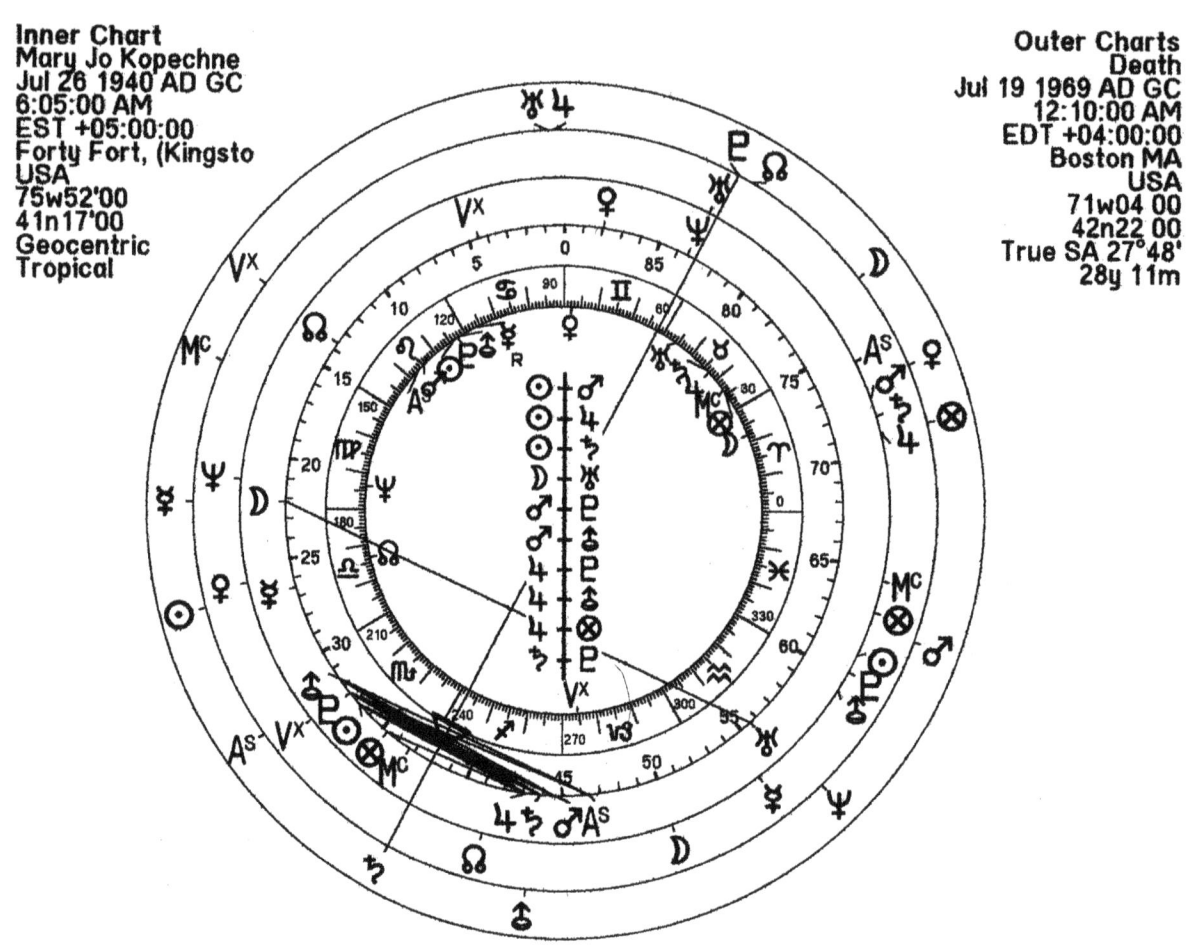

Cosmogram, 90°00' H4 Dial Format

Inner Radix	Middle Directed	Outer Transits
☉ 03♌17	☉ 01♍05	☉ 26♋19
☽ 22♈10	☽ 19♉58	☽ 16♍59
☿ 26♋30R	☿ 24♌18	☿ 22♋16
♀ 27♊56	♀ 25♋44	♀ 13♊12
♂ 14♌38	♂ 12♍26	♂ 02♐31
♃ 13♉09	♃ 10♊57	♃ 00♎30
♄ 13♉54	♄ 11♊42	♄ 08♉00
♅ 25♉36	♅ 23♎24	♅ 00♎38
♆ 23♍27	♆ 21♎15	♆ 26♏02R
♇ 02♌30	♇ 00♍18	♇ 22♍58
☊ 13♎39	☊ 11♏27	☊ 22♓28R
As 16♌25	As 14♍13	As 01♉35
Mc 06♉43	Mc 04♊31	Mc 16♑48
Vx 04♑29	Vx 02♒17	Vx 13♎27
⚸ 01♌37	⚸ 29♌25	⚸ 13♌36
⊗ 05♉18	⊗ 03♊06	⊗ 10♓55

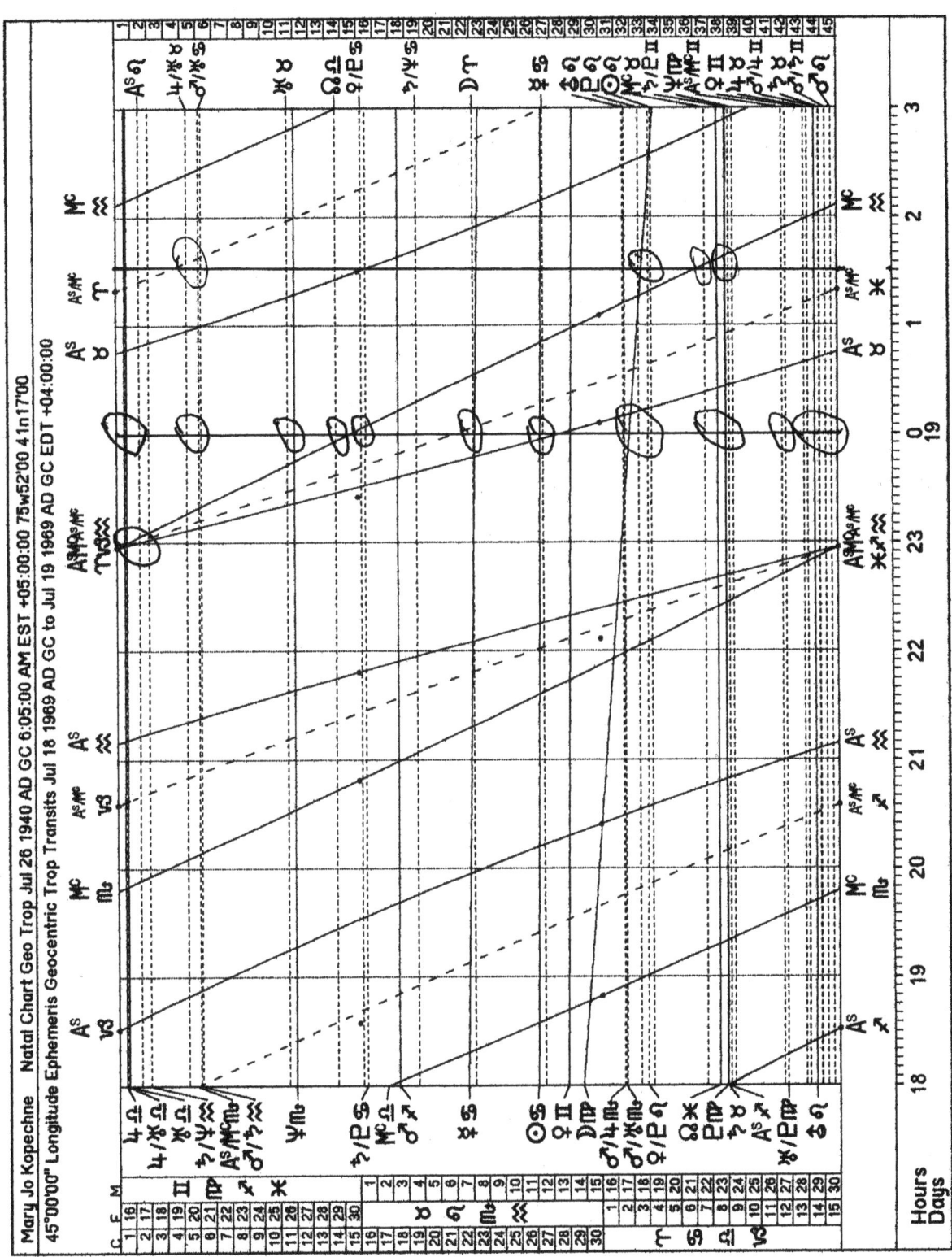

the midpoint of Saturn/Pluto and Saturn/Transpluto, Uranus indicates being unafraid of danger and sudden violence.

Transits

The transiting planets and midpoints for around midnight of July 18-19 are terribly frightening. By following the applicable positions on the 45-degree midpoint ephemeris you can clearly estimate the struggle Mary Jo went through before she expired after the car plunged into the water. The most important contacts are listed as follows.

Jupiter at 0 Libra 30 is semi-square natal Ascendant at 16 Leo 25 and so is Uranus in 0 Libra 38, showing shared happiness with others or with a partner.

The midpoint of Saturn/Neptune at 17 Leo 01 is conjunct the Ascendant and shows sharing of grief and sorrow with others and termination of associations or union.

The Mars/Saturn midpoint at 20 Leo 16 is semi-square natal Mars/Uranus and this can be interpreted as a deadly accident.

Neptune at 26 Scorpio 02 opposition natal Uranus equates to lack of stamina and vitality, confused psychic states and particular inclinations and losses.

Midheaven at 16 Capricorn 48 is opposition the natal midpoint of Venus/Pluto and could have an ego-consciousness direction of the sexual urges. Furthermore there could have been deep feelings of love of karmic union. However, there is also the midpoint of Saturn/Pluto at 15 Cancer 29 involved, showing the capacity for a tragic love or immortality.

Mercury at 22 Cancer 29 is square natal Moon and implies an exchange of thoughts with women, the extension of one's mental horizon and journeys or travels.

The Sun at 26 Cancer 19 is conjunct Mercury and adds good chances of developing the practical and mental facilities and success in business.

When observing the transiting Moon at 16 Virgo 59 on the graph notice it approaches the natal Sun and Pluto, suggesting a positive effect of establishing a position of leadership or the realization of new ideas. The negative effect could easily produce brutal suppression of the feelings, physical suffering and a danger to life or separation by Providence.

The Node at 22 Pisces 28 semi-square the Midheaven shows individual relationships, the establishment of an association of the attainment of joint objectives, unions based on inner understanding and the cropping up of difficulties. Pluto at 22 Virgo 58 and Saturn at 08 Taurus 00 are conjunct Neptune and Saturn respectively, representing the pursuit of peculiar aspirations and a progressive spiritual evolution but also peculiar states of soul-experiences, fantastic ideas, self-torment, confusion of a grievous loss. Saturn is conjunct its natal position, completing a Saturn return.

Transpluto at 13 Leo 38 and midpoint Uranus/Pluto at 26 Virgo 48 are contacting the natal midpoint of Mars/Jupiter and Mars/Saturn, which represents sudden incidents between partners in business or marriage, extraordinary and unusual powers of resistance, brute force, intervention of Higher Power, a sudden accident and separation or a case of death.

Scuba diver John Farrar, who retrieved the body of Mary Jo from the Kennedy car, maintained that Miss Kopechne could have lived up to two hours in an air pocket and quick action could have saved her life. This is reported from a conversation between John Farrar with Mary Jo's father Joseph Kopechne when he visited Chappaquiddick.

Note: Transpluto was sesquisquare the fixed star Scheat. Reinhold Ebertin, in his book *Fixed Stars*, has the following to say about Scheat: "Tied up with a malefic, this could lead the native to lose his life in catastrophes, such as floods, shipwrecks."

Bruno Richard Hauptmann

Infamy, according to the dictionary is: "Evil fame or reputation. An evil or criminal act that is publicly known." In astrology/cosmobiology, this is reflected in the natal chart of. Social or financial position does not protect a person from becoming infamous, it is the deed performed that produces infamy.

Bruno Hauptmann, after three attempts, finally succeeded in entering the United States illegally as a stowaway in the early 1920s. He had been imprisoned in Germany and was awaiting trial. After his arrival he worked at odd jobs and then as a carpenter. On October 10, 1925, he married Anna Hauptmann, and had a son born in 1933.

Charles A. Lindbergh III, was kidnaped March 1, 1932. A ransom of $50,000 was paid that month, and the body was found May 12, 1932.

On September 19, 1934, Bruno Hauptmann was arrested in New York after passing one of the ransom bills. He was put on trial for kidnaping, January 2, 1935, found guilty of kidnaping and murder, February 15, and sentenced to be electrocuted March 8, 1935. After exhausting his appeals, he was executed April 3, 1936.

The trial was sensational and became famous all over the world. The publicity surrounding the case was enormous. Jaded with police incompetence, media and public bias, Bruno Hauptmann was considered guilty from the moment he was arrested. They called it the "Trial of the Century."

The birth time of Hauptmann is listed in the Penfield Collection as 1:10 p.m., source *Sabian Symbols*, and with a note that says "mother gives the time of 1:00 p.m." From my experiences with mother's memories, I opted for the 1:10 p.m. time.

Hauptmann's chart is very unusual; it gave me the chills as it appeared on the computer. Twelve positions out of 13 are packed within 22 degrees on the 90-degree dial. Nine of the planets are in Sagittarius.

The time of his arrival in the US is unknown to me, but it could have occurred when the solar arc Uranus reached the zero degree of the 90-degree dial, which would have been around 1922-23. His marriage would fit the solar arc placement of Jupiter-Moon, Mars, Mercury, Venus, and Node.

Very interesting is the change of the locality. While the focus was very much on his Midheaven in his native land, in the United States it shifted to the Ascendant and the public. The structure pattern of fame-infamy is symbolized by Pluto at the Ascendant/Midheaven in both charts. In 1932, when the kidnaping took place, the solar arc shows Neptune (leading the 10 planets) in aspect to the natal chart for years to come. Neptune is a symbol for kidnaping and kidnapers.

Solar arc Directions

The arrest took place September 19, 1934, two and a half years after the kidnaping. The midpoint generally indicating arrest is Saturn/Uranus and was at 15 Sagittarius 48. The solar arc Pluto at 21 Cancer 19 and the Saturn/Uranus structure were within a few minutes of a sesquisquare to his natal Sun/Uranus midpoint at 6 Sagittarius, showing a limitation of freedom, harm through force majeure, placed into difficult circumstances, tragic experiences and the fate of standing alone and imprisonment.

Solar arc Neptune at 1 Leo 36 retrograde meanwhile moved into orb of natal midpoints Moon/Pluto

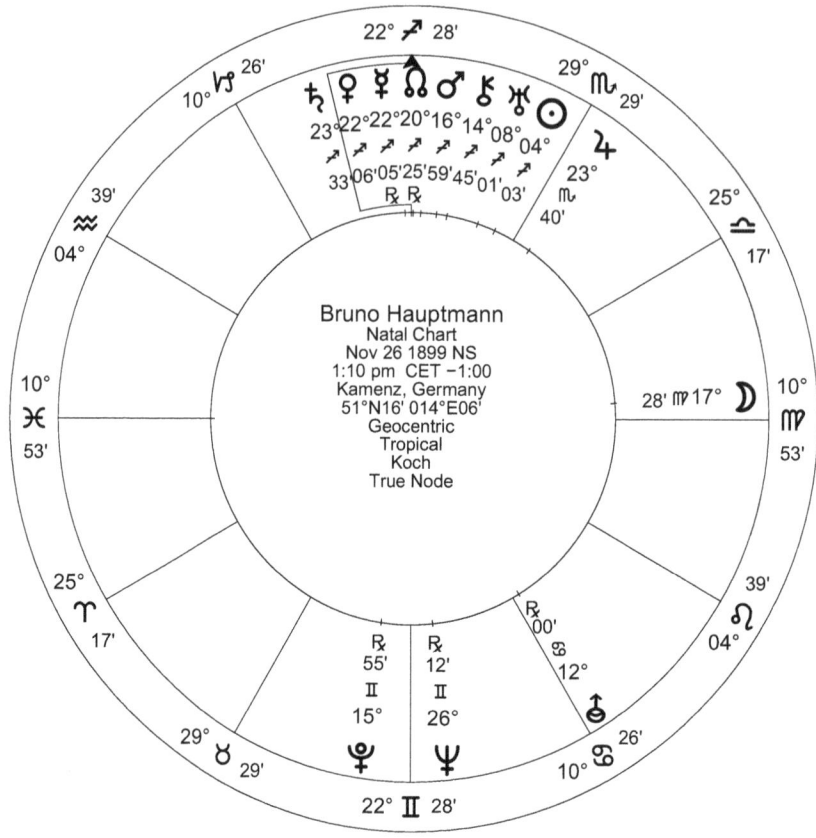

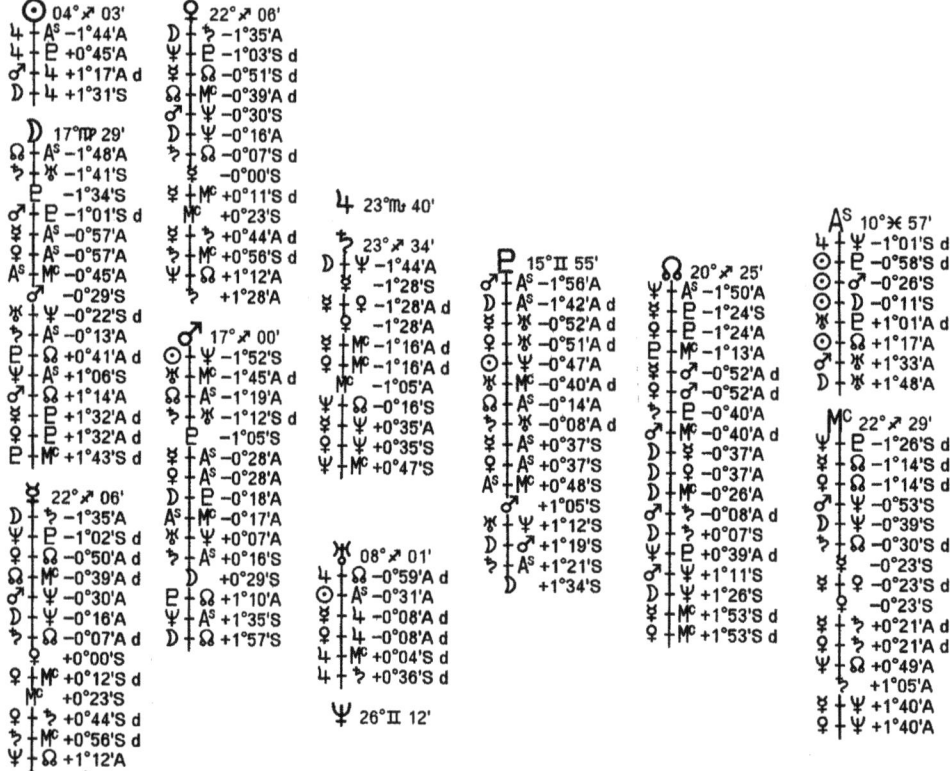

Hauptmann's Midpoints

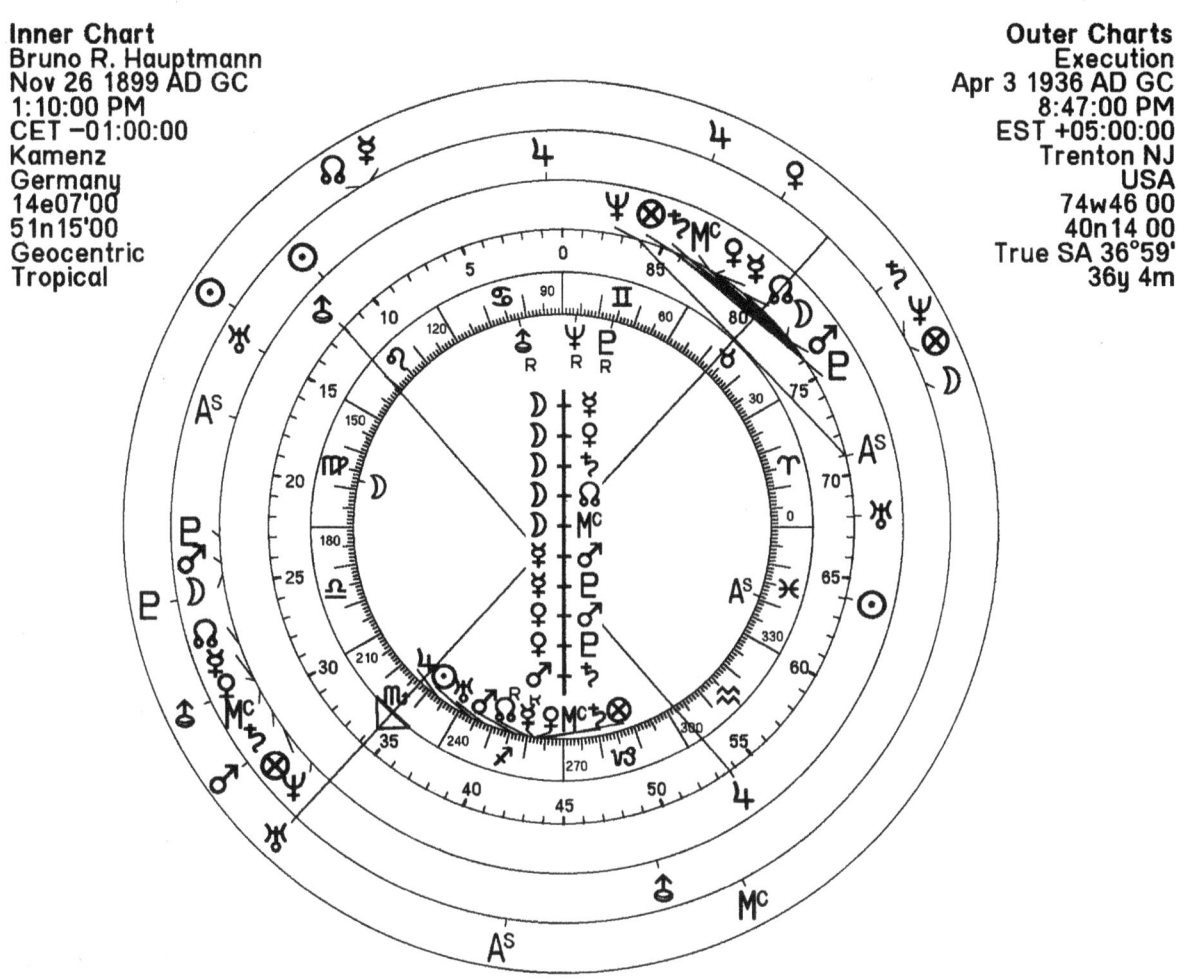

Inner Chart
Bruno R. Hauptmann
Nov 26 1899 AD GC
1:10:00 PM
CET −01:00:00
Kamenz
Germany
14e07'00
51n15'00
Geocentric
Tropical

Outer Charts
Execution
Apr 3 1936 AD GC
8:47:00 PM
EST +05:00:00
Trenton NJ
USA
74w46 00
40n14 00
True SA 36°59'
36y 4m

Cosmogram, 90°00' H4 Dial Format

Inner Radix	Middle Directed	Outer Transits
☉ 04♐03	☉ 11♑02	☉ 14♈08
☽ 17♍29	☽ 24♎28	☽ 12♍47
☿ 22♐06R	☿ 29♑05	☿ 07♈23
♀ 22♐06	♀ 29♑05	♀ 21♓27
♂ 17♐00	♂ 23♑59	♂ 01♉37
♃ 23♏40	♃ 00♑39	♃ 24♓22
♄ 23♐34	♄ 00♒33	♄ 16♓35
♅ 08♐01	♅ 15♑00	♅ 04♉15
♆ 26♊12R	♆ 03♌11	♆ 14♍39R
♇ 15♊55R	♇ 22♋54	♇ 25♋10R
☊ 20♐25R	☊ 27♑24	☊ 07♑43R
AS 10♓57	AS 17♈56	AS 12♏52
MC 22♐29	MC 29♑28	MC 21♌49
⊕ 12♋00R	⊕ 18♌59	⊕ 29♋00R
⊗ 24♐23	⊗ 01♒22	⊗ 14♊13

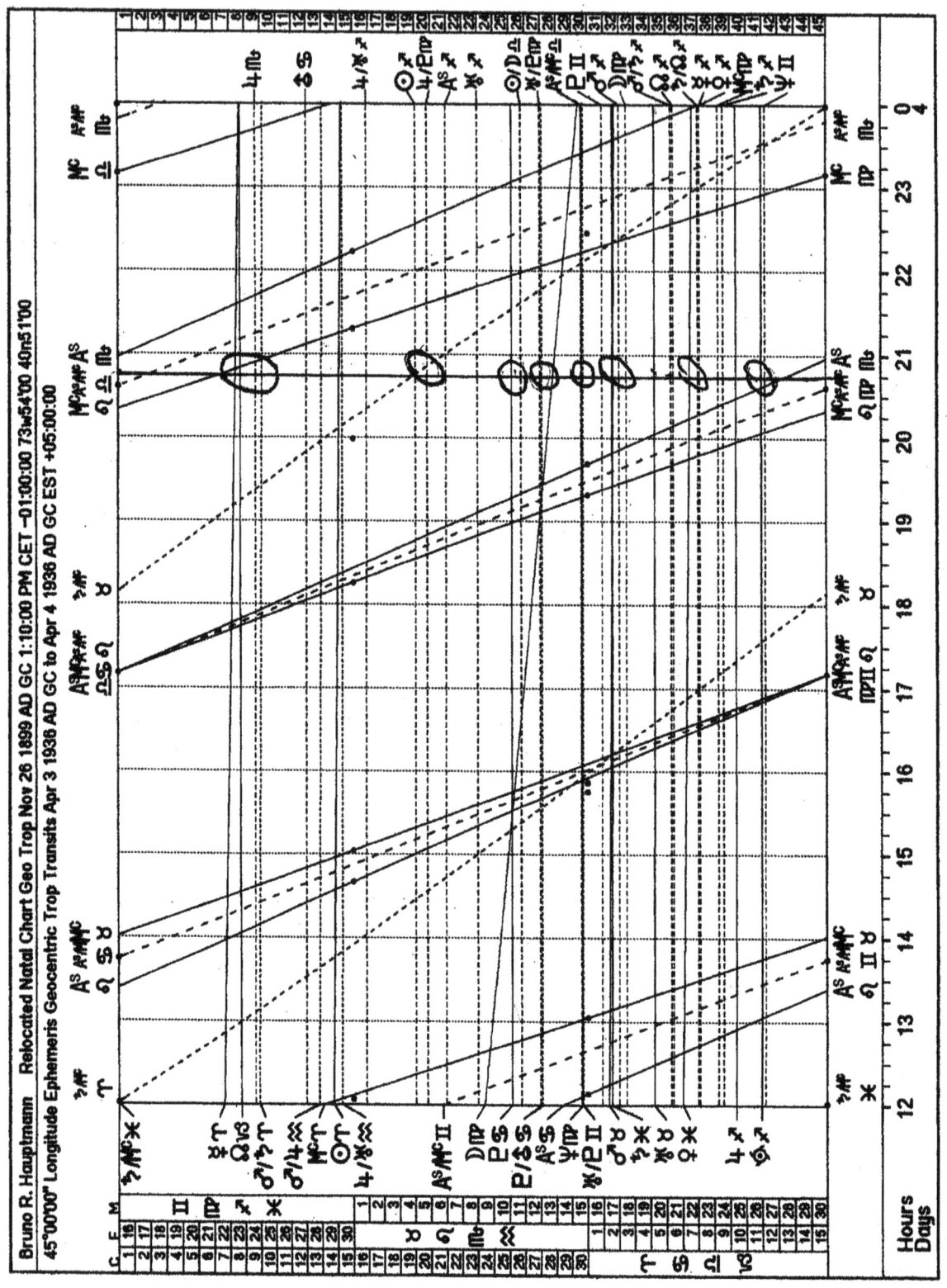

at 1 Leo 34, Mars/Pluto at 16 Pisces 28, Uranus/Neptune at 17 Virgo 07, Neptune/Ascendant at 3 Taurus 39 and Moon/Mars at 2 Scorpio 06, which together indicate the real and clouded emotional outburst of the public, cunning and deceitfulness, peculiar inclinations, fretfulness and grief, and undermining circumstances.

Solar arc Saturn at 28 Capricorn 58 was sesquisquare natal Pluto at 15 Gemini 55 retrograde and conjunct the Mars/Ascendant midpoint at 29 Capricorn 03: inhibitions, the inability to express the capabilities correctly, defeat, and the forcible adjustment to new circumstances and conditions. Solar arc Jupiter at 29 Sagittarius 05, like Uranus at 13 Capricorn, made no significant contacts; however, solar arc Mars at 22 Capricorn 24 was conjunct the natal midpoint of Sun/Ascendant at 22 Capricorn 35 and reflects a fighting spirit and cooperation but also quarrels. Solar arc Venus at 27 Capricorn 31 is semi-square his natal Ascendant at 10 Pisces 57 and can be positive as far as the relationship with a wife, but negatively shows a disharmonious relationship to the environment.

The trial started in January, lasted only six weeks and was over February 15, 1935, when Hauptmann was convicted and sentenced to be executed in the electric chair in Trenton, New Jersey. Appeals were exhausted, and on April 3, 1936 at 8:00 p.m. the sentence was carried out.

Transits

The actual positions of the transits would write the final chapter. The time of the execution was set for 8:00 p.m. in Trenton. Following some delays the time was later and Hauptmann was pronounced dead at 8:47 p.m. The 45-degree ephemeris to show the exact positions of the planets for that time, including some midpoints pertaining to the death.

Pluto at 25 Cancer 10 retrograde was on his marriage midpoint, meaning the forceful elimination of his marriage.

Neptune at 14 Virgo 39 retrograde and the Uranus/Pluto midpoint at 15 Cancer 13 were exactly on his most personal natal midpoint of Ascendant/Midheaven at 1 Aquarius 58, showing the enforcement of decisions, the mania of destruction and application of force.

Uranus at 4 Aquarius 15 was a little more then a degree away from the natal death midpoint at 20 Sagittarius 17 and Node at 20 Sagittarius 25, retrograde reinforcing the event of the execution as intervention of Higher Power, associations with mourners or prisoners.

Saturn at 16 Pisces 35 contacted natal Pluto at 15 Gemini 55 retrograde, Mars at 17 Sagittarius and Moon at 17 Virgo 29, representing brutality, the rage or fury of destruction and violent outbursts of feelings.

Jupiter at 24 Sagittarius 22 was just past natal Saturn at 23 Sagittarius 34 and the Midheaven at 22 Sagittarius 29: Change of abode or residence.

Mars at 1 Taurus 37 with natal Mars at 17 Sagittarius, Pluto at 15 Gemini 55 retrograde and Moon at 17 Virgo 29: See Saturn, as those two planets were semi-sextile.

Venus at 21 Pisces 27 moved toward natal Mercury at 22 Sagittarius 06 and midpoint Saturn/Node at 22 Sagittarius 00: self-discipline, renouncing love.

Moon at 12 Virgo 47 was conjunct natal Uranus/Pluto at 11 Virgo 58 midpoint exactly at 6:45 p.m.: Bringing about changes by force.

The Saturn/Midheaven midpoint at 4 Sagittarius 12 was within nine minutes of a conjunction with natal Sun at 4 Sagittarius 03 and square within minutes of natal Jupiter/Pluto 4 Virgo 48: Insufficient powers of defense in regard to other people, and the misfortune to lose everything. Hauptmann's last words were, "I am innocent."

Charles Stuart

In early fall 1989, amidst several drug related shootings in the Boston area, a more spectacular murder unfolded, piece by piece, revealing a complex web of premeditated intrigue.

Charles Stuart, a man not yet 30, rose from a humble upbringing and without a college education landed a lucrative and prestigious position as general manager for an elegant fur store in Boston. His salary was reported to exceed $100,000 per year.

He married a charming young woman in 1985, an attorney who had just passed the bar. Together with their combined incomes they purchased a comfortable home in the suburbs with a pool and Jacuzzi. His wife was ready to start a family and had begun talking about having a baby a year earlier. It coincided with the Satum return both were experiencing, which is generally a time of assessment in life. She happily became pregnant in April 1989, and both seemed to look forward to the birth of their child.

How did Charles reassess his life at that particular time? He had been nurturing a lifelong dream of owning a restaurant and had actually enrolled in a course to leam how to operate a restaurant business. Was he perhaps worried how the coming child and loss of Carol's income would hamper his objectives?

On October 23, 1989, the couple attended a childbirth class at a hospital a few blocks from where the above-mentioned drug related shootings occurred. On the way home, according to Charles, they were robbed and shot by a black man who jumped into their car at a traffic light. Carol was killed and Charles wounded.

Immediately police and authorities suspected this tragedy a blueprint of a "perfect crime." The onset of police investigations brought unforeseen details to light such as the purchase of additional life insurance policies and a secret lover. Thus, an incredible tale of bumbling dishonesty exposed itself.

In August, Charles confided to his brother Michael that he was tired of his wife and asked Michael to kill his wife. Michael turned down the crazy proposal but Charles didn't stop there. As his sinister thoughts continued to unfold and Carol refused to agree to an abortion, he approached an old high-school friend and asked him to kill his wife. He too told Charles he was crazy.

Suffering from obsession and delusion, Charles turned to his younger brother Matthew. Matthew idolized Charles and was responsive to the plans to help out. With five people closely entangled but lacking in loyalty and conviction, this crime was sure to be revealed if carried out. On October 23, 1989 the murder was committed with a sensational aftermath of publicity that spread throughout the nation.

In this disastrous scheme, the pretended carjacker killed Carol; their baby was born about a half an hour after the murder by emergency caesarean section following her death. However, due to lack of oxygen during the attack the baby died about two weeks later. As the story unfolded the sensational crime revealed more details about Charles' life while he was in a hospital recuperating. The brothers were quiet about their involvement to protect their parents; however, the tension apparently became too much to bear. They went to the police January 2, 1990 after Matthew, the younger brother, told the family. Faced with confronting his deed Charles could not help but make his exit in a sensational fashion. The next day, January 3, he checked into a hotel, and then checked

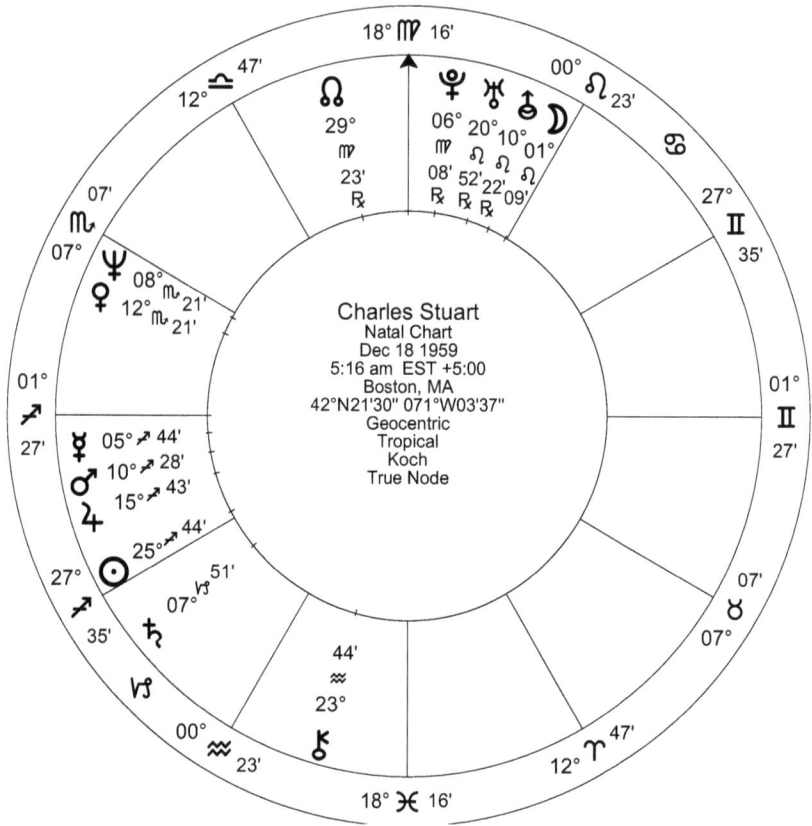

Stuart's Midpoints

out the next day at 5:00 a.m., drove to the Tobin Bridge from which he jumped to his death at 6:45 a.m. The suicide note he left stated that he did hot have the energy to go on to face the allegations.

Natal

At first glance one might think Stuart's chart is all about the Sagittarius joviality that is often associated with this sign. However, a deeper look at his natal chart and the structure patterns reveal an altogether different picture. The good luck he experienced by landing and acquiring a good position to earn more than a normal salary came with apparent ease. However, the looming Saturn return of which none of us is excluded struck with a fury of force equal to the evil of his heinous plans. Saturn brings just deserts.

The Sun at 25 Sagittarius 45 is prominent and the trine to Uranus shows his originality. The Sun square the Node at 29 Virgo 23 retrograde, points toward the importance of associates and blood-relatives in his life. The square to the MC at 18 Virgo 10 and the midpoint structure truly reflect the influence he had on people, his unique individuality, unconventional behavior and business sense.

The Moon in the proud sign of Leo at 1 Leo 10 does unusually well with Jupiter at 15 Sagittarius 44 making a trine to Mercury and square to Neptune, sextile the Node and trine the Ascendant at 1 Sagittarius 27; this combination accounts for the fortunate material success Charles enjoyed and his great imagination. Mercury at 5 Sagittarius 44 is tied to the power of persuasion and in his chart linked with Pluto and Mars and filtered through the Ascendant, which he used abundantly in contact with the public.

Venus at 12 Scorpio 21 shows that on the other hand his love life might have been one of the more mysterious qualities of his personality. The conjunction and parallel of Venus to Neptune at 8 Scorpio 21 and tied to Saturn points toward dissatisfaction with his sexual prowess.

Mars at 10 Sagittarius 29 with a conjunction and parallel to Jupiter reflect his success, but the parallel to Saturn and square Pluto contain the excessive cruelty that was directed toward his wife and then later unto himself. It might have nurtured the greed for more and being unappreciative of all the favors that came his way. The sesquisquare to the Moon typically fits the success that can be enjoyed, but when used negatively it spells squandering and wasteful ways.

Saturn at 7 Capricorn 52 is a comfortable position for Saturn but in relation to the whole chart is a sheer disaster. Saturn is linked with the rest of the so-called malefic planets. The prominent influence of Neptune in the structure pattern points to egoistic ideas and pursuit of twisted plans to the point of obsession. The barbarity of the way the crime was committed is also buried in this structure.

Uranus at 20 Leo 52 adds the tension Charles may have been experiencing throughout his marriage. Neptune is the intrigue and Pluto at 6 Virgo 09 creates an invisible force that contributed heavily to accomplishing his aim.

The Node at 29 Virgo 27 retrograde seems to play a special role in Charles' life. At first it does not appear that way since the aspects are limited compared to the rest of the chart, and on closer examination we find the Node to be very prominent by declination. It is located in the first degree of north declination, occupying a very prominent role in life. The implication of two of his brothers would clearly identify the connection and prove the entanglement with blood-relatives that the Node embraces.

This is only a glimpse into this complicated picture of a natal chart. A precise delineation would certainly add a lot more to this complicated human being.

Solar Arc Directions

Saturn at 8 Aquarius is square natal Neptune at 8 Scorpio 21 and brings tormenting emotional inhibition, strong preoccupation with self and renunciation, and the cunning and deceitfulness, causing harm to others, disasters or catastrophe caused by water. This aspect was still in effect at the time of his suicide.

Pluto at 6 Libra 34 is semi-square natal Uranus at 20 Leo 52 retrograde and brings transformation, the collapse of the old order of things and the construction of the new, enforcement of decisions like "putting a gun to someone's head" and brutality, leaving no stone unturned in the persuit of a particular task and acts of violence.

Node at 29 Libra 48 is semi-square natal Jupiter at 15 Sagittarius 44 and indicates good luck in finding a good partner, in his case his brothers.

The Sun at 26 Capricorn 10 is semi-square Mars. This is the same position as in secondary progressions.

Moon at 1 Virgo 36 is square the natal Ascendant at 1 Sagittarius 27 and has a tendency to be influenced by the female sex, a dishannonious relationship to wife or mother and women in the environment. Since Jupiter at 16 Capricorn 09 also influences the Ascendant and aids the capacity to be merry and cheerful, it indicates fortunate contacts and the creation of a harmonious environment.

Ascendant at 1 Capricorn 52 is square the natal midpoint of Venus/Uranus and brings romantic love, passing love bonds, unfaithfulness, a high degree of excitability in love life and popularity.

MC at 18 Libra 41 is semi-square natal midpoint of Mercury/Ascendant at 3 Sagittarius 36 and may reflect an individual attitude toward others, individual criticism of other people, the act of speaking or negotiating with others and revealing one's own opinion. Conjunct natal Pluto/Ascendant at 18 Libra 48 it manifests as the attainment of authority and power as well as success in career and a fascinating personality. On the negative side it also can apply for violent disputes and a drastic change in one's circumstances in life.

Mercury at 6 Capricorn 10 is sesquisquare natal Uranus at 20 Leo 52 retrograde and this renders the power to influence people, innovations and sudden perceptions of the mind. On the negative side it can indicate a scattering of energy, eccentric actions, upsets and excitements.

Transits

I was astonished when I took a look at the 45-degree ephemeris for a six-month period from August 1 to February 1 covering the transiting planets throughout the comprehensive twisted plan, including the murder-suicide.

Earlier that year Pluto moved into a conjunction with Charles' natal Venus at 12 Scorpio 21 and was

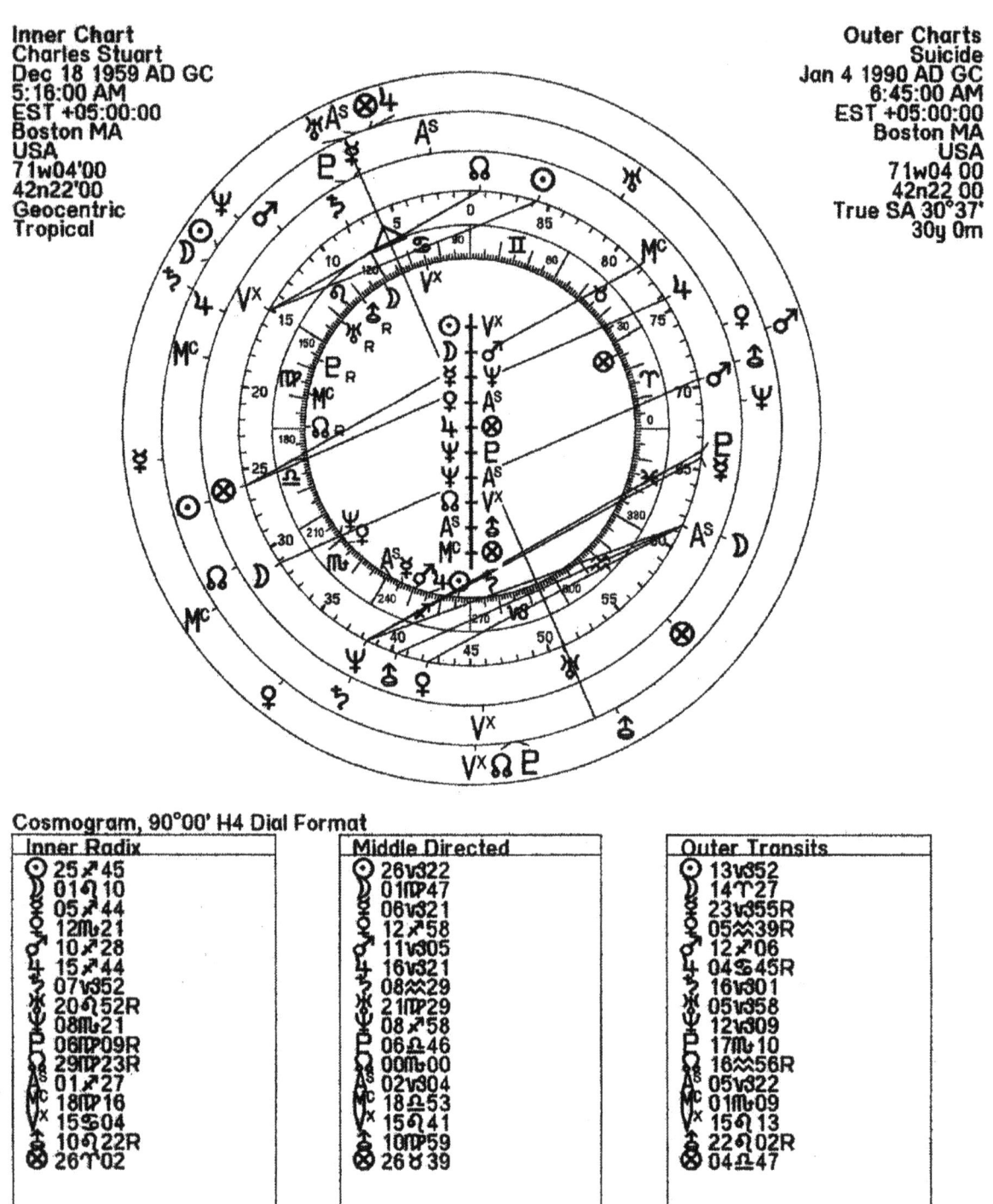

Cosmogram, 90°00' H4 Dial Format

Inner Radix	Middle Directed	Outer Transits
☉ 25♐45	☉ 26♑22	☉ 13♑52
☽ 01♌10	☽ 01♍47	☽ 14♈27
☿ 05♐44	☿ 06♑21	☿ 23♑55R
♀ 12♏21	♀ 12♐58	♀ 05♒39R
♂ 10♐28	♂ 11♑05	♂ 12♐06
♃ 15♐44	♃ 16♑21	♃ 04♋45R
♄ 07♑52	♄ 08♒29	♄ 16♑01
♅ 20♌52R	♅ 21♍29	♅ 05♑58
♆ 08♏21	♆ 08♐58	♆ 12♑09
♇ 06♍09R	♇ 06♎46	♇ 17♏10
☊ 29♍23R	☊ 00♏00	☊ 18♒56R
As 01♐27	As 02♑04	As 05♑22
Mc 18♍16	Mc 18♎53	Mc 01♏09
Vx 15♋04	Vx 15♌41	Vx 15♌13
⊕ 10♌22R	⊕ 10♍59	⊕ 22♌02R
⊗ 26♈02	⊗ 26♉39	⊗ 04♎47

starting to form a semi-square to his Node at 29 Virgo 23 retrograde. This could have been the time that the relationship with his new love Deborah became very intense and with the influence of Pluto became an inseparable union as well as the shaping of destiny shared with others.

In January 1989, Saturn contacted his natal Saturn at 7 Capricorn 52, the first Saturn Return for Charles and his wife Carol. By August 1990, when his heinous plans began to manifest, Saturn passed over the second time and was retrograde, moving direct in September, but within one half of a degree until the

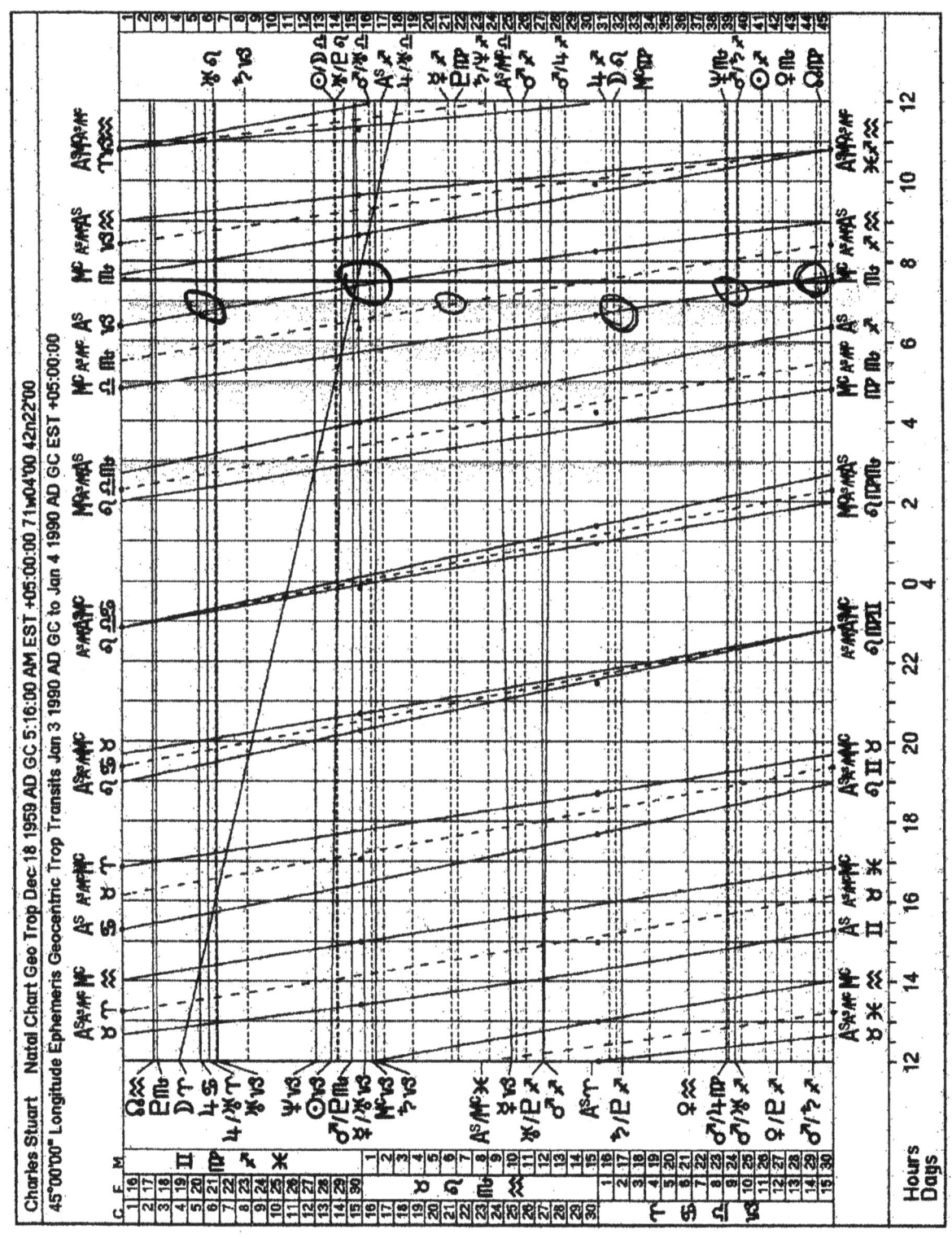

middle of October, about 10 days short of the murder when it passed the third time.

Jupiter at 5 Cancer seems to have aided Charles, contacting Uranus at 20 Leo 52 retrograde around the September 1, forming a "Thank the Lord" combination and moved on to an opposition to natal Saturn about two weeks later, bringing a tendency to have sudden inhibitions before the attainment of an objective, disadvantages and losses.

Mars at 22 Libra 34 at the time of the murder was very close to natal Mercury and Pluto, suggesting a desire to attack others.

By entering various midpoints pertinent to the deeds, one cannot help wondering about the sheer awesome working of the Universe. Following some of the transiting midpoints like Mars/Pluto at 3 Scorpio semi-square natal MC at 18 Virgo 16, resulting in a tendency to proceed in a brutal manner. The Venus/Pluto midpoint at 0 Sagittarius 45 conjunct natal Ascendant at 1 Sagittarius 27 tends to offer the ability to wield great influence over others.

Mercury/Neptune at 29 Scorpio 30 conjunct natal Ascendant shows being open to other people's influences and Mars/Saturn at 0 Sagittarius conjunct the Ascendant brings obstacles caused by others, separation, mourning and bereavement. One can see how all these forces came together when the murder took place and how the forces scattered and focused toward the morbid termination of Charles' earthly existence.

As Charles was recovering in the hospital from the suggested self-inflicted wounds the case started to unravel slowly. The brothers confided with the rest of the family and as the Christmas holidays waned and the transiting midpoint of Mars/Saturn moved toward natal Node, representing contact with prisoners, bereavement and mourning, the brothers went to the authorities January 2, 1990. The Saturn/Pluto midpoint was moving toward the Moon and Jupiter.

On the January 3, Charles checked into a hotel. He checked out the next day at 5:00 a.m. and drove to the Tobin Bridge. He parked the car and leaped to his death at 6:45 a.m. Saturn at 16 Capricorn 01 was semi-square natal Ascendant at 1 Sagittarius 27, and Mercury/Uranus at 14 Capricorn 57 intensified the desire to liberate himself from tension and separation from others. The Ascendant at 5 Capricorn 22 came to natal Uranus at 20 Leo 52 retrograde and the MC at 1 Scorpio 09 square his natal Moon at 1 Leo 10 and square his natal midpoint of Sun/Pluto at 0 Scorpio 57, culminating the experience of physical interference or violence from physical or emotional consequences. His decision was perhaps a blessing for the families of his wife and lover as well as his own, being spared a very unpleasant trial.

This case is a study in cosmobiology to learn the intricate motives that generally are outlined in a person's natal chart. Many times one can ask whether this or that is fate. The answers to that can only be found in the metaphysical realms. The case of Charles Stuart, however, is a pure case of egotism, cruelty and cowardice.

Brandon

You may wonder why someone would write about accidents and fatalities. You certainly are not alone. I asked myself the same question. However, since tragedy struck my own life many years ago, I became more and more aware of how much we are exposed to the fast pace we live in today. The statistics of highway accidents are staggering and have become a daily routine. We listen to the daily news reports, but not until a fatality occurs close to home do we realize that it can happen to any one of us.

We all have the so-called "malefic" influences in the natal chart and transiting progressions, and we are exposed to accident-prone situations daily. Many conditions present themselves by another human factor, which is mostly symbolized by Uranus and Mars, and conditions beyond that are interferences by Pluto. Pluto has always been identified as a symbol for higher power or circumstances beyond anyone's control.

I have done quite a bit of research over the years and often have found that an accident-prone natal chart does not always mean that the individual encounters a serious confrontation. In those charts you find a very strong Saturn, either by sign position, aspects or midpoint connections. Saturn represents the part of our personality that causes us to become responsible drivers and makes us apply self-discipline. This factor is quite important and the query as to why people die prematurely is much of the time difficult to determine.

The following is a brief account of events that involved my 3½-year-old grandson. My daughter-in-law, Pat, and young grandson, Brandon, came to my house for a visit. Brandon was an energetic busy little boy, the joy of our lives. This day he was happily playing a game of going back and forth from the porch to the living room. Suddenly he was distracted, by what we do not know, and he crossed the street. Living on a one-way street, in the middle of a block, traffic does not slow down when the light is green. On his way back to the house, Brandon dashed out from between two parked cars into the path of an oncoming vehicle. The driver of the vehicle was not speeding but it did not matter; the injuries sustained to the child's head at the time of impact were too extensive for survival.

Pat, Brandon's mother, sharing personal thoughts and feelings said, "to have a child die means pain which penetrates every ounce of your being and for which there is no immediate remedy. A car fatally hit our 3½-year-old son, Brandon Ray Kimmel, July 21, 1981, while he was trying to cross the street. He was immediately pronounced "brain dead" and took his last breath only an hour after the accident. How to cope with the feelings of numbness, the intense desire to have him back, and the dreaded reality of never seeing him again were mind-boggling questions. What about our feelings regarding our second child to be born in one month? The feelings were unsettling, but the new life about to be born seemed to be all we had to live for."

Kathryn was born early, 10 days after her brother's death. Due to her precipitate birth, she was kept in the hospital for one week. Once home, her presence was treasured, although obviously not replacing the life gone on before. Therefore, the temporary term of our "bitter-sweet" child came to be. The contrasts of the death and birth experience were seen everywhere, as in the long-stemmed solemn red roses standing next to the dainty gay pink carnations

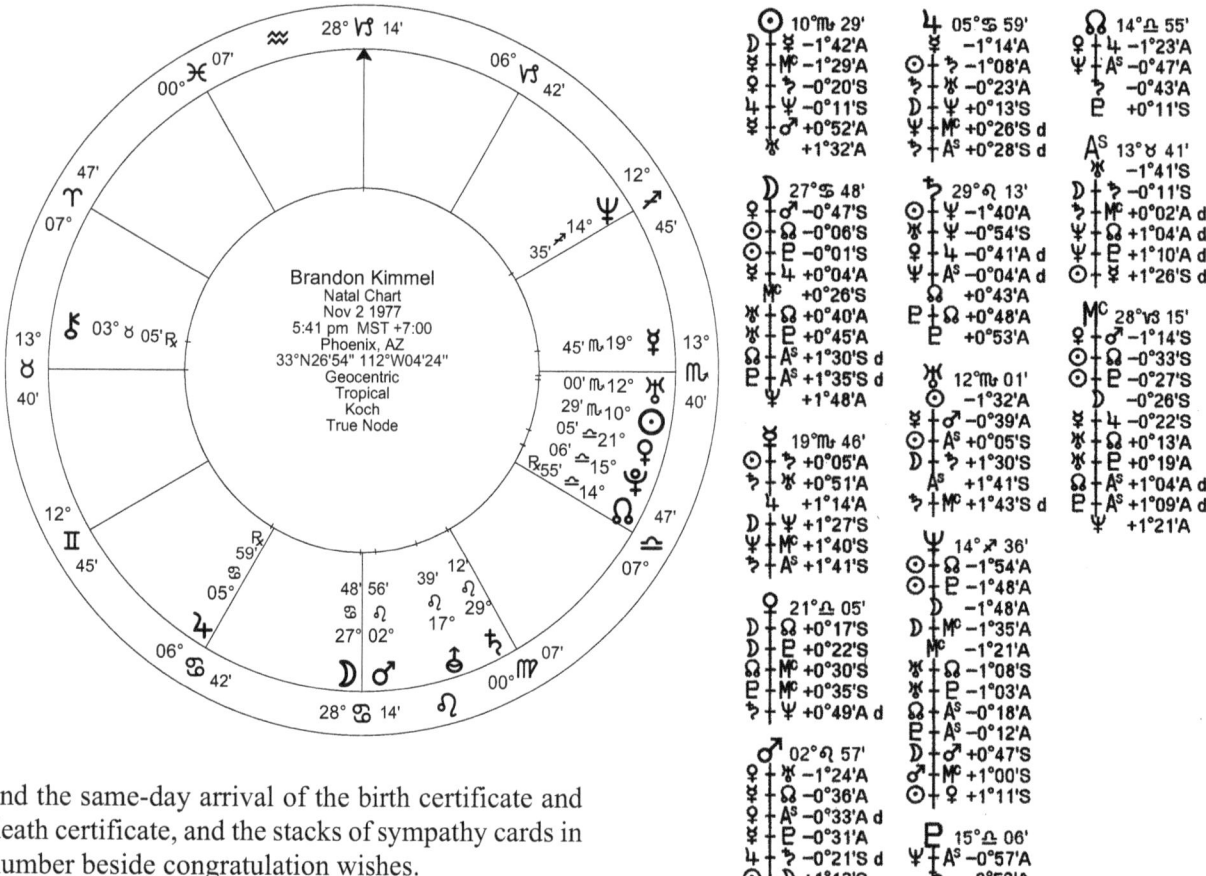

Brandon's Midpoints

and the same-day arrival of the birth certificate and death certificate, and the stacks of sympathy cards in number beside congratulation wishes.

"Life's two greatest mysteries, birth and death," says Pat, "were joyfully—painfully—intertwined, forever changing our lives, our values, and increasing respect for Our Creator." Only those who have personally experienced it can understand the trauma that followed. The effect of such a tragedy reflects upon and influences the entire family and each member suffers in a different way. Some suffer more outwardly, while others in silence. Everyone goes through a period of blame, guilt and accusations which is, as specialists in bereavement tell us, a normal way of healing the loss of a loved one.

Brandon was the first grandson born and my first comment to my son after this very happy occasion was, "he will be accident-prone." Brandon was an exceptional child enrolled in a Montessori preschool and showed great promise. His personality was filled with sunshine.

Natal Chart

Let us examine the natal chart and outline the combinations that make an individual accident-prone. The conjunction of the Sun at 10 Scorpio 29 with Uranus at 12 Scorpio 01, both in opposition to the Ascendant at 13 Taurus 41, indicates a person of physical unrest, mobility, sudden incidents and accidents. All three of these positions are contacting the midpoint of Mercury/Mars at 26 Virgo 21 that shows this young personality as having traits of easy excitability, quick decisions to act in lightening speed, action without deliberation, the danger of catastrophes, turbulent or stormy proceedings. These positions also contact the midpoint of Mercury/Transpluto at 10 Leo 19 and show rash determination, precipitate action or basically the proverbial bull in the china shop. Also, Saturn at 29 Leo 13 is semi-square both Pluto at 15 Libra 06 and the Node at 14 Libra 56 retrograde and indicates violent separations from associations or blood-relatives and suffering mourning and bereavement. These are just a few of the natal aspects and their response to accidental conditions.

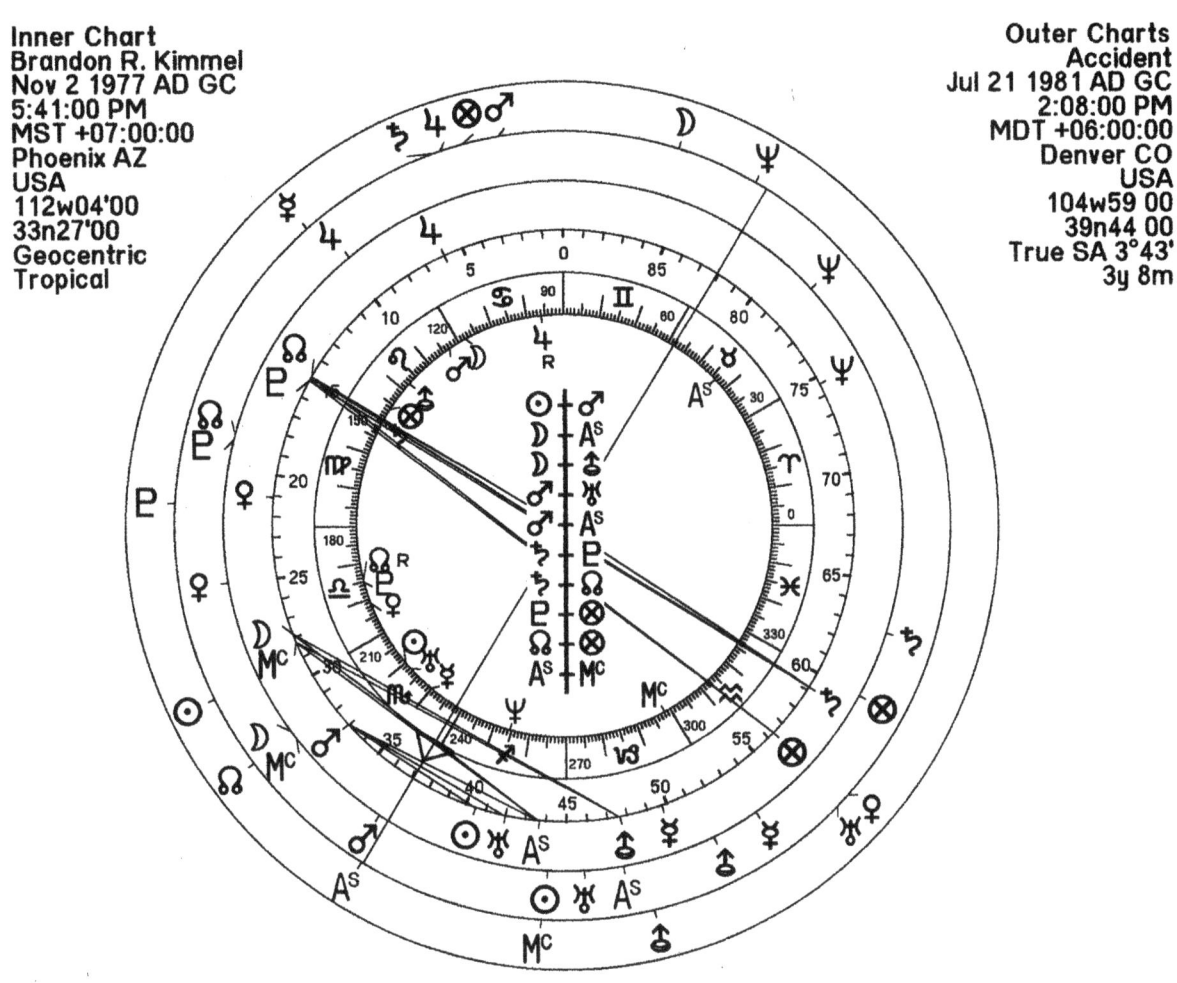

Cosmogram, 90°00' H4 Dial Format

Inner Radix	Middle Directed	Outer Transits
☉ 10♏29	☉ 14♏12	☉ 28♋57
☽ 27♋48	☽ 01♌31	☽ 25♓40
☿ 19♏46	☿ 23♏29	☿ 10♋16
♀ 21♎05	♀ 24♎48	♀ 26♌41
♂ 02♌57	♂ 06♌40	♂ 02♋20
♃ 05♋59R	♃ 09♋42	♃ 04♎36
♄ 29♌13	♄ 02♍56	♄ 04♎46
♅ 12♏01	♅ 15♏44	♅ 26♏08R
♆ 14♐36	♆ 18♐19	♆ 22♐34R
♇ 15♎06	♇ 18♎49	♇ 21♎39
☊ 14♎55R	☊ 18♎38	☊ 01♌41
AS 13♉41	AS 17♉24	AS 07♏01
MC 28♑315	MC 01♒58	MC 14♌03
⊕ 17♌40	⊕ 21♌23	⊕ 18♌15
⊗ 26♌22	⊗ 00♍05	⊗ 03♋44

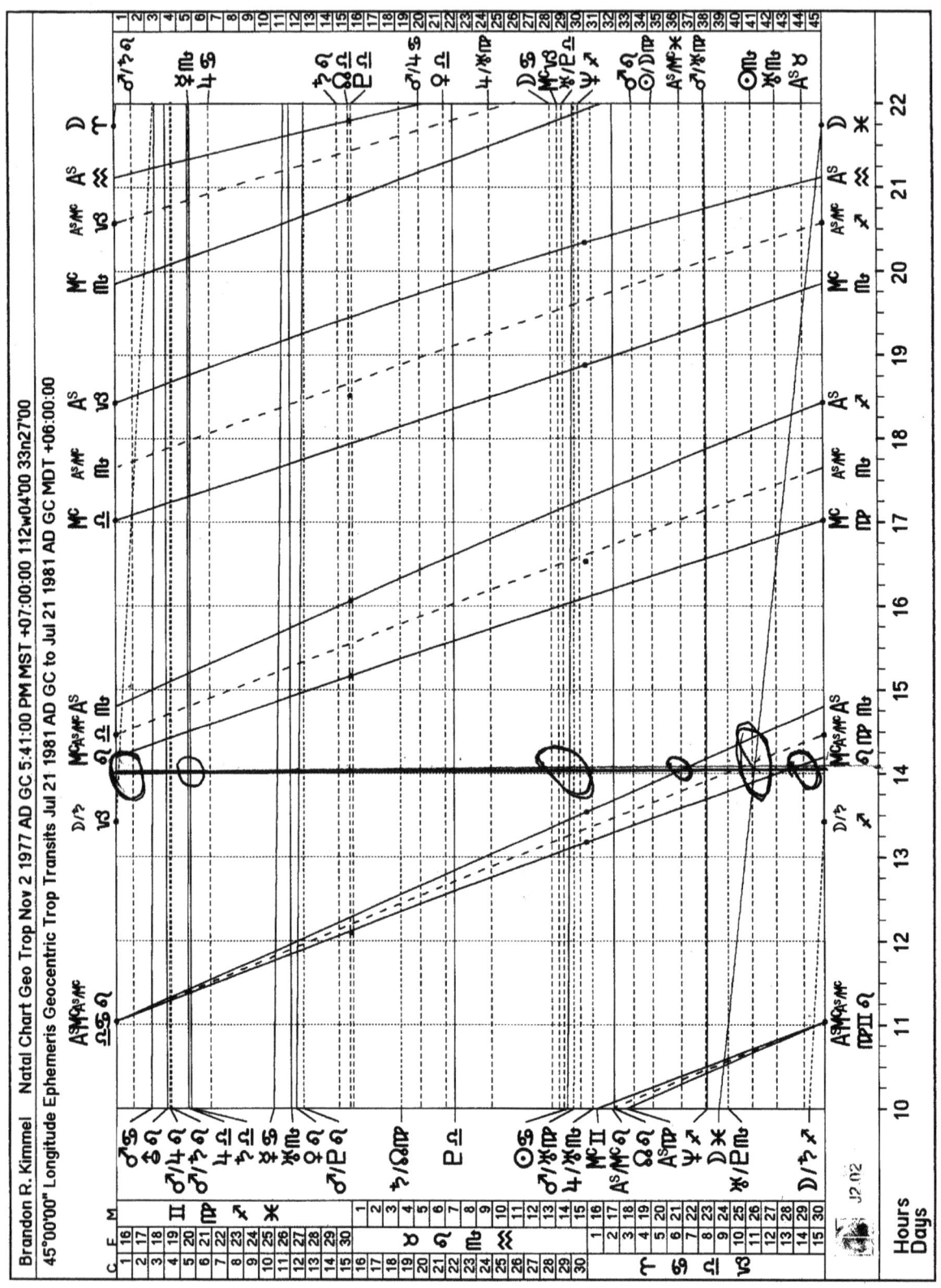

Solar Arc Directions and Transits

Solar arc Uranus at 15 Scorpio 45 and the Sun/Ascendant midpoint at 15 Leo 49 are conjunct the natal Mars/Saturn midpoint at 16 Leo 05 which is known as the death-axis and may indicate brute force, intervention of higher power, a sudden accident and separation by death. In addition, all of this energy released itself at a highly sensitive personal point of transiting Midheaven at 14 Leo 03.

The solar arc midpoint of Mars/Uranus, a symbol for accident and injury, is at 26 Virgo 13 and is within two minutes of perfect orb semi-square natal Sun/Uranus at 11 Scorpio 15; this is a symbol for sudden turns in life or a fated connection with accidents or catastrophe. The solar arc personal midpoint of Ascendant/MC that represents an important event in life is at 24 Virgo 42 semi-square natal Sun at 10 Scorpio 29, adding a boldness and assertive nature. Furthermore, the configuration was in contact with the transiting Moon at 25 Pisces 40, indicating activity of impulse and instinct in the hour.

After arriving at the hospital, Brandon was put on life-support system. At the request of the family, the system was disconnected and he was pronounced dead at 5:19 p.m. By that time the transit Ascendant/Mc midpoint was at 10 Scorpio 05 and the Moon at 27 Pisces 28 exactly within minutes on the natal Sun 10 Scorpio 29.

Solar arc Saturn at 2 Virgo 56, Pluto at 18 Libra 49 and Node at 18 Libra 38 retrograde were set off by the transiting Saturn/Node midpoint at 3 Virgo 13. The biological correspondence of this combination indicates separation from the astral body, the mystery of the three days and the organism as affected by shock events. This axis is prominently displayed and repeatedly points to accidents as described.

The death chart's Saturn at 4 Libra 46 conjunct Jupiter at 4 Libra 36 was semi-square solar arc Mars/Saturn at 19 Leo 48 and semi-square natal Mercury at 19 Scorpio 46 with almost perfect orbs; this implies news of mourning, a quick dissolution (of the body) and a very pleasant and easy death.

Patricia

The following chart is that of the child's mother. In many ways this is an unusual chart since not many women experience the phenomenon of birth and death in a very short period of time. Only a very few contacts are presented for this tragic event.

The transiting midpoint of Mars/Saturn in the accident chart at 18 Leo 33 was on her natal Pluto at 18 Leo 01 retrograde: brutality, the rage of fury of destruction, the intervening of Higher Power. It was square solar arc Neptune at 19 Scorpio 06: Weak vitality, self-torment, a grievous loss. Patricia was eight months pregnant; the accuracy is phenomenal.

As the Moon 25 Pisces 40 in the accident chart moved to the time when the death of Brandon was announced to 27 Pisces it also contacted her natal midpoint of Mars/Jupiter 27 Pisces 17, the configuration of the expecting mother and the Jupiter/Uranus midpoint 12 Taurus 29 (Moon-Jupiter/Uranus) indicates a fortunate grasp and understanding of things. The new life had to be protected as well of the condition of her son was concluded. This is indeed an event that to know the worst can act as a partial release of tension at that point.

The most sensitive midpoint of Ascendant/MC 25 Virgo 32 in the accident chart was opposition the transiting Moon at 25 Pisces 30 as the few hours elapsed until death was pronounced. The transiting Moon at 25 Pisces 30 and Neptune at 22 Sagittarius 34 retrograde were semi-square: The experience of being gripped by foreboding (she did express the fear of Brandon's death, while awaiting his fate in the emergency room). The transiting Ascendant/MC midpoint at 25 Scorpio 32 was within minutes of an opposition to the natal Moon.

As the transiting Midheaven entered Libra it contacted the natal Mars/Saturn midpoint at 2 Cancer 29, Pluto at 18 Leo 01 retrograde, Mars at 5 Aries 01 and Uranus at 5 Cancer 25 retrograde: separation, mourning, bereavement, and the ability to bear the suffering of the soul with dignity and without complaint.

Kathryn Frances

Kathryn was born 10 days after the tragedy. She was three weeks premature and in intensive care for one week. Following are some of the most prominent aspects for the birth of the child:

The position of Kathryn's midpoint of the Ascendant/MC 23 Gemini 14, Neptune 22 Sagittarius 22 retrograde and Sun 9 Leo 09 contacted the natal

Inner Chart
Patricia Kimmel
Mar 8 1951 AD GC
3:13:00 AM
MST +07:00:00
Boulder CO
USA
105w17'00
40n01'00
Geocentric
Tropical

Outer Charts
Accident (Brandon)
Jul 21 1981 AD GC
2:08:00 PM
MDT +06:00:00
Denver CO
USA
104w59 00
39n44 00
True SA 30°07'
30y 4m

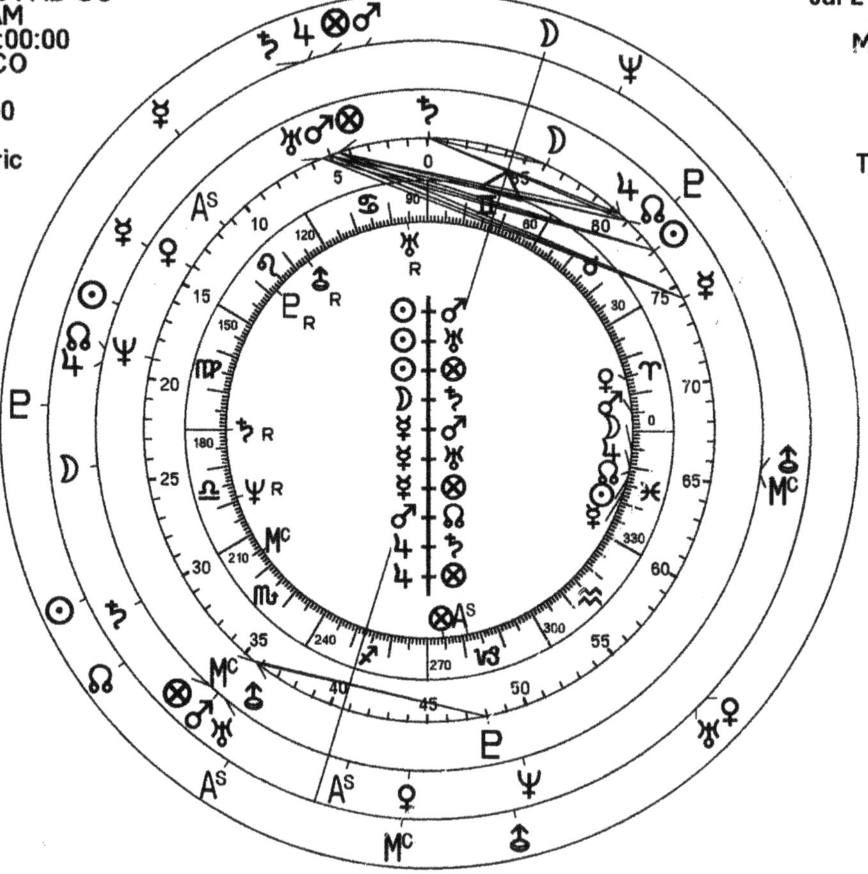

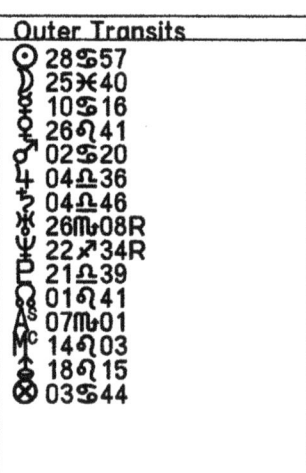

Cosmogram, 90°00' H4 Dial Format

Inner Radix	Middle Directed	Outer Transits
☉ 17♓02	☉ 17♈09	☉ 28♋57
☽ 23♓55	☽ 24♈02	☽ 25♓40
☿ 14♓18	☿ 14♈25	☿ 10♋16
♀ 14♈07	♀ 14♉14	♀ 26♌41
♂ 05♈01	♂ 05♉08	♂ 02♋20
♃ 19♓32	♃ 19♈39	♃ 04♎36
♄ 29♍56R	♄ 00♏03	♄ 04♎46
♅ 05♋25R	♅ 05♌32	♅ 26♏08R
♆ 18♎59R	♆ 19♏06	♆ 22♐34R
♇ 18♌01R	♇ 18♍08	♇ 21♎39
☊ 19♓00	☊ 19♈07	☊ 01♌41
As 11♑27	As 11♒34	As 07♏01
Mc 05♏35	Mc 05♐42	Mc 14♌03
↑ 05♌48R	↑ 05♍55	↑ 18♌15
⊗ 04♑34	⊗ 04♒41	⊗ 03♋44

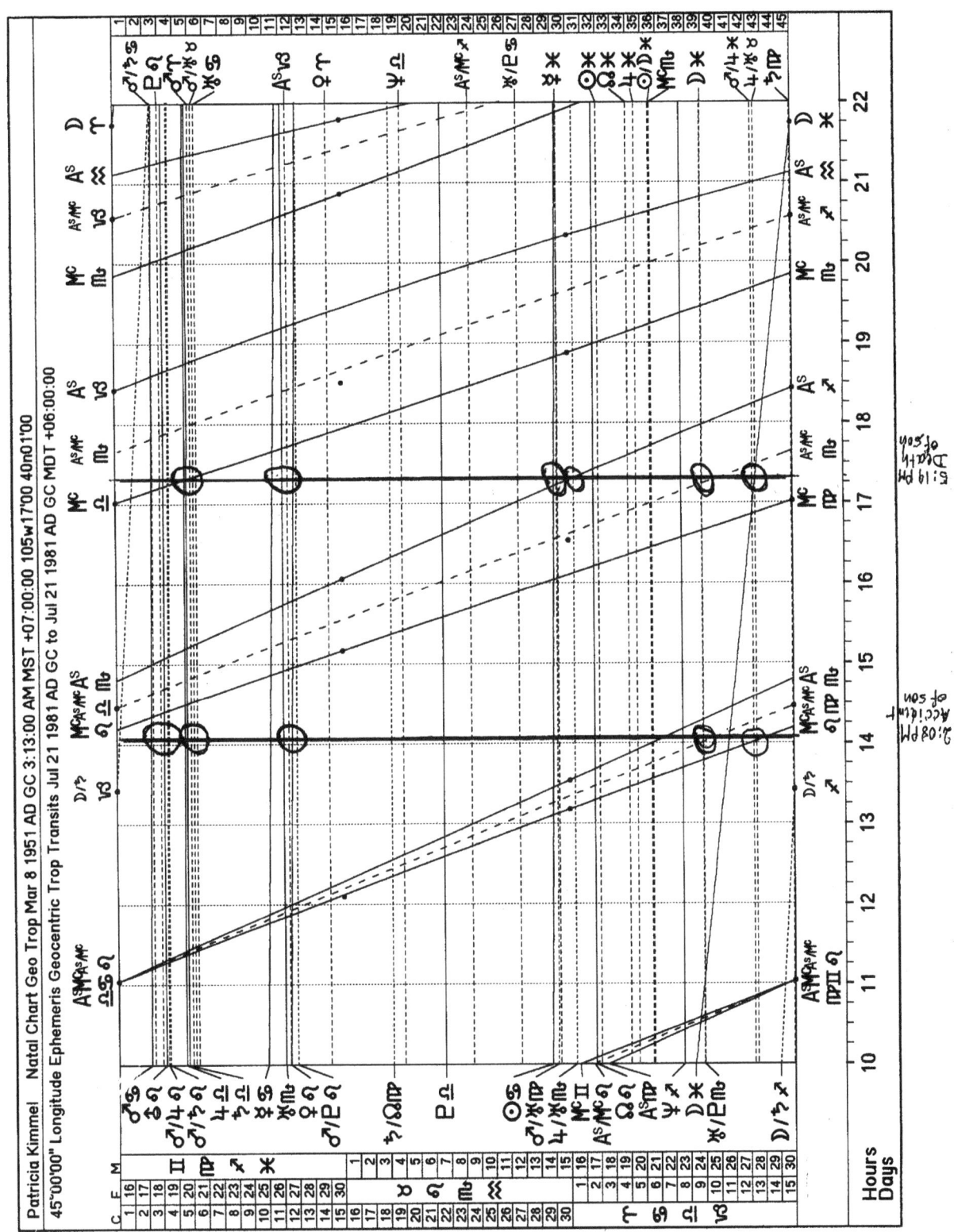

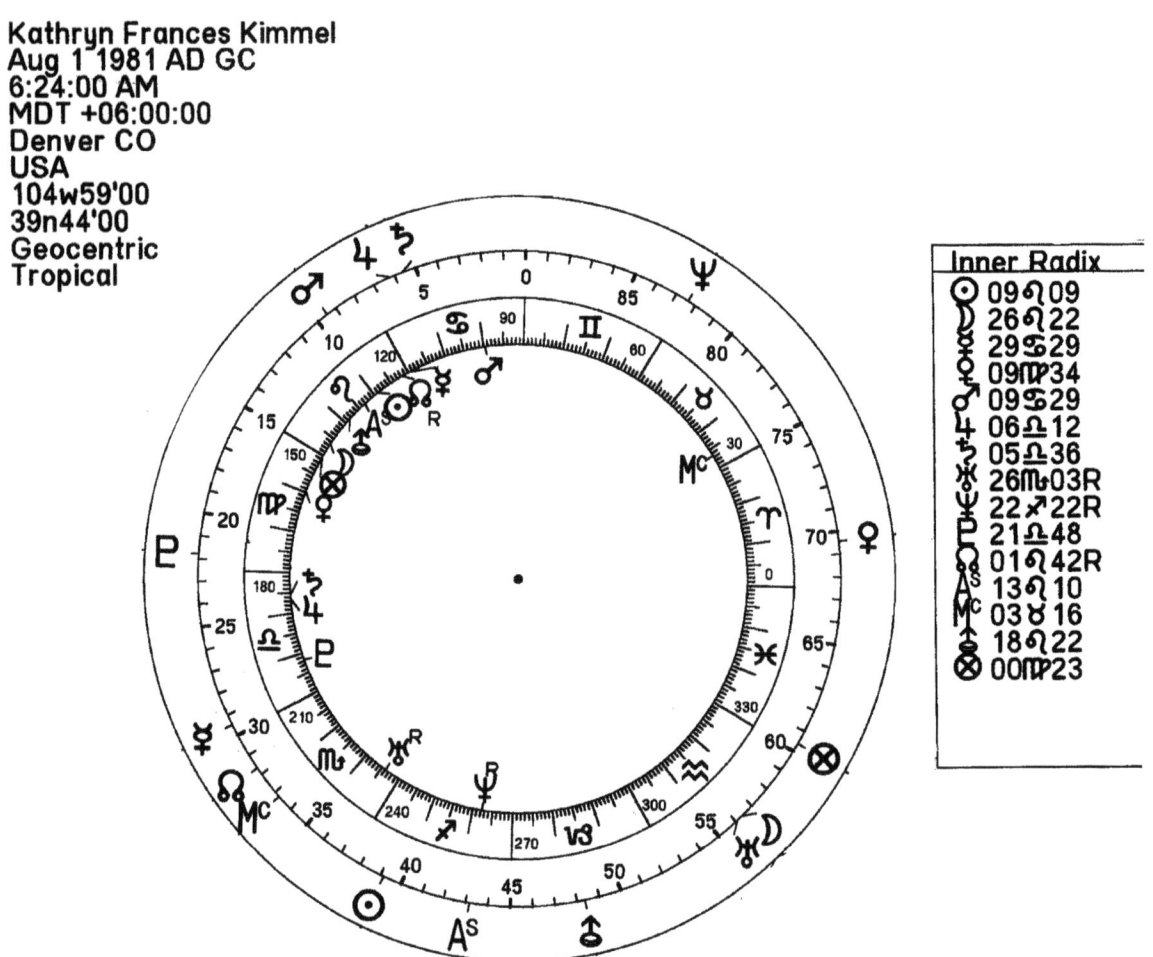

structure of Patricia's Moon 23 Pisces 55-Sun/Saturn configuration (sesquisquare). Husband and wife shared this moment of birth with a faint notion of happiness.

Transiting Sun/Saturn at 7 Virgo 23 and Pluto at 21 Leo 48 contacted Patricia's directed Ascendant/MC at 8 Capricorn 40: forced separation of living being, and transiting Mars/Jupiter midpoint 22 Leo 51 to that midpoint: one of the typical birth constellations.

Kathryn's Ascendant at 13 Leo 11 semi-square Patricia's natal Mars/Jupiter 27 Pisces 17, square natal Jupiter/Uranus 12 Taurus 29 and semi-square directed Venus/Ascendant 27 Virgo 55 brought shared happiness and showed union through the bonds of love.

Wolfgang Amadeus Mozart

When describing Mozart, Paul Henry writes, "The elements of Mozart's greatness are beyond analysis and discussion. Other great musicians can be discussed, his music does not offer any opening—is pure, unbroken, finished to the very end. There is no such harmonious phenomenon in the entire history of music."

Many books have been written about Mozart's life and his music; however only a few important milestones of his short stay on Earth are recorded here. His exceptional genius is certainly reflected in his birth chart that reveals his uniqueness.

His fame was clearly established during his lifetime and has increased, lasting more than 200 years throughout the world. He was born into a musical family and was educated by his father, Leopold Mozart. He nurtured young Wolfgang's talent from the earliest age of childhood.

Natal

A brief analysis of his personal astrological points begins with the Sun at 7 Aquarius 23 and this reveals the qualities of good powers of observation, intuitive understanding of others, readiness to help others, the realization that one's rise in life comes from one's own efforts but also from others and having a rebellious nature toward tutelage. The conjunction to Mercury reveals good chances of developing practical and mental faculties while also leading to nervousness through overwork.

The opposition and parallel to Neptune can bring about many influences like abundant experiences in the spiritual realm, but also being easily influenced by others, being exploited by others, great disappointments and entanglement in scandals. The close trine to the MC certainly represents the tremendous success Mozart enjoyed.

The structure of the Sun is equally strong. One very powerful contact is the midpoint of Mars/Pluto that has the capacity to produce a person who can work to the point of collapse and violent measures caused through the intervention of Higher Powers.

The Moon at 17 Sagittarius 48 takes on a most prominent position in Mozart's birth chart, being within one degree of a conjunction to Pluto and square to Uranus, Node and Ascendant. Reinhold Ebertin comments on this combination, writing, "The Moon describes emotions and soul life that are strongly connected with the unconscious. The accentuated feelings of lust and aversion could be decisive whether the goals in life are pursued with enthusiasm or whether the undermining of feelings impairs the creative and enterprise. In most cases the emotions are very strong and seek expression in some form of creativeness. Individuals with strong Moon-Pluto aspects are often not integrated personalities, one can move in a highly artistic and creative prowess and is able to accomplish exceptional achievements, while the other links itself with inferior instincts, addictions and even criminal peculiarities."

The Moon is furthermore connected with important midpoints. While Sun/Saturn and Mercury/Saturn are very revealing of opportunities to gain abundant experience and the absorption and digestion of many different impressions, the Sun-Neptune opposition would cause depression and persecution mania which is suggested by some of Mozart's biographies.

The Ascendant at 12 Virgo 41 is perhaps the most

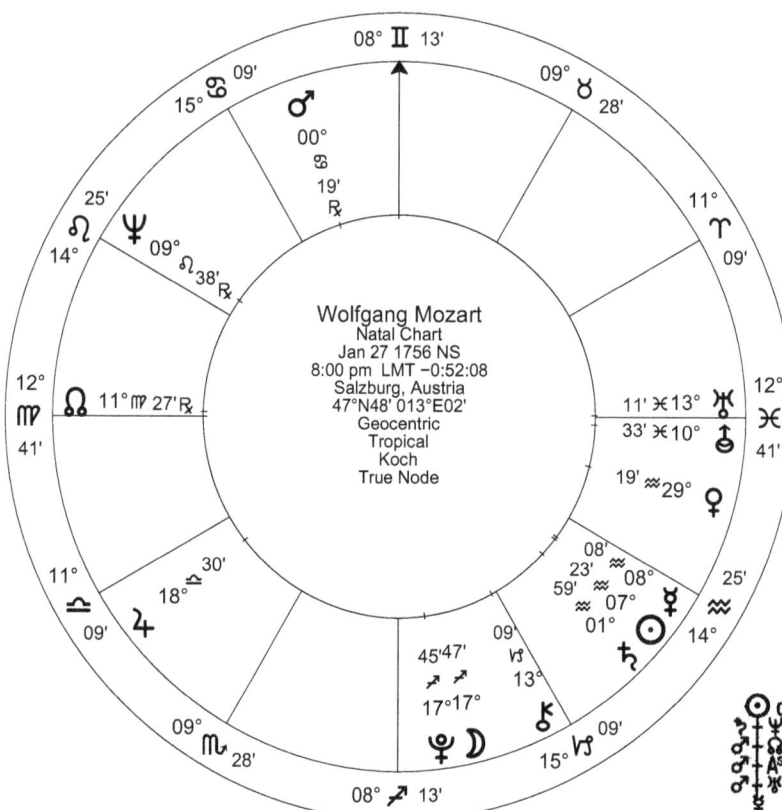

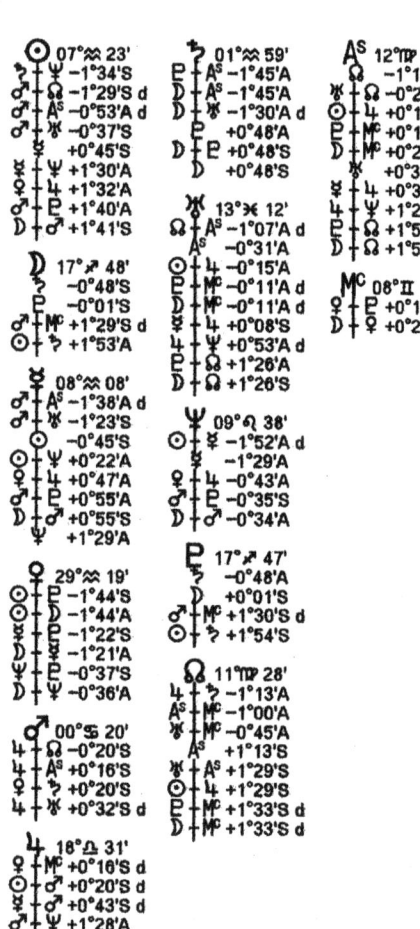

Mozart's Midpoints

fantastic structure I have ever seen in my many years as an astrologer/cosmobiologist. The very personal electrifying point is opposition Uranus within a 30-minute orb. The Ascendant is connected to all positions of the planets in the natal chart. Referring to *The Combination of Stellar Influences*, this reveals a quick response to the influence of the environment, making new contacts suddenly, originality, a quick-responding personality, an unusual degree of emotional excitability, nervousness, crisis and upsets with females in the environment.

The conjunction to the Node at 11 Virgo 28 and opposition to Uranus at 13 Pisces 12 is at the midpoint of Pluto/MC at 13 Virgo 01 and perfectly defines the unusual fame Mozart achieved during his short life and after his death. This point is also responsible for the procurement of important positions, sudden attainment of objectives, sudden changes and irresponsible power.

The MC at 8 Gemini 14 trines the Sun, Mercury and Saturn and also squares Uranus, Node and Ascendant. Most of the influence is already reflected within the Ascendant. The MC at the midpoint of Venus/Pluto at 23 Capricorn 33 and Moon/Venus at

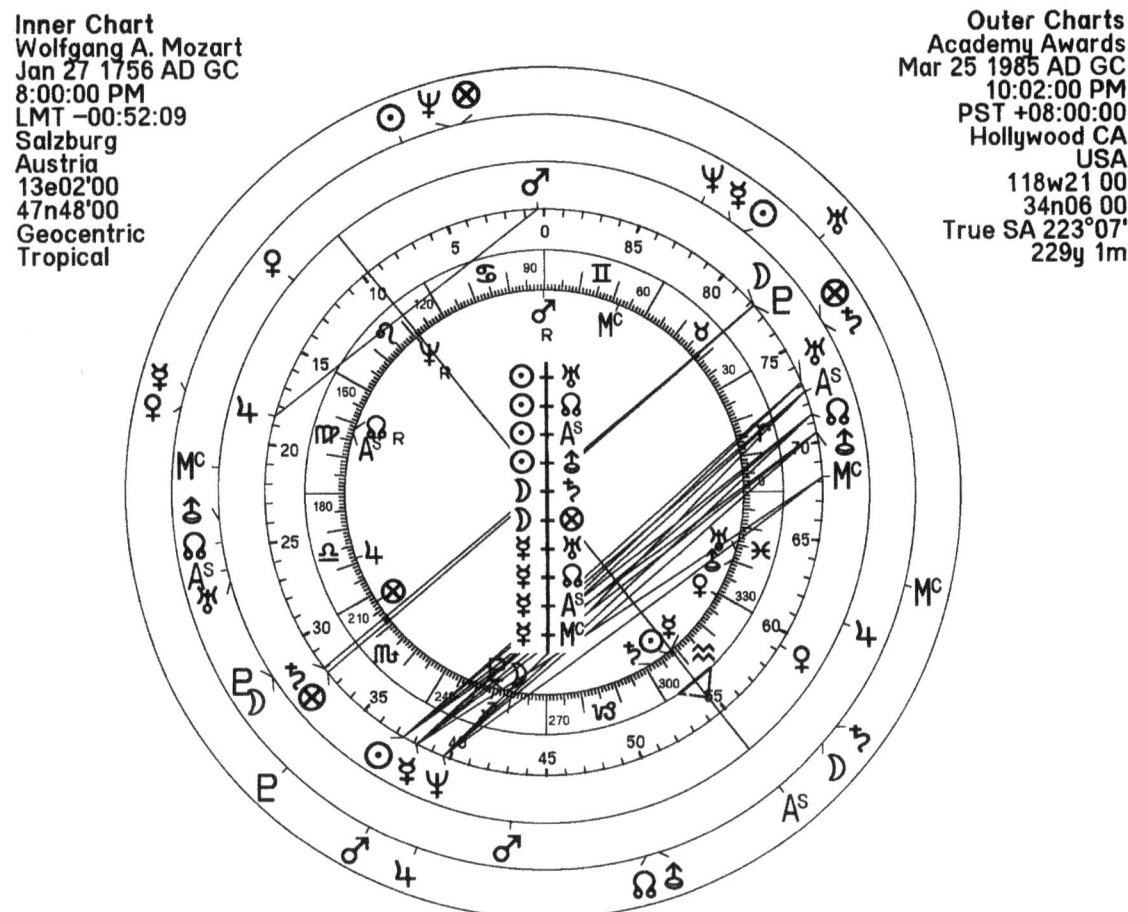

23 Capricorn 34, both semi-square the MC, show an ego-conscious direction of the sexual urges and a strong feeling of love, artistic creation and deep feelings of love, karmic union, a heart filled with love and a loving wife and/or mother.

Solar Arc Directions

At age 13, Mozart began to achieve great honors. He traveled to Italy with his father to give a concert. The week of April 11, 1770, Mozart went to St. Peter's to hear Allgeri' Misereri sing in the Sistine Chapel. Later, he wrote it out from memory. At that point the solar arc Moon-Pluto conjunction, a very important point in his birth chart, reached natal Mars, Transpluto, the Nodes and the natal midpoint of Venus/Jupiter, and the solar arc structure of Jupiter-Venus/MC came to the natal Moon-Pluto conjunction.

The time around age 21 was perhaps one of the most critical periods in Mozart's life. He fell in love with Aloysia Weber, his mother died in Paris in July 1778 and he suffered the disregard of the aristocrats of Europe. That time was marked by solar arc Moon-Pluto-Saturn axis moving into many midpoint structures, creating a period of disappointments and suffering.

On August 4, 1782, at age 26, Mozart married Constance Weber. The solar arc was almost 27 degrees with solar arc Venus moving to many natal positions. One of the most prominent is the natal Moon-Pluto/Jupiter midpoint.

His greatest achievements occurred around age 30 when the solar arc Moon-Pluto conjunction reached natal Jupiter, at which time he composed the operas "Don Giovanni," "The Marriage of Figaro" and other great works. In addition the solar arc Jupiter was precisely at the midpoint of Venus/Neptune and solar arc Sun and Mercury contacted the natal MC.

The following five years Mozart gave concerts all over Europe. In May 1787 his father died in Salzberg. In July 1791 his sixth child was born. On

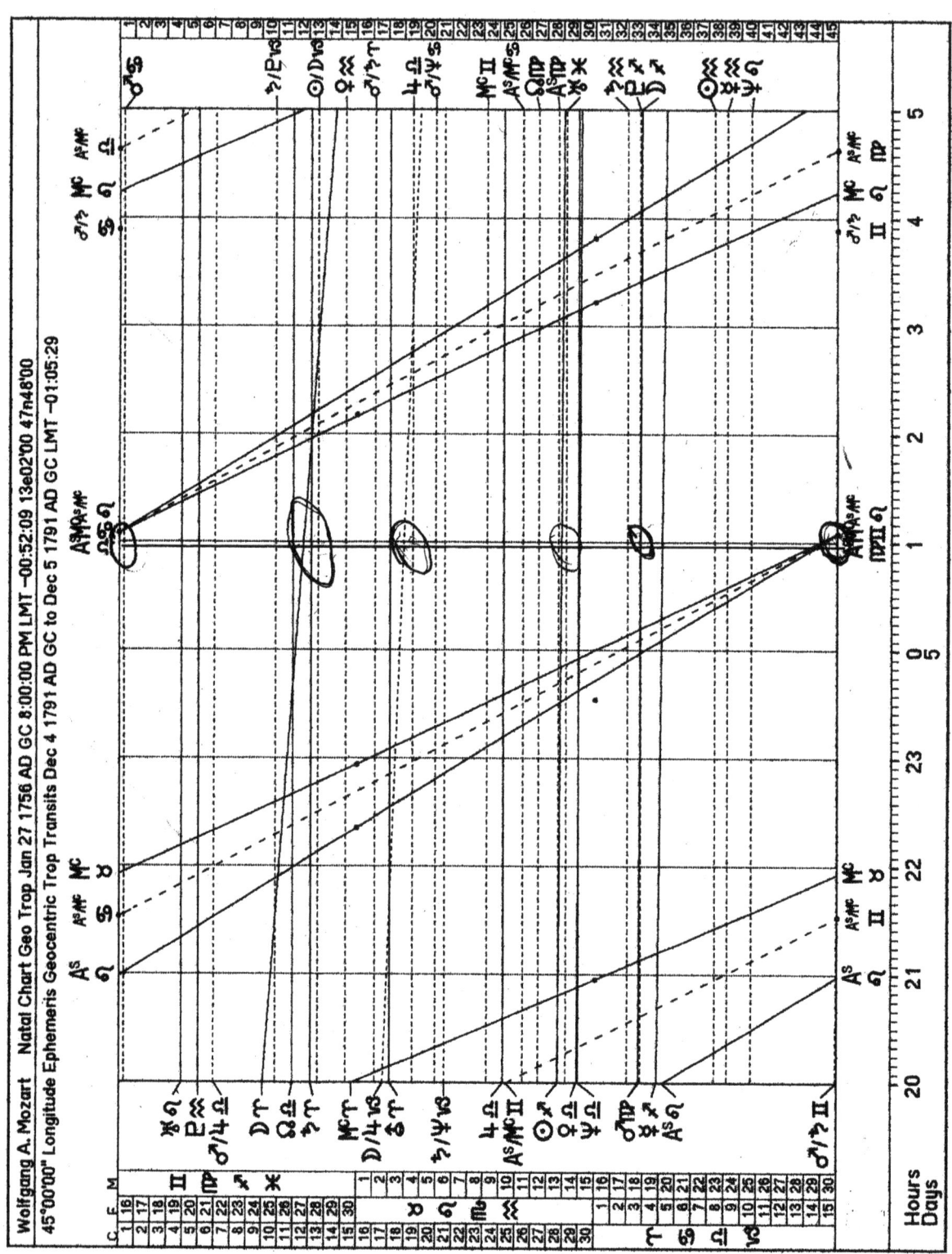

September 30 of the same year the opera "The Magic Flute" premiered in Vienna, Austria. On November 20, 1791 Mozart became ill and died two weeks later on December 5, 1791 at 0:55 LMT in Vienna.

Transits

Mozart's death has been recorded as December 5, 1791 at 00:55 in Vienna, Austria. The following are some of the most important contacts circled on the 45-degree midpoint ephemeris starting at the top.

Moon at 11 Aries 36 and Saturn at 12 Aries 09 are square natal Sun/Moon midpoint at 12Capricorn36 referring to inner inhibitions or repressions, separation from the community, marriage, shared suffering and illness.

The Moon/Jupiter midpoint at 17 Cancer 57 is square natal Jupiter at 18 Libra 31 and this combination is seen in many charts at the time of expiration.

The Sun at 12 Sagittarius 53 is square natal Ascendant at 12 Virgo 41 and Uranus at 13 Pisces relating to physical unrest and much excitement within the environment.

Mars at 17 Virgo 48 is exactly square natal Pluto at 17 Sagittarius 45 and Moon at 17 Sagittarius 47, showing great changes in mood and easy excitability.

The transiting midpoint of Mars/Saturn at 29 Gemini 58 and the MC at 27 Gemini 41 are both approaching the Aries point where natal Mars is located, thus marking the time of his death and bearing the suffering of the soul with dignity and without complaint.

Note: It is interesting to mention that in 1985 when the motion picture "Amadeus" won eight Academy Awards that natal Uranus-Ascendant structure of fame was activated by the midpoints Moon-Pluto-Ascendant, Venus/Mars and Jupiter/Node, manifesting attainment of recognition and fame, unusual success and unusual powers of attraction.

I like to compare Mozart's genius with powerful waves coming ashore, sometimes more intense than others, yet never ceasing to exist. At that time in 1985 I advanced the solar arc positions to the two hundred year anniversary of Mozart's death in 1991 and projected that "another colossal wave would come ashore. Once again the music of Mozart will receive prominence and the truth of his genius will be celebrated the world over." This was realized when in December 1988 New York's Lincoln Center for the Performing Arts announced that its "Mozart Bicentennial," which began in January 1991.

Robert

Robert grew up with three brothers and a sister and was quite a happy lad. To fortify his individuality he instinctively became a fighter in his early years. He started kindergarten when he was 4½ years old and was a favorite of the teacher. Going on to first grade was even more exciting for him. Being rambunctious, dashing and tumbling at play, he acquired many bruises, scrapes and cuts and some broken bones.

As the years passed, Robert began to grow up and it was in the sixth grade when he felt emotionally charged through his involvement in school. He became very athletic and by the eighth grade also developed great interest in science and music. Due to some difficulties concerning his father he found himself with low confidence and depression until the following year when he met a history teacher who showed him a direction that changed his life.

One day after graduating from high school, Robert enlisted in the armed forces to become a professional soldier. After basic training and further schooling to become a paratrooper in 1967, he was sent to Viet Nam; he was 18 years old. The following year on the battlefield he described in his own words that he had "no fear of death and met God face to face." The next three years were extremely intense, filled with the danger of enemy fire and suffering battle wounds. The date of his first injury is not clear, but the following two engagements of war Robert recalls clearly.

On February 18, 1969 at 4:20 p.m., "I was on a Battalion Search and Destroy Mission in the jungle mountains region of South Viet Nam," he said, "especially in the mountains of An-Ke, 40 kilometers south of Kotum and 46 kilometers west of Qui-Nhon, in II Corp near the camp of the First Air Calvary Division with whom we shared occupancy." Several days before this incident, "we had sporadic hostile contact with small units of the First North Vietnamese Infantry Division," he explained. In the afternoon of this day, "we suddenly made heavy contact with enemy forces at the base of a hill known as Hill 805."

"A massive amount of small arms and automatic weapons fire," he continues, "started and did not let up for over 30 minutes." During this fight, "I was near the point of a company size column that eventually surrounded the north side of Hill 805. Moving slowly and carefully in force up the hill, we had planned to surround the enemy at the top of the hill and totally destroy them." While maneuvering, other members of First Platoon were in selected places to avoid casualties. "I stood behind a large jungle fern using it as a shield from the enemy fire." While returning as much fire as possible, "a bullet hit the tree," he said, "went through it, and struck me in the left side of the chest, after penetrating through an M-16 magazine of bullets that I had draped across my chest like a bandoleer. I was blown backwards and fell into unconsciousness."

Two days later Robert woke up in the 67th EVAC Hospital in Qui-Nhon. He had been returned to his original unit, B Company first Battalion 503rd Airborne Infantry 173rd Airborne Brigade. "I was told that I had received a socking chest wound," he said. The medic who administered treatment placed a piece of plastic from a bandage over the wound and laid it across Robert's chest until an evacuation helicopter could take Robert and several others wounded from the field. "The bullet had broken the seventh rib

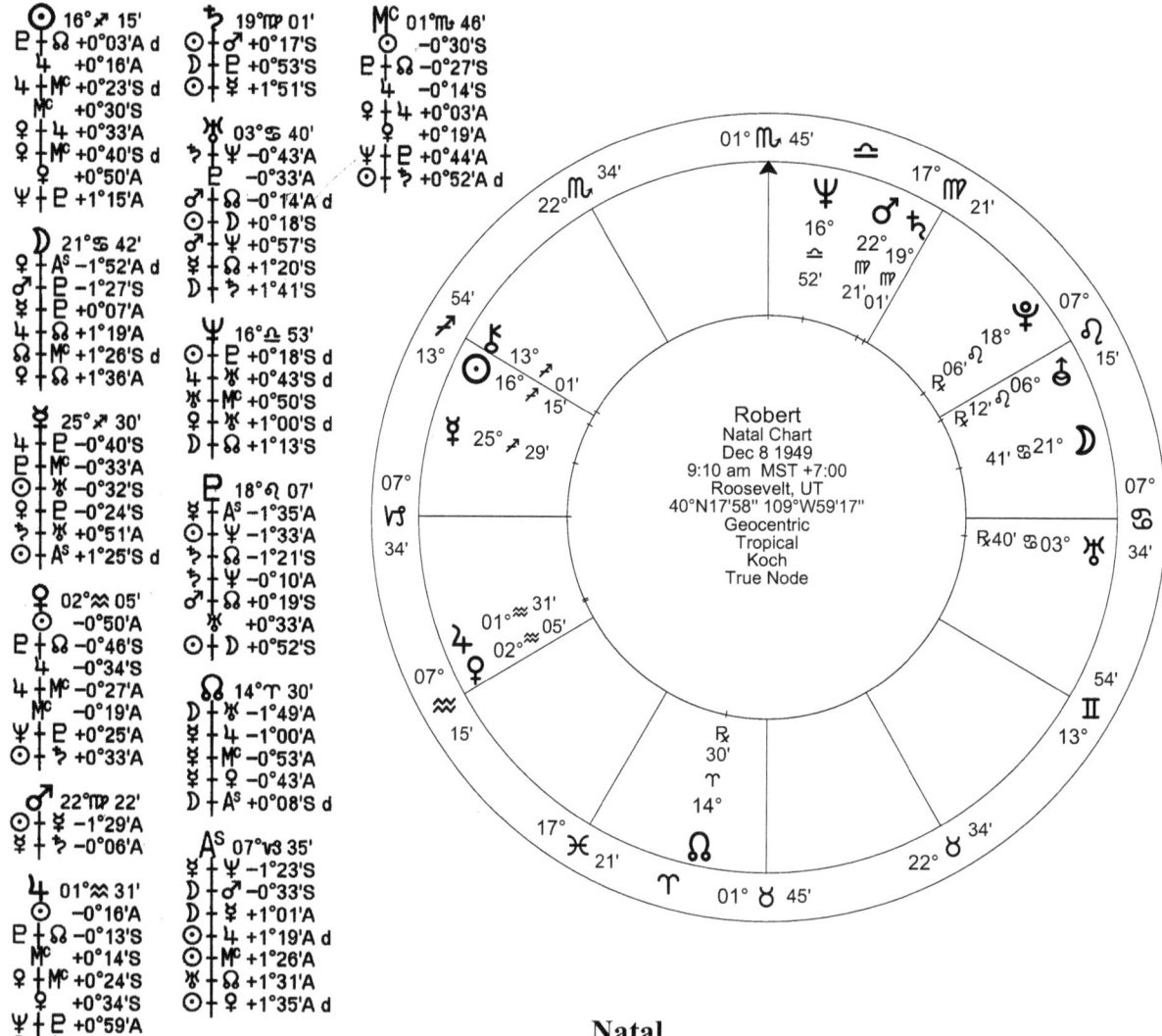

Robert's Midpoints

on the left side of my chest," he described, "just to the right below my heart. This was the second of three wounds I received in the Republic of South Viet Nam."

Robert was awarded a second Purple Heart for a wound received May 9, 1969 at 9:40 a.m. Similar to the previous battle wound, a bullet ricocheted off of a tree before striking Robert in the leg, shattering his thighbone.

In 1970 his tour of duty was over. Among his Service Decorations are three Purple Hearts, a Silver Star and a Distinguished Service Cross. Instead of continuing on as a professional soldier he changed direction and became a science teacher.

Natal

The Sun at 16 Sagittarius 15 clearly describes a mobile and ready for action personality. Robert has a love of sports and his idealism has no bounds; a dual nature and striving for a secure position in life are equally pronounced. Being enthusiastic and sociable is also a positive trademark for him. The regular aspects are numerous. The square to Mars at 22 Virgo 22 emphasizes a great fighting spirit, the will to live and great vitality. The courage and desire to lead is pronounced as well. The square to Saturn at 19 Virgo 01, however, points to inhibition and separations. At times he would have a difficult struggle in regard to advancement in life and little help through elderly people. The feeling of loneliness would come also with the just stated aspects.

The structure pattern of the Sun is equally strong, again pointing toward a powerful personality, especially the midpoint of Pluto/Node. The Jupiter/MC

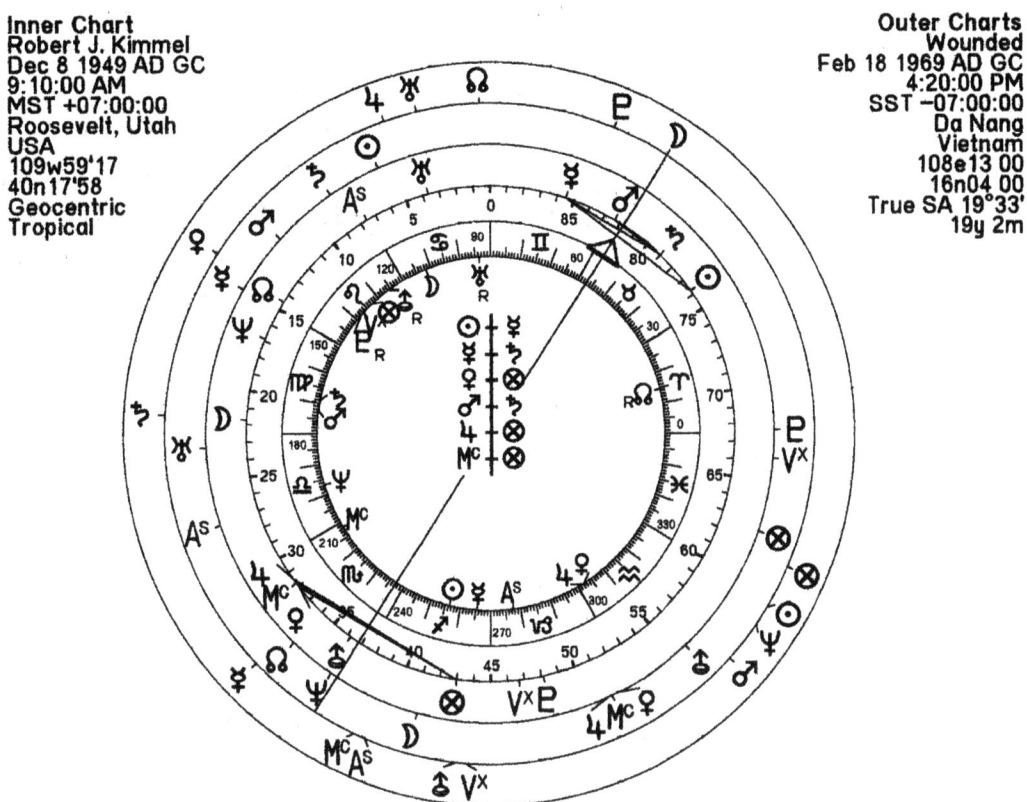

midpoint stands for a healthy physique and striving toward a particular aim. The midpoints of Venus/Jupiter at the MC indicate the joy of love, while Neptune/Pluto can bring about peculiar diseases such as Agent Orange poisoning from Viet Nam.

The Moon at 21 Cancer 41 describes the emotional life, which is contrary to the enthusiastic personality stated by the Sun. The square to Neptune at 16 Libra 53 heightens the sensitivity and provides a vivid dream life. It also points toward the ability to understand other people's troubles. The negative connotation can bring about the danger of being exposed to peculiar and strange influences, and crises in life caused by laziness or self-indulgence.

The structure pattern of the Moon is much more complex, citing the strongest as Mars/Pluto, Mercury/Pluto and Jupiter/Pluto, and Jupiter/Node pointing to impulsiveness and daring, as well as injuries, the power to speak with heart and soul and consequently convince people, and attaching great importance to spiritual relationships.

The Ascendant at 07 Capricorn 35 stands for a responsible attitude, self-control, concentration and diplomacy, and determination to improve his social position and establish a sufficient income. The opposition to Uranus alters the personality considerably, adding tension, quarrels, separations and difficult but successful battles in life to overcome complicated conditions.

The structure pattern for the Ascendant alters the behavior even more with midpoints Sun/Jupiter and Sun/MC and represents devoting life to a good objective, individual progress and advancement.

The MC at 01 Scorpio 46 brings about perserverance, a sympathetic understanding of others and the right grasp of every situation, but also a tendency to overtax one's powers and energy. The close square to Jupiter and Venus shows success, generosity and optimism, love and affection, a sense of beauty and art and, at times, self-torment and confusion.

Solar Arc and Transits

The solar arc was 19 degrees 33 minutes. A few distinct solar arc directions are quite revealing, like the Sun, Jupiter, MC and Venus on the natal midpoint of Uranus/Ascendant and Mercury in contact

73

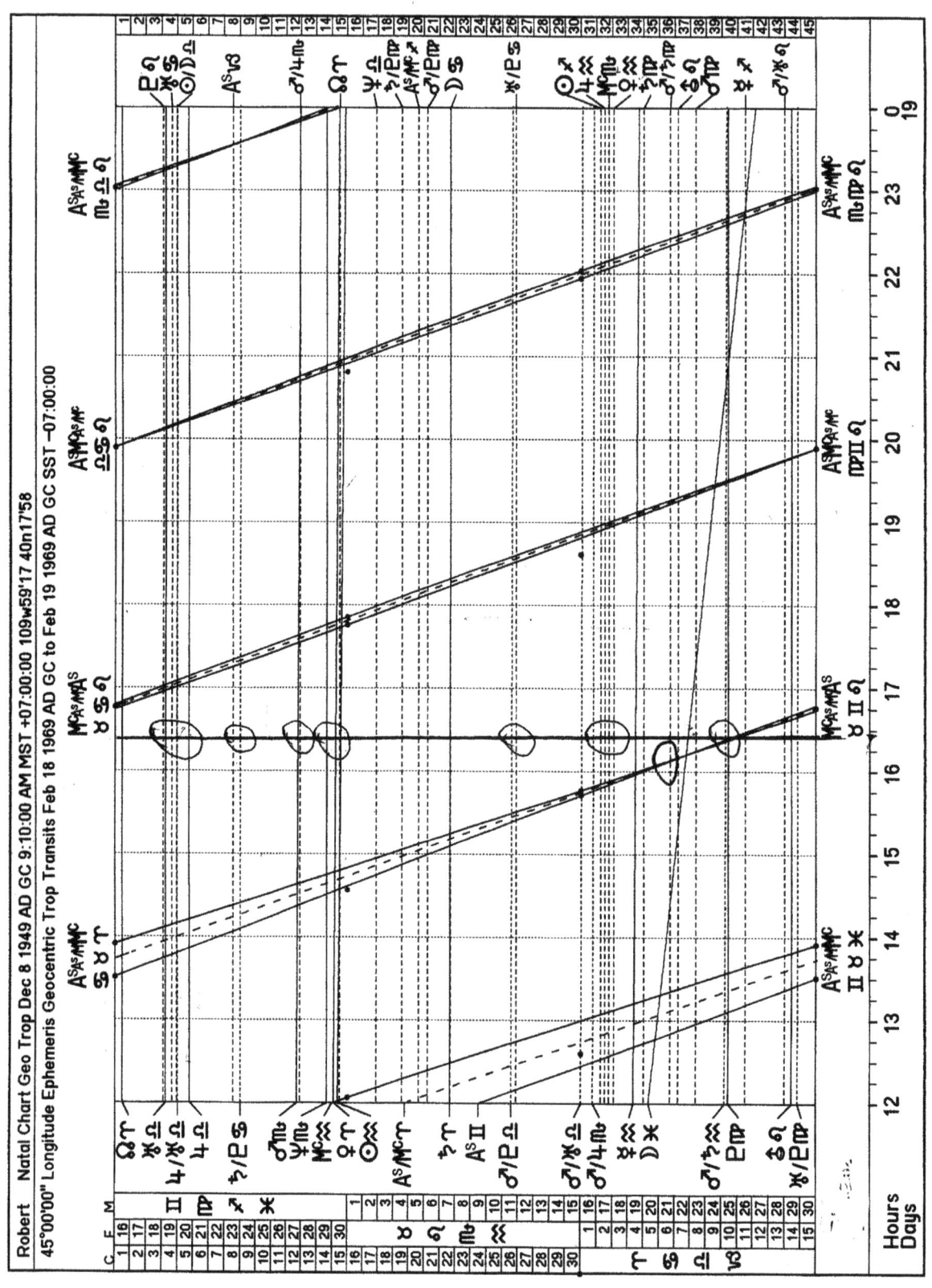

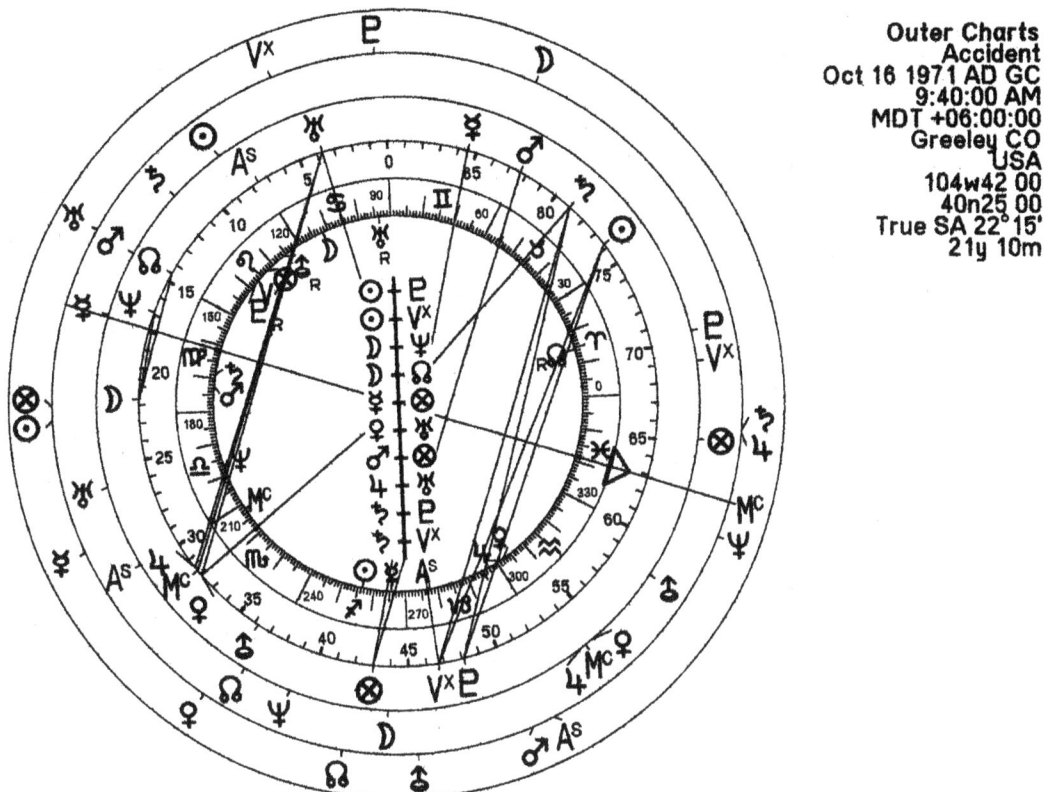

with the Node. The transits are more numerous.

Transiting Uranus retrograde was in 03 Libra 26 square natal Uranus in 03 Cancer 40 and semi-square natal Pluto in 18 Leo 07 and so was the transiting Jupiter/Uranus midpoint, perhaps saving his life. Transiting Mars 26 Scorpio 48 was conjunct natal Mars/Jupiter, also a fortunate combination to have at a time of great peril. Transiting Saturn in 21 Aries 41 was exactly square his natal Moon at 21 Cancer 42. The transiting midpoint of Mars/Pluto was contacting natal Uranus/Pluto, certainly a life changing combination. Transiting Mars/Jupiter in Scorpio was in tune with his fortunate cluster of planets, Sun, Jupiter Venus and MC. Transiting Sun at 20 Aquarius and Venus at 14 Aries 15 on the natal Node identifies the help he received by being flown to the hospital. The Moon in 21 Pisces 47 was just approaching natal Mars in 22 Virgo 22.

Accident

Two and one half years later, on October 16, 1971, 5:20 a.m. while attending college, another accident occurred. Robert was warned that the coming weekend showed transits that were not suitable for traveling. However, this suggestion met deaf ears. Robert and his friend Gregg were traveling on a highway at an excessive speed, and drizzling rain caused the pavement to be wet.

The car slid only a little onto the shoulder of the highway; but, because of the high speed the car went out of control, flipping over three times, plowing down a fence and several posts and finally landing completely demolished but right side up. Both young men stepped out of the car and shook hands with amazement. Neither one of them was injured except for minor bruises.

Solar Arc and Transits

The solar arc clocked in at 22 degrees 15 minutes. Some of directions for this event include solar arc Pluto at 10 Virgo 33 and Uranus at 25 Cancer 55, while the midpoint of these two planets at 18 Leo 09 is only two minutes away from natal Pluto at 18 Leo 07, revealing a process of transformation, an accident and the mania of destruction.

Solar arc Mars at 14 Libra 17 was opposite natal Node at 14 Aries 30, solar arc Transpluto at 28 Leo

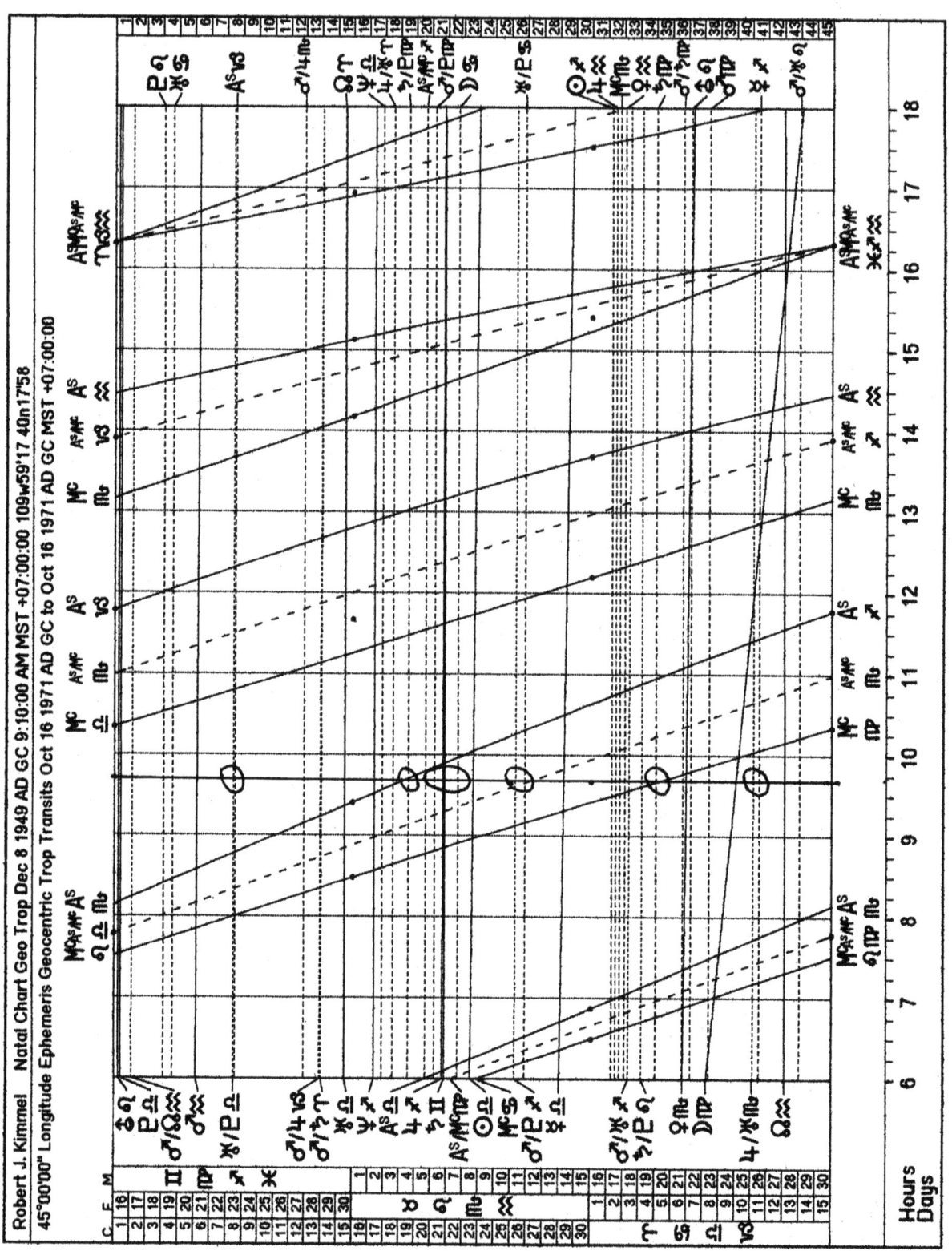

28 and transiting Uranus at 14 Libra 30 indicate the cooperation between Robert and Gregg when the car overturned three times.

Transits

The Uranus/Pluto midpoint at 07 Libra 27 was only minutes away from a square to natal Ascendant at 07 Capricorn 35, showing an unusual or restless environment, application of force and accident. From traditional astrology we know that Capricorn rules the knees and Aries the head. The bruises incurred were to the knee and the head (black eye).

The transiting Jupiter/Uranus midpoint at 10 Scorpio 07 in a semi-square to natal Mercury at 25 Sagittarius 30 shows short travels, having the ability to adapt to every situation, a fortunate release of tension, damage to buildings and motor damage. According to the report and after discussing the situation with Robert, it was determined that the quick decision by the young men prompted them to brace themselves while the car was rolling over three times. The fortunate release of tension was demonstrated by the fact that there were no serious injuries. The accident damaged a farmer's fence and rendered the car completely useless.

Ronald Goldman

Ronald Goldman is one of the murder victims of the notoriously publicized "Trial of the Century" of O.J. Simpson in 1994. While the other victim, Nicole Simpson, and her life activities were much more scrutinized, it is assumed Ronald Goldman was an innocent bystander. But was he?

Ronald was 25, good looking, energetic and admired and loved by his family and friends. His dream and objective in life was to own a large restaurant. He worked occasionally as a male model to supplement his income. His downside was perhaps a fondness for the good things in life. During the trial, reports surfaced that credit-card debt led to a bankruptcy of around $12,000 for liabilities in 1992.

At the time of his death he was working at a restaurant as a waiter to acquire experience for his ultimate dream. In order to achieve that sooner he liked to mingle with the rich and famous in upscale Los Angeles where he felt comfortable expressing his cheerful, pleasurable and warm personality. He was confident that would help him take advantage of opportunities, should they arise. An acquaintance and friend, Nicole Simpson, was perhaps one of those people.

At the Mezzaluna restaurant where Nicole Simpson often dined, rumors of drug trafficking floated around, and that five young men were in jeopardy. Within the past three years, two had been killed and two were missing, and now Ronald had been murdered.

Prior to his murder, Goldman had received anonymous telephone threats and one of his managers at Mezzaluna Restaurant had angrily warned him, "If you're fucking her (Nicole) you are in trouble!" A witness reported that the manager was furious about the circumstances surrounding Ronald's activities but was not referring to threats from O.J. Simpson.

According to sources and friends close to Goldman and his place of work, Ron was the object of an obsessive and abusive man who was jealous to the point of violence. This man, it is reported, expressed a raging hatred for Nicole and was stalking Ron, and threatening both of them if Ron did not break off his affair with her.

Perplexing burglaries led to sensationalized headlines in newspapers and television. Defense attorney Robert Shapiro's office was broken into and robbed during the trial. Faye Resnick's apartment was broken into in 1994, her journals rifled through and stolen, and she blamed the Simpson legal team. According to journalist Geraldo Rivera, another close friend of Faye Resnick's had been murdered some years before in San Francisco.

Dr. Jennifer Ameli, a clinical psychologist who had counseled both Ron and Nicole, was harassed and threatened in 1994 and 1995. Her offices were burglarized and case files stolen. A specialist in relationship, marriage and family counseling, Dr. Ameli also works with drug-related problems at the Tarzana Rehabilitation Center, and has a number of clients in the entertainment field. In March 1996, she detailed for an interviewer, Ian Bowater, this list of intimidations.

Early in 1995, an anonymous telephone caller asked to purchase the files of Nicole Simpson and Ronald Goldman. Dr. Ameli refused and a few days later her office in Santa Monica was broken into and some files were stolen. Police investigating the

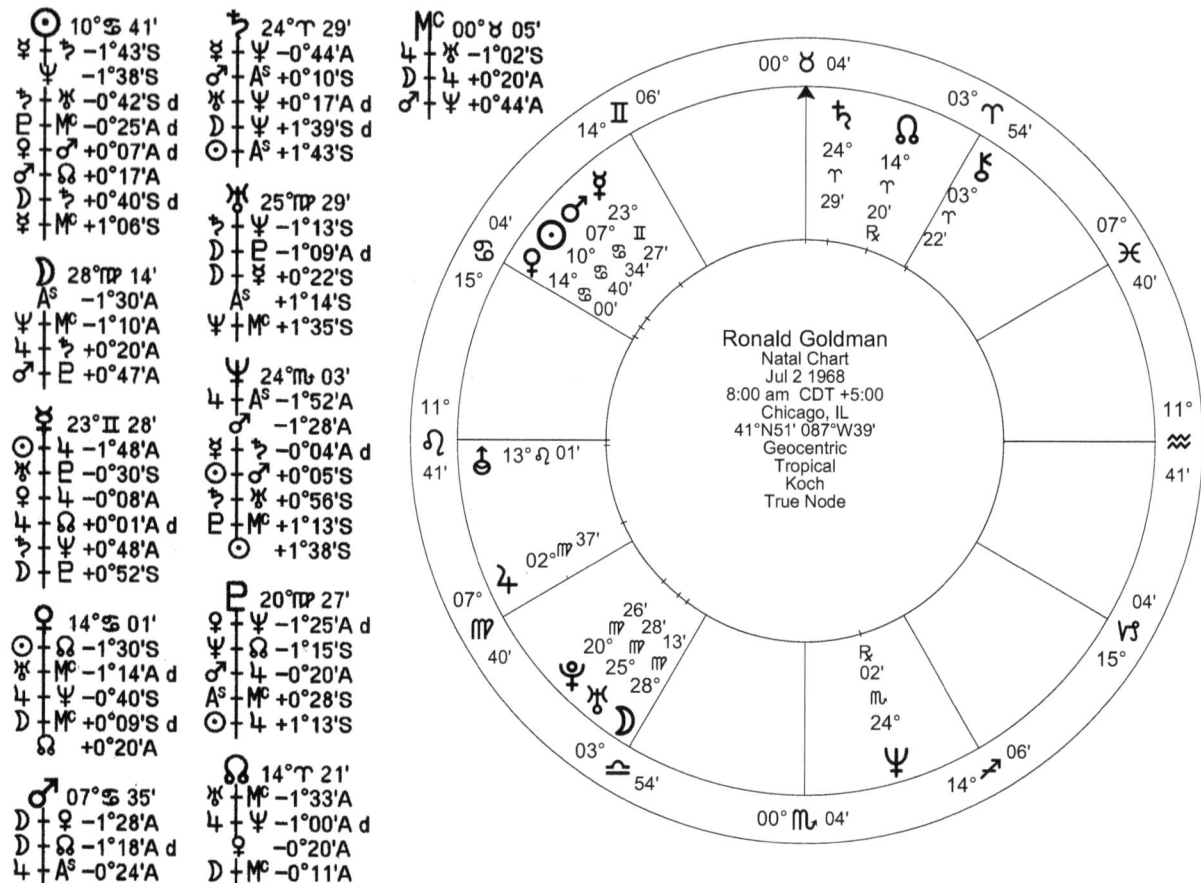

Goldman's Midpoints

break-in removed from the scene other files and a bill addressed to Goldman. Concerned with therapist/client confidentiality issues, Dr. Ameli reported this to the board of Behavioral Sciences at the Consumer Protection Agency.

A few weeks later an unknown assailant approached Dr. Ameli from behind. He pushed and threatened her, telling her to keep her mouth shut about the Simpson case. She did not see his face or recognize his voice and could only tell he was tall. During this time she also received threatening telephone calls. Sometime later she was confronted near her Malibu home, which houses her second office. Subsequently someone broke into her house.

Fearing for herself and her family, Dr. Ameli reported all incidents to the police and asked for protection, but found them unsympathetic. She admits that her answers to police inquiries had to be evasive because she did not want to violate client confidentiality. She believes this may have antagonized the police. One of the Simpson detectives investigated the incidents, but neither the prosecution nor the defense did anything about it.

The fateful night of the murder was June 12, 1994 at 10:30 p.m. Ronald had borrowed a car from a friend to return a pair of lost sunglasses belonging to Nicole Simpson's mother. After he had entered the gate to Nicole's residence they were both viciously and brutally killed with a knife.

Solar Arc Directions

The solar arc in 1994 was 25 degrees 45 minutes. There were several distinct solar arc directions that determined 1994 as an eventful year. Solar arc Uranus at 20 Libra 14 semi-square natal Jupiter at 2 Virgo 38 points toward the fast life Ronald was already involved with for some time.

Inner Chart
Ronald Goldman
Jul 2 1968 AD GC
8:00:00 AM
CDT +05:00:00
Chicago IL
USA
87w38'00
41n53'00
Geocentric
Tropical

Outer Charts
Murder
Jun 12 1994 AD GC
10:30:00 PM
PDT +07:00:00
Brentwood, Ca
USA
118w28 00
34n03 00
True SA 24°45'
25y 11m

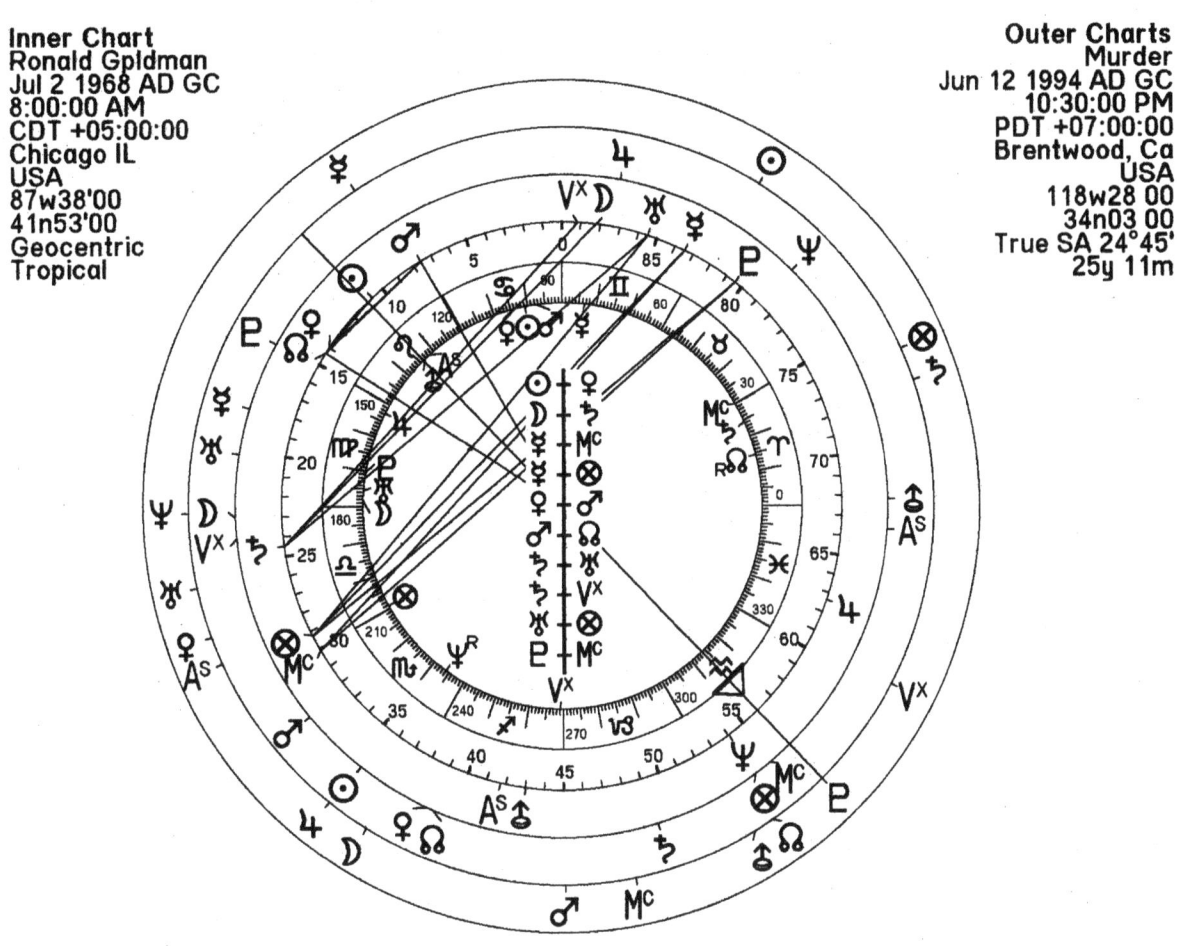

Cosmogram, 90°00' H4 Dial Format

Inner Radix	Middle Directed	Outer Transits
☉ 10♋41	☉ 05♌26	☉ 22♊00
☽ 28♍14	☽ 22♎59	☽ 07♌01
☿ 23♊28	☿ 18♋13	☿ 08♋24R
♀ 14♋01	♀ 08♌46	♀ 27♋33
♂ 07♋35	♂ 02♌20	♂ 15♉03
♃ 02♍38	♃ 27♍23	♃ 05♏18R
♄ 24♈29	♄ 19♉14	♄ 12♓19
♅ 25♍29	♅ 20♎14	♅ 25♑37R
♆ 24♏03R	♆ 18♐48	♆ 22♑46R
♇ 20♍27	♇ 15♎12	♇ 25♏59R
☊ 14♈21R	☊ 09♉06	☊ 23♏30R
As 11♌43	As 06♍28	As 28♑38
Mc 00♉05	Mc 24♉50	Mc 17♏48
Vx 29♐09	Vx 23♑54	Vx 00♍29
⚷ 13♌01	⚷ 07♍46	⚷ 22♌45
⊗ 29♎16	⊗ 24♏01	⊗ 13♐36

81

Solar arc Saturn at 19 Taurus 15 contacts multiple midpoints. Starting with the natal midpoint of Neptune/Transpluto at 3 Libra 32, Saturn here defines as impractical dreamers, drug-pushers and being overly impressionable. Saturn contacting Venus/Pluto midpoint at 17 Leo 14 shows a tragic love, and contacting Pluto/Node at 2 Cancer 24 indicates violent termination of a relationship, while Saturn contacting Sun/Uranus at 18 Leo 05 may manifest as sudden separation from another person. Saturn in relation with the midpoint of Moon/Mars at 17 Leo 55 reflects separation from the mother.

Jupiter at 27 Virgo 23 connecting with natal Ascendant at 11 Leo 43 may appear as having a pleasant and agreeable manner, and having generous and wealthy people in the environment. Jupiter contacting Neptune/MC at 12 Leo 34 emphasizes having a tendency to dream of good fortune and contacting Moon/Uranus at 26 Virgo 52 shows aims and objectives on a grand scale and a lucky hand in enterprises. All the while Mars at 2 Leo 20 at midpoint of Saturn/Ascendant at 18 Gemini 06 acts out as separation, mourning and bereavement.

Solar arc Venus at 8 Leo 46 is semi-square natal Mercury at 23 Gemini 28 and semi-square natal midpoint of Moon/Pluto at 24 Virgo 21, the Uranus/Pluto at 22 Virgo 58 and Saturn/Neptune at 9 Leo 16, adding up to thoughts of love, love union with extreme emotions pursued with fanaticism, bringing about the collapse of the old order of things and suffering.

Mercury at 18 Cancer 13 is semi-square natal Jupiter at 2 Virgo 38 and natal midpoint Sun/Saturn at 2 Gemini 35, indicating serious problems and a fortunate separation from someone.

Solar arc Sun at 5 Leo 26 semi-square natal Pluto at 20 Virgo 27 and midpoint Ascendant/MC at 20 Gemini 54 shows someone with a fascinating personality in unusual surroundings. The Node at 9 Taurus 06 retrograde contacting natal midpoint Saturn/Neptune at 9 Leo 16 and Jupiter/Node at 23 Gemini 30 and natal Mercury/Uranus at 9 Leo 29 beckons good relationships, but also represents giving, receiving stimulated suggestions along with mourning and bereavement.

The solar arc Moon at 22 Libra 59 and Ascendant at 6 Virgo 29 are contacting natal midpoint Node/MC at 22 Aries 13 and approaching natal Saturn at 24 Aries 29, representing the creation of a relaxed atmosphere with common interests and the fear of being exposed by indiscreet action.

The solar arc Midheaven at 24 Taurus 51 had just passed natal Neptune at 24 Scorpio 03 retrograde, yet contacting midpoints Jupiter/Transpluto at 22 Leo 50, Saturn/Uranus at 9 Cancer 59, Venus/Mars at 10 Cancer 48, Mars/Node at 25 Taurus 58 and Sun at 10 Cancer 41, offering the energies of living life to its fullest, a wasteful and excessive social life, making the highest demands on self, the establishment of a sexual relationship, a good team-worker and the pursuit of objectives.

The solar arc midpoint of Mars/Saturn (known as the death midpoint) at 25 Gemini 48 on natal Uranus 25 Virgo 29 may facilitate the application of brute force, separation and death. One of the significant constellations associated with murder is solar arc Mars mentioned above at 2 Leo 20 in midpoint of Saturn/Pluto at 2 Leo 13 and may be a symbol for brutality, assault, ruthlessness and the necessity to fight for life. That fell on natal midpoint of Sun/Neptune at 17 Virgo 22 very close to natal MC at 00 Taurus 05. A little more then two degrees of orb is allowed with the Ascendant or MC.

Secondary Progressions

Since the slow-moving planets do not move very much in such a short life, a few of the most significant aspects are as follows:

The Mars-Mercury/Saturn configuration at 24 Cancer 40 moved to a square to natal Saturn, forming the death constellation, plus indicating disputes and a change through force of circumstances.

Venus at 15 Leo 56 in natal midpoint of Sun/Pluto shows a tragic love, and in natal Mercury/Mars refers to quick decision in love-matters.

The Sun at 5 Leo 26 contacting natal Pluto and Ascendant/MC midpoint facilitates the power of attainment, danger to life and separation by Providence. The Node at 11 Aries 42 retrograde contacting natal midpoint of Sun/Venus, Pluto/MC and Jupiter/Ascendant indicates the desire to get together and influence lovable people, a love of pleasure and social meetings, and with Neptune, a lack of judgment.

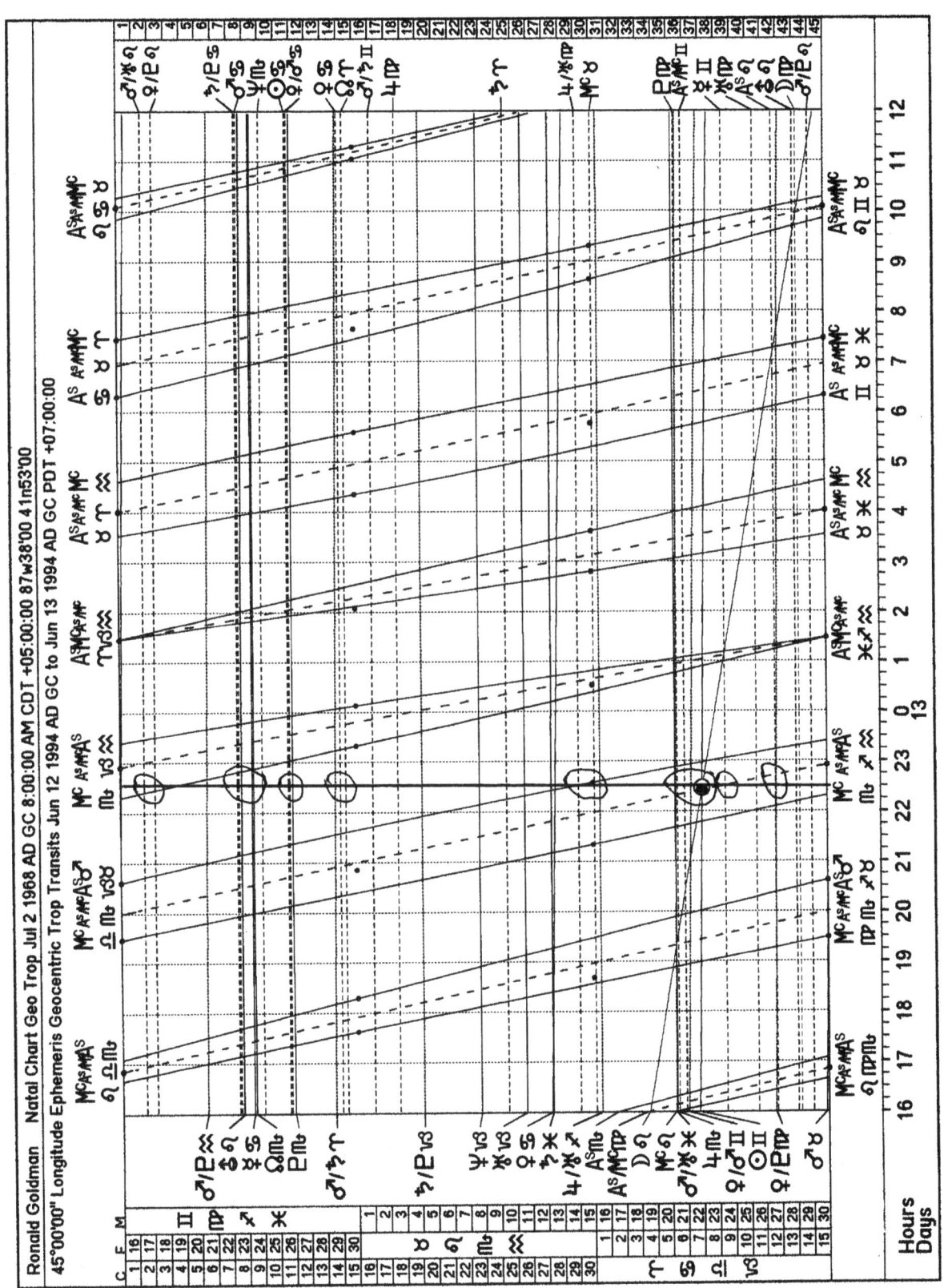

Transits

Using progressions and directions reveals a year of warning. However, the environment and circumstances surrounding Ronald Goldman is a key component and triggered this tragic event evidenced by the transits in the following delineations of the 45-degree ephemeris.

The transiting Midheaven at 17 Scorpio 48 square natal Mars/Uranus at 16 Leo 34 and Venus/Pluto at 17 Leo 14 reveal the execution of violent and drastic actions and deep feelings of love (Karmic union).

Mercury at 8 Cancer 24 retrograde and Node at 23 Scorpio 30 retrograde were contacting Mars at 7 Cancer 35, Neptune at 24 Scorpio 03 retrograde and Saturn/Pluto midpoint at 7 Cancer 26, delivering the desire to solve a difficult problem, common suffering shared with others, the necessity to fight for life and failure through faulty judgment.

Pluto at 25 Scorpio 59 is sesquisquare the Sun and the Venus/Mars midpoint within minutes of orb. This contact can manifest as an urge to establish a union between the sexes and strong sexual contacts.

The Mars/Saturn midpoint at 13 Libra 41 on natal Venus at 14 Cancer 01 and Node at 14 Aries 21 retrograde shows loss of a female associate (death).

The Ascendant at 28 Capricorn 35 and Jupiter/Uranus at 15 Sagittarius 28 were contacting natal Midheaven at 00 Taurus 05 and this may appear as shared happiness and optimism with a partner.

Jupiter at 5 Scorpio 18 retrograde, Sun at 22 Gemini 00, Moon at 7 Leo 01, Mars/Uranus at 20 Virgo 20, Venus/Mars at 21 Gemini 18 and Ascendant/Midheaven at 20 Gemini 54 were all on natal Pluto at 20 Virgo 27 and the most individual midpoint of Ascendant/Midheaven at 21 Gemini 18 becomes a powerhouse of contacts exercising power, force, violent intervention and Higher Power with feelings of social activities and successful popularity and seeking understanding from others and association with females. However, lurking in the background is violent intervention and action.

The Venus/Pluto midpoint at 26 Virgo 46 was semi-square natal Ascendant at 11 Leo 43 (three minute orb) and becomes an attractive and fascinating personality, and an unusual love affair.

John P.

When astrologers or students of astrology experience a tragic event in their lives, the validity of astrology is often doubted due to the emotional involvement, guilt feelings or misunderstandings.

Recently I was asked, "Where in this chart is it indicated that this young man would use his energies to destroy himself?" First is a brief history of this young man who committed suicide by hanging.

John and his sister were very young when their parents divorced. A stepfather physically abused the boy on different occasions but John never confided in any one about this mistreatment. Both children were more or less shuffled between mother and father. When they stayed with their father they had to live by his code of standards, which was totally different from that of their mother.

At approximately age 18, John went into the armed forces to get away from the insecure home and the problems of not being able to find a job to support himself. He was sent to Korea where he met his future wife. While in Korea, John started to use drugs that were easily obtainable and he had difficulties with his superior officers.

At the time of his death his wife was six months pregnant and his discharge from the service was approximately six months away. He did not like the service but was more afraid of getting out and facing the responsibilities of civilian life.

The night of the tragic event, John sent his wife shopping and after she returned she found him dead. The coroner ascertained the time of death as 8:30 p.m. CDT, September 20, 1977, 97W44, 32N07.

Natal

The Sun at 13 Virgo 37 is indicative of a methodical mind, sense of criticism, simplicity and contentment. The close conjunction with Jupiter at 12 Virgo 25 indicates success and advancement; however, in a negative connotation this contact can produce conflicts that are caused by arrogance, differences with people within the environment or with superiors as well as with the laws of the land. The semi-squares to Neptune and Venus refer to awakening from emotional infatuations, disillusionment and a sense of reality.

The Moon at 3 Libra 41 has fairly good aspects but the midpoint structure is extensive and has some disturbing contacts like the Uranus/Pluto midpoint that symbolizes restlessness, daring, determination and bringing about change by force. The Uranus/Ascendant midpoint represents the emotional response, getting excited easily through the influence of others. The Moon in Cancer heightens all the above. The Jupiter/Neptune midpoint adds little sense of reality, instability and wastefulness.

The Ascendant at 5 Gemini 21 depicts a lively and versatile environment. Furthermore it represents an obliging manner, quick responses, adaptation, superficiality and inconsistency. While some of the aspects are very good, the square and parallel are very disturbing. Some of the interpretations are control over the environment, the attainment of success at all costs, readjustments to circumstances, violent disputes, injuries accidents and drastic or radical changes of circumstances in life.

The MC at 14 Aquarius 11 indicates new and modern aims and aspirations, occasional and sudden

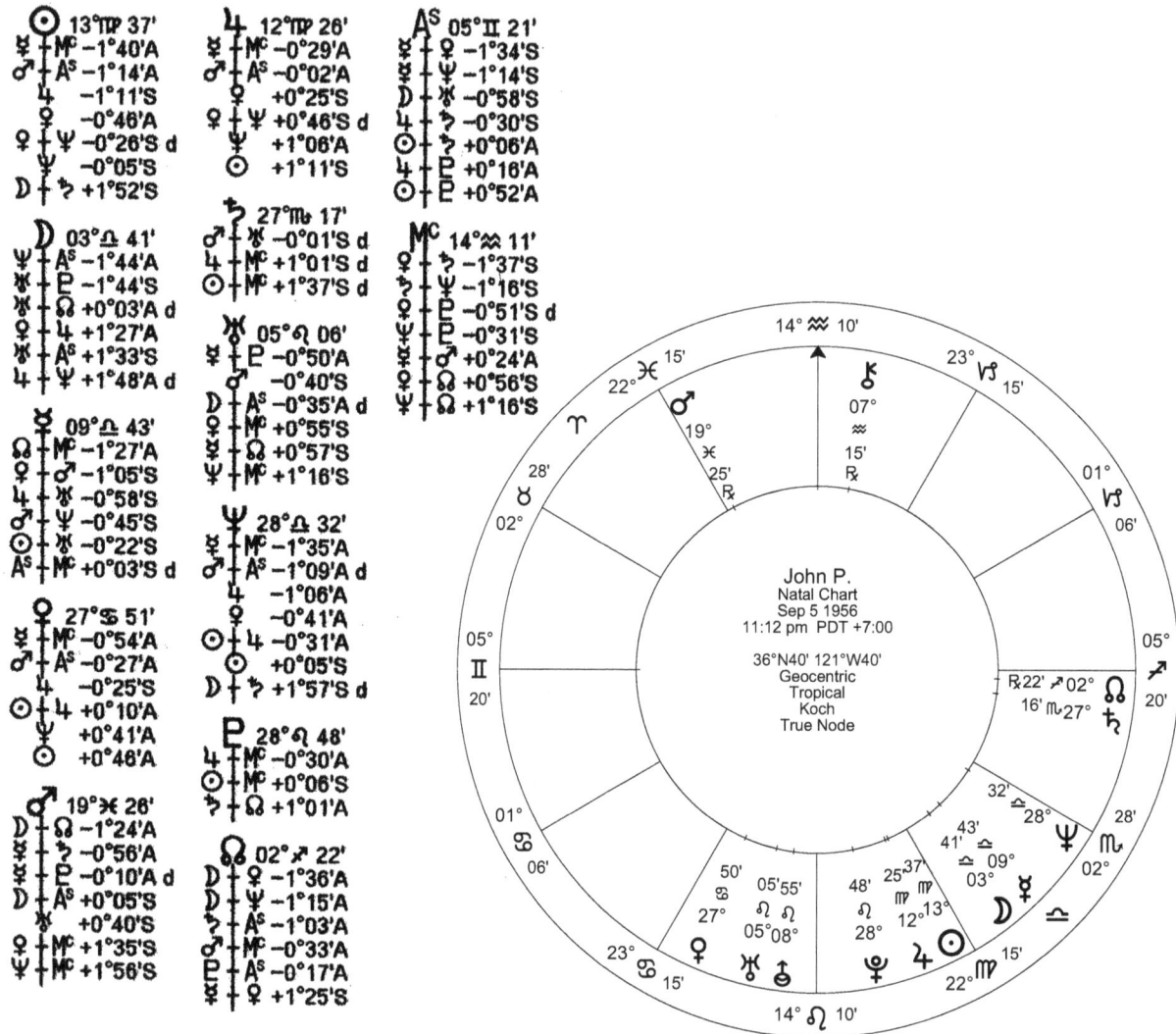

John's Midpoints

assertions, the grasping of the best opportunities, but also quite the opposite of scattered energy through too much planning. Some of the midpoints are very disturbing, such as the Venus/Saturn midpoint combined with the MC, referring to emotional inhibitions or inhibited desires, jealousy, the urge to seek solitude and separation in love. The Saturn/Neptune midpoint additionally indicates a frequent change in mood, emotional suffering and wavering between material and idealistic inclinations. The Neptune/Pluto midpoint, perhaps the most disturbing, refers to peculiar soul experiences, manias, a craving for alcohol or drugs and confusion.

The structure patterns are given here for your examination and only a few references are made to the most important configurations. The square of Saturn and Pluto and Saturn at the midpoint of Marts/Uranus describe cruelty, the application of force and self-destructive energy, clearly indicating that this force was in operation when John killed himself. From the negative and violent environment of his childhood it was only a matter of time until the natal chart would be activated by progressions and transits and the pressures and responsibilities would become too much for John to confront properly.

Solar Arc

The solar arc directions for 1977 indicate some rather significant combinations, of which the following are only a few.

Sun 4 Libra 09 had shortly before formed a conjunction with the natal Moon at 3 Libra 41, and Jupiter at 2 Libra 58 approaching natal Moon showed the

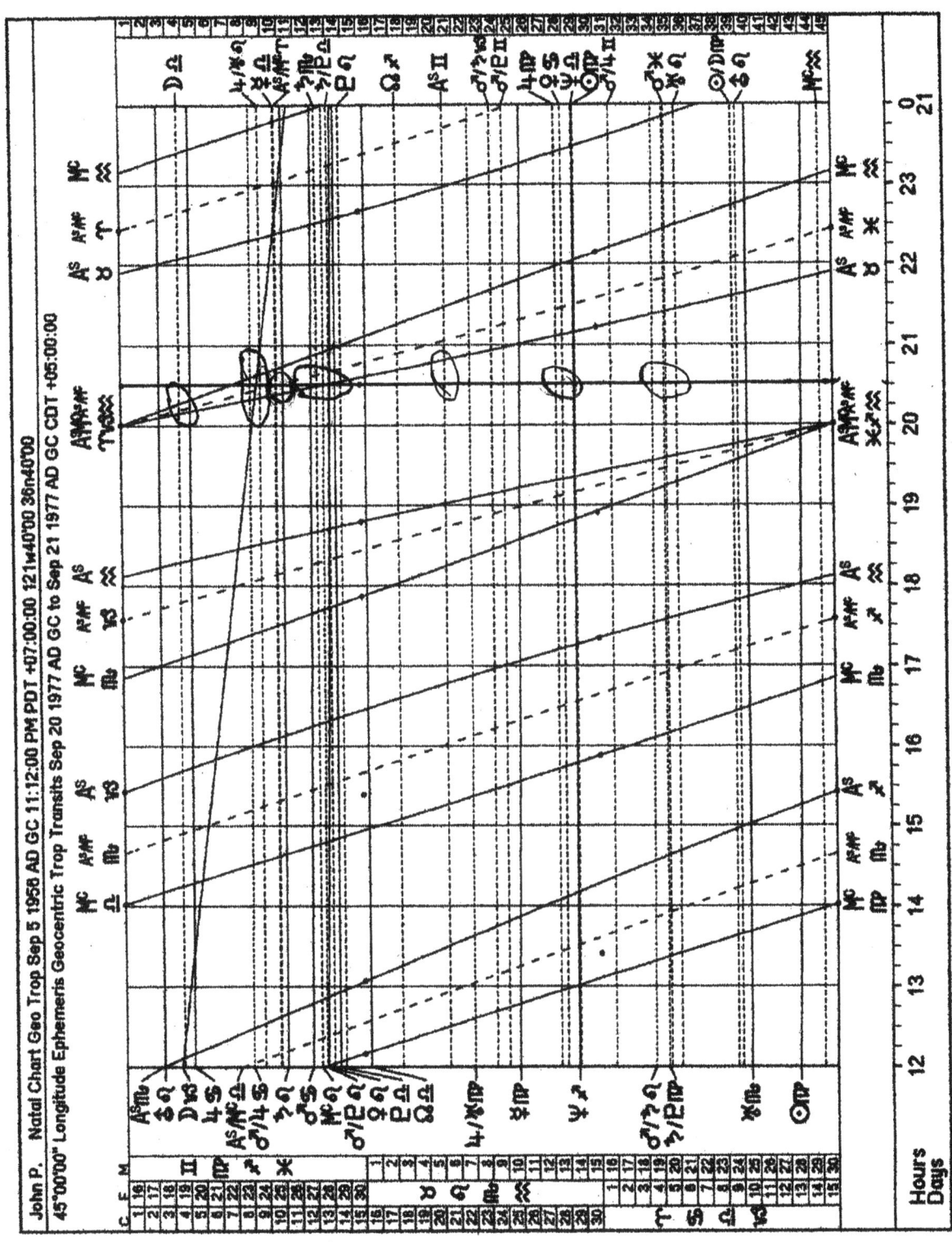

new baby which was due in about three months.

Mars at 9 Aries 58 almost in exact opposition to natal Mercury at 9 Libra 43 points toward achievements thought out well in great detail.

The Moon at 23 Libra 13 reached the square of the natal Mars/Saturn midpoint, showing a fit of depression or weakness of will.

Mercury at 0 Scorpio 15 moved to the natal midpoint of Moon/Saturn and interprets as a reflection, meditation, thinking of separations, feeling sad and saying good-bye.

Pluto at 19 Virgo 20 opposite natal Mars at 19 Pisces 26 retrograde implies brutality, to proceed in a brutal manner, violent assault.

As you can see, the solar arc directions for that particular time in 1977 are numerous and as the transiting planets set off the various directions and natal positions, the pressure of everyday living and responsibilities mounted constantly.

Transits

The 45-degree graphic ephemeris for the day of his death September 20, 1977 from 12:00 noon until midnight is shown with significant midpoints added to demonstrate how the whole pattern fits together.

Pluto at 13 Libra 27 is semi-square natal Saturn at 27 Scorpio 17 and semi-square natal Pluto at 28 Leo 48 and is known for cruelty, hard struggling for success, the pursuit of egotistic goals and the application of force.

Mars at 11 Cancer 56 also contacted the above two planets and its sesquisquare to Saturn at 27 Scorpio 17 tends toward harmful or destructive energy, separation, cases of death.

Venus at 28 Leo 06 joins the combinations above, making a square to natal Saturn and a conjunction to Pluto, showing extraordinary strain in love life, coldness of feelings and the desire to renounce love.

Neptune at 13 Sagittarius 34 moved back and forth on the natal Sun at 13 Virgo 37, Jupiter at 12 Virgo 26 and Venus at 27 Cancer 51 and natal Neptune at 28 Libra 32, bringing depression, high sensitivity, weakness and awakening from emotional infatuation.

Uranus at 9 Scorpio 30 is square natal Transpluto at 8 Leo 56 and brings sudden emotional shock and upheaval, rebelliousness and bull-headedness.

Saturn at 25 Leo 11 is semi-square natal Mercury at 9 Libra 43 and is conjunct natal Ascendant/MC midpoint at 9 Libra 46, fostering seclusion and preoccupation with own thoughts and separation.

Sun at 27 Virgo 58 is very close sequin-square to natal MC at 14 Aquarius 11 and manifests as a loss of interest in life.

Moon at 8 Capricorn 31 is approaching square natal Mercury at 9 Libra 43 and sesquisquare the natal Jupiter/Uranus midpoint at 23 Leo 46, describing the hour of thinking is influenced by his feelings and perceptions.

Ascendant at 21 Aries 15 as of 8:30 p.m., the time the coroner determined as the time of death had just passed a semi-square to natal Ascendant at 5 Gemini 21 and is a contact that has been found many times when birth charts are correct.

MC at 13 Capricorn 26 is semi-square natal Saturn at 27 Scorpio 17 and sesquisquare natal Pluto at 28 Leo 48 and shows separation, mourning, being placed in cumbersome and difficult circumstances, self-sacrifice and flight.

Observe the midpoints of Saturn/Pluto at 19 Virgo 19, Saturn/Node at 20 Virgo 16 in close opposition to natal Mars at 19 Pisces 26 retrograde and Mars/Saturn at 3 Leo 34 conjunct natal Uranus at 5 Leo 06, which are some very violent combinations for self-destruction.

Jayne Mansfield

It has been said that Jayne Mansfield's close involvement with satanic priest Anton LeVey was responsible for her death. At the time Miss Mansfield became involved with the man associated with the First Church of Satan she was having an affair with her attorney, Sam Brody.

Jayne joined the church and took it very seriously. She even wore a medallion that Anton had chosen for her. Brody was a very jealous man and did not want Jayne seeing LeVey. In turn, Anton did not want Mr. Brody to be so much a part of her life.

While the three were together one night, Mr. Brody began making fun of the church's religious objects. At one point, he lit a skull-shaped candle that was used only for destructive rituals. LeVey, seeing the lit candle blew it out and became outraged. He said he didn't know what the outcome of the act would be, but warned of impending danger. Brody laughed it off but Miss Mansfield took it quite seriously.

Shortly after the incident Jayne promised to take her six-year old son, Zoltan, to see LaVey's pet lion, but LeVey would not allow it. She took her son to a private zoo instead. While she was posing for some photographs, Zoltan stepped in the lion's path. The "tame" lion quickly lunged for the boy; he was mauled and nearly died. Jayne attributed this to the stigma created by Brody's attitude and lighting the evil candle.

At one point in the heat of the love triangle, LeVey exploded and told Brody that he would be dead within one year. He warned Miss Mansfield to stay away from him or she too would be in danger merely by being near Brody.

Six months later Jayne and Brody were in Biloxi, Mississippi where she was appearing in a club. One evening the owner of the club, Jayne, Mr. Brody and three of her children were driving at high speed to New Orleans. Suddenly they encountered a cloud of fog; a truck was spraying insecticide. Within moments they rammed into the rear of the vehicle; the three adults died instantly, but the children survived. Jayne, who was sitting in the passenger's seat to the extreme right, was decapitated.

Natal

Compared to other natal charts, Jayne Mansfield's Ascendant at 2 Cancer 57 is not known as a degree symbolizing being accident-prone, however her natal Uranus at 23 Aries 41 is truly a sight to behold. Uranus is at the midpoint of Pluto/Transpluto and termed as a most destructive combination, which is not shown on the midpoint structures.

Solar Arc Directions

The solar arc for the time of her death was 33 degrees and 6 minutes. The solar arc Uranus had moved to 26 Taurus 47 and the natal midpoint of Pluto/Ascendant at 12 Cancer 07, which is reinforced by transiting Saturn at 11 Aries 54.

The delineation for this combination is indeed ominous, interpreting as sudden changes through calamities and forces beyond one's personal control, sudden disasters, times of crises, the misfortune to live in constant anxiety, restlessness, extraordinary incidents and upsets, accidents, and suffering from forcible suppression.

These combinations move to an area of 25 degrees

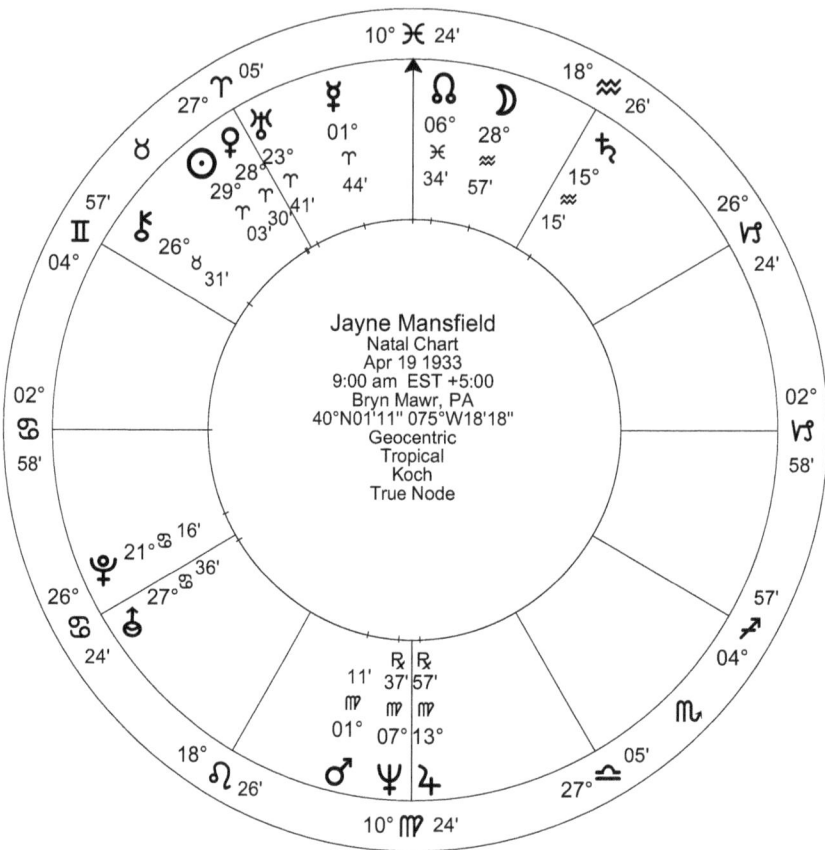

of a fixed sign, and include Taurus, Leo, Scorpio and Aquarius. On the 90-degree circle they all show up at the same spot, 25 degrees Taurus, and the degree of the fixed star Algol.

In Ebertin Hoffman's book, *Fixed Stars*, he states, "Algol: (approximately 25 Taurus 15 in 1980) Head of Gorgo Medusa, is a name derived from Arabic 'Al Ghoul' meaning Demon, Evil Spirit or Devil. Derived from the same root is 'Golem' and 'Alcohol' of Prague. Algol is part of a double star system. Its darker brother circles the brighter star in about 69 hours in such a manner that an occultation for 9 hours appears as viewed from Earth, and this gives a periodical change in brightness. Continually, its brightness alternates between values 2,2 and 3,5. It is assumed that other dark stars belong to the solar system of Algol." Dr. Lomer wrote in *Kosmobiologie*, August 1950, page 302 that "Arabic commanders in chief, in times of conquest, made it a point that no important battles were begun when the light of Algol was weak."

The solar arc directed sensitive midpoint of Ascendant/MC at 9 Gemini 46 sets off the above natal Uranus destructive combination and is supported by transiting Ascendant/MC at 10 Pisces 16 and shows taking the wrong path in life, the pursuit of wrong objectives, and devotion to peculiar objectives. The directed axis of Mars/Uranus at 0 Leo 33 and Mars/Pluto at 14 Virgo 20 is met by transiting ASC 0 Taurus 34 within one minute of orb and reflects an accident or physical injury.

Solar arc Mars at 4 Libra 19 squares natal Ascendant at 2 Cancer 57 and is in the midpoint of Jupiter/Uranus, a very fortunate combination to have, and the transiting Sun/Moon midpoint in 19 Taurus 13 shows Jayne's involvement at the time, being in love with Mr. Brody and a lot of activity in her career.

The solar arc Ascendant at 6 Leo 03 and Jupiter/Uranus midpoint at 6 Leo 55 reach the natal Ascendant/MC midpoint at 6 Scorpio 40 and natal Saturn/Transpluto at 6 Scorpio 25. The biological correspondence for Saturn/Transpluto is spinal bones supporting the neck and neck bone. Transiting Jupiter came to 6 Leo 50 and Uranus is semi-square at 20 Virgo 43. This normally would be a life saving combination at the last moment, however, when the time comes for us to die, no aspect will prevent it. In fact,

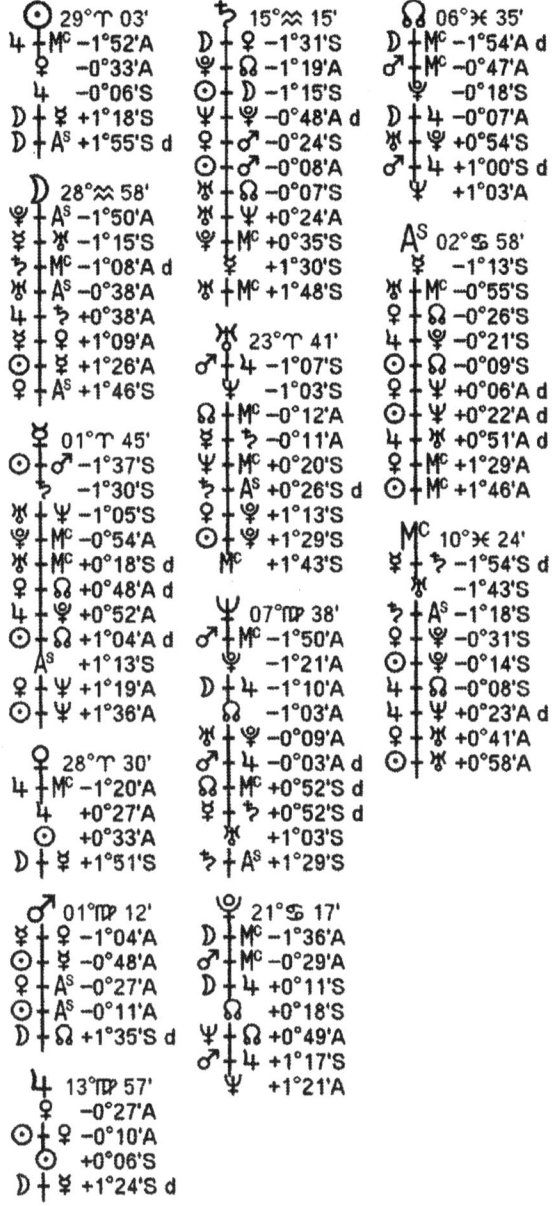

Mansfield's Midpoints

at the time of death, many harmonious aspects are present especially Moon Jupiter contacts.

Transits

The transiting death axis of Mars/Saturn at 16 Cancer 40 is sesquisquare natal Mars at 1 Virgo 12 and contacting the solar arc directed Sun at 2 Gemini 09, Venus at 1 Gemini 36, Transpluto at 0 Virgo 43 and Jupiter at 17 Libra 03 and all this is interpreted as a quick dissolution of the body or instant death. Contributing farther description to the incident. Mars at 21 Libra 26 is square Mercury at 21 Cancer 39 retrograde and contacting natal Pluto at 21 Cancer 17 and the Node at 6 Pisces 35. This describes the impatience of rash and speedy driving and the misfortune of suffering intense attacks.

Jupiter at 6 Leo 50, along with the midpoint Mars/Neptune at 6 Scorpio 40, were within minutes of a square and conjunction to the natal sensitive midpoint of Ascendant/MC at 6 Scorpio 40. This shows the possibility of suffering misfortune, unhappiness or ill luck, soul suffering and disappointments.

Transpluto at 12 Leo 35 was on the natal Mars/Uranus midpoint 27 Gemini 27, providing a potential for violent intervention. Saturn/Node at 22 Aries 23 was contacting natal Neptune at 7 Virgo 38 retrograde and Uranus at 23 Aries 41 and shows the tendency to sacrifice oneself for others, mourning, and bereavement while Mars/Jupiter at 14 Virgo 08 is conjunct natal Jupiter at 13 Virgo 57 retrograde, and sesquisquare Venus at 28 Aries 30 and Sun at 29 Aries 03 combined showing hastiness, opportunities slipping away and termination of relationships. Compounding it all is transiting Ascendant/MC midpoint at 12 Virgo 16 passing natal MC at 10 Pisces 23 representing a fateful moment as Jupiter/Uranus at 28 Leo 46 and Uranus/Ascendant at 14 Cancer 38 contact natal Moon at 28 Aquarius 58 describing the sudden changes of the moment and there is possibly disagreement between Jayne and Brody at the time of the accident.

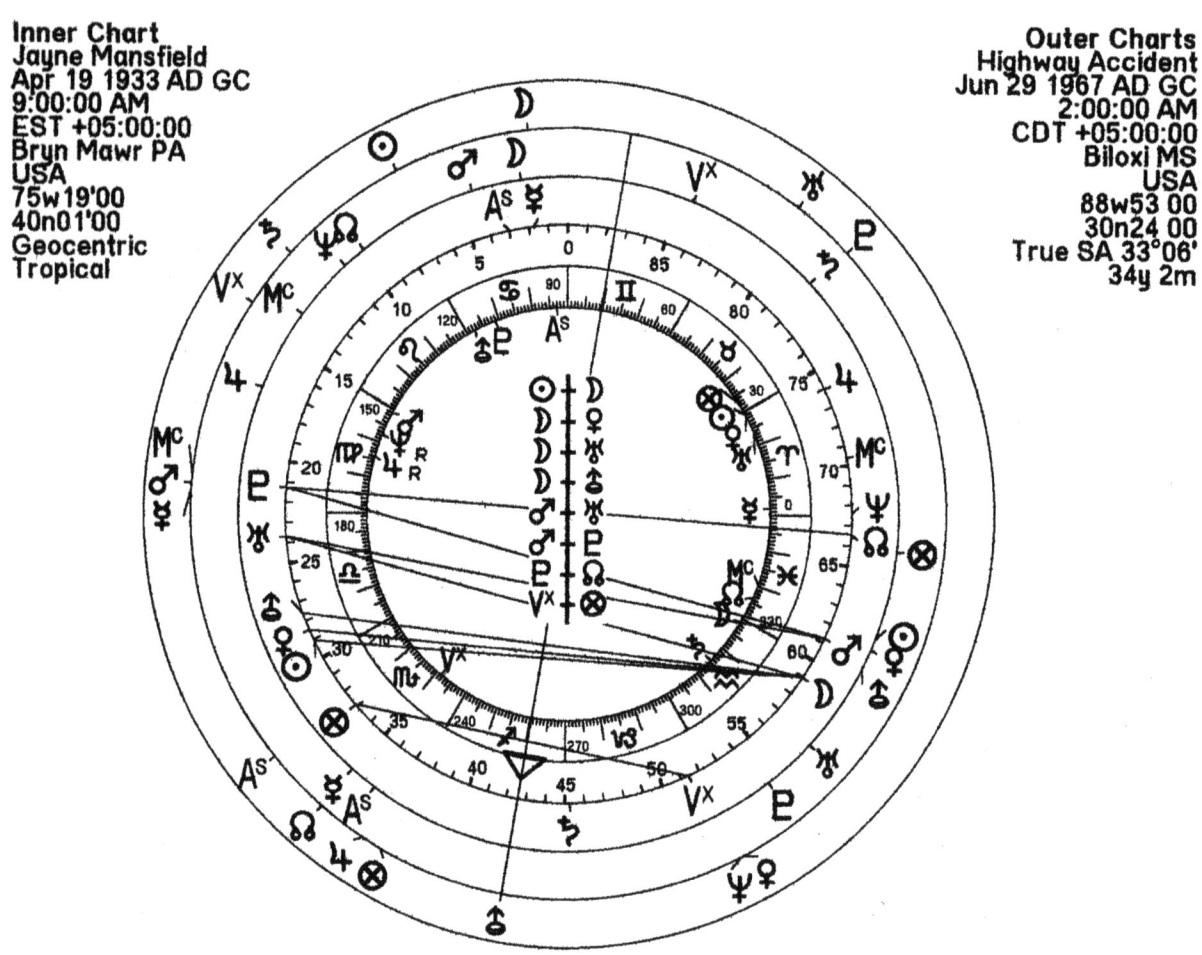

Cosmogram, 90°00' H4 Dial Format

Inner Radix	Middle Directed	Outer Transits
☉ 29♈03	☉ 02♊09	☉ 06♋52
☽ 28♒58	☽ 02♈04	☽ 01♈33
☿ 01♈45	☿ 04♉51	☿ 21♋39R
♀ 28♈30	♀ 01♊36	♀ 21♌58
♂ 01♍12	♂ 04♎18	♂ 21♎26
♃ 13♍57R	♃ 17♎03	♃ 06♋50
♄ 15♒15	♄ 18♓21	♄ 11♈54
♅ 23♈41	♅ 26♉47	♅ 20♍43
♆ 07♍38R	♆ 10♎44	♆ 21♏54R
♇ 21♋17	♇ 24♌23	♇ 18♍13
☊ 06♓35	☊ 09♈41	☊ 04♉51R
As 02♋57	As 06♌03	As 02♉19
Mc 10♓23	Mc 13♈29	Mc 21♑05
Vx 21♏24	Vx 24♐30	Vx 14♎16
☒ 27♋37	☒ 00♍43	☒ 12♌35
⊗ 02♉52	⊗ 05♊58	⊗ 07♌37

Inner Chart
Jayne Mansfield
Apr 19 1933 AD GC
9:00:00 AM
EST +05:00:00
Bryn Mawr PA
USA
75w19'00
40n01'00
Geocentric
Tropical

Outer Charts
Highway Accident
Jun 29 1967 AD GC
2:00:00 AM
CDT +05:00:00
Biloxi MS
USA
88w53 00
30n24 00
True SA 33°06'
34y 2m

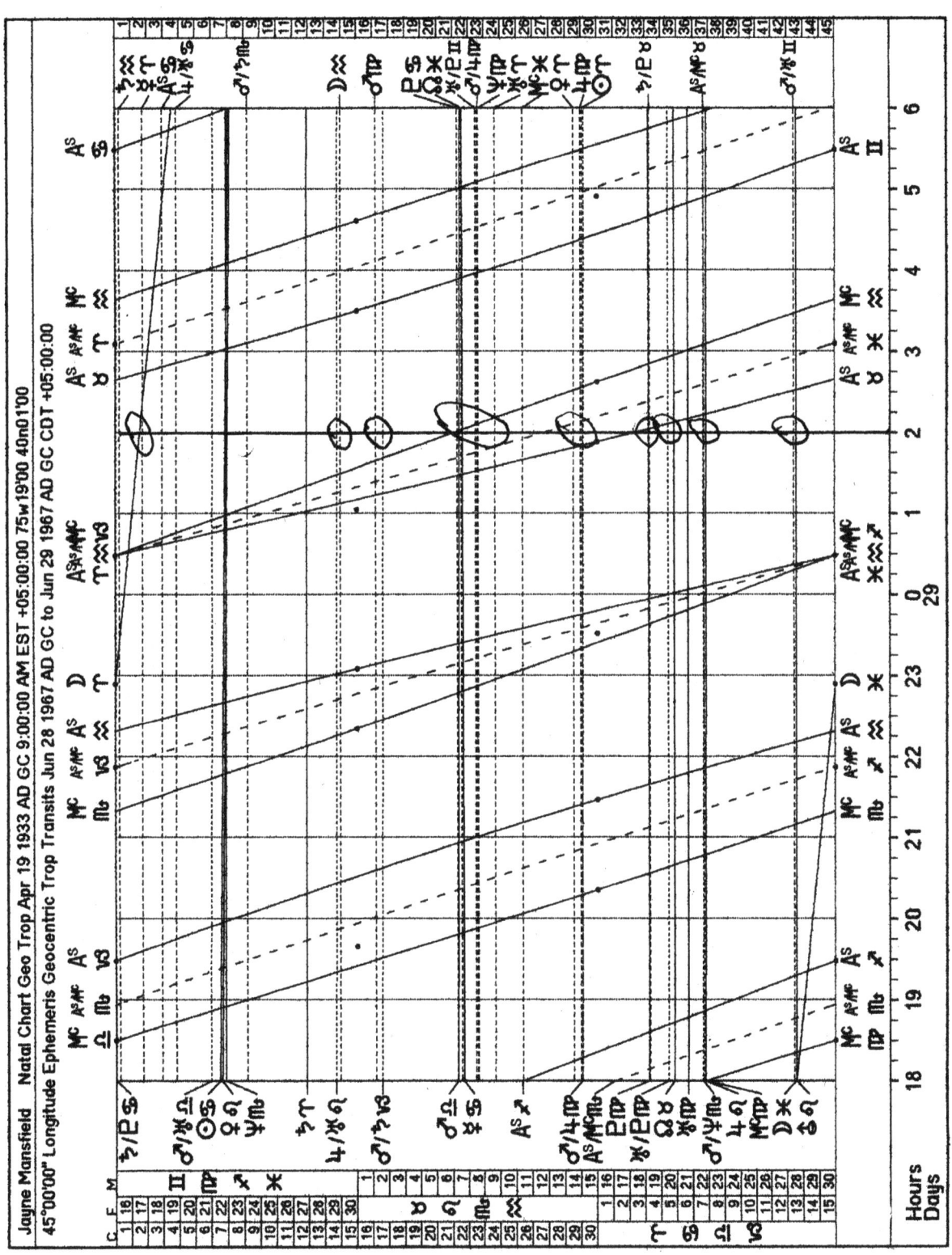

Evelyn

"What happened to me," exclaimed Evelyn as she regained consciousness. There were medics administering first aid, police cars and ambulances screeching to a halt with sirens blaring midst shattered glass from a windshields scattered on the street.

Evelyn drove the 1967 Mustang down a busy one-way street and a crane boom crushed her car February 22, 1971, 1:45 p.m. She was knocked unconscious when the steel roof of her car came down on her head and caused serious head, back and internal injuries. The 50-ton crane with a drilling attachment was being used to dig the foundation for an apartment complex. "It was approved by the most experienced operator and used in a normal way as usual," the spokesman for the construction firm stated. This particular case was one of the very first I outlined after being introduced to cosmobiology. The accuracy of this event is incredible.

As is usual with accidents, the natal chart shows potential. The Ascendant structure contained the midpoint Mars/MC. Also, Mars is at the midpoint of Uranus/Pluto, Uranus is on midpoint of Mars/Ascendant and Pluto at the midpoint of Mars/Transpluto, representing a certain accident-prone pattern indicating that at some time in this person's life and under proper circumstances this pattern would be activated.

There are two different types of accidents: those we cause ourselves, usually by negligence and hastiness, and those that we have no control over. The first is a typical Mars/Uranus pattern while with the second I have found many Pluto connections. This particular case can fit well into the later category.

The almost perfect square, within minutes of natal Pluto at 8 Cancer 06 and the Node at 8 Libra 38, showing that the native is bound to experience connections or associations that will influence her life drastically in some manner. That alone, however, does not show how, but when you look a little further, this Node is also conjunct Jupiter (Pluto, Node and Jupiter) and all are trine the MC. The woman did receive a rather comfortable settlement after all the court proceedings were over. What a way to get that is another matter, which we will now explore.

Solar Arc Directions

Solar arc Uranus at 29 Aries 24 was approaching a conjunction to the natal Sun at 0 Taurus 37. The MC at 26 Pisces 13 and Mars at 10 Aquarius 46 axis were moving toward the natal midpoint of Jupiter/Uranus at 27 Sagittarius 06, the "Thank the Lord" configuration that shows surprise winnings through wealthy associations.

Solar arc Ascendant at 18 Cancer 09 reached the natal midpoint of Jupiter/Uranus/MC at 18 Capricorn 07 and represents shared happiness with others or partners, to shape the environment according to one's ideas, to furnish the home to own taste. She used the money from the settlement to pay the mortgage and furnish the home.

Solar arc Sun at 17 Gemini 43 is at the natal Mars/Uranus midpoint at 2 Aquarius 59, pointing to the accident and injuries suffered.

Transits

Transiting Pluto at 29 Virgo 01 retrograde, Transpluto at 14 Leo 15 retrograde, and MC at 28 Pisces 13 moved to contact natal Neptune at 13 Leo

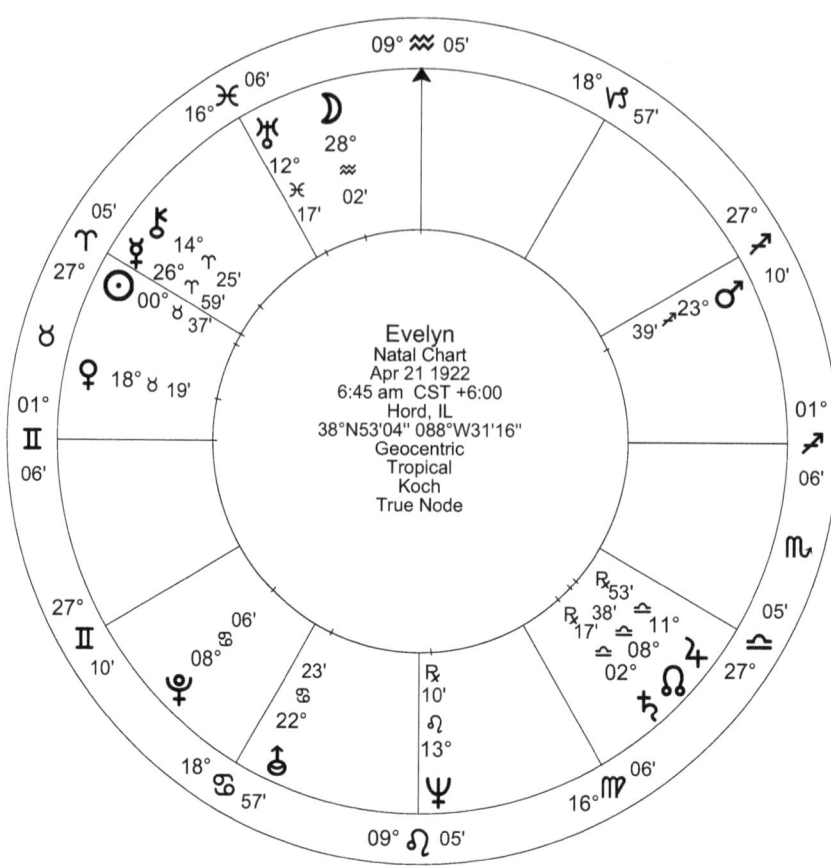

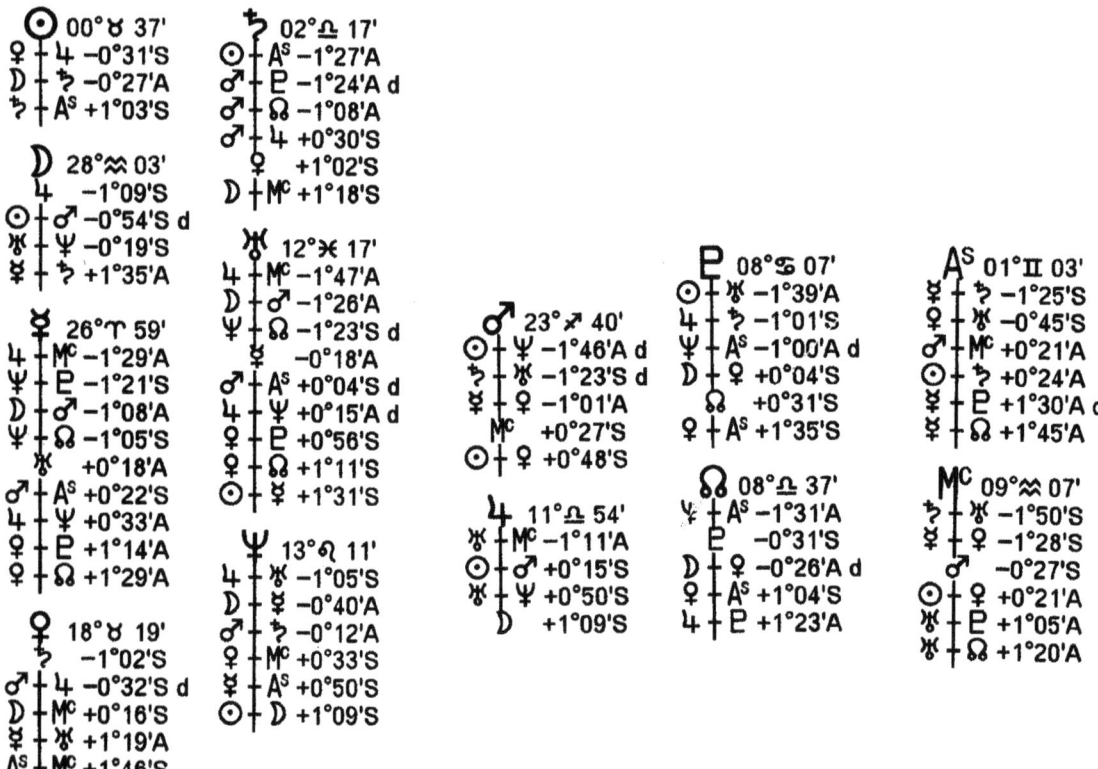

Evelyn's Midpoints

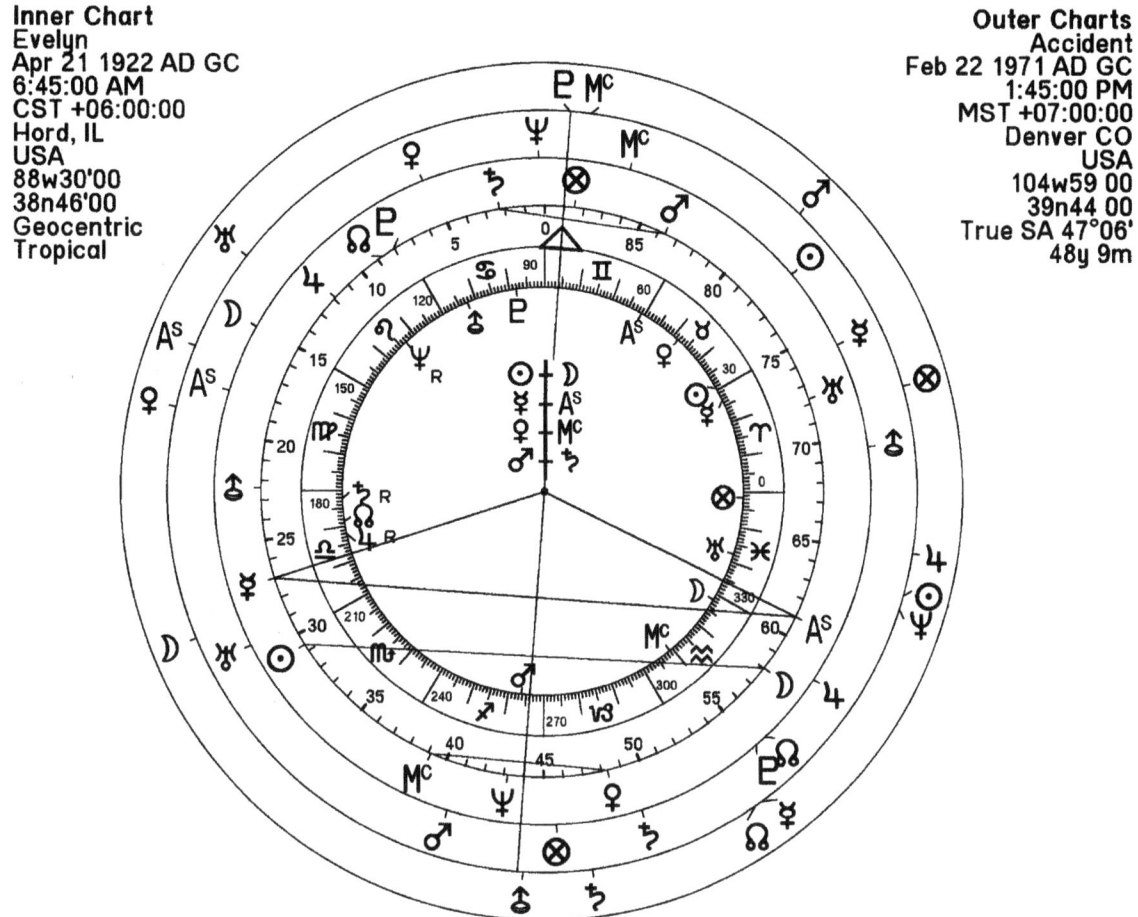

11 retrograde, Mars/Saturn midpoint at 12 Scorpio 58 and Jupiter/Uranus at 27 Sagittarius 05 all together indicate weak vitality, the rage and fury of destruction, the intervening of Higher Power, bodily injury, and sudden change of financial circumstances.

Uranus at 13 Libra 00 retrograde is close to natal Jupiter at 11 Libra 54 retrograde, forming once more the "Thank the Lord combination. The brutality midpoint Mars/Pluto at 9 Scorpio 08 is right on the natal MC at 9 Aquarius 07 and may indicate fortunate turns in life and sudden recognition. Evelyn's picture was on the front pages of both major local newspapers.

Transiting Saturn at 16 Taurus 54 and midpoint Mars/Uranus at 16 Scorpio 07 came within natal Saturn at 2 Libra 17 retrograde and Mars/Pluto at 0 Libra 53, truly combinations for having to suffer violent assaults and destruction as well as a struggle for survival.

The Sun at 3 Pisces 35 and Neptune at 3 Sagittarius set off the solar arc Ascendant at 18 Cancer 09, producing associations with weak or sick people. The transiting Moon, generally indicating the hour, is at 28 Capricorn 12 and the attached midpoints were semi-square to Uranus at 12 Pisces, all pointing to an accident.

Transiting Mercury at 23 Aquarius 59 and Node at 23 Aquarius 39 came to natal Pluto at 8 Cancer 06 and Node at 8 Libra 37, bringing about the eventual fortunate settlement and a common and tragic destiny shared with others, referring to the contractor, crane-operator and insurance company.

A year later, April 6, 1972, the woman suffered a heart attack and also survived. Solar arc Uranus was in exact contact with the Sun, which is an established combination for tension, as the woman was 5'2" tall and weighed 200 pounds.

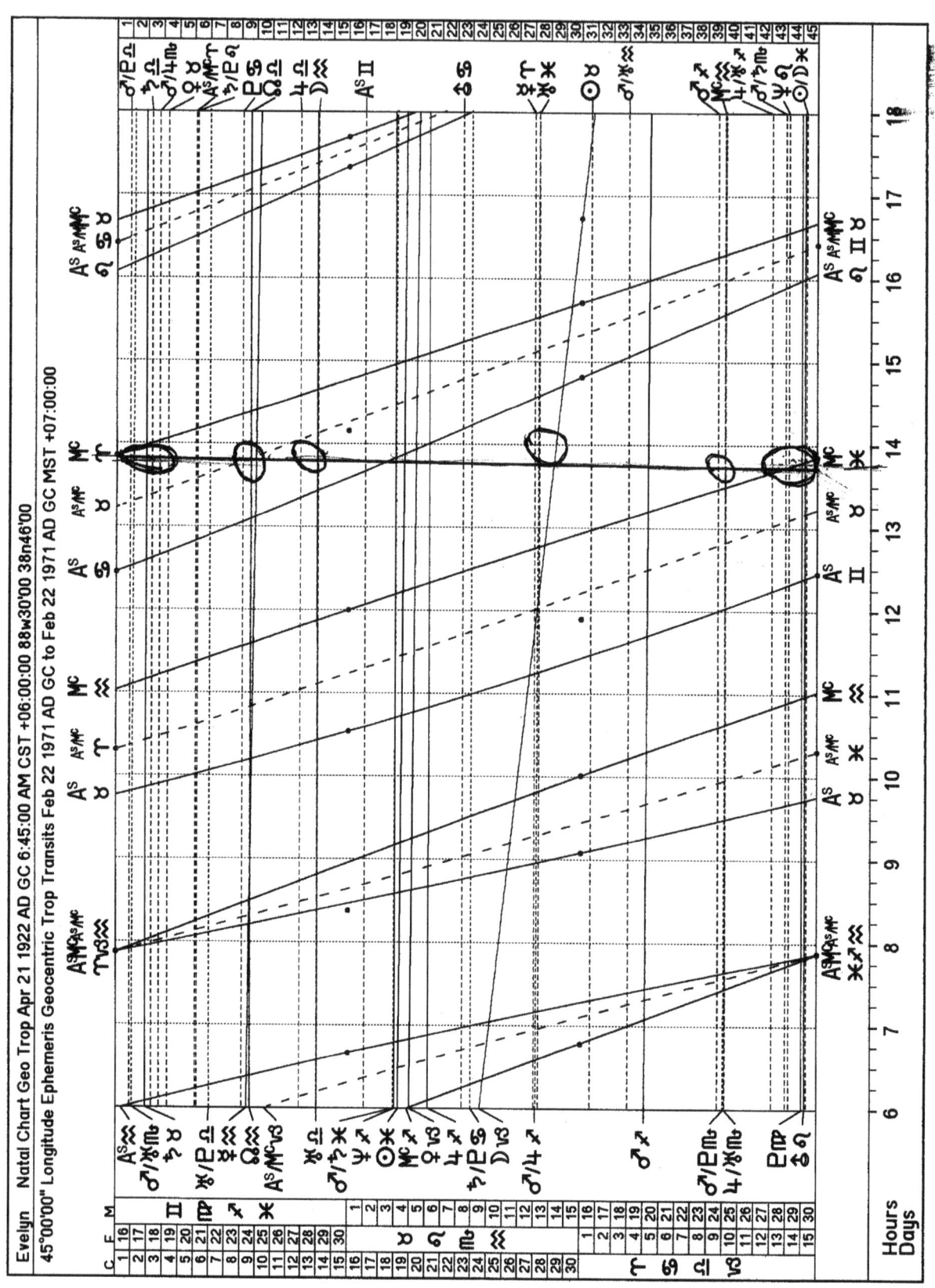

John F. Kennedy, Jr.

In July 1999, the nation and the world again shared the tragic experience of the untimely deaths of young people—John F. Kennedym Jr. (son of the late President John F. Kennedy), his wife Carolyn Bessette Kennedy and sister-in-law Lauren Bessette. The trio were flying in John Jr.'s plane en route from Caldwell, New Jersey to Martha's Vineyard, Massachusetts on July 16, 1999 to attend the wedding of Rory Kennedy, a cousin, scheduled for the next day, when they vanished only 10 miles from their destination, Gay Head, Massachusetts. The plane crashed at 9:39 p.m. EDT, 70W40, 41N25.

For more than four and a half days the sea kept the victims. They were finally located and retrieved from the ocean floor by the most sophisticated technology available. By observing the hour-by-hour happenings on television, my thoughts again drifted toward the unexplained, the mysteries of life and death and searching for an answer which of course cannot be found unless you turn toward the spiritual side of our existence. The age-old question of fate and free will comes to mind especially when the inexorable tragedy of death abruptly intervenes.

Following that dreadful event unfolding on television, rekindles the worst agony a human soul can experience, especially in those who have suddenly lost someone young. The healing process will be slow and different for each of the Kennedy and Bessette families.

As astrologers-cosmobiologists we can find answers by analyzing the planetary components for events. However, we can never penetrate those mysteries, which always shall be forever unobtainable to us. The following is a brief analysis of the tragic event. The times have been officially verified and reflect the circumstances revealed in those agonizing hours.

Natal

A brief analysis of the personal points of his birth chart shows the Sun in 2 Sagittarius 57, which is always ready for action. The generous nature is full of enthusiasm for new things and the temperament is changeable. Most Sagittarians strive for a secure position in life and also seek important associations.

The Moon in 27 Aquarius 25 would make the native concerned for others and their troubles and he would always be available to help others in need. There is a great love of independence, there are abundant hopes and wishes and change is also a definite signature.

The Ascendant in 11 Virgo 58 reveals his personality as he appears to the outside world and at the same time points to stable conditions and circumstances. There is care and attention and tidiness, which is often in conflict with the luminaries and therefore could cause difficulties.

All of this is even more emphasized with the Node at 11 Virgo 45 retrograde, doubling the effect of associations as well as blood relatives. Disagreements through excessive criticism can create unpleasant periods. The Midheaven at 9 Gemini 18 reveals his ego-consciousness, showing multiple aims amd interest establishing his own individuality, but at the same time a scattering of energies.

Solar Arc Directions

At the time of the accident some interesting solar arc directions were in effect: Solar arc Sun at 12 Cap-

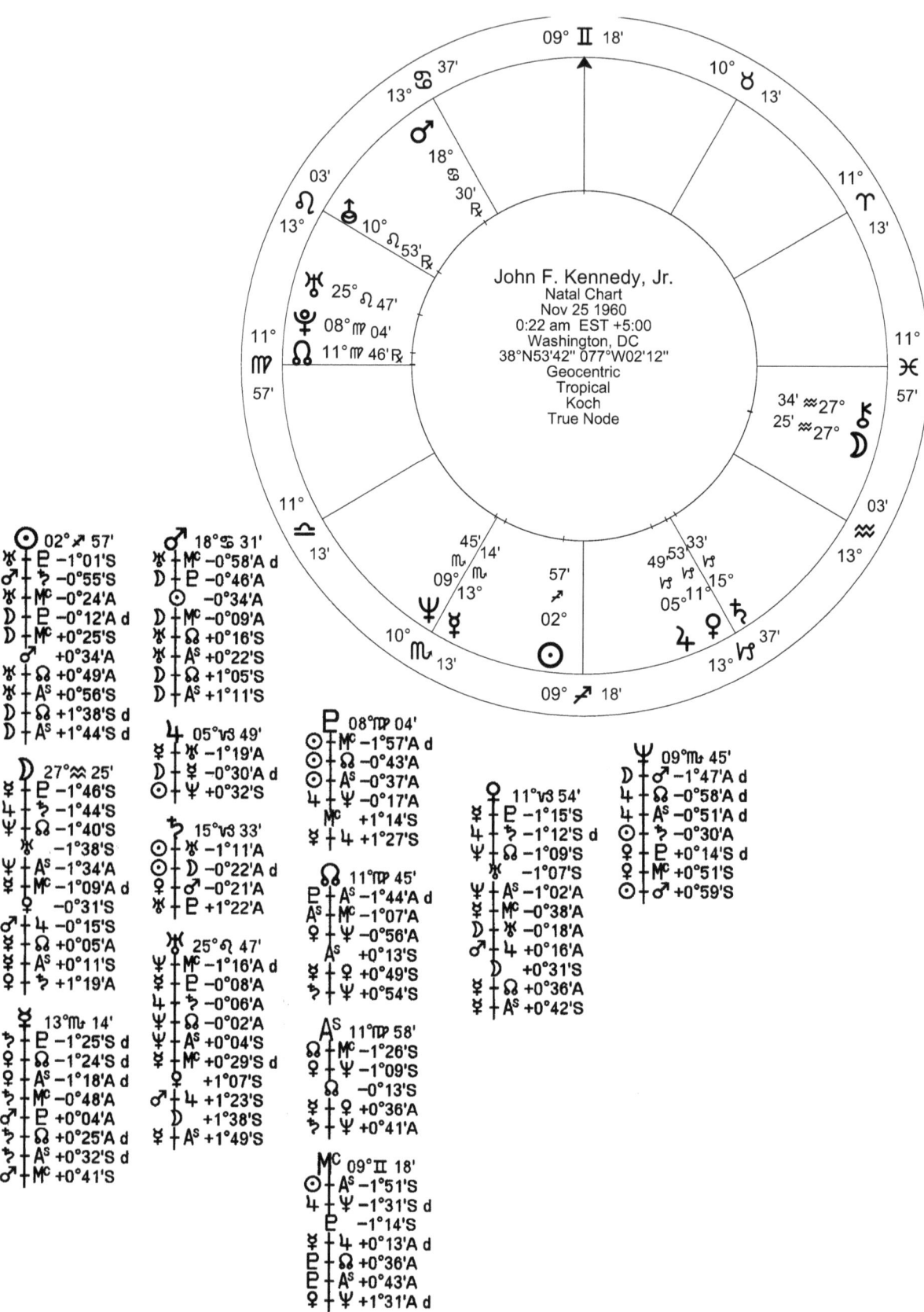

Kennedy's Midpoints

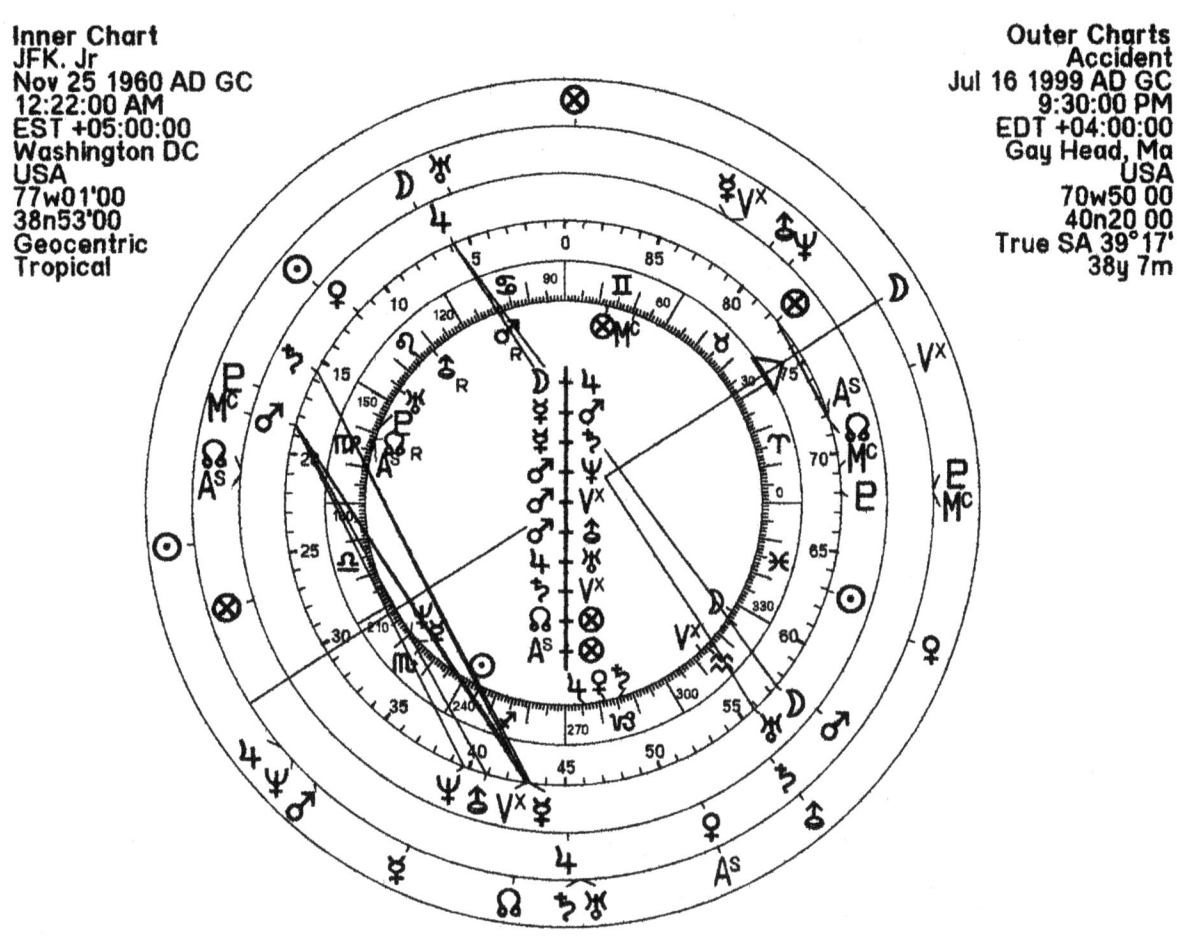

Inner Chart
JFK. Jr
Nov 25 1960 AD GC
12:22:00 AM
EST +05:00:00
Washington DC
USA
77w01'00
38n53'00
Geocentric
Tropical

Outer Charts
Accident
Jul 16 1999 AD GC
9:30:00 PM
EDT +04:00:00
Gay Head, Ma
USA
70w50 00
40n20 00
True SA 39°17'
38y 7m

Cosmogram, 90°00' H4 Dial Format

Inner Radix	Middle Directed	Outer Transits
☉ 02♐57	☉ 12♑14	☉ 24♋04
☽ 27♒25	☽ 06♈42	☽ 15♍32
☿ 13♏14	☿ 22♐31	☿ 08♌50R
♀ 11♑54	♀ 21♒11	♀ 02♍09
♂ 18♋31R	♂ 27♌48	♂ 04♏28
♃ 05♑49	♃ 15♒06	♃ 02♉36
♄ 15♑33	♄ 24♒50	♄ 15♉32
♅ 25♌47	♅ 05♎04	♅ 15♒39R
♆ 09♏45	♆ 19♐02	♆ 03♒14R
♇ 08♍04	♇ 17♎21	♇ 08♐01R
☊ 11♍45R	☊ 21♎02	☊ 13♌02
As 11♍59	As 21♎16	As 21♍03
Mc 09♊19	Mc 18♋36	Mc 07♐53
Vx 13♒02	Vx 22♓19	Vx 12♍47
⚷ 10♌54R	⚷ 20♍11	⚷ 24♌49
⊗ 17♊31	⊗ 26♋48	⊗ 29♐34

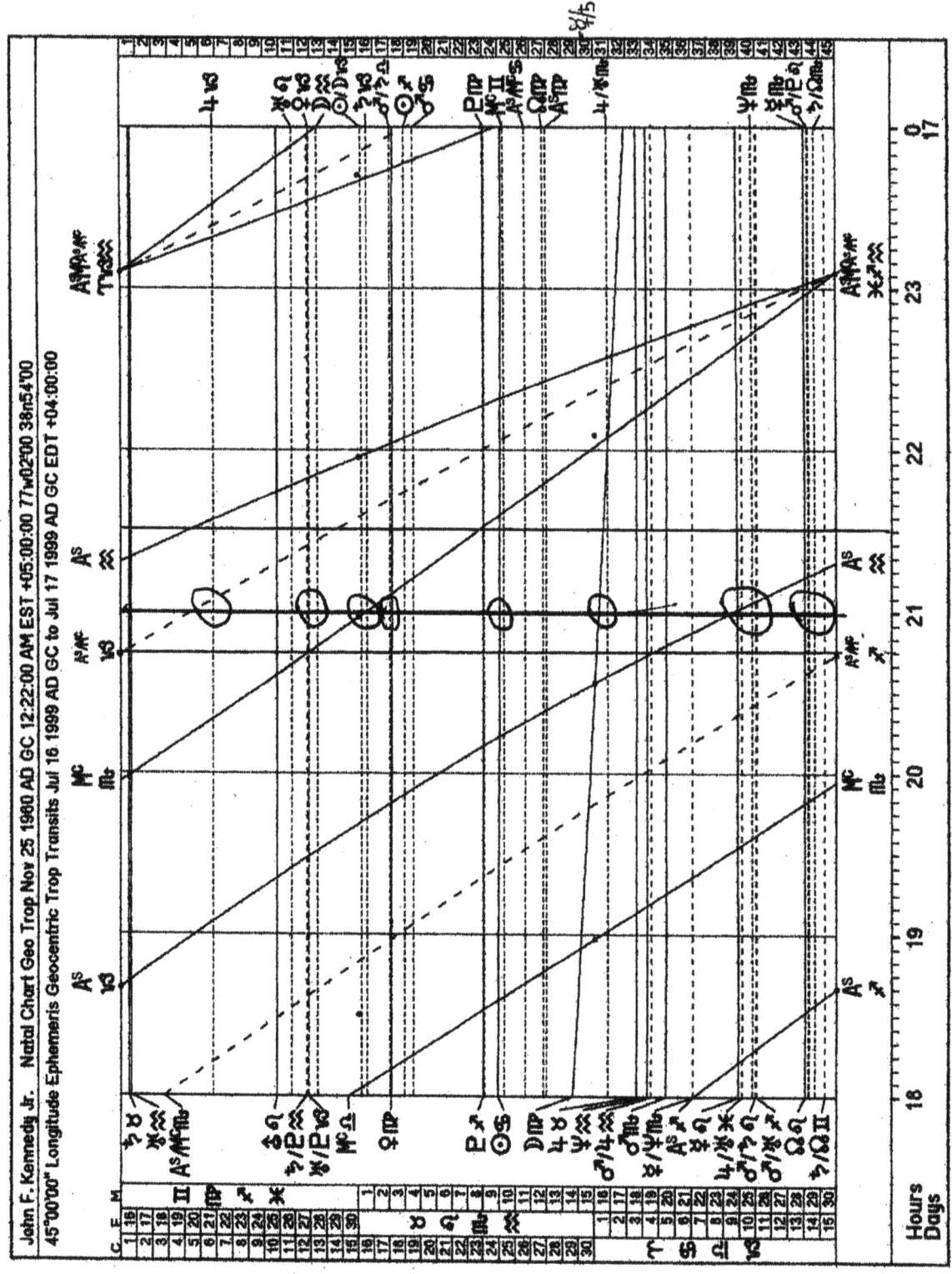

ricorn 14 is semi-square the natal Moon at 27 Aquarius 25 and describes a nature that, when expressed positively, indicates a good relationship with a partner; when negative there may be a disharmony in relationships. Solar arc Mars at 27 Leo 48 is conjunct natal Moon, showing excitement, expression of intense emotions, marital differences, frankness and honesty.

Solar arc Uranus at 5 Libra 05 square natal Jupiter at 5 Capricorn 49 implies lucky chances, sudden change in destiny, successful speculation and urge for independence. The solar arc Moon at 6 Aries 42 square natal Jupiter displays happiness, kindness and popularity, generosity and also inner conflicts and marital differences. Solar arc midpoint Mars/Saturn at 26 Scorpio 20 square natal Uranus at 25 Leo 47 brings unusual power of resistance, a test of nervous strength, intervention by Higher Power or by Providence and a sudden accident, bodily injury or separation or case of death.

Secondary Progressions

The Progressed Midheaven at 18 Cancer 37 is conjunct natal Mars at 18 Cancer 31 and refers to ego conscious action, attainment of aims in life as well as failures caused through wrong arrangements or instructions and quarrels or disputes. The progressed North Node at 7 Virgo 33 is retrograde and conjunct natal Pluto at 8 Virgo 04 with the possibility of a common and tragic destiny shared with others. The progressed Ascendant at 15 Libra 56 is square natal Saturn at 15 Capricorn 33 and may show process of gaining experiences, suffering caused through the environment and the tendency to separate from others.

The progressed Sun at 12 Capricorn 14 conjunct natal Venus at 11 Capricorn 54 is a combination representing physical love, popularity and a sense for beauty, music and nature; but in negative expression everything is done for the sake of external appearance. Progressed Jupiter at 14 Capricorn 31 conjunct natal Saturn at 15 Capricorn 33 may manifest patience, happy feelings through separation and happiness in seclusion or angry upsets and annoyance. Progressed Venus at 27 Aquarius 25 is exactly conjunct the natal Moon and offers the feeling of love and devotion or perhaps irritability, moodiness and conflicts in love.

Transits

The 45-degree midpoint ephemeris displays the slow motion movement of the planets toward the positions in the natal chart. The vertical lines drawn for the time of 8:45 p.m. on July 16, 1999 at take-off, and the time radar contact was lost show some of the most noteworthy contacts.

Transiting Pluto at 8 Sagittarius 01 is square natal Pluto at 8 Virgo 04 and opposite natal Midheaven at 9 Gemini 19. These form a very close mutable T-cross, including the fixed star Antares that fits the popular saying, "none are so blind as those who will not see." Transiting Neptune at 3 Aquarius 14 is retrograde and square the natal midpoint of Venus/Uranus at 3 Scorpio 50 and defines as sensitivity, tendency to listen to other people's suggestions too readily, a peculiar love-relationship and the necessity to renounce love suddenly.

Transiting retrograde Uranus at 15 Aquarius 39 is inconjunct the natal midpoint of Mars/Neptune at 14 Virgo 08 and is opposite natal midpoint Mars/Ascendant at 15 Leo 15, bringing changing energy levels, states of weakness emerging suddenly, a crises in life, illness or accident, illness caused through others and discordant environment. Saturn at 15 Taurus 32 trine the Mars/Neptune and square Mars/Ascendant and can indicate unfortunate consequences due to a weak will, dispute or the sharing of worries, anxieties, suffering or mourning with others.

Jupiter in transit at 2 Taurus 35 is inconjunct the midpoint of Uranus/Neptune at 2 Libra 46 and may cause a tendency to rely on others or to be in a confused psychic state. Meanwhile, retrograde Mercury at 8 Leo 51 is sesquisquare natal midpoint Sun/Saturn at 24 Sagittarius 15 and has to do with having depressing thoughts, tackling serious problems and thinking of separation. Additionally, Venus at 2 Virgo 08 is semi-square natal midpoint Mars/Saturn at 17 Libra 02 and suggests a combination of coldness of feeling, a loveless disposition, loss of female persons and the inability to love. Compounding this is the Moon at 15 Virgo 04 square natal midpoint Mercury/Saturn at 14 Sagittarius 24, perhaps causing temporary inhibited mental comprehension and lack of clear thinking and reduced quality of eyesight as it was dark and foggy. Surely in the last moments John Jr. was totally disoriented while thinking he was flying horizontally, yet his plane was in a vertical nose dive as Moon at Mercury/Saturn midpoint can be the absorption and digestion of many different impressions.

Further evaluation of transits shows a continuum of theme. The slow moving midpoints of Saturn/Pluto and Uranus/Pluto come very close to the natal Moon and Venus, suggesting a tragic destiny, estrangement and alienation, a loss of fortune and a self-destroying energy, forced decisions and an accident. Transiting Venus is exactly on his natal death axis and carries the possibility of separation, loss, death and death of females. By the time of last radio contact the transiting midpoint of Ascendant/Midheaven passed over that position as well as the natal Sun and Mars, expressing going together into separation mourning and bereavement.

Transiting Ascendant connected with the Mercury/Neptune midpoint just after take-off and is energy for the power of imagination, but also a lack of clarity and failures through incorrect behavior and inner confusion. By 9:00 p.m., the Ascendant contacted transiting Mercury, Jupiter/Uranus, Mars/Saturn and Mars/Uranus midpoints, causing a reeling into wrong judgment, missed opportunities, sudden application of effort and a struggle for survival and accident. About 10 minutes later, the Ascendant reached transiting Node and natal Mars/Pluto and Saturn/Node, showing the intensity of personal relationships, daring and foolhardiness, suffering under difficulties together with others and separation and increasing difficulties with relationship between people sharing the same residence. At 9:30 p.m. the Ascendant was on natal Jupiter, showing John Jr. overestimating his abilities; the most experienced veteran flyers refused to fly that dark foggy night. At the time of last contact with the flight tower, the transiting Midheaven beamed over the natal Ascendant/Midheaven, showing the young trio entering a point of no return before the entire world.

Accidental Drowning

Allen

Allen Sjomeling was to be 25 years old on April 25, 1971. He was married, but was separated from his wife. He had survived combat in Vietnam, only to be caught up in the turmoil of everyday life—mentally, physically and emotionally. I met this man through my son. They had developed a close friendship while working together as employees of the same firm and had shared many adventures together. As a result of one of their adventures, Allen met a girl named Jeanette and quickly fell in love with her. The couple was happy and began planning their life together. On the fateful night of March 7, 1971, a rendezvous at a nightclub was arranged between Allen and my son. The night was intended to be a youthful spree of drinking and dancing. The meeting never came about. The forceful hand of fate guided Allen to his destiny.

Allen, Jeanette, and another young man named Dale went instead to a mountain village in Colorado. The time spent there was jovial but Jeanette and Allen sensed that there was "something wrong." The intensity of their intuitive feeling increased as the evening wore on. As the three drove down the mountain, conversation in the automobile was very modest.

Coming around a curve on this dry mountain road, Dale, the young man driving, missed the curve. At that moment, the car went out of control and plunged into Bear Creek. Bear Creek, at that time was swelled with freezing waters from the first thaw. The car had overturned, pinning Allen and Jeanette inside.

Dale, able to move, freed himself from the car and ran for help. As the auto began to sink into the icy waters, Allen and Jeanette realized the peril of their predicament. There was no panic—on the contrary, there seemed to be a calmness and understanding. As the car continued to sink, the water slowly began to cover Allen's head. Jeanette tried in vain to hold his head above the water as long as she could. Neither Allen nor Jeanette could do anything to save his life. They embraced, kissed, and Allen whispered, "I can't breathe." Both lost consciousness. Help arrived on the scene only seconds later. Allen could not be revived; Jeanette lived to experience the grief fate had provided.

After an incident has occurred, retracing the correlation of the planets with the event is a simple matter, but it is a necessary step in the process of research. I gathered authentic information surrounding these tragic moments and will now give a brief account of how accurately cosmobiology mirrored the experience.

Allen's natal structure patterns show various accident-prone configurations, the most noteworthy are: The Ascendant at 7 Libra 07 in the midpoint of Uranus/Transpluto shows being placed in unfortunate circumstances and parting from others.

The MC at 8 Cancer 39 gives much information. It is in the midpoint of Saturn/Node, Saturn/Neptune, Uranus/Pluto and Venus/Neptune, meaning disadvantages or painful and grievous loss through associations with others, accident, failures through incorrect behavior and emotional suffering.

Uranus at 11 Gemini 02 in midpoint of Pluto/Node can show emotional suffering through separation and sudden tragic destiny shared with others.

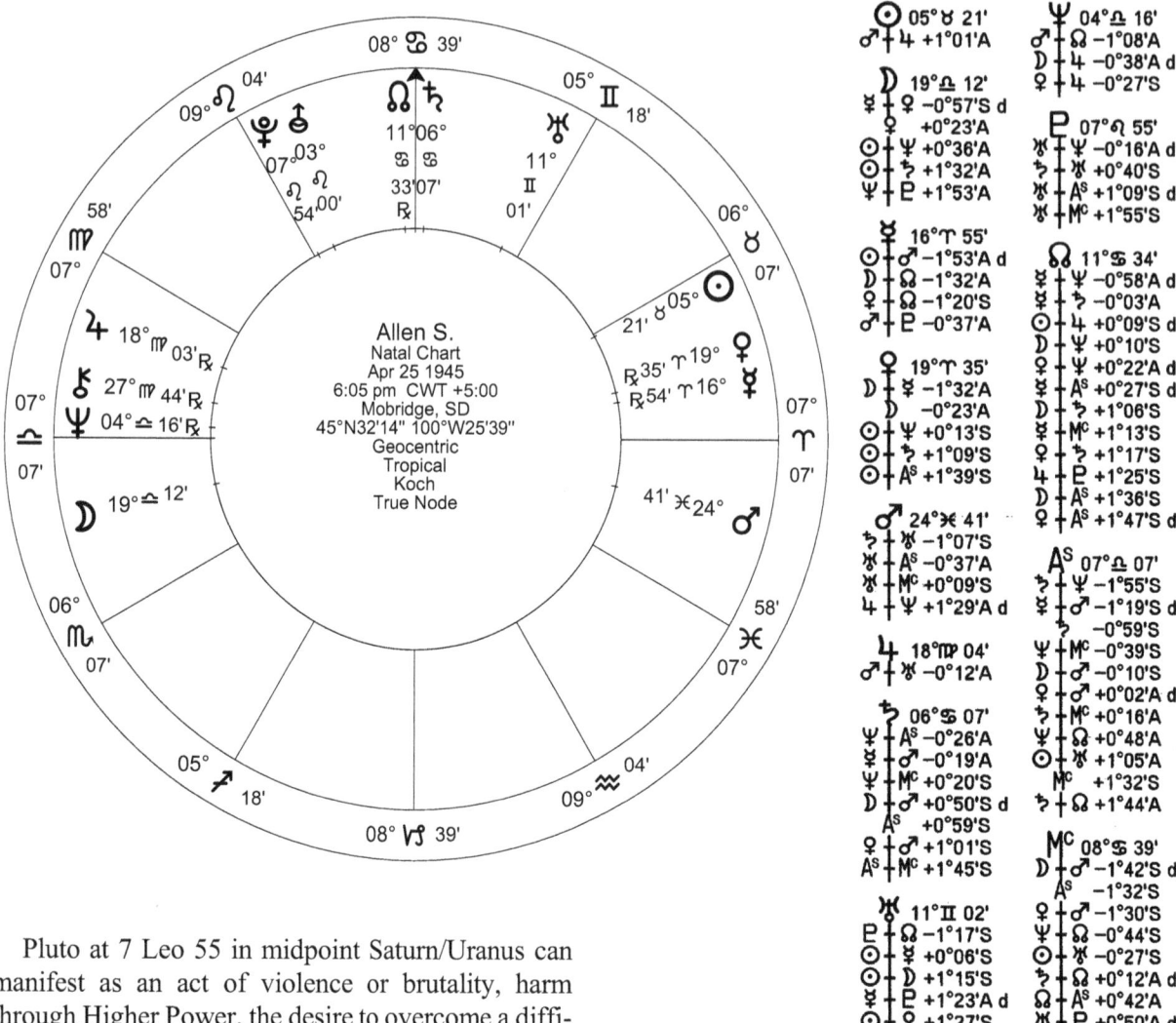

Allen's Midpoints

Pluto at 7 Leo 55 in midpoint Saturn/Uranus can manifest as an act of violence or brutality, harm through Higher Power, the desire to overcome a difficult situation. Pluto contacting Uranus/Neptune points toward the abandonment of resistance, the necessity to give in, losses, calamities and catastrophes.

Mars at 24 Pisces 41 in the midpoint of Uranus/Ascendant equates a vigorous or active intervention within the environment (the environment at the time was the car) and again injury, accidents and having to suffer violent assaults.

Solar Arc Directions

The solar arc directions for the year ahead were overflowing with aspects to further emphasize the accident-prone nature of Allen. The solar arc Pluto at 2 Virgo 56 made contact to the natal Moon at 19 Libra 12 and the Mercury/Venus midpoint at 18 Aries 55 identifies the strong love attachment and the tragic realization for the necessary adjustments that loomed ahead.

Solar arc Node at 6 Leo 35 contacted natal Sun/Pluto at 21 Gemini 38 and Mars/Jupiter at 21 Sagittarius 23 midpoints, pointing to that fateful association, separation and marital differences (Jeanette was still married).

Solar arc Uranus at 6 Cancer 03 made the following contacts: an almost perfect conjunction to natal Saturn at 6 Cancer 07, and the natal midpoints of Neptune/Ascendant at 5 Libra 42 and Mercury/Mars. While the Saturn-Uranus contact indicates much emotional tension, a limitation of freedom and unrest within the environment (the environment was in that instant the car), the midpoint combinations indicate the danger of catastrophe and sudden predicaments through others.

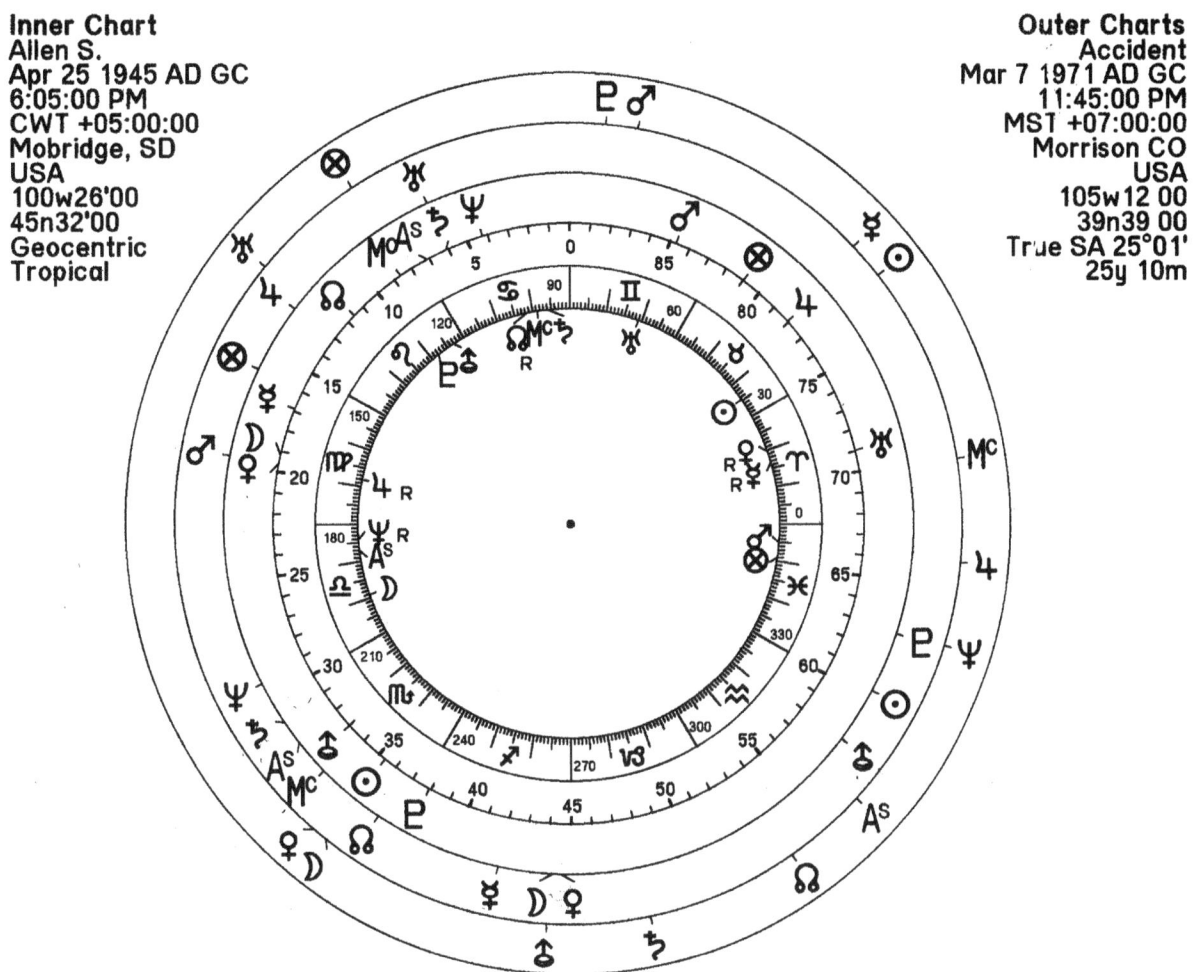

Solar arc Saturn at 1 Leo 08 in the following structures of Neptune/Ascendant, Neptune/MC, Venus/Mars, Moon/Mars and Uranus/Transpluto came to aspect natal Jupiter at 18 Virgo 04 and magnified circumstances by greatly exaggerating the strange contacts, insecurity, worry, separation from a lover and restriction due to new circumstances or environment.

The solar arc axis of Jupiter at 13 Libra 05-Transpluto at 28 Leo 02 made contact to natal Mercury/Ascendant at 12 Cancer 01, Mercury/MC at 27 Taurus 47, Moon/Saturn at 27 Leo 39 and Venus/Saturn at 27 Taurus 51, again pointing to the separation of a love relationship without sadness.

The solar arc structure of Mars at 19 Aries 42 contained all the accident-prone contacts imaginable, namely Saturn and Uranus with the two personal points of Ascendant and MC adding again accident, injury, deprivation of freedom, sudden drastic changes and intervention in the environment.

Solar arc Mercury at 11 Taurus 56 in the midpoint of Mars/Pluto at 26 Gemini 19 was in close range with natal Mars at 24 Pisces 41. This implies the misfortune to suffer violence and, to top it off, when you add transiting Mars at 27 Sagittarius and Pluto at 28 Virgo 41 retrograde to all the above it gives an incredible force and power of release to the energy.

Solar arc Sun at 0 Gemini 22 in the midpoint of Pluto/Transpluto at 0 Virgo 29 in contact with natal Mercury at 16 Aries 54 retrograde shows the most destructive power, violent brutality, crises of life and death, leaving chaotic conditions and pandemonium.

Solar arc Moon at 14 Scorpio 13 and Venus at 14 Taurus 36 took on an exceptional position. Both contacted the natal Mars/Saturn midpoint at 15 Scorpio

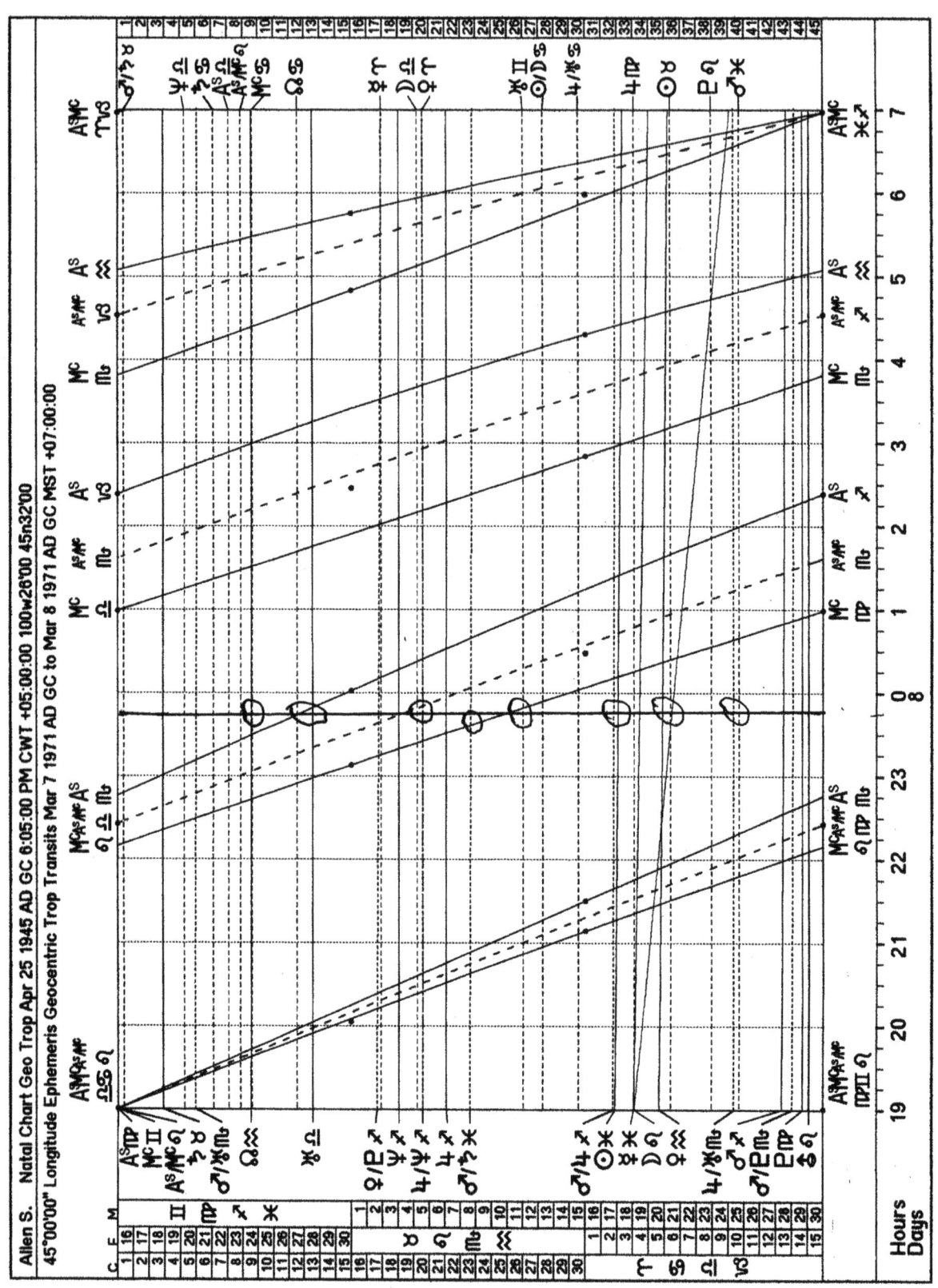

24 and Mars/Neptune midpoint at 29 Sagittarius 29, defined as death and dissolution of the body.

The solar arc Ascendant at 2 Scorpio 08 and MC at 3 Leo 40 were in contact with the Jupiter-Transpluto axis and the accident prone midpoint of natal Mars/Uranus.

One more significant factor is the solar arc midpoint of death. Mars/Saturn at 11 Gemini 26 was within 20 minutes conjunct natal Uranus at 11 Gemini 02 and shows the potential for sudden accident, separation, death and intervention of Higher Power.

Transits

Of course the transits always have to align with the directions and the natal chart.

Using cosmobiology we also have the 45-degree midpoint ephemeris where we can chart a period for many years as well as several hours. In Allen's case the following graph is for a 12-hour period, for March 7, 1971 from 7:00 p.m. to 7:00 a.m. the next morning. The line drawn vertically is for 11:45 p.m., when the accident happened, and the contacts from the transiting planets to the natal positions are circled.

The Node at 23 Aquarius is within four minutes of a sesquisquare to the natal MC. This combination indicates two people with the same outlook on life at the time, and with Uranus at 12 Libra 33 retrograde and the Ascendant at 26 Scorpio 41, the situation they suddenly found themselves in.

The next circle is the transiting midpoint of the Ascendant/MC making contact to natal Moon at 19 Libra 12, Venus at 19 Aries 35 retrograde and the Jupiter/Neptune midpoint at 4 Sagittarius 35 revealing that feelings and seeking a cordial understanding was all that mattered in those moments of entrapment. Add to the above the influence of Jupiter and Neptune and you have the explanation of sharing great hopes with others and the harm and damage through their thoughtlessness and driving at high speed on a dangerous road while intoxicated. A few minutes earlier, about 11:35 p.m., the transiting MC at 9 Virgo 50 met the Mars/Saturn midpoint at 7 Pisces 42, forming the death configuration.

The transiting Pluto/MC midpoint at 19 Virgo 15 and Mercury at 18 Pisces 25 reached natal Jupiter at 18 Virgo 04 retrograde. At about midnight the Moon at 5 Leo 27 and Venus at 4 Aquarius 52 reached the natal Sun in 5 Taurus 21.

Transiting Pluto at 28 Virgo 41 retrograde and Transpluto at 14 Leo 06 retrograde arrived at the natal Mars/Saturn death-axis. In addition, Pluto was in opposition to the fixed star Scheat at 28 Pisces 43. The following interpretation is from Ebertin-Hoffman's book *Fixed Stars*—Scheat tied up with malefic planets could lead the native to lose his life in catastrophes such as floods, shipwreck etc."

Jeanette

In contrast, the following are some significant accident-prone configurations in Jeanette's natal chart: Mars at 8 Aries 13 and Mercury at 9 Aries 29, and Neptune at 8 Libra 50 retrograde are in the midpoint of Pluto/Ascendant at 8 Cancer 53, pointing toward foolhardiness and daring, and the tendency to invite danger, injury and accidents; however these combination also can have a positive influence toward others and successful teamwork.

The Mars/Saturn (death axis) at 5 Gemini 15 and the Jupiter/Uranus ("Thank the Lord") midpoint at 7 Virgo 12 aims toward separation, mourning and bereavement, and shared happiness with others.

Neptune at 8 Libra 50 retrograde is positioned in the midpoint of Saturn/Uranus: the abandonment of resistance, weakening strength, separation, mourning and bereavement.

In the midpoint of Pluto/Ascendant at 9 Cancer 53: Accidents, and the experience of most awkward and unfortunate situations. The Ascendant/MC midpoint again points to experiencing grave disappointments.

Venus at 26 Pisces 56 contacts the Ascendant and Pluto at 10 Leo 59 retrograde, indicating strong attachments as well as strange providence in love relationships.

At the time of this life-threatening event, there were six important solar arc directions in Jeanette's chart: solar arc Mars at 1 Taurus 21 within minutes conjunct natal Sun at 1 Taurus 34 and square natal Saturn at 2 Leo 16 and solar arc Neptune at 1 Scorpio 59 retrograde, showing both the will to live and mourning. The Neptune influence depicts the entanglement in scandal.

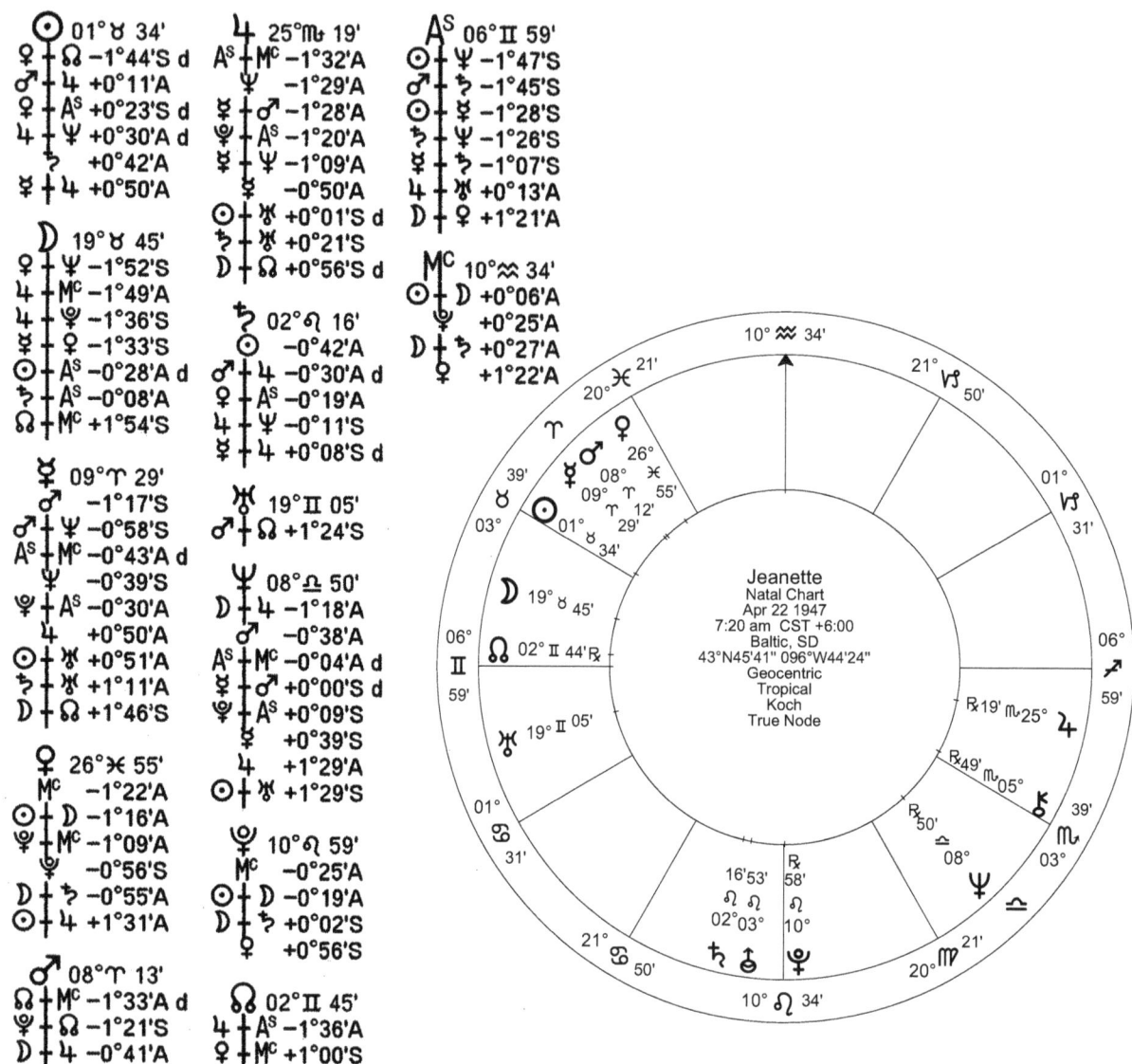

Jeanette's Midpoints

Solar arc Pluto at 4 Virgo 07 and the MC at 3 Pisces 42 both were square natal Node at 2 Gemini 45 retrograde, suggesting the potential for a strange providence or a common and tragic destiny shared with others. Solar arc Node at 25 Gemini 53 square natal Venus at 26 Pisces 56 would be the love union, and solar arc Venus at 20 Aries 03 is at the midpoint of natal Node/Ascendant at 4 Gemini 46 and Mars/Saturn midpoint at 5 Gemini 15: death of a love union.

The solar arc accident midpoint of Mars/Uranus at 6 Gemini 47 is conjunct natal Ascendant at 6 Gemini 47 exactly to the minute, and solar arc Ascendant at 29 Gemini 55 is semi-square natal Mars/Uranus at 13 Taurus 39, referring to an accident and struggle for survival. This was like a double indemnity.

Many of the March 7 aspects indicated love, happiness and passion; however, the most conspicuous factor is concentrated on Jeanette's natal Ascendant-Jupiter/Uranus configuration at 6 Gemini 47, when at the time of peril the transiting Jupiter-Mars/Saturn axis at 6 Sagittarius 06 was in close conjunction, representing a pleasant disposition, a lucky chance, fortunate turns in life, a sudden change in destiny, a fortunate separation, a quick dissolution of the body, a very pleasant and easy death, intervention of Higher Power or by Providence, a sudden accident.

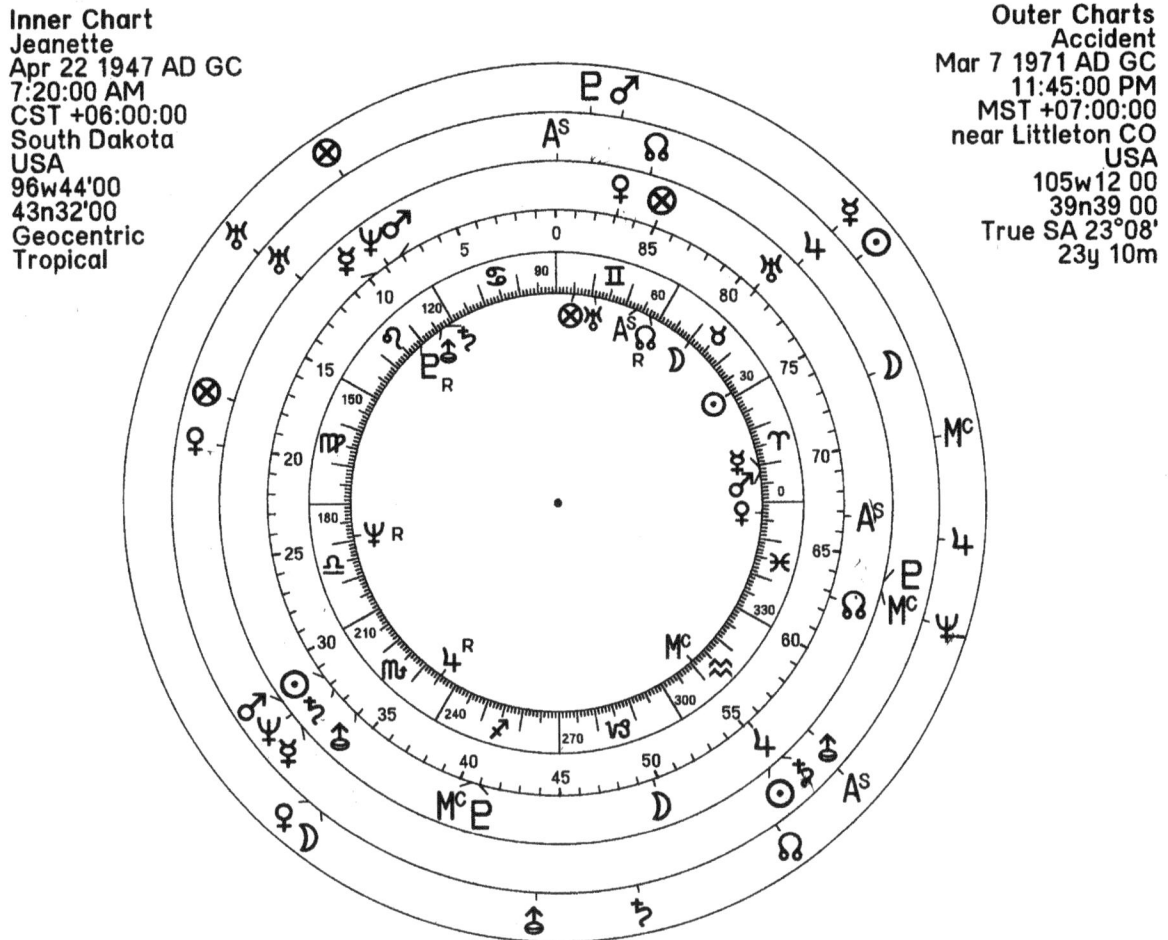

At this point a few words from Jeanette, who wrote a four-page letter to my son describing the last comments: "Since I was there with Allen, I know he did not suffer. I am sure he knew he was going to die, and even then he was so content. He was as cold as I was, and if I had not gotten out, I would have gone into such a peaceful state like Allen had—no suffering and how fortunate to die that way."

This is but a small account of the delineation; however, the pertinent points are precise enough to draw definite conclusions. Please note: The transiting Ascendant/MC midpoint at 18 Libra 15 and Neptune at 3 Sagittarius 04 retrograde was within one degree of orb of a sesquisquare and opposition the natal Node at 2 Gemini 45 retrograde in Jeanette's chart, displaying the importance of associations in this person's life.

Several months after the accident I found out that Jeanette had a twin sister born one hour earlier at 6:20 a.m. April 22, 1947. After inquiring about the sister's activities on the day of the accident, I was told that March 7 was a very routine and uneventful day. In Jeanette's 45-degree midpoint ephemeris, the natal Ascendant and MC of Jeanne are dotted in to show that her personal points were not at all in such a precarious position.

The driver of the car, Dale, was born December 17, 1945. No time and place of birth was available. After the rescue, Dale and Jeanette were treated at a hospital and released. On December 26, 1971, Dale was sentenced to 10 days in jail. Originally he was charged with vehicular homicide, causing the death of another while under the influence of alcohol. A lesser plea was accepted because there was no felonious intent shown in his driving.

It is noteworthy to show that transiting Jupiter/Uranus at 9 Scorpio 19 contacted Dale's natal Sun at 25 Sagittarius 30 with a 45-degree angle: sudden physical happiness. The transiting death axis at 7 Pisces 42 was sesquisquare his natal Saturn at 23

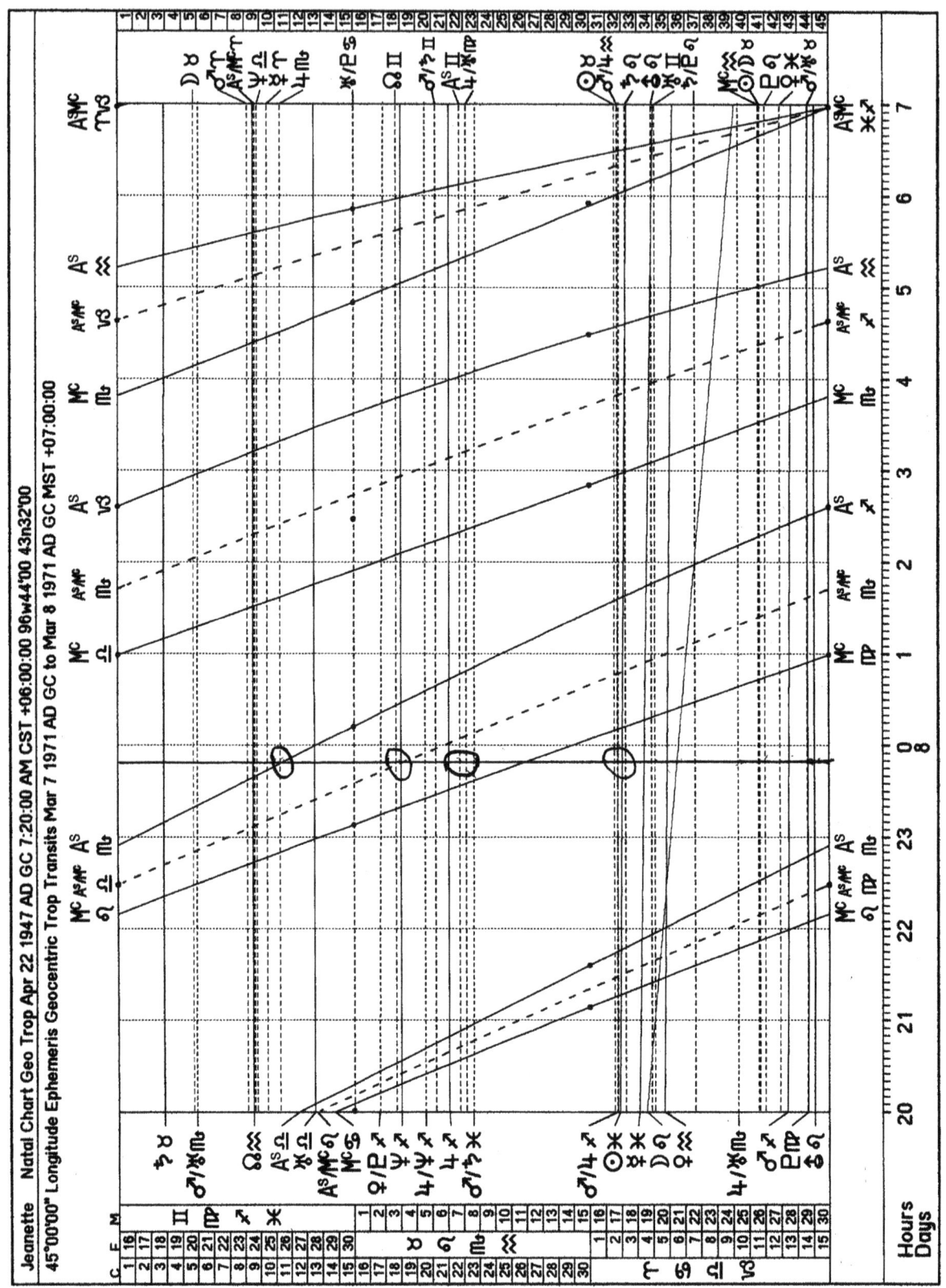

Cancer 24 retrograde and Jupiter at 22 Libra 55. He, like Jeanette, escaped death within a hair's breadth: an easy death.

Dale's natal structure of Neptune at 8 Libra 28 is in midpoints Mars/Uranus and Mercury/Pluto. The first: a fainting fit when overtaxing strength, a car accident (highway suicide). The second: slow mental alertness taxing the energies and powers because of self-underestimation of intoxication. The transiting Ascendant/MC midpoint at 18 Libra 15 was between his natal Sun and Pluto or the midpoint of it at 18 Libra 23, showing the crises of self-preservation, consciousness of purpose or objective, and the quality of leadership, the experience of physical interference or violence with physical or emotional consequences. Dale was able to get out of the car and instantly run for help.

John Ritter

Following is a short biography of this talented actor, Jonathan Southworth Ritter. He was the son of the legendary country-singing star and actor Tex Ritter, yet he became famous in his own right. In high school he was a leader as student body president. Later he attended the University of Southern California where his major was psychology and minor was architecture. Several years later he was encouraged to join an acting class and in 1971 graduated with a bachelor of fine arts degree.

During this period he was performing in stage plays around Europe while his father was entertaining troops in Germany. John also performed at an air base there. His father passed away before John achieved the celebrity status of "Three's Company" (1977-1984) for which he earned an Emmy Award.

His 1977 marriage to Nancy Morgan produced three children and his 1999 second marriage to Amy Yasbeck, one child. His second successful series, "8 Simple Rules for Dating My Teenage Daughter," started in 2002 and continued until his death.

John collapsed on stage while an episode of the series was being taped September 11, 2003, and died shortly afterward around 10:00 p.m. The Providence St. Joseph Medical Center in Burbank announced that he suffered from aortic dissection, an unrecognized flaw in the heart. What follows is a description of his natal makeup, progressions, solar arc direction and transits for the time of his sudden demise.

Natal

This brief description is to cover especially the personal points, Ascendant, Midheaven, Sun, Moon and the Node. It seems John lived his life to the fullest on the stage and in his private life. The Ascendant at 20 Aries 23 certainly describes environment with the power to obtain and to maintain his place in the world. I have often wondered whether his private life was also as rambunctious as the role he portrayed as John Tripper. He was a leader and had a clear objective of what he wanted in life. Courage, boldness and enthusiasm also belong to an Aries Ascendant as well as being quarrelsome, having self-confidence and ambition.

His Sun at 25 Virgo 06 demonstrates an individual who is concerned about details, correctness, diligence and analytical ability. Enmity is caused by fault finding and good opportunities are often missed. The Sun is also in close opposition to the Moon at 22 Pisces 02 causing friction within him and a tendency to allow conflicts to manifest. Positive influences would be making contacts with partners and friends and joint success having to do with public life. Negative expression could bring about disharmony with parents or partners and differences caused by inner tension. The structure of the Sun at midpoint of Venus/Mars adds tremendously to his artistic creativeness, passionate love and sexual desire. The Jupiter/Uranus midpoint adds a good intellectual grasp and an inventive mind.

The Moon in Pisces would make him susceptible to external influences and moodiness. Sometimes there might even be a feeling of inferiority. The sesquisquare to Mars and square to Uranus certainly would contribute too much tension and upsets, and cardiac problems, as well as successes.

The MC at 12 Capricorn 18 stands for the ego-consciousness and spiritual awareness. It would depict the intense striving for the attainment of ob-

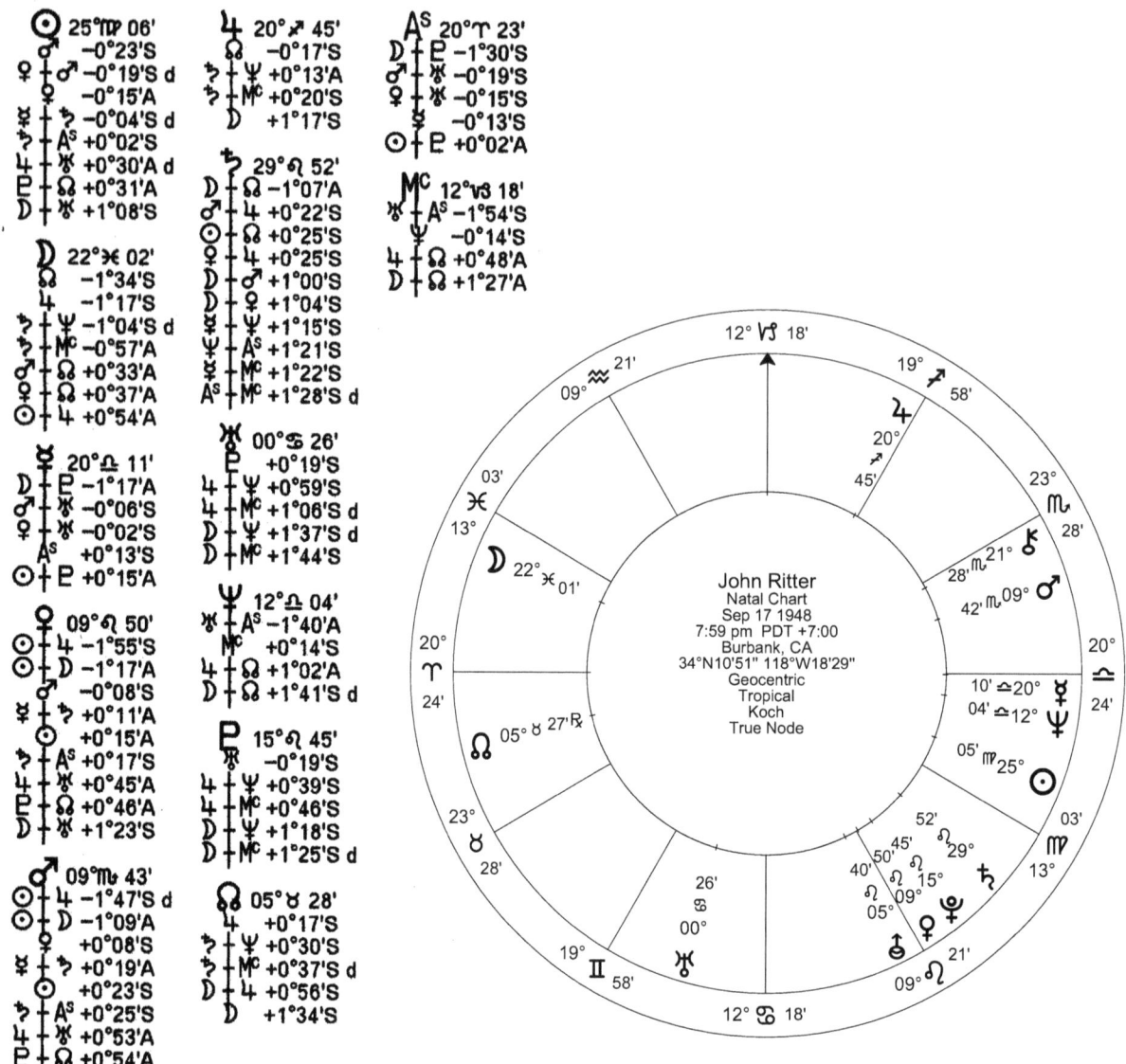

Ritter's Midpoints

jectives. A conservative attitude and sense of reality would certainly contribute to the eventual prominence of his profession.

The Node at 5 Taurus 28 shows that associations and alliances would call for permanent unions and striving for personal advantage through others. Jupiter sesquisquare the Node would enhance and bring about harmonious relationships, gain in business with others and the luck of finding a good partner.

In addition, by using the Anatomical Chart, the 26-degree rules the physical heart organ and creates a structure pattern, giving us a little more information. The 26-degree Leo is semi-square Neptune, representing weakness, and the 26-degree Leo is also at the midpoint of Mercury/Uranus that represents tension.

Solar Arc Directions

While the secondary progressions show no significant contacts of this tragic event, the solar arc directions indicate several. John's solar arc was 54 degrees 32 minutes. The solar arc Moon at 16 Taurus 34 had passed natal Pluto at 15 Leo 45 (square) the year before and produced extreme emotions, and solar arc Jupiter at 15 Aquarius 17 was already influencing natal Pluto and Uranus at 0 Cancer 26 (semi-square), forming the "Thank the Lord combination. All the above progressions and directions created stress on the emotional level and, in the bio-

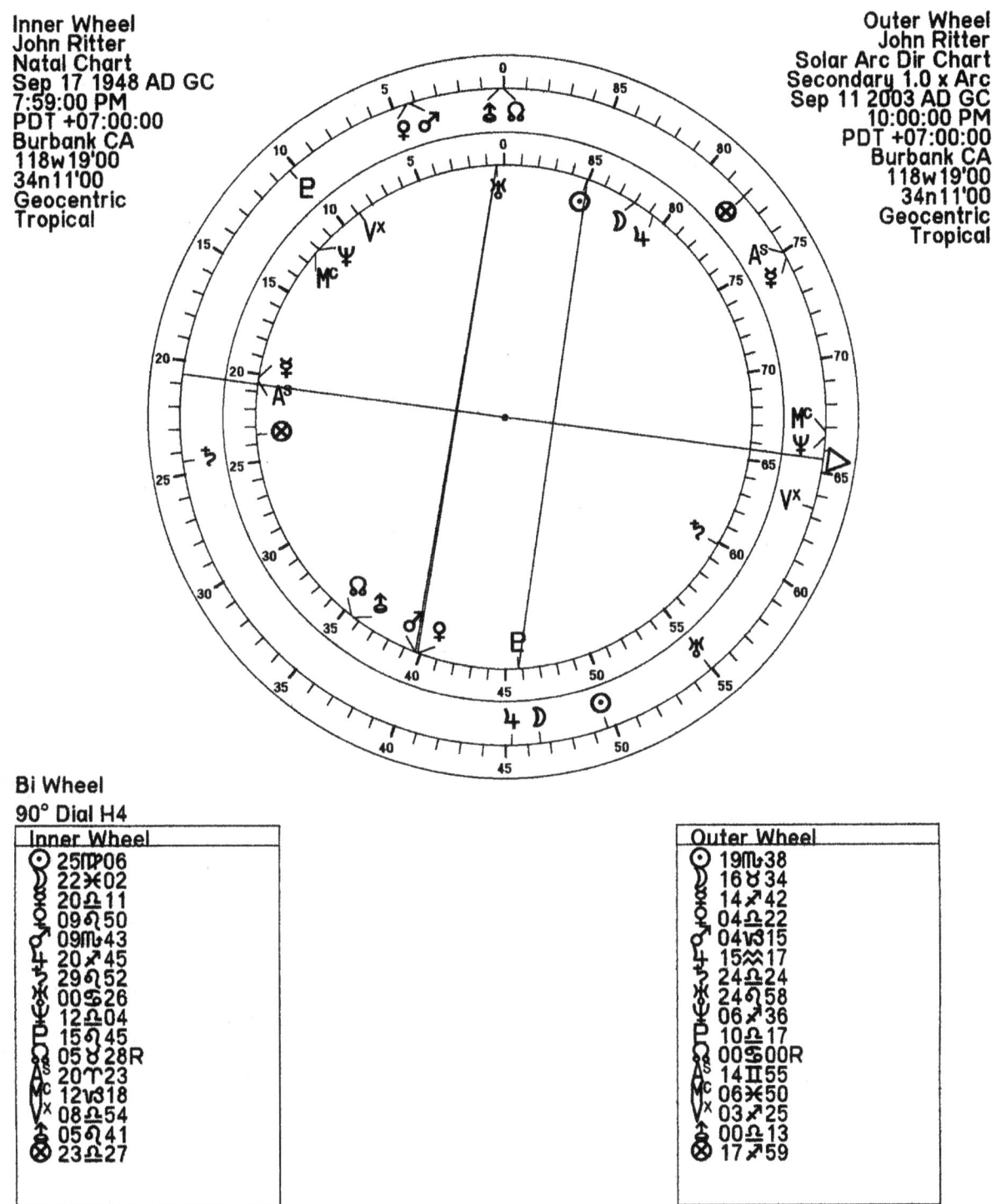

logical correspondence, disturbances of the blood pressure.

Solar arc Uranus at 24 Leo 58 and Pluto at 10 Libra 17 are within range of influencing natal Neptune at 12 Libra 04, causing among other things insecurity and fatigue. This transformation semi-square is within minutes of contact with the degree of the heart that could have been weak from the start with the semi-square to Neptune.

Solar arc Saturn at 24 Libra 24 is on natal midpoint of Node/MC at 8 Virgo 53, pointing toward difficulties in associations and career. When the 26th

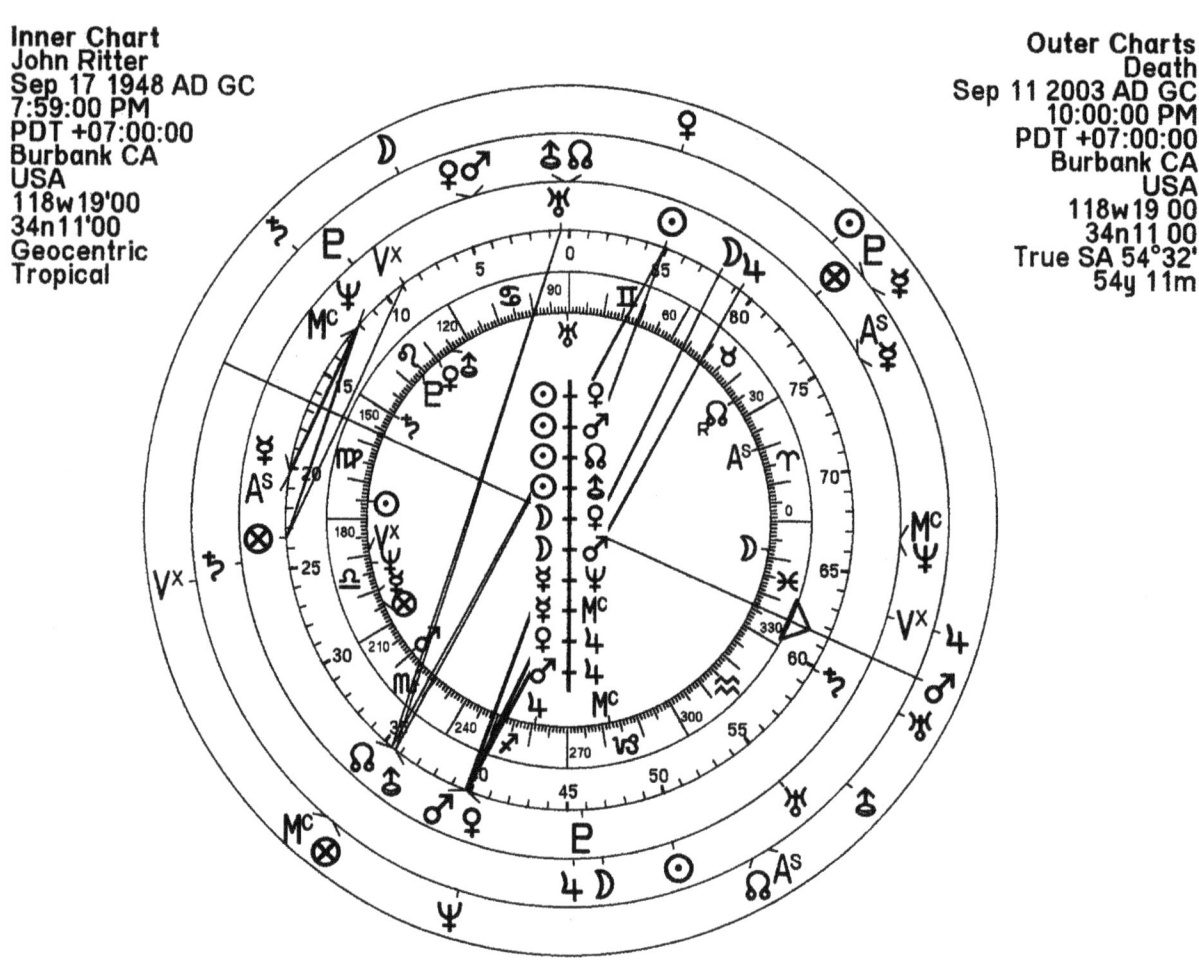

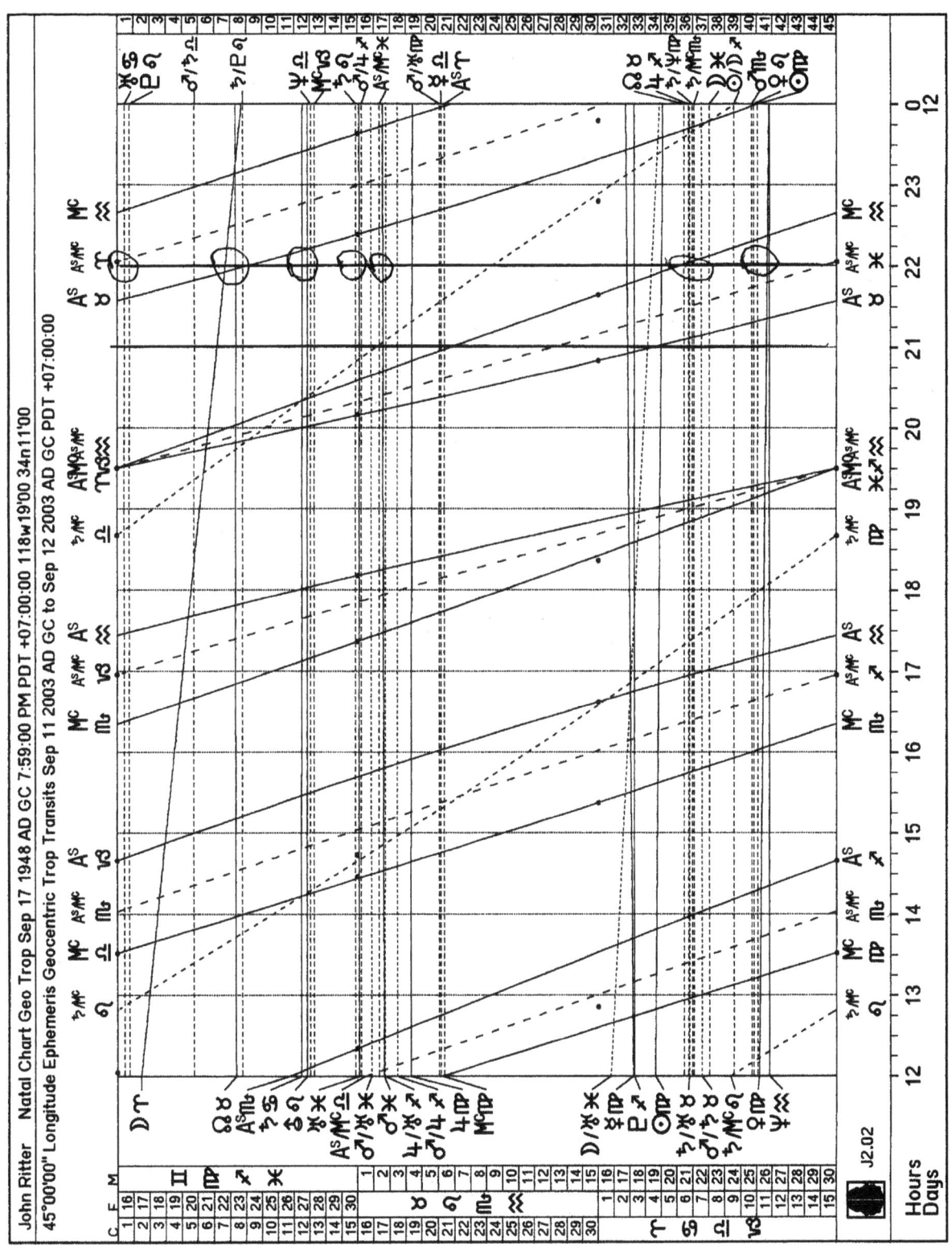

degree of Leo is advanced by solar arc it falls on 20 Libra 32 within minutes of a conjunction to natal Ascendant at 20 Aries 23 and Mercury at 20 Libra 11, emphasizing the environment and communication.

Transits

On the 45-degree ephemeris two vertical lines are drawn between 9:00 and 10:00 p.m. The transit planets are calculated for 10:00 p.m., Burbank, California. The Node at 22 Taurus 21 retrograde is square natal Saturn/Pluto at 22 Leo 48 and symbolizes common suffering shared with others. Many times this combination refers to being prevented by others from reaping successes and at the same time it can be self-destructive in regard to physical energy.

Saturn at 11 Cancer 32 is square natal Neptune at 12 Libra 04 and opposition natal MC at 12 Capricorn 18. This transiting T-Cross is a combination implying frequent mood changes, losing courage quickly, wavering between material and idealistic inclinations and emotional suffering. Uranus at 00 Pisces 06 is opposite natal Saturn at 29 Leo 52 and may produce a tendency to cause unrest within the environment, which can apply at home as well as at the job, and sudden intervention in one's destiny with a limitation of freedom. Mars at 1 Pisces 35 retrograde is conjunct the most sensitive natal midpoint of Ascendant/Midheaven at 1 Pisces 21 and creates a signature individual in action and successful teamwork. Venus at 25 Virgo 42 and Neptune at 10 Aquarius 50 retrograde are sesquisquare natal Sun at 25 Virgo 05 within orb of a semi-square to natal Venus at 9 Leo 50 and natal Mars at 9 Scorpio 43, offering an awakening from emotional infatuation with the awareness of disappointment.

The Moon at 6 Aries 42 is semi-square the Node at 22 Taurus 21 retrograde, approaching the natal midpoint of Saturn/Pluto at 22 Leo 48, forming a powerful combination pointing toward melancholy and suffering through associations, but also blood relatives. The Ascendant at 23 Taurus 02 at 10:00 p.m. reached the natal midpoint of Saturn/Pluto, setting off the above mentioned powerhouse energies bringing about separation, mourning and bereavement.

The MC at 05 Aquarius 07 is approaching natal Jupiter at 29 Sagittarius 45, the natal Moon at 22 Pisces 02, natal Node at 5 Taurus 28 retrograde and natal midpoint Saturn/Neptune at 20 Virgo 58 and midpoint Saturn/MC at 06 Scorpio 05, ushering in emotional suffering and diseases with causes difficult to ascertain. The most sensitive transiting midpoint of Ascendant/Midheaven at 29 Virgo 05 is applying to natal Uranus at 00 Cancer 26 and natal Pluto at 15 Leo 45, expressing excitements and upsets. The principle of Uranus and Pluto is basically a transformation and combined with the most sensitive midpoint describes exactly what happened to John Ritter at that time.

Highway Inferno

This story is from a newspaper account taken from the *Rocky Mountain News,* Denver, on September 4, 1982. "Two women were critically burned after they were blasted out of their motor home when its leaking propane tank exploded and engulfed the vehicle in flames at a highway rest stop. The explosion destroyed the motor home and a pickup truck parked next to it. The two women were airlifted to a Denver hospital. Both were listed in critical condition with second and third degree burns over 80 to 90 percent of their bodies. The husband of one of the women and the companion of the other escaped unharmed from the motor home moments after the explosion."

Since one of the women involved in this accident is also a professional astrologer, she was aware of the time factor in the whole ordeal and was kind enough to supply me with many details which generally are not known. In order for you to get the most information, her detailed account is included here.

"You asked about previous violence in my life, the answer is, there has not been any. In the spring of 1943, at age 12, I was in a car accident. My mouth and gums were badly cut and my teeth were loosened but everything completely healed in a short time. Mid-November 1949, at age 18, I had a cervical cyst. By the end of the month I hemorrhaged and developed a critical infection. An operation and blood transfusion followed. This was a very critical time for me, it was the first quarter of college and I was pulling straight A's but ended up with all B's because I missed so much of the last part of school and finals. I was also in emotional turmoil over a romance I feared was about to end after a year (the love in my life at that time ended up becoming my husband). I nearly died at this time but I have no record of exact dates.

"I have never experienced any other life-threatening situation, notably never been hit, attacked, raped, broken bones, etc. I have spent a fortune on dental work and some Saturn health problems.

"When I first entered astrology in January 1974, I was alarmed to read harrowing potentials in my chart. I learned, with time, that when you experience the event, you can always find the correlations. There are many times the chart is activated but the energy is used positively.

"Then came 1982. Early that year I had a D&C and extensive dental work, then on May 24, 1982, I had a hysterectomy. I hoped that all this would use up the secondary progressed Mars square the natal Moon. I went to Europe in 1975, 1978, 1979 and 1981. I planned again to go in September of 1982; the trip did not come about.

"On September 3, 1982, at approximately 9:30 a.m. MDT, my husband and I picked up friends at Stapleton airport in Denver. They flew in from Houston for a trip to Wyoming. About 10:15 a.m., in the parking lot of the Merchandise Mart, Denver, the propane fuel tank valve released and did not reclose. I was the only one there (the others were in the Mart). I was very frightened, my knees started shaking, and my throat was dry. A black dockworker witnessed this and laughed at my fears. I ran up to the fourth floor and returned with my husband and friends. The hissing noise was gone and most of the gas was gone out by now. No one seemed very alarmed. I did not want to continue, but because of my guests, I hid my apprehension. Harry, my husband, started the coach, no event. We all got in and drove to the propane bulk station to have the valve checked and to refuel.

"A part-time employee, not on duty, looked at the valve, tapped it with a hammer and said it was okay to proceed but advised us to have the valve checked after the trip. Around noon the attendant refilled our tank and, unknown to us, over-packed it. Just after noon, a small foreign car drove into our right tire. There was no damage to us but he was disabled. We were on our way again.

"At 1:10 p.m. we pulled off at a rest stop for lunch. We parked in an end slot; a pickup camper was on our right, nothing on the left. Immediately after setting the brake, the valve again released. Harry noticeably became excited and got us gals out at once. After running about 20 feet, I turned and saw my husband still in the coach. Ignition occurred simultaneously, I was engulfed in flames! It was a blowtorch-like searing heat; flames were sizzling on my arms. I took a couple of steps and immediately called out to Marcie, "fall and roll!" The grass was barely damp but it put out the flames. My top layer of skin was falling off, my hands felt like bursting and the pain was excruciating. People in a fifth-wheel trailer allowed me to lie on the bed until first-aid arrived. Fortunately, I had the presence of mind to remove my watch, wedding ring and earrings before I started to swell.

"The fire-truck came from Fort Collins and a helicopter came from Greeley. Marcie and I were airlifted to Denver. TV cameras were at the scene as we were put into the chopper. I had an IV in the jugular vein en-route to the hospital; there was no other vein available. In the hospital, saline, etc. was administered. I swelled to 205 pounds. Although small amounts of morphine or equivalent are occasionally given, it has little discernable value since the pain is so very great and so constant.

"With the skin gone, aura is very weak, you seem to absorb the pain and suffering of others as well as your own. I was very vulnerable and sensitive at that time to TV special effects and violence on TV was traumatic.

"I was in the Intensive Care Unit for one month, in a regular private room for one month, and then, left the hospital on October 30, 1982. Daily tanking and debridement was indescribable for some time; later I enjoyed tanking. After six weeks on my back, I had to stand up and walk. Again the pain was beyond description. My legs burst and blood flowed each time I tried for several days. I was exhausted and upset for two to four hours afterwards.

"The blessings: Incredible support from my family, relatives and friends. I never felt so much love from prayers (and they are still going on). I did not require psychological help. While my own "true grit" and positive thinking are responsible in part, support from those close to me had much to do with my mental health.

"No one wants to be unattractive and I am no exception to that notion, however, character has always been more valuable to me. There are times I have trouble accepting the alterations. The recuperating part is the incredible, endless journey, layers to go through. The separate one-out-of-the-million's feeling at times was overwhelming. No matter how much help and support I felt, I still had to suffer it myself physically. More than once I did not want to live. I can appreciate that side of pain too. It was not really depression but logical deduction. It did not seem worth the trouble, I have not really changed in this regard. Obviously, I still anticipate a good life. If I had to go through it again, I would feel the same.

"I had such a wonderful full life and had accomplished most of what I wanted to; the rest was just a continuation. What I am saying is, going through this has shown me what I can survive. I have not built up any greater defense against pain and suffering and have no hesitation toward the future operations for release, grafts, and subsequent rehabilitation therapy. One finds oneself needing to be grateful that doctors can intervene to help eliminate the limiting factors but at the same time, there is difficulty handling the anger.

"Valves and openings are ruled by Uranus. Why didn't the ignition occur the first time when the gas leaked out? There was no live flame source to ignite on. Harry had not lit the pilot light on the refrigerator (he forgot) but then at noon, the time of refueling, he did light the pilot light. When the fire occurred, Uranus was rising. It is presumed the gas vapor found the pilot light flame source. Also, propane ignites on the perimeter (outer boundary) not at the source one would expect. Although we gals were out, we were in exactly the wrong place. The fire enveloped the

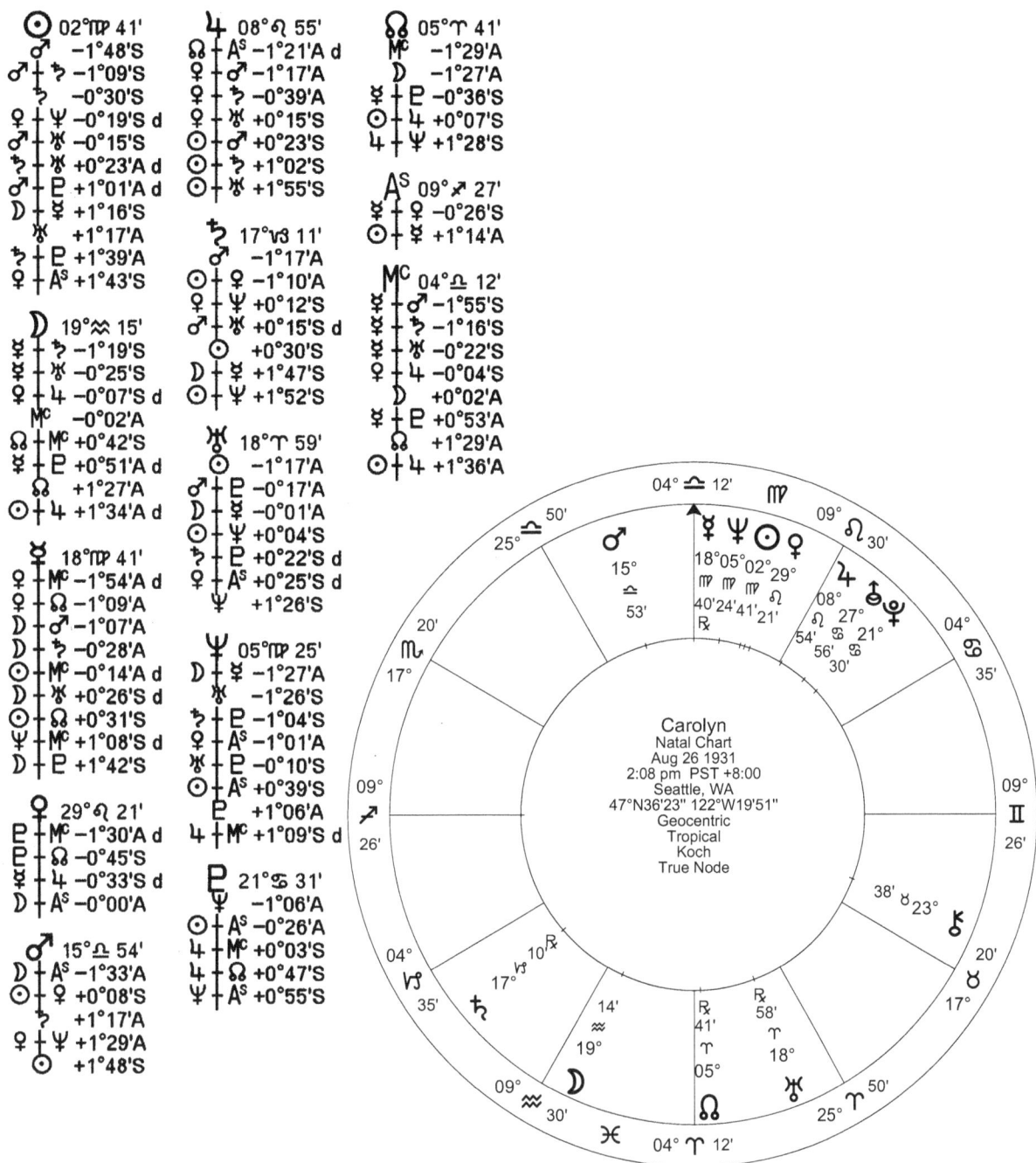

exterior first, allowing the men to jump through it.

"The entire motor home burned in seven or eight minutes. The interior temperature reached 3,500 degrees, quite a spectacle! Unlike gasoline, the fire consumed, but did not throw debris like usual explosions. Fire also destroyed the adjacent camper. The couple and their dog were not injured but they lost everything including his glasses and wallet. All they had left was a jar of pickles."

Carolyn

The individual has a remarkable accident-prone pattern. In the 360-degree circle notice the cardinal grand cross. In the 90-degree circle Mars, Saturn, Uranus and Pluto are within six degrees of each other and yet only at age 12, in 1982, was an accident experienced. The earlier took place when solar arc MC contacted natal Mars.

Inner Chart
Carolyn
Aug 26 1931 AD GC
2:08:00 PM
PST +08:00:00
Seattle WA
USA
122w20'00
47n36'00
Geocentric
Tropical

Outer Charts
Inferno
Sep 3 1982 AD GC
1:10:00 PM
MDT +06:00:00
Fort Collins CO
USA
105w05 00
40n35 00
True SA 49°55'
51y 0m

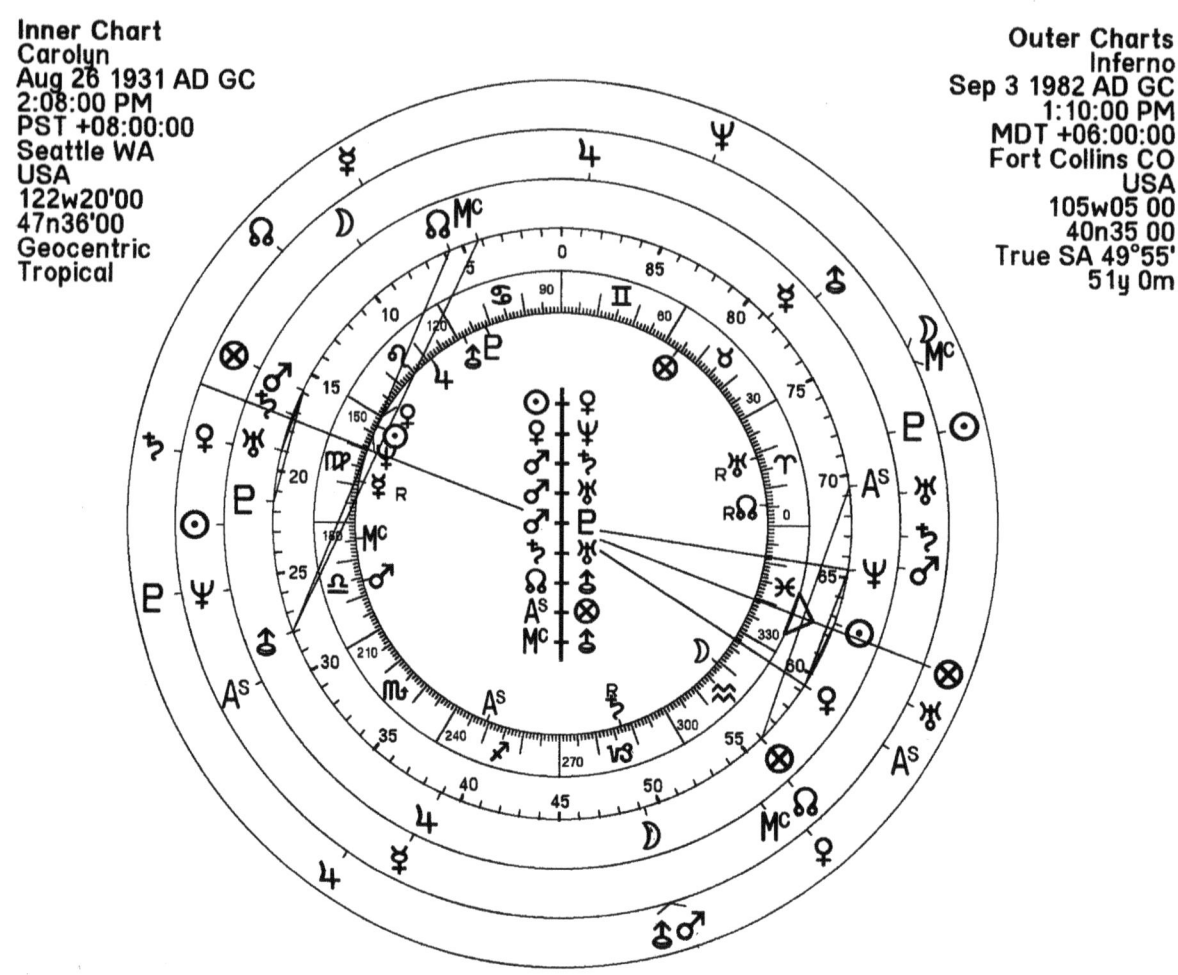

Cosmogram, 90°00' H4 Dial Format

Inner Radix	Middle Directed	Outer Transits
☉ 02♍41	☉ 22♎36	☉ 10♍57
☽ 19♒15	☽ 09♈10	☽ 14♓14
☿ 18♍41R	☿ 08♏36	☿ 07♎49
♀ 29♌21	♀ 19♎16	♀ 24♌56
♂ 15♎54	♂ 05♐49	♂ 19♏10
♃ 08♌55	♃ 28♍50	♃ 06♏35
♄ 17♑11R	♄ 07♓06	♄ 19♎58
♅ 18♈59R	♅ 08♊54	♅ 00♐51
♆ 05♍25	♆ 25♎20	♆ 24♐17R
♇ 21♋31	♇ 11♍26	♇ 25♎08
☊ 05♈41R	☊ 25♉36	☊ 11♋41R
As 09♐27	As 29♑22	As 29♏06
Mc 04♎12	Mc 24♏07	Mc 13♍43
⚷ 27♌57	⚷ 17♍52	⚷ 19♌07
⊗ 26♉00	⊗ 15♋55	⊗ 02♊23

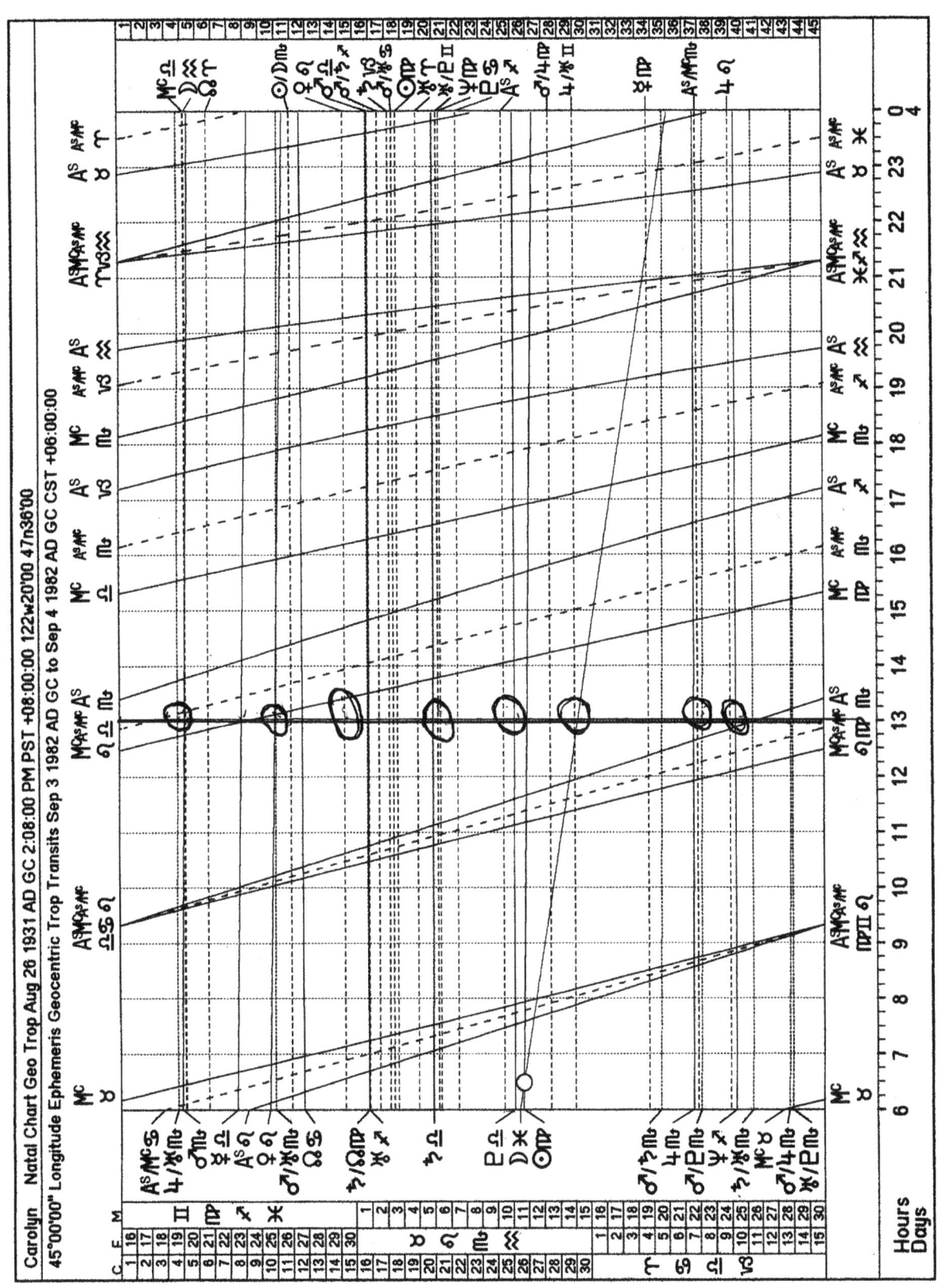

The natal Sun at 2 Virgo 41 and Saturn at 17 Capricorn 11 retrograde are in the midpoint of Mars/Uranus at 17 Cancer 26, indicating a person who is able to act quickly, allowing for sudden adjustments to new conditions and circumstances in life, accidents and operations. This complex combination is also at the midpoint of Mars/Pluto at 3 Virgo 43, causing injury, violent measures, upsets or shocks caused through the intervention of Higher Power. It reaches further through the midpoint of Saturn/Uranus at 3 Pisces 05 that represents physical exposure to severe tests of strength, powers of resistance and separation plus the midpoint of Saturn/Pluto that may show physical toil, over-exertion, renunciation and privation.

The major life-changing event on September 3, 1982 has many contacts which I will outline beginning with the cardinal grand cross mentioned earlier. The natal Ascendant at 9 Sagittarius 27 is contacting the midpoint of Pluto/Transpluto at 24 Cancer 44, and according to John Hawkins in his book, *Transpluto Or Should We Call Him Bacchus*, this combination indicates "destructive or constructive power and force suddenly released leaving chaotic conditions and pandemonium." In the psychological correspondence he further notes, "this is the most destructive two-combinations in astrology. The after-affects create an entirely new set of conditions, sudden blowups that have been seething underneath for some time or crises of life and death."

Natal Uranus at 18 Aries 59 retrograde is also contacting the midpoint of Sun/Neptune at 4 Virgo 03, which can bring about sudden upsets and excitements, sudden emerging weakness or illness and extremely high sensitivity. At the same time a tragic deception or illusion is triggered when the whole structure by solar arc of 49 degrees 55 minutes advances to 8 Gemini 53 opposing the natal Ascendant at 9 Sagittarius 27, setting off the above and unleashing the description of Pluto-Transpluto. In addition it shows sudden disasters or calamities of great consequence, the ability to make sudden decisions in the most difficult situations, danger through water, poison or gas.

Solar Arc Directions

The solar arc Ascendant at 29 Capricorn reaches the natal midpoint of Jupiter/Uranus, the "Thank the Lord" aspect at 13 Gemini 57. Also, the transiting Moon at 14 Pisces 14 and MC at 14 Virgo 43 reveals that the hour and minute were forming a powerful picture and clearly indicating the exactness of the planetary positions.

Transits

Then came the transits that put the whole year's activity into great detail. Transiting Pluto at 25 Libra 08 semi-square the Sun at 10 Virgo 57 contacts the solar arc Pluto-Neptune semi-square, which caused the sensitive physique, proneness to external influences and later the gradual commencement of therapy. Furthermore this Pluto at 25 Libra 08 represents causing chaotic conditions under a tragic illusion as the party thought the valve of the gas tank was repaired.

Neptune at 24 Sagittarius retrograde semi-square solar arc Mercury at 8 Scorpio 36 indicates the lack of clarity, but support comes from natal Jupiter at 8 Leo 55, adding great hope for the future. Uranus at 0 Sagittarius 51 on the other hand sets off natal Mars at 15 Libra 54 and Saturn at 17 Capricorn 01, revealing the life-threatening situation.

Saturn at 19 Libra 58 contacting the natal midpoint of Uranus/Pluto at 5 Gemini 15 and semi-square natal Neptune at 5 Virgo 25 begs the exposure to extreme pressure by others, as in the hospital staff. It also indicates a sympathetic understanding of others, deep study of a subject of special interest such as astrology, and delving into the supernatural realms, all of which was very much fulfilled after the initial hospital stay.

Jupiter at 6 Scorpio 35 is conjunct the most sensitive natal midpoint of ASC/MC at 6 Scorpio, indeed a life-saving contact. Mars at 19 Scorpio 10 is square, and Transpluto at 19 Leo 07 is opposite natal Moon at 19 Aquarius 15, and the Jupiter/Uranus midpoint at 18 Scorpio 44 set off a multitude of aspects and midpoints describing this terrible unfortunate event.

Venus at 24 Leo 57 semi-square solar arc Moon at 9 Aries 09 and Node/MC midpoint at 24 Leo 52, representing the feeling of love and devotion, good judgment concerning the real value of things and the capacity to love wholeheartedly, as well as the astral body and ego-consciousness, and the psychic or inner stress of the soul. In addition, Mercury at 7 Libra 49 is semi-square natal midpoint of Jupiter/Neptune at 22 Leo 10, offering rising hopes, while the Ascendant at 29 Scorpio 06 is square natal Venus at 29 Leo 21, bringing a harmonious attitude toward others.

Caroline's Injuries

Seventy-five percent of Caroline's body was burned, mostly third-degree, and she had grafts on arms and legs. She suffered heavy second-degree burns on face, ears, chin and throat, and third degree burns under the nose that cannot be grafted. Future grafting for right arm at elbow joint, on her sides and right wrist are planned. She needs release for constructors on fingers and grafts for same on palm side of fingers of both hands. Her left hand is quite bad and requires grafts after removal of scar tissue, making tight web spaces on both hands, especially on the left hand. She also needs full thickness grafts on the backs of both hands for cosmetic and functional reasons.

Graft operations took place:

September 13, 1982, Left leg, Denver 9:35 a.m.

September 18, 1982, Left leg, remove cast, total anesthesia at 12 noon; more, grafts, left leg, left hip, both arms, all in cast.

September 27, 1982, Casts removed for constructors

November 12, 1982, Right hand released, grafted 2-3 p.m.

November 20, 1982, Cast changed

November 27, 1982, Cast off

December 10, 1982, Left hand constructors released, grafted pins put in four fingers 2:00 p.m.

December 24, 1982, Cast off

December 29, 1982, Pins removed, left hand

January 3, 1983, To Seattle for 5½ months daily therapy

May 17, 1983, Returned to Denver

On October 6, 1982 at 2:00 p.m. MDT hundreds of stapales were removed. They were holding grafts in place even though casts had previously been removed. Since the end of June 1983, she said, "I can care for myself, drive, cook and do light housekeeping. Operation times are given for those I know; the rest I do not have a record of."

Note: Her blood pressure, temperature and pulse were pretty normal all the time except for September 16, 1982 (13 days after burn) when her blood pressure rose due to a catheter infection, amazingly lucky that way.

Harry

Harry's most prominent feature for accidents in his natal chart is Mars at 26 Leo 00 sesquisquare Uranus at 11 Aries 14. In 1982 the solar arc was 50 degrees and 52 minutes and Mars had reached 16 Libra 51 and Uranus 2 Gemini 05, with both planets contacting natal Pluto at 17 Cancer 34. This combination can cause violent intervention, a struggle for survival, accidents and injuries.

The solar arc Sun at 26 Leo 23 set off the volatile accident axis at the midpoint of Saturn/Uranus at 9 Libra 46 with a very close square to solar arc Part of Fortune at 9 Cancer 58. Harry's natal Jupiter/Uranus midpoint at 7 Taurus 18 protected him, keeping him from being injured in this horrific accident.

Transiting Sun at 10 Virgo 56 and Pluto at 25 Libra 08 met with Transpluto at 26 Cancer 16, signifying a highly destructive combination. Transiting Mars/Uranus midpoint at 25 Scorpio 01 and Venus at 24 Leo 56, with the Node at 11 Cancer 41 contacted various solar arc positions reflecting the people involved in the accident. The Jupiter/Uranus midpoint at 18 Scorpio 46, Mars at 19 Scorpio 10 and Transpluto at 19 Leo 07 in aspect to natal Sun at 5 Cancer 32 indicate good fortune in a dangerous situation. The transiting midpoint of Mars/Saturn at 4 Scorpio 34 indicates great danger to life and is semi-square natal Ascendant at 17 Virgo 53, showing the great difficulty of the moment.

The next two transiting personal points, the Moon at 14 Pisces 14 and MC at 13 Virgo 43 to the natal Mercury at 15 Gemini 27 produce indicate the emotional and mental contact he could give his wife afterwards; however it lacked the close contact to accidents in comparison to the chart of Carolyn and friend Marcie. The transiting Ascendant at 29 Scorpio 06 is within minutes of perfect orb in contact with natal Neptune at 29 Leo 13 and Uranus/Pluto

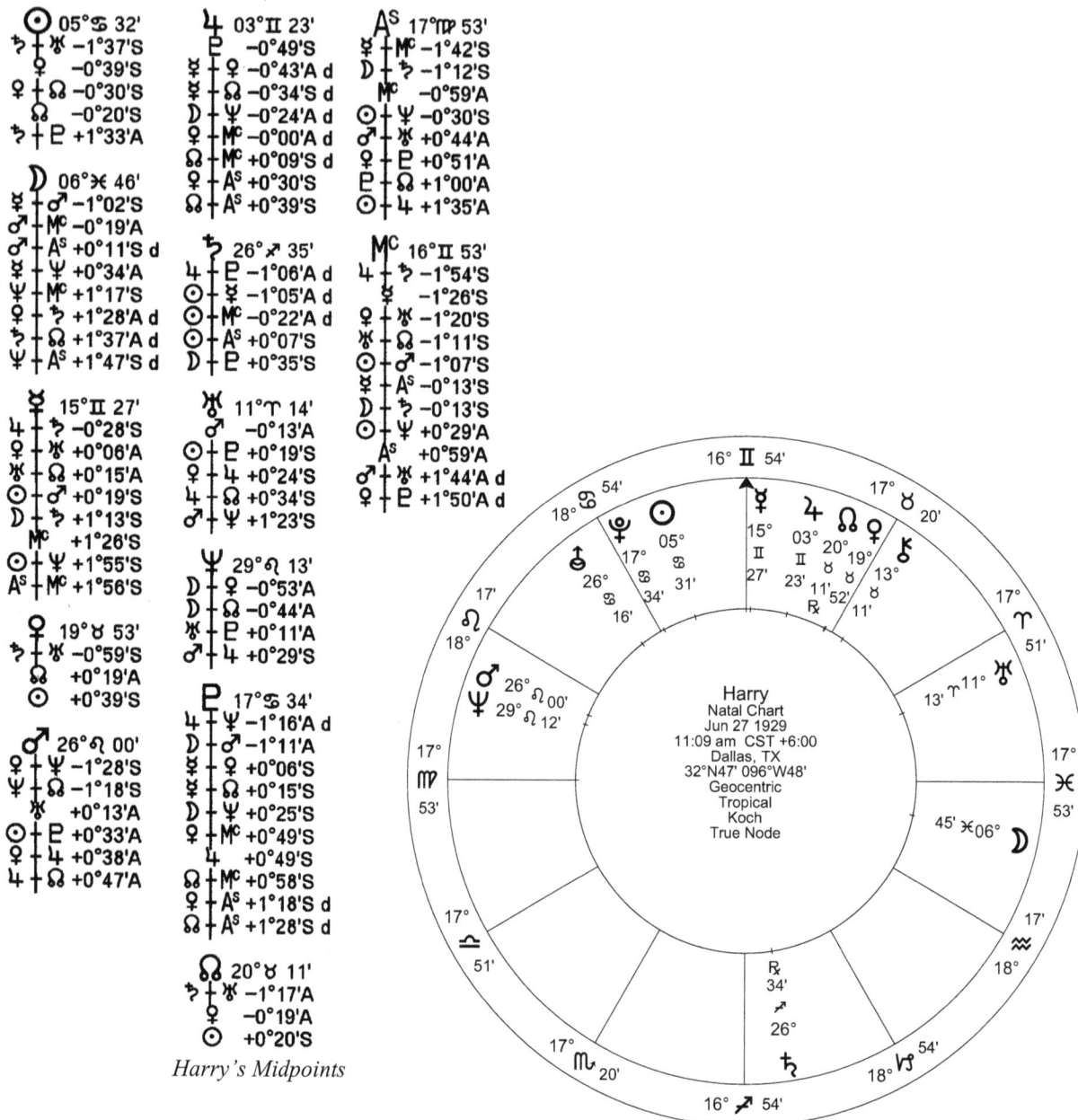

Harry's Midpoints

midpoint at 29 Taurus 24, creating insecurity and uncertainty and an accident. Uranus at 0 Sagittarius 01 moved to natal Neptune at 29 Leo 13, clearly showing the confusion and sudden impact of what happened. The midpoint of ASC/MC at 21 Libra 24 is with the Sun/Part of Fortune midpoint at 21 Cancer 40 and is an extremely fortunate combination.

Marcie

Marcie was 20 feet from the motor home at the time the fire ignited. She had burns over 50 percent of her body, mostly second-degree. She had superficial facial burns and second-degree burns on her legs and arms, no body burns, but her hands and one ankle were burned badly. She almost died due to very bad blood infections, high temperatures, high blood pressure and an erratic pulse. Doctors were unable to graft.

Marcie left the hospital after six weeks to return home. She almost had open-heart surgery the second week while hospitalized due to blood clods. In November she returned from Houston to San Diego, and by December she had returned to work part-time.

Inner Chart
Harry
Jun 27 1929 AD GC
11:09:00 AM
CST +06:00:00
Dallas TX
USA
96w49'00
32n47'00
Geocentric
Tropical

Outer Charts
Inferno
Sep 3 1982 AD GC
1:10:00 PM
MDT +06:00:00
Fort Collins CO
USA
105w05 00
40n35 00
True SA 50°51'
53y 2m

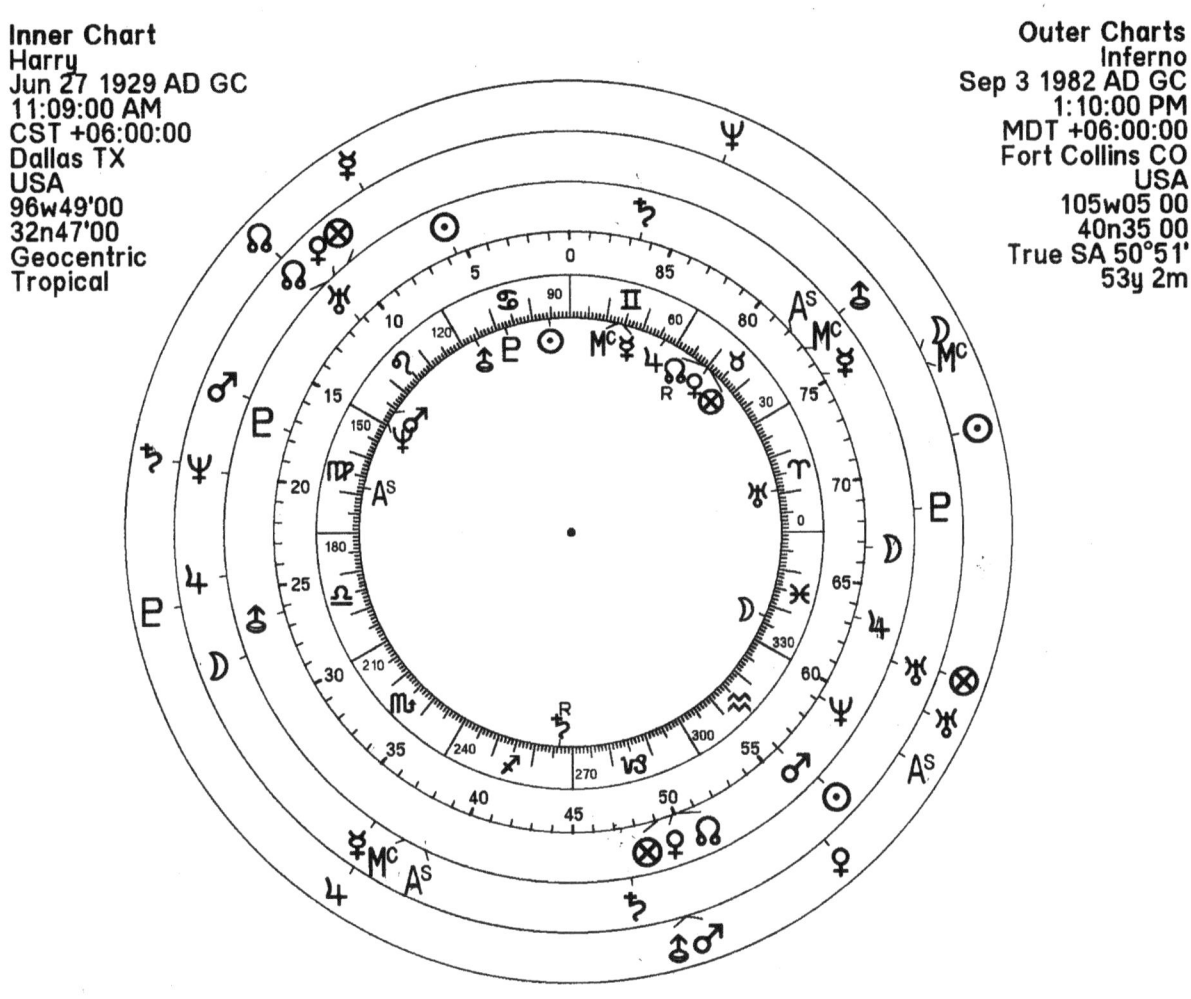

Cosmogram, 90°00' H4 Dial Format

Inner Radix	Middle Directed	Outer Transits
☉ 05♋32	☉ 26♌23	☉ 10♍57
☽ 06♓46	☽ 27♈37	☽ 14♓14
☿ 15♊27	☿ 06♌18	☿ 07♎49
♀ 19♉53	♀ 10♋44	♀ 24♌56
♂ 26♌00	♂ 16♎51	♂ 19♏10
♃ 03♊23	♃ 24♋14	♃ 06♏35
♄ 26♐35R	♄ 17♒26	♄ 19♎58
♅ 11♈14	♅ 02♊05	♅ 00♐51
♆ 29♌13	♆ 20♎04	♆ 24♐17R
♇ 17♋34	♇ 08♍25	♇ 25♎08
☊ 20♉11R	☊ 11♋02	☊ 11♋41R
As 17♍53	As 08♏44	As 29♏06
Mc 16♊53	Mc 07♌44	Mc 13♍43
⚷ 26♋16	⚷ 17♍07	⚷ 19♌07
⊗ 19♉07	⊗ 09♋58	⊗ 02♊23

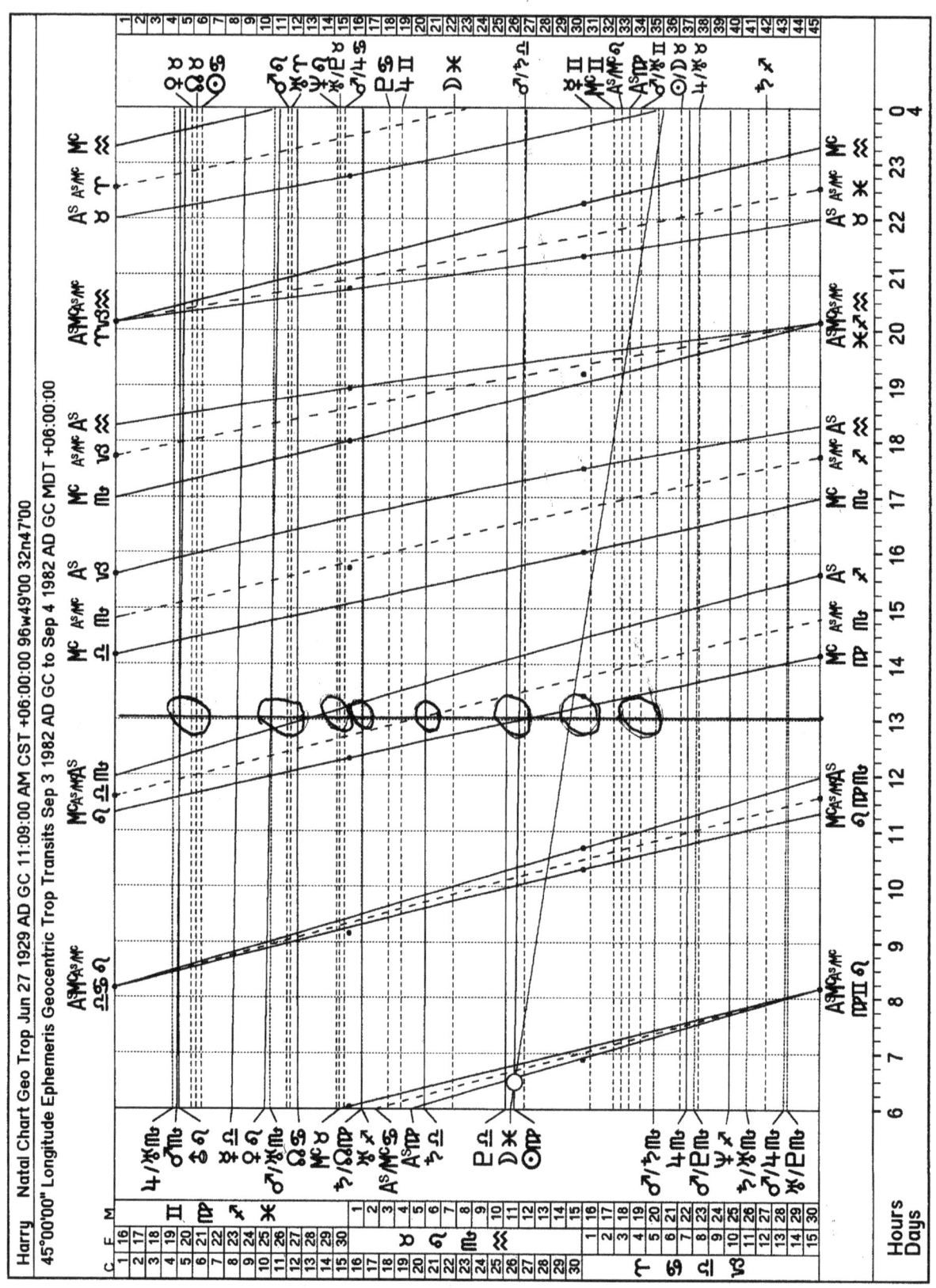

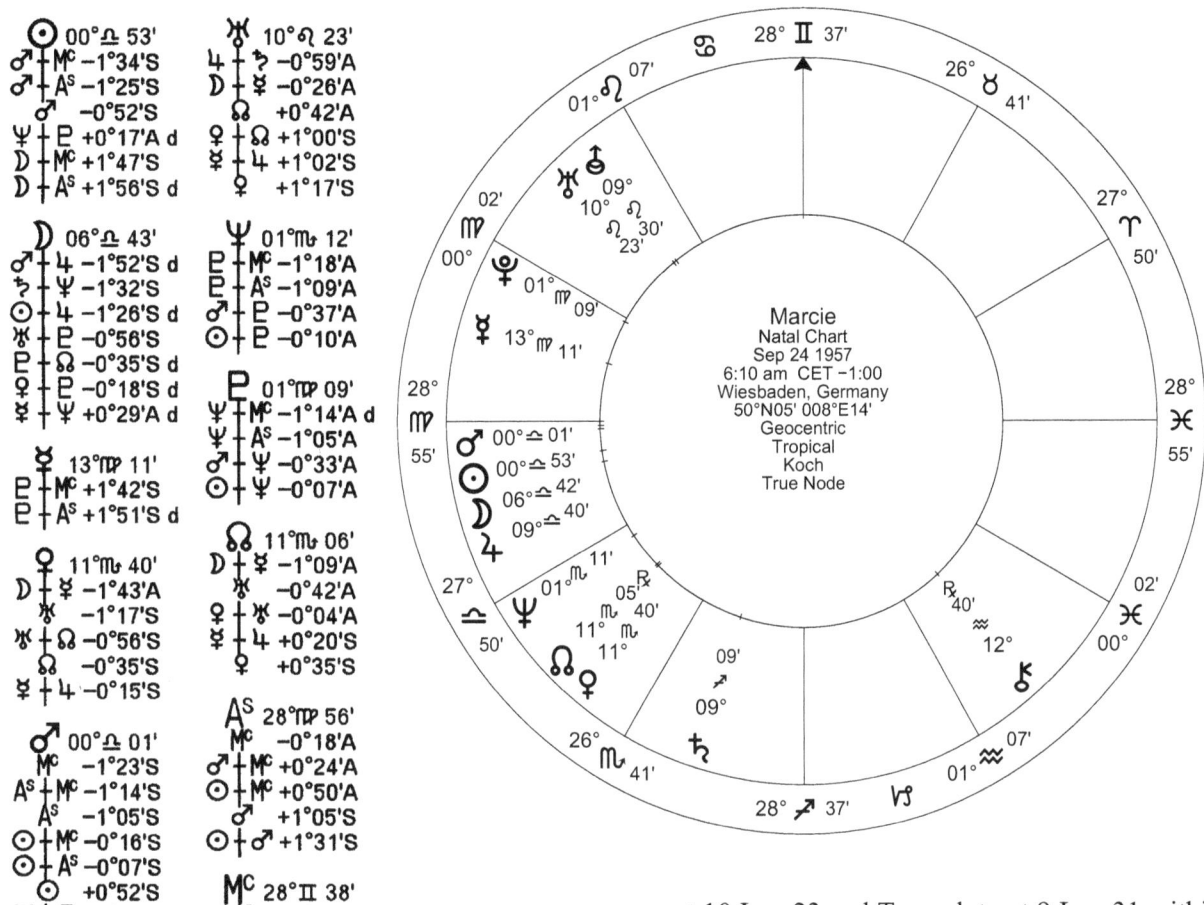

Marcie's Midpoints

Natal

Marcie does not have a vivid accident-prone natal chart, as does Carolyn. She has a very vulnerable square with MC at 28 Gemini 38, Ascendant at 28 Virgo 56, Mars at 0 Libra 01, and Sun at 0 Libra 53. These four positions are within three degrees in the 90-degree circle chart or the structure pattern of Mars, which is the focus point.

A second constellation that is striking is Venus at 11 Scorpio 40 and Node at 11 Scorpio 06 square Uranus at 10 Leo 23 and Transpluto at 9 Leo 31 within three degrees in the 90-degree circle. The first, makes her prone to accidents, while the latter vividly shows the activity in her love life.

Proceeding with the solar arc directions for 1982 at 24 degrees 37 minutes, the accident midpoint, Mars/Uranus at 29 Virgo 49, is within orb of her natal Sun, Mars, MC and Ascendant, activated by transiting Pluto at 25 Libra 08 that is intensifying the natal tendency toward accidents. Since each cluster of planets, natal and solar arc, stretches between three and four degrees it indicates a four-year period of major events unfolding in Marcie's life that lead to the desire to renounce love, estrangement, common suffering with others and brutality. There are some midpoints in cosmobiology that are especially vulnerable for disaster and that fall under the category of accidents involving gas explosions.

Transits

Transits by slow moving planets are especially powerful due to the length of time they are in effect. Looking at Marcie's chart shows Uranus at 0 Sagit-

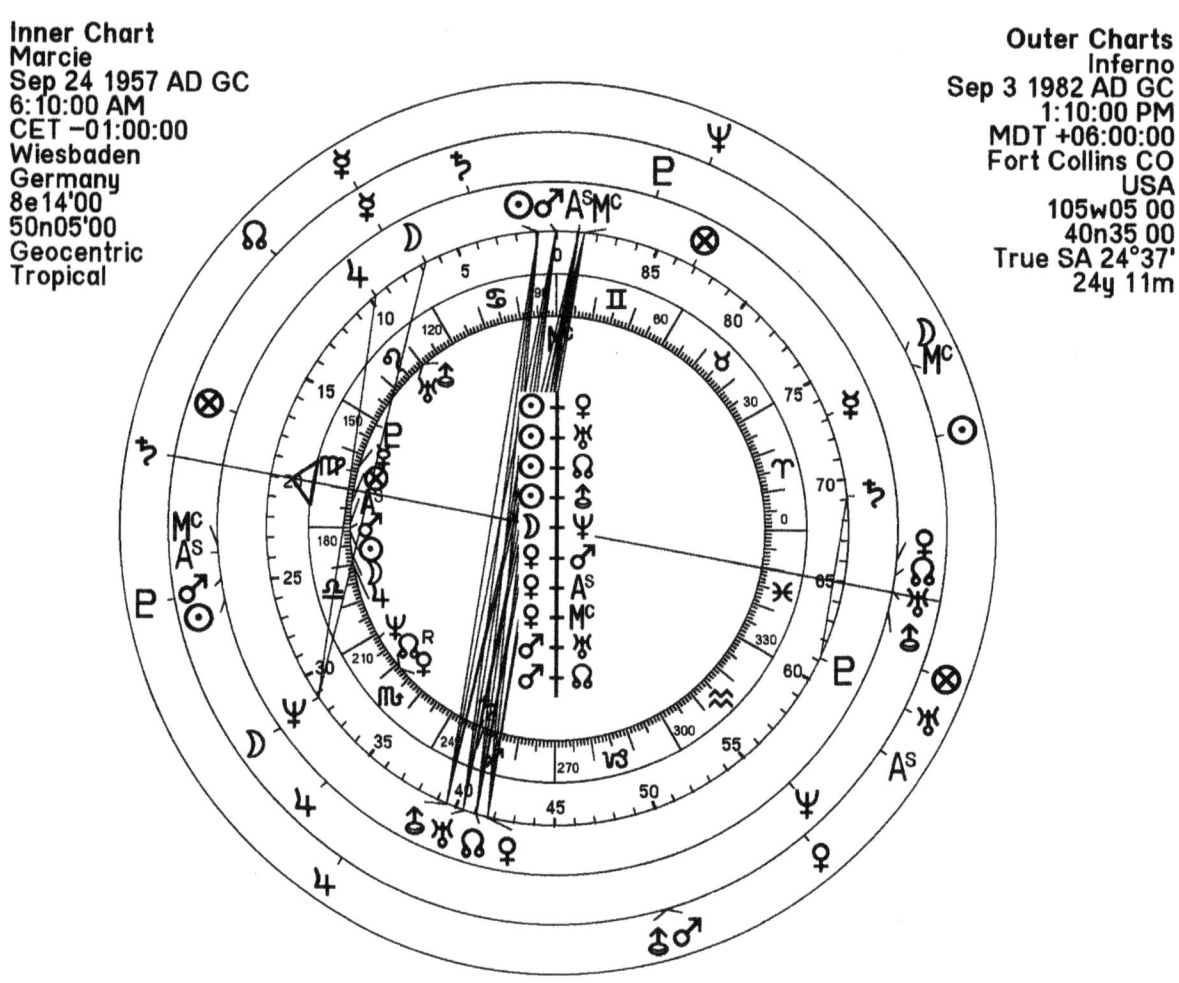

Inner Chart
Marcie
Sep 24 1957 AD GC
6:10:00 AM
CET −01:00:00
Wiesbaden
Germany
8e14'00
50n05'00
Geocentric
Tropical

Outer Charts
Inferno
Sep 3 1982 AD GC
1:10:00 PM
MDT +06:00:00
Fort Collins CO
USA
105w05 00
40n35 00
True SA 24°37'
24y 11m

Cosmogram, 90°00' H4 Dial Format

Inner Radix	Middle Directed	Outer Transits
☉ 00♎53	☉ 25♎30	☉ 10♍57
☽ 06♎43	☽ 01♏20	☽ 14♓14
☿ 13♍11	☿ 07♎48	☿ 07♎49
♀ 11♏40	♀ 06♐17	♀ 24♌56
♂ 00♎01	♂ 24♎38	♂ 19♏10
♃ 09♎40	♃ 04♏17	♃ 06♏35
♄ 09♐09	♄ 03♑46	♄ 19♎58
♅ 10♌23	♅ 05♍00	♅ 00♐51
♆ 01♏12	♆ 25♏49	♆ 24♐17R
♇ 01♍09	♇ 25♍46	♇ 25♎08
☊ 11♏06R	☊ 05♐43	☊ 11♋41R
As 28♍56	As 23♎33	As 29♏06
Mc 28♊38	Mc 23♋15	Mc 13♍43
↑ 09♌31	↑ 04♍08	↑ 19♌07
⊗ 23♍06	⊗ 17♎43	⊗ 02♊23

132

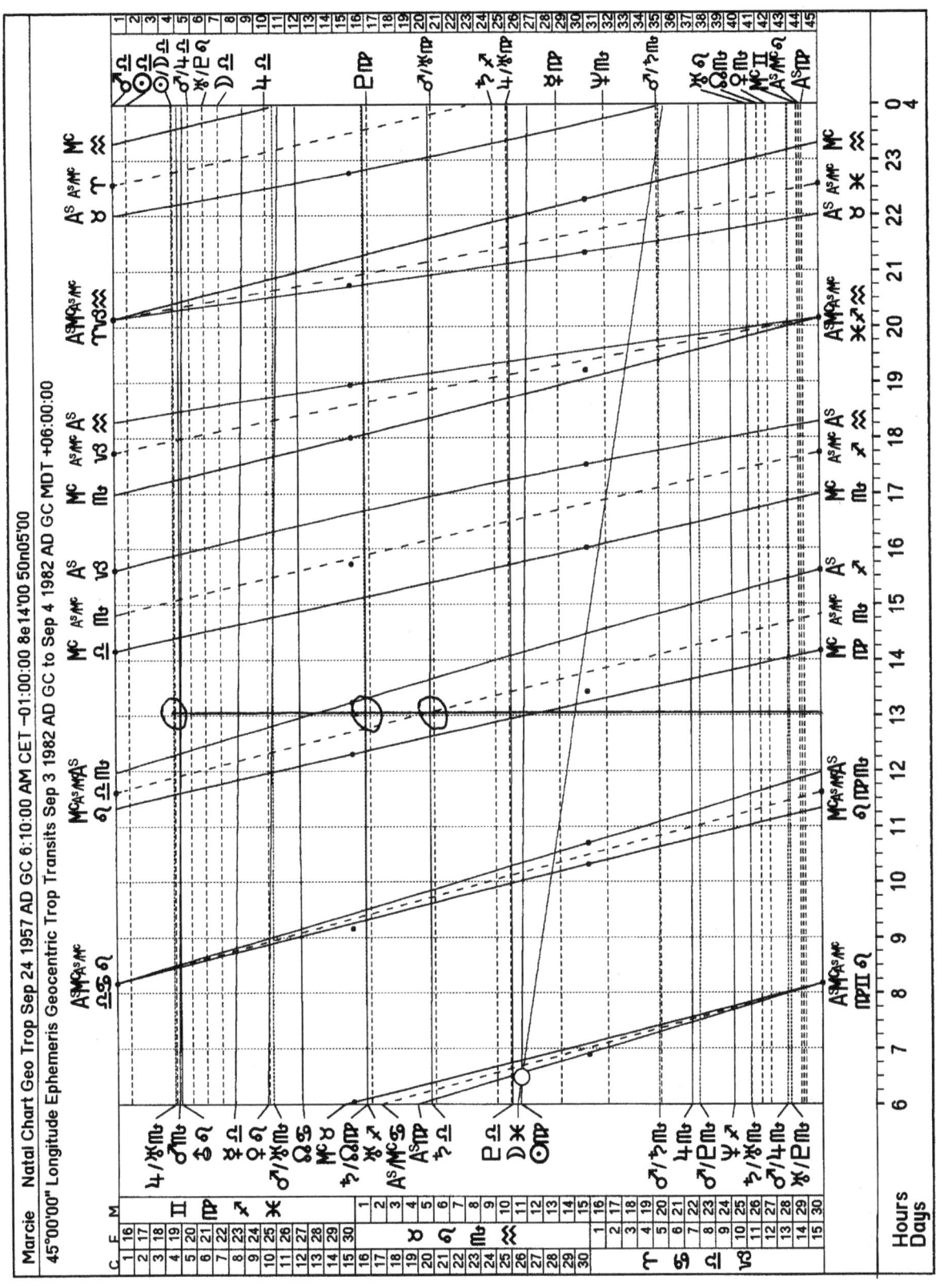

tarius 51, bringing about sudden events, and is square to natal Pluto at 1 Virgo 09, pointing toward life-altering experiences that take away old conditions and bring new ones into focus.

Saturn always plays a big role in such a drastic events. This planet has midpoints attached that especially affect Marcie's love life, delaying marriage.

Jupiter, extremely strong and making powerful contacts to natal and solar arc positions, especially Neptune, brought about infections. The blood-pressure disturbance is caused by the midpoint of Uranus/Moon at 3 Libra 10, reinforced by Mars at 19 Scorpio 11 and the "Thank the Lord" combination of Jupiter/Uranus at 18 Scorpio 44. Neptune at 24 Sagittarius 17 retrograde, moving ever so slowly toward a natal Venus-Node semi-square, shows the breaking of the engagement. One year later, Neptune was moving toward the Ascendant and MC when confusion, disappointment and emotional suffering made it necessary to see a psychiatrist.

The house in Galveston, Texas was swept away by Hurricane Alicia, when aspects in Marcie's chart were again activated, causing loss of fortune or possessions. The area where Peter and Marcie work and live was hit badly by the storm but she was not in town that week. By the time she returned, the phone and electricity were back on.

Peter

Natal Ascendant at 14 Pisces 12 and Uranus at 16 Gemini 51 retrograde are the most prominent in Peter's chart, indicating that throughout his lifetime many activities would come about unexpectedly. To be involved in such a horrifying accident as a guest must have been an experience beyond comprehension; thus it would be helpful to analyze the Node.

The solar arc for Peter was 37 degrees and 10 minutes. The danger to life came about by the solar arc Pluto at 18 Virgo 56 contacting the natal midpoint of Uranus/MC, and the solar arc Sun at 15 Sagittarius 12 at the midpoint of Uranus/Ascendant. Solar arc Node at 8 Leo 45 is conjunct the natal Sun at 8 Scorpio 02, but is in semi-square transiting Neptune at 24 Sagittarius 17, supporting shared experiences.

Solar arc Transpluto at 11 Virgo 46 is semi-square natal Mars at 26 Cancer 35 and Saturn at 24 Cancer 52, indicating great danger to life.

Transits

At the time of the accident, transiting Node at 11 Cancer 41 was sesquisquare natal Mercury at 25 Scorpio 32, an intricate combination containing energy of the actual happenings and adding a tremendous luck factor. He was not in the vicinity as were the women involved.

Transiting Pluto at 25 Libra 08 had just passed solar arc Uranus at 24 Cancer 00 and natal Saturn at 24 Cancer 52, but was coming toward natal Mars at 26 Cancer 35. This represents a complete transformation of events and a tremendous amount of tension, completely new conditions, but accidents as well.

Transiting Saturn at 19 Libra 58 and Part of Fortune at 2 Gemini 23 were both concentrating on solar arc Mars and Saturn, depicting the luck factor at a life-threatening event. Jupiter at 6 Scorpio 35 came close to the natal Sun at 8 Scorpio 02. Moon at 22 Virgo 44 and MC at 21 Sagittarius 33 and the solar arc Jupiter/Uranus midpoint at 22 Virgo 45 show the great luck factor and also a typical marriage formula that actually came about later. Mars in transit at 19 Scorpio 10, Transpluto at 19 Leo 07 and the Jupiter/Uranus midpoint at 18 Scorpio 43 stimulated solar arc Mercury at 2 Capricorn 42 and the natal Node at 1 Cancer 35, offering a great luck factor to the highway accident formula. The transit of Mercury at 7 Libra 49 was with natal Neptune at 7 Libra 19 as well as with solar arc Venus at 22 Scorpio 51 and Jupiter at 21 Scorpio 30.

Transiting Venus at 24 Leo 57, along with the accident-prone Mars/Uranus midpoint at 25 Scorpio 01, were exact within minutes of natal Mercury at 25 Scorpio 32, identifying traveling (Mercury), with lover (Venus), and others (Node) experiencing an accident (Mars/Uranus).

Transiting Moon at 14 Pisces 14 and MC at 13 Virgo 44 contacted the natal ASC structure at 14 Pisces 11 plus the solar arc Sun at 15 Sagittarius 12, Moon at 29 Libra 54 and MC at 28 Capricorn 43. The activation for an accident is clearly shown, however. The heavy aspects of Mars, Saturn, Uranus, Pluto and Transpluto are not as prominent and frequent compared to the two women and the location they were standing at the time of the explosion. The most sensitive transiting midpoint, ASC/MC at 21 Libra 25, applies auspiciously to the natal midpoint of

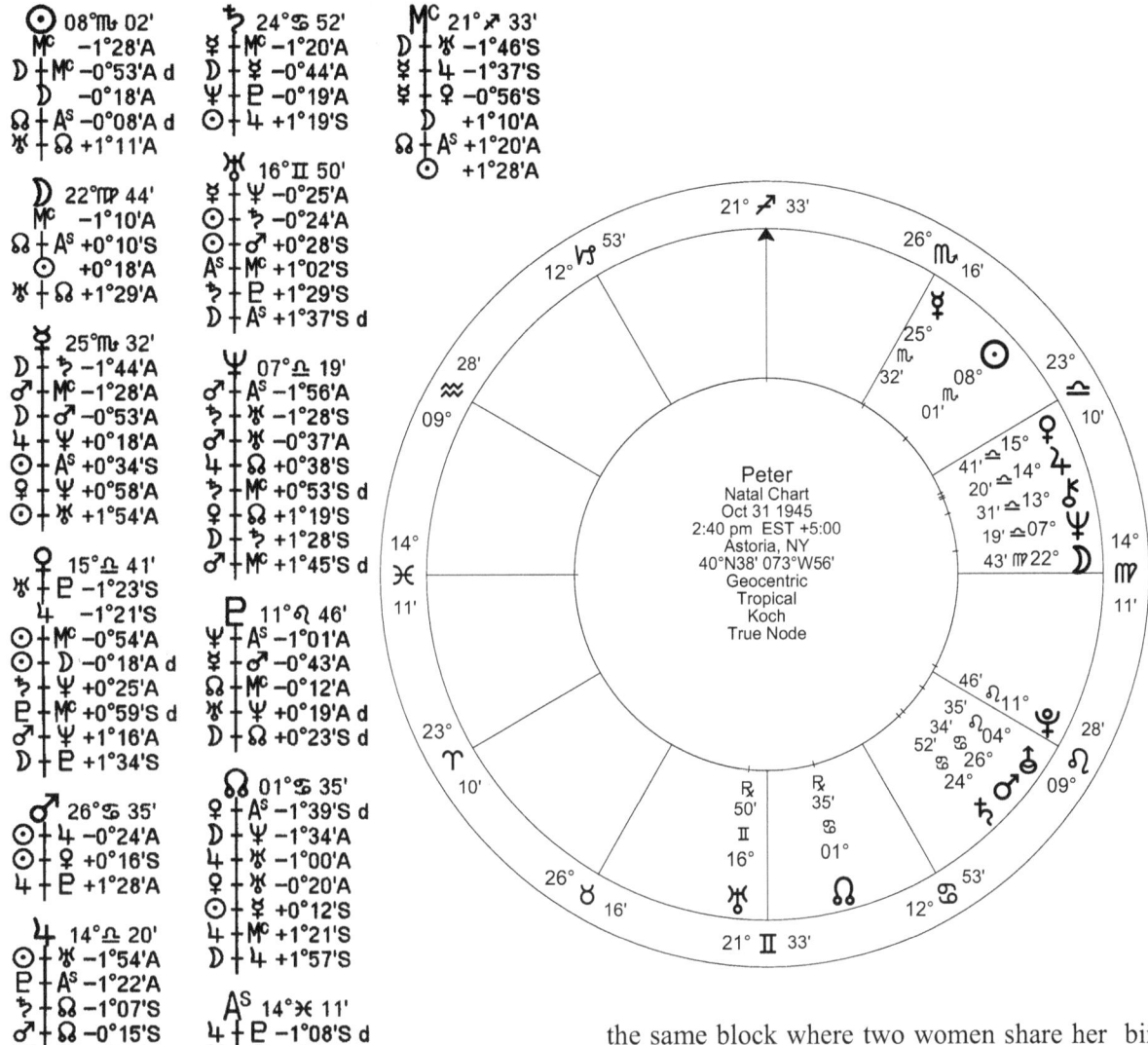

Peter's Midpoints

Mercury/Uranus at 6 Virgo 11 and solar arc Ascendant at 21 Aries 21.

In addition to all the people involved is something that we find every once in a while. Carolyn lives on the same block where two women share her birthday, within a period of two hours. All three were married to men with June birthdays with strong Gemini and Taurus placements. Two of the women married in November 1952 to men born one week apart. The Moon in all three charts is within the same degree; only the Ascendants and MCs are different. There is one very important detail: two of the women were not traveling down the highway with a leaking gas tank at the time of these transits.

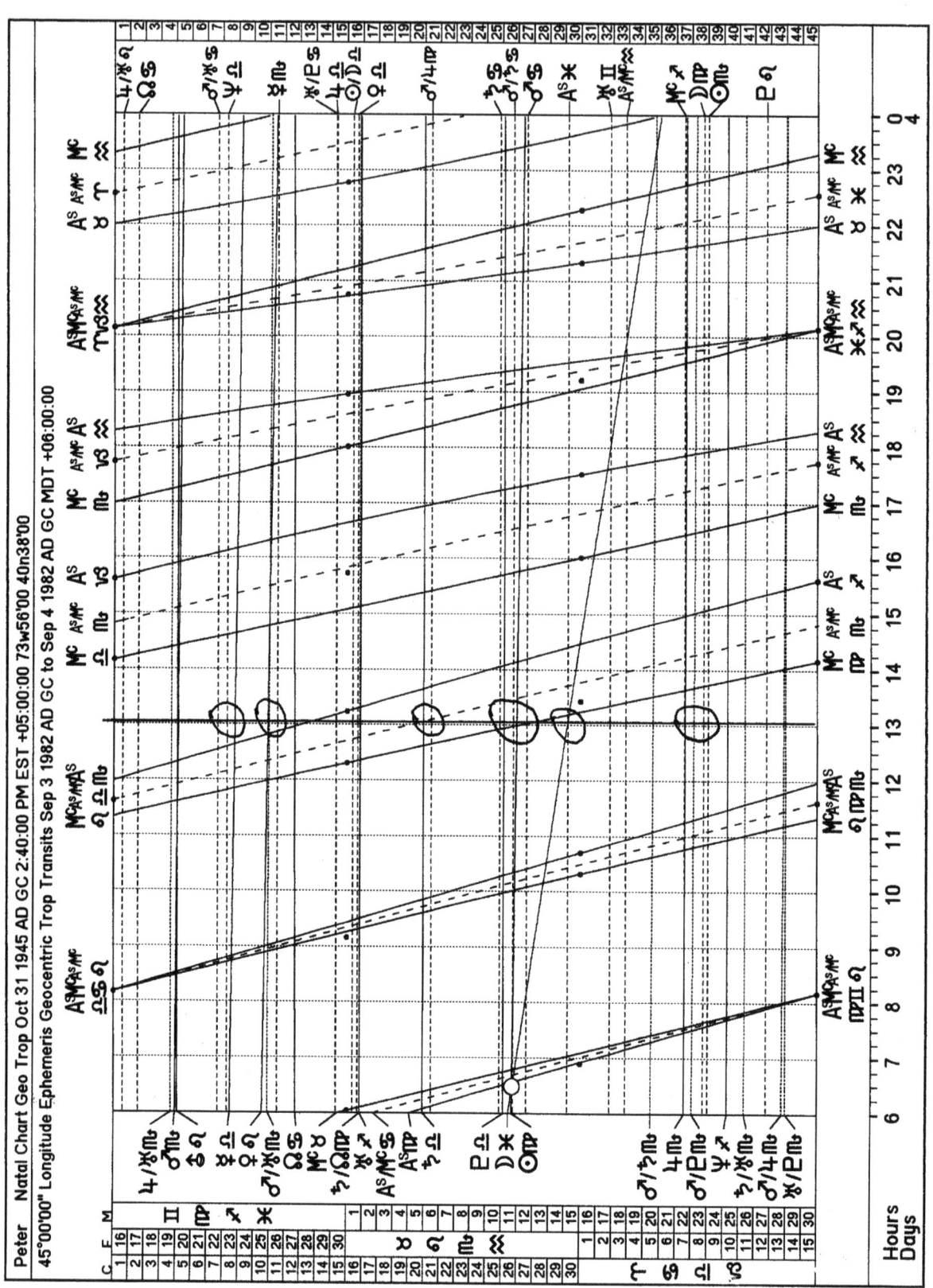

JonBenet Ramsey

JonBenet Ramsey was murdered December 25, 1996 in Boulder, Colorado. So far, no killer has been found and the case is shrouded in mystery. Ineptness by the police department, difficulties within the district attorney's office, separate attorneys for each parent and media exposure have contributed to the frustrations this case has created. Various suspects have been cleared; only the parents are still under the umbrella of suspicion.

JonBenet was the daughter and second child of enchanting southern socialite Patricia Paugh from West Virginia and her wealthy millionaire businessman husband John Bennett Ramsey from Lincoln, Nebraska. It was the second marriage for John Ramsey who also had two adult children from the first marriage. The family lived in a 15-room Tudor style home in Boulder, where he operated his very successful business.

Patsy Ramsey had trained and educated JonBenet to participate in beauty and talent contests, dressed in sophisticated costumes. After a visit with friends on Christmas Day, JonBenet was put to bed between 9:30 and 10:00 p.m. MST. Sometime between bedtime and dawn she was killed; her skull was fractured, she was strangled with a cord and sexually molested, and her mouth was taped with duct tape. Her body was carried to the basement to a small remote room where she was later found with her feet taped together and her arms above her head.

The following morning Patsy, in her daily routine, found JonBenet missing from her bed. She called 911 for help at 5:52 a.m. after finding a ransom note demanding $118,000 from an apparent kidnaper. This leaves a window of time of about eight hours when the murder occurred. During that time the murderer took the little girl from her bed, sexually abused, tortured and killed her, wrote a 2½-page ransom note, left it on the staircase and disappeared into thin air.

The police arrived about 6:00 a.m. to investigate the site of the apparent kidnaping, but found nothing. A second search occurred at a later time when her body was discovered at 1:05 p.m. John Ramsey carried the corpse into the living room and placed it by the Christmas tree, thus destroying much of the evidence. According to Dr. Cyril Wecht, "rigor mortis" had already occurred by the time she was found.

Cyril Wecht, M.D., J.D. is a forensic pathologist who in early 1998 wrote the book, *Who Killed JonBenet Ramsey?* He is considered the best in his field of forensic medicine. The findings of Dr. Wecht's analysis entered into public records were the first of appalling and shocking new conclusions. One of his striking opinions expressed in his many interviews on television is that the death was a tragic accident, and he describes the details of his findings as a sick sex game that has tragic consequences and is known as autoerotic asphyxiation.

The time of the actual killing is unknown and a coroner or forensic expert can only estimate it. John E. Meyer, M.D., Boulder County coroner, issued the original complete autopsy report on August 13, 1997. It is speculated that the death occurred about midnight.

Natal

Just as the murder case itself is extraordinary, so is the natal chart of this beautiful little girl. The most striking figure is the fixed grand cross engulfing the

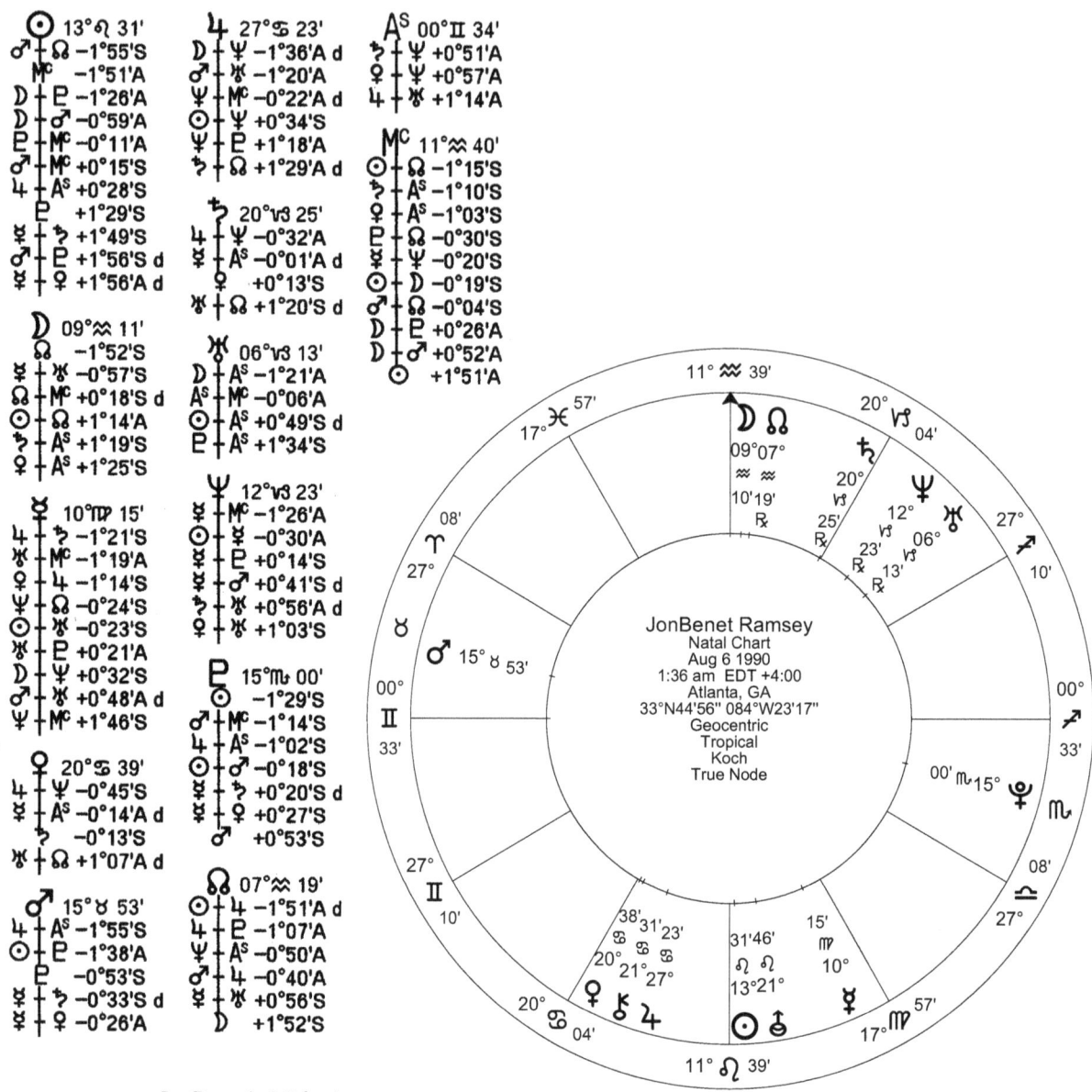

JonBenet's Midpoints

Sun at 13 Leo 31, the Moon at 9 Aquarius 11, Mars at 15 Taurus 53 and Pluto at 15 Scorpio 00. This configuration can send a chill down anybody's spine and cause one to wonder what the mission in life was supposed to be, and what the eventual outcome has in store for those who hopefully can be brought to justice.

Another natal structure that is especially disturbing is the Sun contacting the midpoint of Mars/Pluto at 15 Leo 27. This combination shows tendencies to cause injuries, accidents, violent measures and upsets or shock caused through the intervention of Higher Power.

The vast successes within the world of beauty contests, in contrast to the horrifying murder of JonBenet Ramsey at a very young age, is clearly shown by applying the progressions and the transits at the time of this event.

Solar Arc Directions

At the time of JonBenet's death the solar arc was 6 degrees and 8 minutes. The Sun, Mercury and MC were the most active planets. The fixed grand cross was activated by solar arc Mars at 22 Taurus 01 square natal Transpluto at 21 Leo 47 and sesqui-square natal Uranus at 6 Capricorn 13 retro-

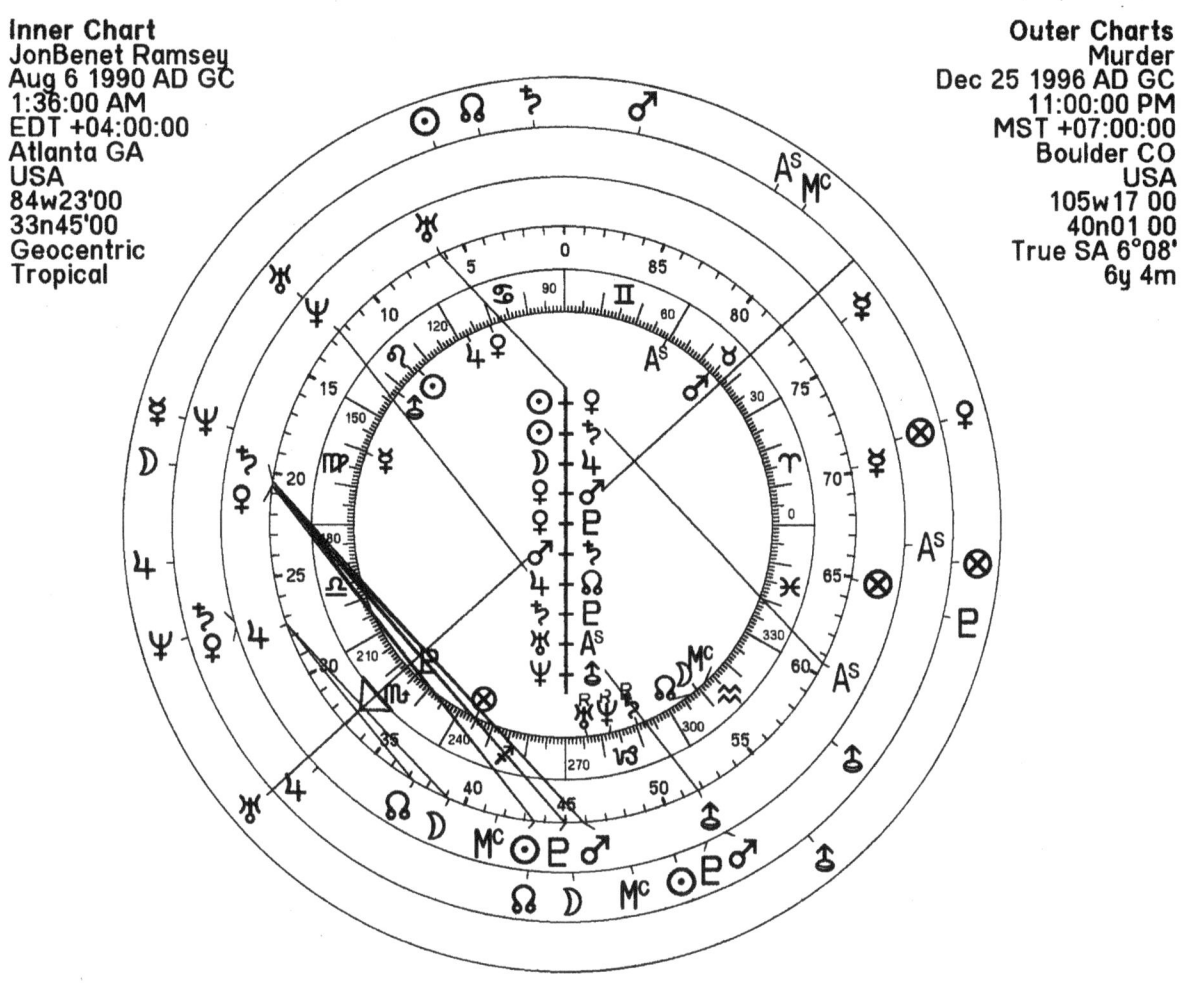

Inner Chart
JonBenet Ramsey
Aug 6 1990 AD GC
1:36:00 AM
EDT +04:00:00
Atlanta GA
USA
84w23'00
33n45'00
Geocentric
Tropical

Outer Charts
Murder
Dec 25 1996 AD GC
11:00:00 PM
MST +07:00:00
Boulder CO
USA
105w17 00
40n01 00
True SA 6°08'
6y 4m

Cosmogram, 90°00' H4 Dial Format

Inner Radix	Middle Directed	Outer Transits
☉ 13♌31	☉ 19♌39	☉ 04♑45
☽ 09♒11	☽ 15♒19	☽ 20♋22
☿ 10♍15	☿ 16♍23	☿ 18♑40R
♀ 20♋39	♀ 26♋47	♀ 11♐15
♂ 15♉53	♂ 22♉01	♂ 27♍13
♃ 27♋23	♃ 03♌31	♃ 23♑51
♄ 20♑25R	♄ 26♑33	♄ 01♈04
♅ 06♑13R	♅ 12♑21	♅ 02♒57
♆ 12♑23R	♆ 18♑31	♆ 26♑37
♇ 15♏00	♇ 21♏08	♇ 04♐11
☊ 07♒19	☊ 13♒27	☊ 03♎04R
AS 00♊34	AS 06♊42	AS 21♍48
MC 11♒40	MC 17♒48	MC 20♊34
⚷ 21♌47	⚷ 27♌55	⚷ 24♌41R
⊗ 04♐54	⊗ 11♐02	⊗ 06♓11

grade. Solar arc Pluto at 21 Scorpio 08 semi-square natal Uranus at the same time. This combination can bring about drastic and violent changes.

In addition, solar arc Node at 13 Aquarius 26 was opposition the natal Sun, and solar arc Moon at 15 Aquarius 18 was square natal Pluto. Furthermore, the solar arc Venus-Saturn opposition touched off natal Jupiter in 3 Leo 31, pointing to the sexual damages of JonBenet. Solar arc Uranus at 12 Capricorn 21 retrograde moved to the natal Neptune-Ascendant sesquisquare. Ebertin's exact delineation for this combination is: "The trait of succumbing to the influence of others easily, as well as sudden troubles through others, also suffering illness through others, and the misfortune to be hindered, harmed or defamed by others."

Secondary Progressions

At age six the secondary progressions are not very many. The progressed Moon at 5 Taurus 55 moving through the twelfth house signifies shrouding the situation in mystery. The progressed Ascendant at 11 Gemini 47 creates a very close 150-degree aspect with natal Neptune at 12 Capricorn 23 retrograde, thus heightening the sudden and mysterious happenings.

Transits

Strangely enough, the parents had December 25, 1996 inscribed on JonBenet's gravestone as her date of death. Generally the coroner determines the approximate time of death. Therefore, my conclusion is to check out the time around 11:00 p.m., December 25.

The graph is calculated from 3:00 p.m., December 25 to 3:00 a.m., December 26, 1996 and the vertical line is drawn for 11:00 p.m. The Sun at 4 Capricorn 47 is moving toward a conjunction to natal Uranus at 6 Capricorn 13 retrograde, and also a square to the natal midpoint of ASC/MC at 6 Libra 07. This interprets as a sudden event, perhaps involving the father producing sudden experiences with JonBenet.

Mercury at 18 Capricorn 39 retrograde is semi-square Pluto at 4 Sagittarius 11 and both moving toward natal Saturn at 20 Capricorn 25 retrograde and Venus at 20 Cancer 39 and implies persuasive suggestions toward unrestrained sex-expression, possibly caused by nervous irritation through over work. The Node at 3 Libra 04 contacting natal Pluto at 15 Taurus 00 generally indicates a union or cooperation.

Venus at 11 Sagittarius 18 and Neptune at 26 Capricorn 37 both contact natal Mercury at 10 Virgo 15 and the Uranus/Pluto and Mars/Uranus midpoints. This combination shows an erotic imagination causing nervous troubles through wrong or misdirected love sensations, along with being prone to seductive influences and amorous aberrations caused through a strong longing to love without attaining fulfillment; a tragic love.

Mars at 27 Virgo 14 is sesquisquare natal MC at 11 Aquarius 40 and refers to quarrels or disputes. Saturn at 1 Aries 05 is sesquisquare natal Pluto at 15 Scorpio 00 and natal Mars at 15 Taurus 53 and indicates brutality, assault or violence and maltreatment. Uranus at 2 Aquarius 57 is within minutes of perfect aspect to the following natal midpoints: Saturn/Pluto, Venus/Pluto and Mars/Saturn, revealing sudden acts of violence, unusual experiences in love and the inclination to apply brute force. It also shows intervention of Higher Power, a sudden accident and separation or a case of death. The Moon at 20 Cancer 44 had just contacted natal Venus and Saturn at 11:00 p.m., and the Midheaven of 20 Gemini 34 and Ascendant of 21 Virgo 48 had contacted the following natal midpoints between 10:30 and 11:00 p.m.: Saturn/Pluto, Venus/Pluto and Mars/Saturn: Temporary or passing states of chaos, separation or death of female, mourning and bereavement.

Dr. Wecht, in his above-mentioned book, refers to a connection with suspected sexual assault: ". . . theorized that the rope had pinched the Vagus Nerve that descends from the brain down each side of the neck to control the functions of many of the body's organs. Among its purposes is the key role of regulating the heart and lungs. If the nerve's electrical messages are interrupted, cardiac and respiratory function may cease, resulting in what doctors call 'electrical death.' The heart and lungs could begin to slow down, develop erratic responses, and eventually stop, leaving no evidence to establish an obvious cause of death."

Using Ebertin's Anatomical Degrees we find the neck nerves connected to the spinal cord are 11, 12 and 13 degrees of Taurus. At the time of the alleged

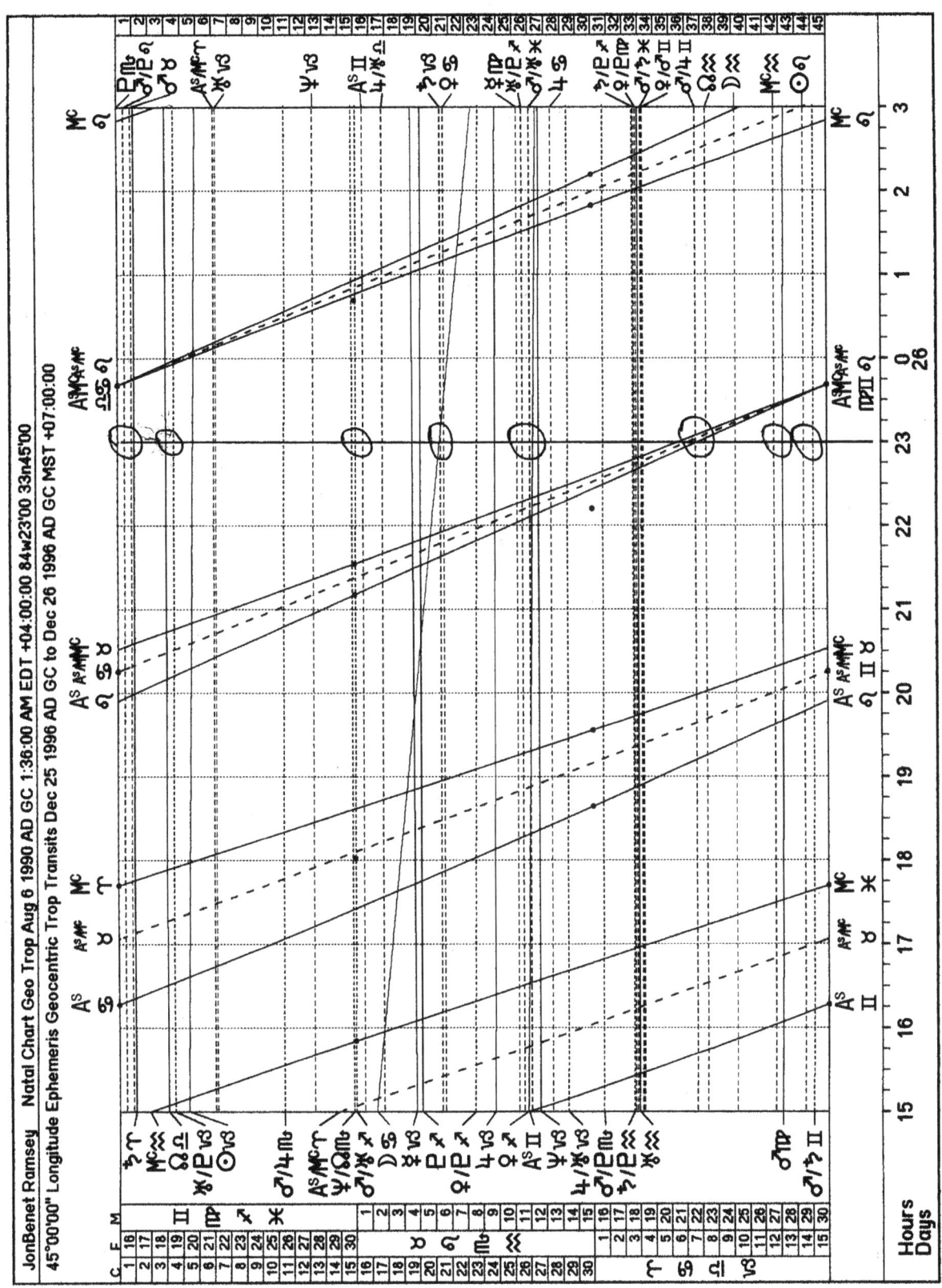

attack at around 11:00 p.m., Mars was at 27 Virgo 14 forming a sesquisquare to those degrees in Taurus. The solar arc directed Anatomical Degrees moved six degrees and seven minutes to 17, 18, and 19 degrees Taurus. The transiting Sun at 4 Capricorn 44 is sesquisquare the degrees of the Vagus Nerve (17, 18, 19 Leo). The transiting Node at 3 Libra 05 retrograde also forms a sesquisquare to those degrees and shortly before midnight the transiting midpoint of ASC/MC was at 18 Leo 03, in a square aspect to the solar arc directed degrees. The transiting Mars/Saturn midpoint at 29 Gemini 09 (which does not change between 11:00 p.m. and 12:00 a.m.) is semi-square JonBenet's natal Sun at 13 Leo 45, within a 13 minute-orb.

Another interesting observation involves the midpoint of natal Pluto/Transpluto at 3 Libra 24 (not shown on graph). The meaning of this midpoint according to John Hawkins is, "utter chaos," the most destructive combination in astrology of two planets. At the time of death (about 11:45 p.m.) the transiting Node (associations, blood relatives) was at 3 Libra 05 with the transiting MC at 3 Cancer 15 and transiting Ascendant at 2 Libra 50.

The birth information for family members came from *Death of Innocents* by John and Patsy Ramsey. On September 15, 1998 a grand jury began hearing the case; however, as of spring 2006 no indictment had been issued.

Many articles and books have been written by numerous reporters, attorneys and others who were associated with the case. Many appearances of attorneys and commentators on TV programs as well as several prominent TV specials featured the parents professing their innocence. With all the media attention the details are pretty much known surrounding the case.

Jimmy

The statement, "too mature to be going that fast," was made by Jimmy's mother to the local newspapers as her son and three others perished in an accident involving his slick 1965 Corvette. Jim loved his car more than anything in his life. He was always working on it, replacing old parts and polishing it up. He was so proud of his car that he only used it for weekends and taking friends out for a spin.

On Saturday April 5, 1975, this beautiful and proud possession became a death machine. Driving under the influence of alcohol and, as a witness stated, at speed that made the car look "like a streak," the Corvette swerved onto the soft gravel shoulder of the road, went into a sideway skid, crossed the double yellow centerline and flashed into the eastbound line of traffic. The westbound car accelerated and rocketed down the straight dry asphalt weaving in and out of traffic. The vehicle exceeded the 45-mile per hour speed limit as witnesses watched as it "whoosh by" with tremendous speed. With tires screeching and smoking, the coupe slid the length of a football field and with horrifying force hit the front end of a Vega.

Jimmy was the life of every party, the center of attention and good friends with everybody. He wasn't the type to sit down and study so he dropped out of high school. He worked a steady job and shared an apartment with a friend. Having the leisure of many hours and the luxury of owning a Corvette at age 22, all of his energies were focused on the car and what it could do. Reports indicated he was a good driver, but after drinking and getting behind the wheel of a charged sports car the atmosphere was not at all favorable for that Saturday afternoon.

Natal

The natal chart of this young man has a conspicuous pattern for accidents. He defies what generally is indicative of a Pisces Sun: passive reactive nature. As you look to the aspects of the Sun at 17 Pisces 30 you will find a very powerful structure pattern, specifically the combination of Sun contacting the Uranus/Pluto midpoint that indicates untiring creative work, the tendency to make the highest demands on one's physical energy, overexcitement of the nerves, a breakdown and the possibility of a catastrophe. Additionally strong is the almost perfect square of Uranus at 14 Cancer 32 retrograde to the Midheaven at 14 Libra 42 and both in the midpoint of Transpluto/Ascendant at 14 Libra 56, portraying a charismatic personality and a braggart, an obnoxious individual who is eccentric and bullheaded. The Ascendant's structure shows without mistake the daring nature, even perhaps the subconscious desire to face danger as the Ascendant at 23 Sagittarius 12 is a focus point, square the Sun at 17 Pisces 30, trine to Mars at 21 Aries 14 and to Pluto at 21 Leo 28, as well as parallel Uranus.

Mercury at 2 Aries 57 has no direct contact to Saturn; however, the midpoint of Mercury/Saturn at 14 Cancer 43 is occupied by the Midheaven and Uranus mentioned above. While the Midheaven on this spot may provide the ability to concentrate, Uranus supplies just the opposite, plus a tendency toward a quick departure or a car ride!

The Mars structure pattern carries multiple midpoints such as Sun/Pluto, showing tendency toward violence, brutality or harm through force, foolhardiness and daring, exposure to danger or accidents and injury. The Pluto/ASC midpoint indicates premature

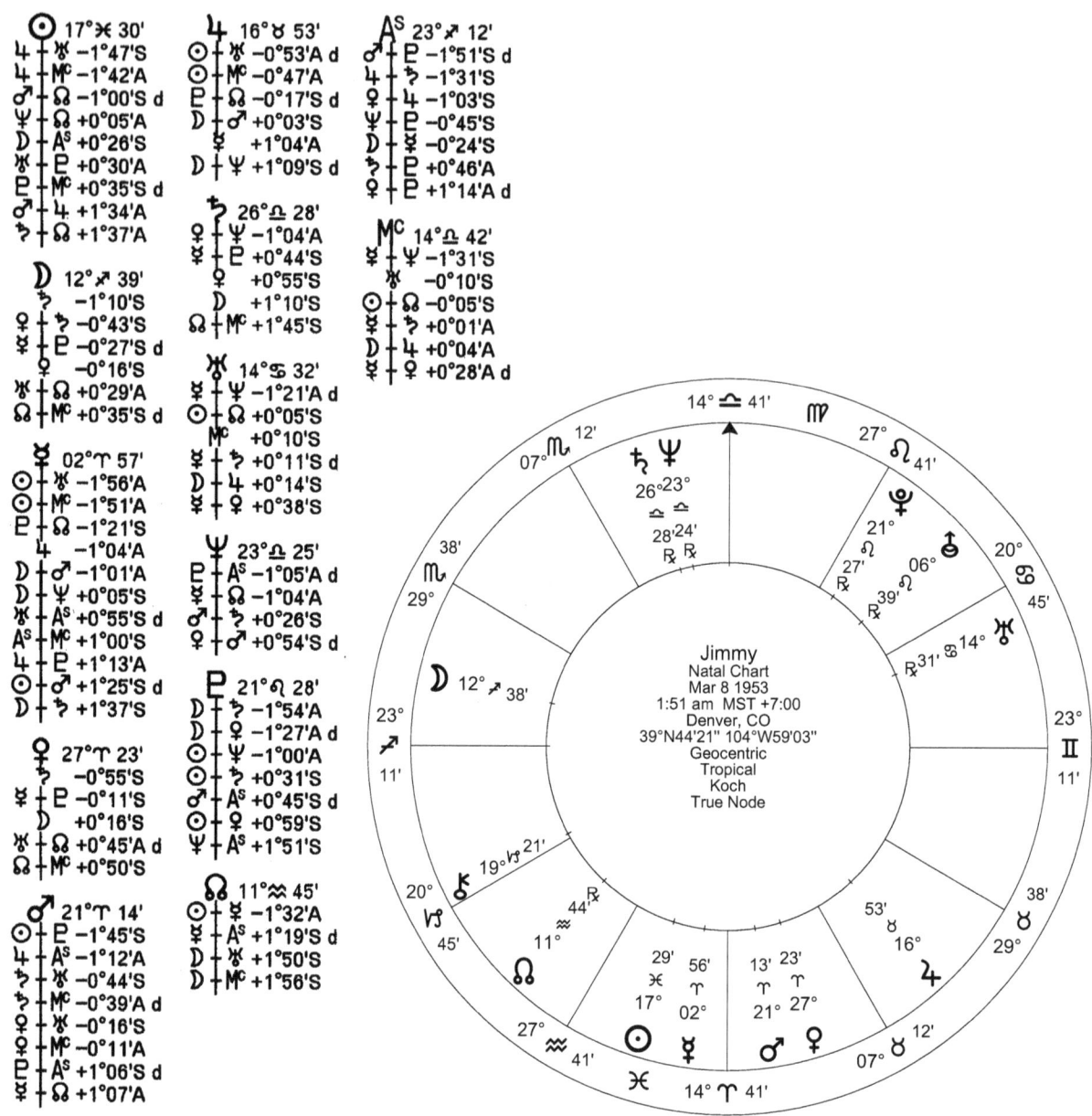

Jimmy's Midpoints

action, violence and the desire to rule others. In addition, Jimmy's Mars at 21 Aries 14 makes regular aspects, including an opposition and parallel to Saturn, that can be a harmful or destructive energy; a square to Uranus that suggests unbridled recklessness; an opposition and parallel to Neptune, showing the use of misdirected powers; and a trine to Pluto and Ascendant and an opposition to the Midheaven that imply the misfortune of suffering violent injuries when careless. During a person's lifetime combinations like these are often activated by progressions and transits. This of course depends upon the way the energies are utilized.

Secondary Progressions

One of the secondary progressed aspects in this tragic event is the progressed Midheaven at 6 Scorpio 35 square natal Transpluto delivering an excessive nervous irritation and presence of mind. For "Presence of Mind" perhaps the comment from his mother to me can be applied here: "He was thrown from the car and landed on his head. It cut his face, his neck was broken and so was his spine. He hemorrhaged internally. The rest of the body was not damaged except his hands. His palms were just black; it looked like he had rope burns. The motor was cut off

Inner Chart
Jimmy Ross
Mar 8 1953 AD GC
1:51:00 AM
MST +07:00:00
Denver CO
USA
104w59'00
39n44'00
Geocentric
Tropical

Outer Charts
Accident
Apr 5 1975 AD GC
4:15:00 PM
MDT +06:00:00
Denver CO
USA
104w59 00
39n44 00
True SA 21°57'
22y 0m

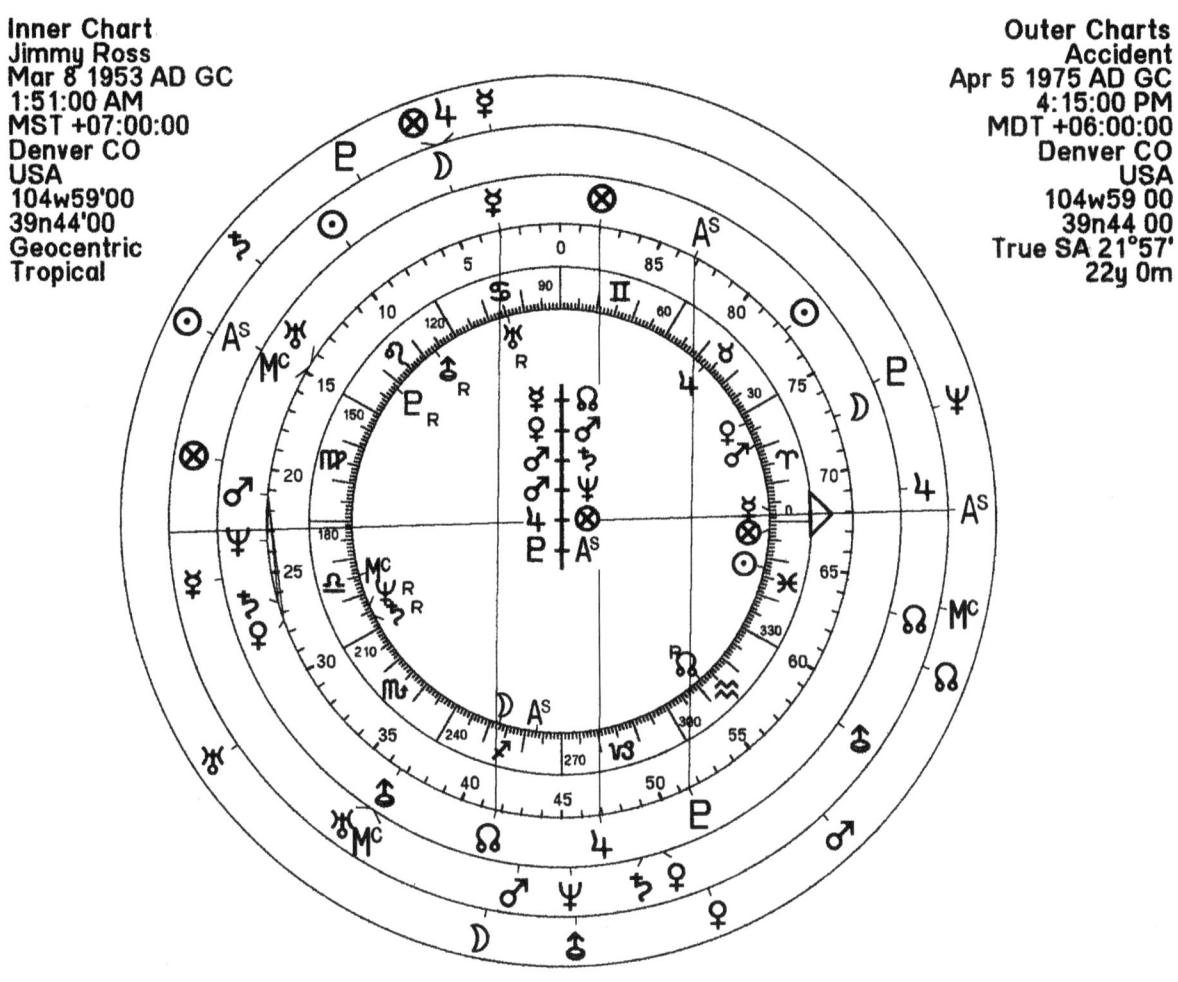

Cosmogram, 90°00' H4 Dial Format

Inner Radix	Middle Directed	Outer Transits
☉ 17♓30	☉ 09♈27	☉ 15♈30
☽ 12♐39	☽ 04♑36	☽ 12♒12
☿ 02♈57	☿ 24♈54	☿ 02♈33
♀ 27♈23	♀ 19♉20	♀ 20♉29
♂ 21♈14	♂ 13♉11	♂ 25♒32
♃ 16♉53	♃ 08♊50	♃ 04♈24
♄ 26♎28R	♄ 18♏25	♄ 12♋25
♅ 14♋32R	♅ 06♌29	♅ 01♏05R
♆ 23♎25R	♆ 15♏22	♆ 11♐40R
♇ 21♌28R	♇ 13♍25	♇ 07♎41R
☊ 11♒45R	☊ 03♓42	☊ 02♐07R
As 23♐12	As 15♑09	As 07♍55
Mc 14♎42	Mc 06♏39	Mc 04♊20
⚷ 06♌40R	⚷ 28♌37	⚷ 15♌30R
⊗ 28♓02	⊗ 19♈59	⊗ 04♋37

145

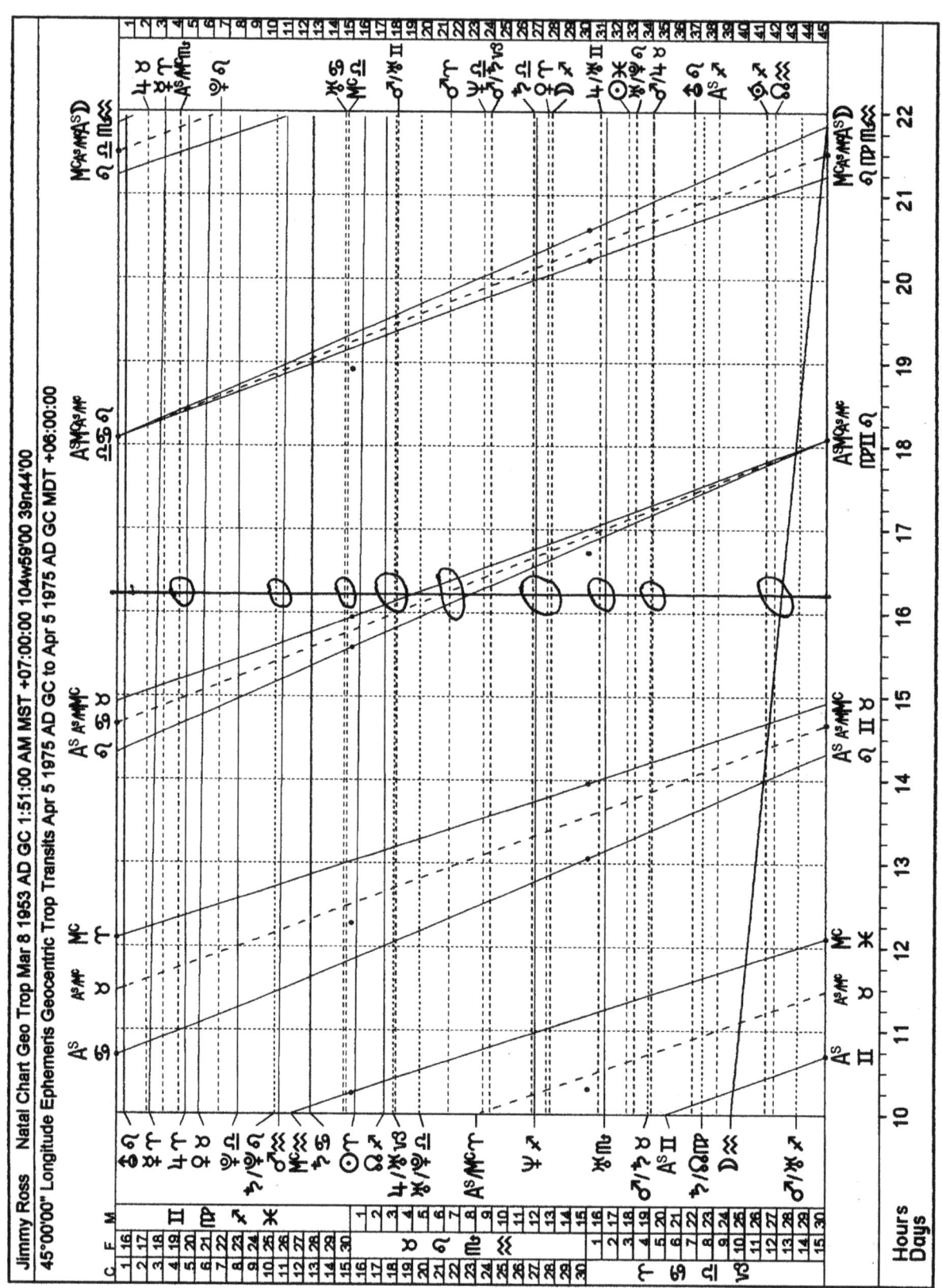

and the ignition key was never found. I felt he tried to stop the car since the key cannot be taken out of the ignition when the motor is running. The other car did have the key in the ignition."

The next important progressed aspect was Mars at 7 Taurus 24 square natal Transpluto at 6 Leo 40 retrograde and sesquisquare natal Ascendant at 23 Sagettarius 11: Determination and persistence to succeed (the biological connotation: decapitation (broken neck), actions are either too fast or too slow and the use of force to obtain goal.

Solar Arc Directions

Some of the following solar arc directions confirm an attitude and the violence. Solar arc Uranus at 6 Leo 29 conjunct natal Transpluto may create an attitude of freedom to do as one pleases, eccentric stubbornness along with being rebellious and bullheaded. Solar arc Ascendant at 15 Capricorn 08 square natal Midheaven at 14 Libra 42 and opposite natal Uranus at 14 Cancer 32 retrograde, activated by the transiting Sun at 15 Aries 30, forms a grand cross in the 360-degree circle that delineates as a lack of self-control, the inclination to behave in a restless and hasty manner in the presence of others, sudden adjustments to new circumstances and a sudden turn of destiny.

Solar arc Mercury at 23 Aries 53 and Jupiter at 8 Gemini 50 were on the midpoint of the natal Saturn/Neptune at 24 Libra 57 and equate to inhibition in thinking or slow or difficult grasp of things, egoism, narrow-mindedness and the tendency to get upset easily. Mercury was supported by the transiting Mars/Neptune midpoint at 24 Libra 47, showing that he was guided by wrong or erroneous perceptions and impressions, all of which are a result of being intoxicated.

Transits

Transiting Transpluto at 15 Leo 29 retrograde contacts solar arc Neptune at 15 Scorpio 22 retrograde and the solar arc Mars/Saturn midpoint at 15 Leo 48, creating a ruthless and cruel approach. Jupiter at 4 Aries 24 is sesquisquare the natal midpoint of Ascendant/Midheaven at 18 Scorpio 57, encouraging the optimist, the desire for gaiety and social entertainment with others and the ability to become popular among others. Then adding Mars at 25 Aquarius 32 along with the Saturn/Pluto midpoint at 25 Leo 03 contacting within one-half degree the solar arc Sun at 9 Aries 26 and solar arc Uranus/Pluto midpoint at 24 Leo 56 combusts into a catastrophe and over-stimulation of the nerves, and all the above is square the fixed star Scheat, which is associated with beheading.

The Sun at 15 Aries 30 square natal Uranus and opposite natal MC is energy of emotional and physical unrest, a lack of self-control and an excitable man. The Node at 2 Sagittarius 07 retrograde and the Jupiter/Uranus midpoint 17 Cancer 45, both sesquisquare the natal Mars/Uranus midpoint at 2 Gemini 53 respectively demonstrates excitement in the presence of others and the ability to share joy with others. Neptune at 11 Sagittarius 49 retrograde is sesquisquare natal Saturn 26 Libra 28 displaying a peculiar character and a strong preoccupation with oneself. Uranus at 1 Scorpio 05 retrograde is semi-square natal midpoint of Jupiter/Uranus at 15 Gemini 43 and confirms an inner tension suddenly released and a sudden change in destiny. The midpoint of Mars/Saturn at 3 Scorpio 59 is opposite the natal midpoint of Mars/Jupiter 4 Taurus 09, which is defined as a complete concentration of energy upon a particular objective to the entire exclusion of other interests, to destroy or eliminate something thoroughly, and a quick dissolution of the body. The Moon at 12 Aquarius 12 is approaching the conjunction of the natal Node in 11 Aquarius 45 retrograde and equals separation.

Now, the most sensitive midpoint of Ascendant/Midheaven at 21 Cancer 08 is square natal Mars and is setting off this powerful and hideous structure that very moment and describes the individual in action, square natal Neptune revealing disappointments, and conjunct natal midpoint Mars/Saturn at 23 Cancer 51 the separation, mourning and bereavement. All of this is extremely fatalistic and sad, but it did not have to be this way. Jimmy chose to drink and drive and that combined with all of these unbalanced energies caused this tragic accident.

Laci Peterson

Laci Peterson, 27, and eight months pregnant, disappeared, supposedly while walking her dog close to her home on December 24, 2002 in Modesto, California. The next day shortly before 6:00 p.m. she was reported missing by her husband Scott Peterson as well as her parents Mr. and Mrs. Roacha.

An extended search by Modesto police followed, that included dogs, horses, helicopters, rafts as well as firefighters, but no trace of Laci. According to other reports she was last seen in a neighborhood park around 10:00 a.m.

Laci's husband, Scott Peterson, 30, when questioned, said he was fishing at the San Francisco Bay. After fishing he tried to call his wife on his cell phone but could not reach her, and after arriving home, found her purse in the house and her car in the driveway. In following weeks Scott Peterson participated in the search, placing posters, talking to police and pleading on television for her safe return. Reward money of $100,000 plus $25,000 more was offered.

As no trace of the woman could be found, Scott became a suspect in her disappearance. A few days later, police issued a warrant to search Peterson's home; nothing suspicious was found. By mid-January the search expanded to other counties. On January 17, 2003 the police reported to Laci's family that her husband had been having an affair. On January 24, Amber Frey, held a press conference to reveal that she had had a recent relationship with Scott Peterson and by mid-February a second search of Peterson's home was conducted. By March 5, the Modesto police classified the Laci Peterson case as a homicide. On April 13, 2003, a fully developed male fetus washed ashore in Richmond, and the following day, April 14, the remains of a badly decomposed body of an unidentified female was discovered, and on April 18 the announcement came that the bodies were those of Laci and her unborn son Conner. Authorities had focused on Scott Peterson since the beginning of the investigation without an arrest, but on April 21, 2003 he was arrested in the San Diego area and brought back to Modesto and booked on two counts of murder.

This short biography is but a fraction of this complicated case. Since Laci's body was decomposed so badly, neither the time nor manner of death could be established. Following is a speculative outline of what could have happened in this highly publicized and tragic case.

Natal

The following are a few comments on the most important personal points in Laci's natal chart. The Sun at 13 Taurus 24 generally stands for a rich soul life, endurance, fixity, a sense of humor and form. Money matters are important, and striving for security is prominent.

The Moon at 27 Aquarius 07 enhances the fixity quite a bit. A great love of independence and concern for other people becomes pronounced. This also is a symbol for moodiness and can be responsible for misunderstandings. The Ascendant at 11 Aries 00 indicates one's appearance or how other people perceive her. The exuberant sign of Aries points toward a restlessness and indicates Laci would have the power to maintain her place in the world. Aries on the Ascendant suggests self-confidence and ambition as well as impulsiveness, while at the same time a certain amount of quarrelsomeness may be present.

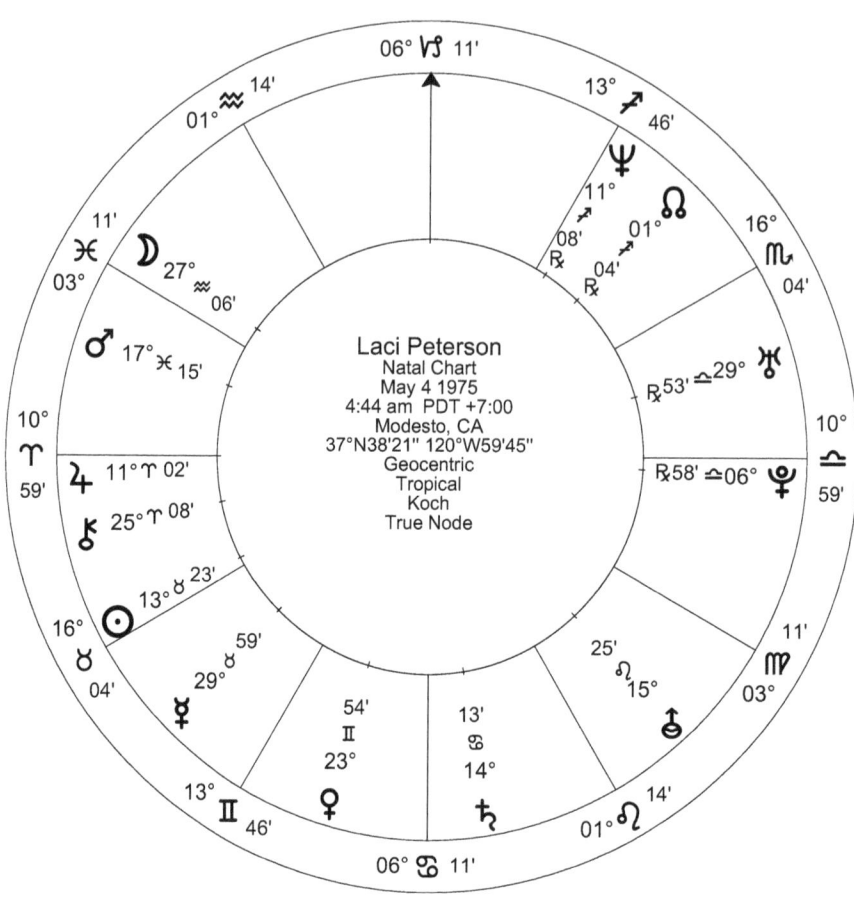

Laci's Midpoints

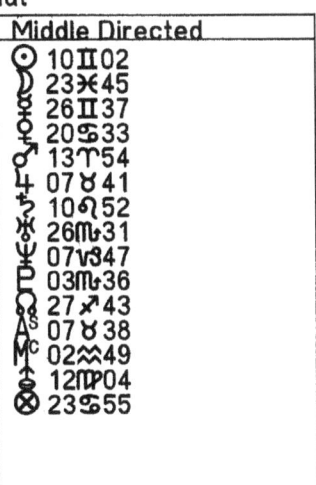

Inner Chart
Laci Peterson
May 4 1975 AD GC
4:44:00 AM
PDT +07:00:00
Modesto CA
USA
121w00'00
37n39'00
Geocentric
Tropical

Outer Charts
Possible murder
Dec 23 2002 AD GC
8:45:00 PM
PST +08:00:00
Modesto CA
USA
121w00 00
37n39 00
True SA 26°38'
27y 7m

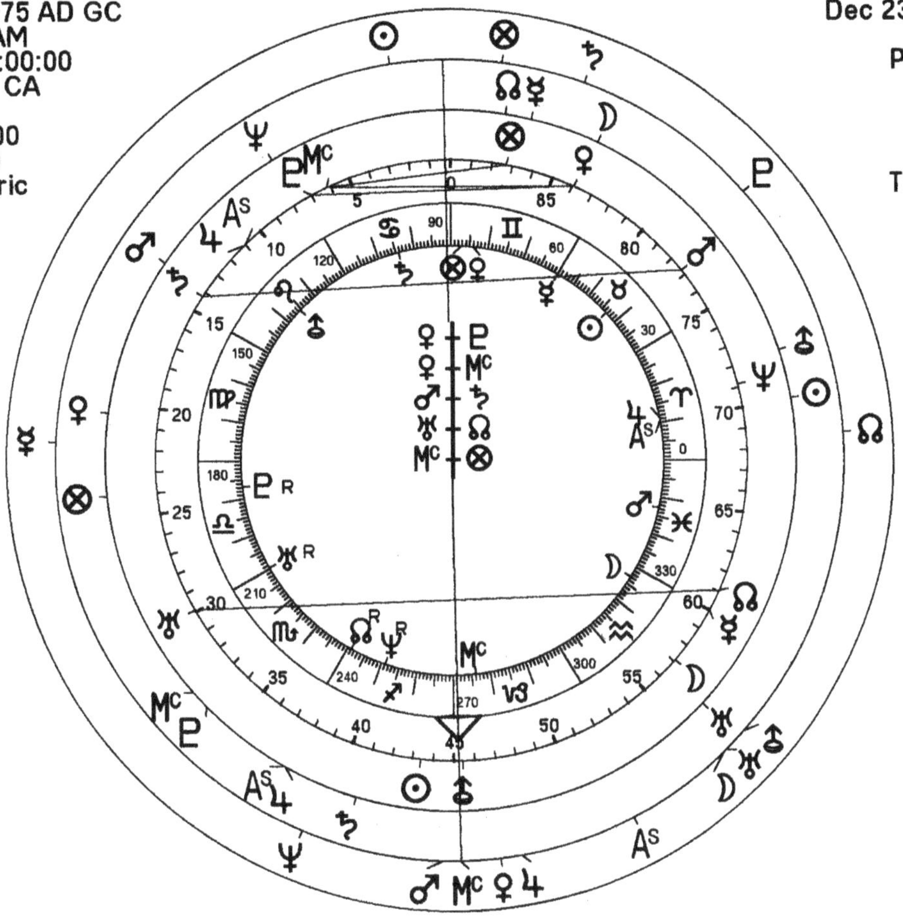

Cosmogram, 90°00' H4 Dial Format

Inner Radix	Middle Directed	Outer Transits
☉ 13♉24	☉ 10♊02	☉ 02♑11
☽ 27♒07	☽ 23♓45	☽ 25♌49
☿ 29♉59	☿ 26♊37	☿ 21♑49
♀ 23♊55	♀ 20♋33	♀ 16♏41
♂ 17♓16	♂ 13♈54	♂ 14♏32
♃ 11♈03	♃ 07♉41	♃ 17♌28R
♄ 14♋14	♄ 10♌52	♄ 25♊04R
♅ 29♎53R	♅ 26♏31	♅ 25♒56
♆ 11♐09R	♆ 07♑47	♆ 09♒19
♇ 06♎58R	♇ 03♏36	♇ 17♐59
☊ 01♐05R	☊ 27♐43	☊ 08♊29R
As 11♈00	As 07♉38	As 21♌44
Mc 06♑11	Mc 02♒49	Mc 15♉15
↑ 15♌26	↑ 12♍04	↑ 26♌52R
⊗ 27♊17	⊗ 23♋55	⊗ 28♐06

151

Most disturbing is the prominent grand cross in cardinal signs that tends toward conflict energy. Compounding this revolving struggle of instinctual conflicting purposes is the Ascendant-Jupiter conjunction that represents exercising a favorable influence on one's environment and relationships, yet, may show up as a disharmonious attitude toward other persons.

The Midheaven represents one's aim in life and at 06 Capricorn 11 describes having the nature toward attaining her objectives, a sense of reality, concentration upon herself and her work are pronounced, yet, there could be times of feeling alone even while in an intimate relationship or in the company of others. The MC is square Pluto and represents a crisis or a sudden turn in destiny.

More troubling however are the structure patterns of those personal points. To mention a few, notice the Sun at the midpoint of Mars/Pluto that may show injury, violent measures or an upset or shock caused through the intervention of Higher Power. Also, the Moon in Aquarius in a most compromising position at the midpoint of Saturn/Pluto that indicates the tragic destiny of a woman is also semi-square to the Ascendant that may suggest being placed in cumbersome and difficult circumstances, and/or experiencing separation mourning and bereavement. These are but a very few of the delineations that describe what Laci experienced in her last hours of life.

Solar Arc Directions

The solar arc for the speculative death of Laci, December 24, 2002, is 26 degrees and 38 minutes. Some of the contacts are indeed indicative of attracting events of a cruel and forceful nature under certain circumstances. The solar arc Sun at 10 Gemini 02 is approaching the opposition of natal Neptune at 11 Sagittarius 09 and is a typical contact of being exploited by others, great disappointments and chaotic conditions. Solar arc Mercury at 26 Gemini 37 applying to the Part of Fortune at 27 Gemini 17 would point toward fortunate discussions.

The most ominous solar arc contact is perhaps that of Pluto at 3 Scorpio 36 retrograde in a close sesquisquare to natal Mars at 17 Pisces 16 with a possibility of experiencing violent assaults and/or injuries. In turn, solar arc Mars at 13 Aries 54 forms an applying square to natal Saturn at 14 Cancer 14 and is the typical death configuration generally indicative of disputes or separation, and solar arc Midheaven at 2 Aquarius 49 in a very close semi-square to natal Mars points toward premature actions and quarrels.

The solar arc directed Moon at 23 Pisces 45 within minutes of a perfect square to natal Venus at 23 Gemini 55 is a combination that is often a difficult period for women in their last month of pregnancy.

Secondary Progressions

The most significant is progressed Mercury at 23 Gemini 22 retrograde in a very tight conjunction to natal Venus at 23 Gemini 55, revealing perhaps lively discussions about her and Scott's love relationship and affection, plus an increased hypersensitivity in those matters.

The Moon had just entered the sign of Pisces about three weeks prior the disappearance and was moving square toward the natal Node at 1 Sagittarius 05 retrograde, an inclination toward estrangement and separation.

Transits

The following are some transits for the estimated time of Laci Peterson's death and calculated for 8:45 p.m., December 23, 2002, Modesto, California. The most important astrological contacts that generally are shown in anyone's death are especially the ones containing the personal points and applicable midpoint configurations.

Pluto at 17 Sagittarius 59 square natal Mars at 17 Pisces 16 (this combination is prominent in the solar arc direction as well) shows the possibility of experiencing violent assaults or injury.

Neptune at 9 Aquarius 19 is sesquisquare natal Venus at 23 Gemini 55 within a few minutes of perfect orb and could mean a difficult realization of ideals and wishes and an awakening from emotional infatuation and the awareness of disappointment.

Uranus at 25 Aquarius 56 semi-square the natal Ascendant at 11 Aries 00 within a few minutes of perfect orb points to the excitement in or with the environment, upsetting and sudden incident or an accident. The opposition to the natal midpoint of Saturn/Pluto at 25 Leo 36 adds the possibility of sudden acts of violence, but also being unafraid of danger.

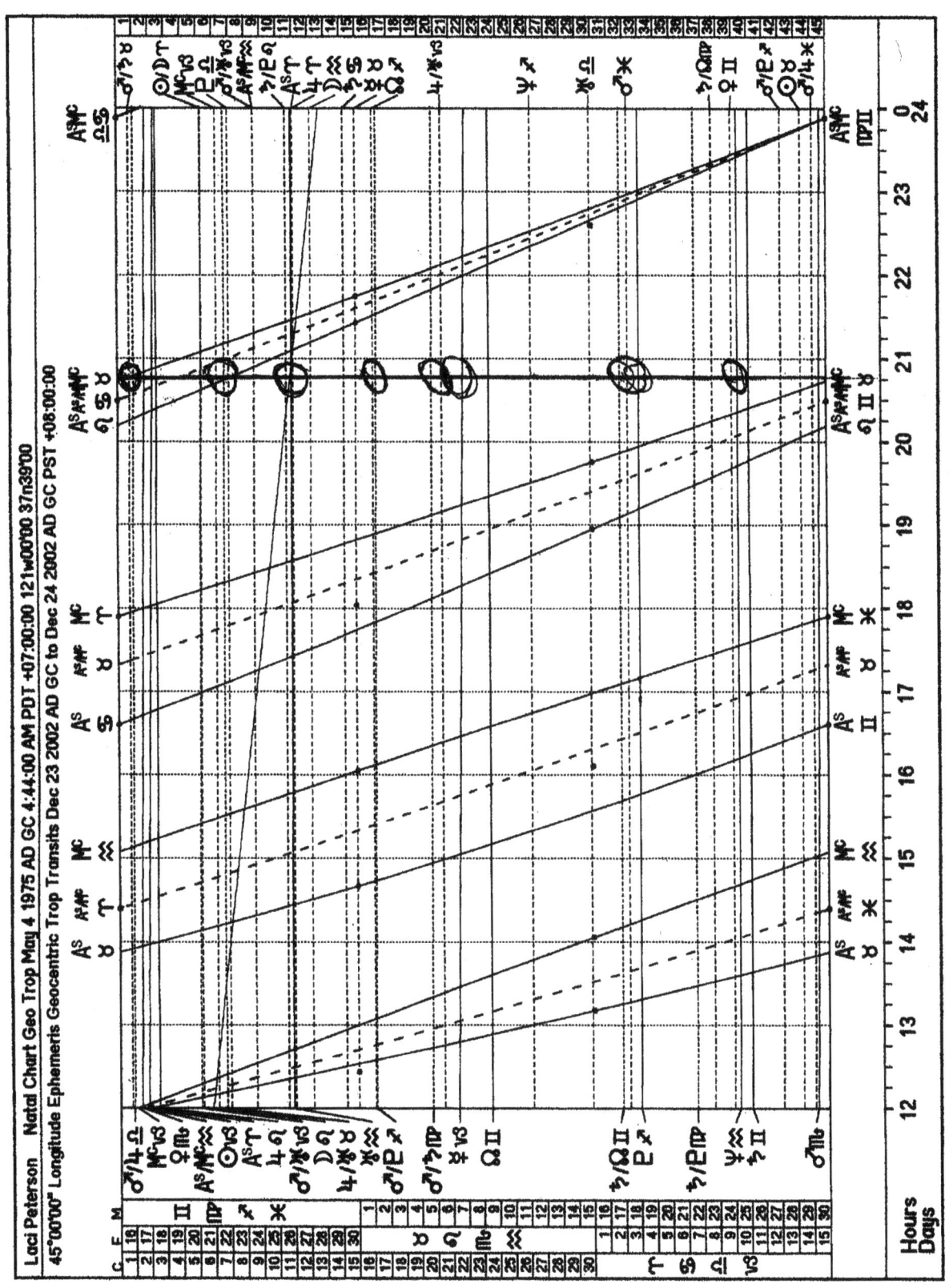

Saturn at 25 Gemini 04 retrograde is conjunct natal Venus at 23 Gemini 55 and creates and energy of difficulties in a couple's love life, scenes of jealousy and the stage of sobering down again.

Jupiter at 17 Leo 28 retrograde and the Sun at 2 Capricorn 01 in transit were sesquisquare and semi-square respectively to natal midpoint of Mars/Saturn at 15 Scorpio 45. This is quite a frightening contact, especially with Jupiter, which would exaggerate circumstances. Ebertin describes this as the quick dissolution of the body. After Laci was washed up on the shores not much was left to identify.

Mars at 14 Scorpio 32 is semi-square the natal midpoint of Mars/Jupiter at 29 Virgo 10 and is a typical birth aspect as well as success, but it can also point to marital difficulties. Venus at 16 Scorpio 41 conjunct natal Mars/Saturn at 15 Scorpio 45 adds the inability to love and express love, separation, death of a female.

Transiting Mercury at 21 Capricorn 49 is in opposition to natal midpoint of Jupiter/Uranus at 20 Cancer 28, the "Thank the Lord" combination, and may show abundant thoughts and coming up with many ideas and a tendency to arguments about life-philosophy.

The Moon at 25 Leo 49 generally indicating the hour is applying sesquisquare to natal Ascendant at 11 Aries 00 within minutes of perfect orb and represents hypersensitivity concerning the environment. Uranus at 25 Aquarius 56 is in opposition to the Moon as well, causing no doubt a lot of tension and with the natal Saturn/Pluto midpoint at 10 Virgo 36 refers to sudden violence indicated in earlier descriptions. The Ascendant at 8:45 p.m. at 21 Leo 44 is approaching semi-square to natal Pluto at 6 Libra 58 retrograde and sesquisquare natal Midheaven at 6 Capricorn wielding a great desire to succeed at all costs, making unusual contacts and readjustments to circumstances.

The transiting Midheaven at 15 Taurus 15 was within one-half degree opposition the death configuration (Mars/Saturn) at 15 Scorpio 45 and the semi-square transit Mars/Jupiter midpoint at 1 Libra 00 and seems to have insured the success of this treacherous mission.

Some transiting midpoints relate to premature and violent death, such as the most intriguing Mars/Jupiter at 1 Libra 00 semi-square natal Mars/Saturn. Ebertin's view is most amazing; he writes: "The complete concentration of energy or particular objective to the entire exclusion of other interests, the ability to render quick work (satisfactorily) the ability to destroy or eliminate something thoroughly, as well as a fortunate separation, a quick dissolution (of the body), a very pleasant and easy death."

The midpoint of Jupiter/Uranus at 21 Scorpio 42 semi-square natal Pluto at 6 Libra 58 retrograde indicates an unusual striving for knowledge and understanding, a strong awareness of purpose or objective in life and a sudden change in financial circumstances. The most personal midpoint of Ascendant/Midheaven by transit at 8:45 p.m. is 3 Cancer 30 and had just passed the natal death axis Mars/Saturn between 8:30 and 8:45 p.m.

Note: After a lengthy trial in Redwood City, California, Scott Peterson was convicted of first and second degree murder in November 2004.

Larry

"Airman Lives After 1000 Ft. Plunge" was the October 8, 1954 headline describing the feat of a 22-year-old airman who survived a 1000-foot fall from the Million Dollar Highway into the Animas River Canyon in southern Colorado. "My number just wasn't up" summed up the young airman.

Doctors described Larry's survival as miraculous. He only suffered deep cuts around his right eye, arm and scalp, and a possible fracture of his right arm. He was en route to Arizona to see his wife; he had driven from Denver to Durango, Colorado, where he mistakenly took the wrong direction onto the Million Dollar Highway. After Larry was rescued, the only thing he recalled was that he was smoking and listening to the radio, and that the road was muddy right before he went over the side.

A passing motorist found him staggering along the Rio Grande Railroad narrow gauge tracks, miles from the crash scene. The county sheriff said Larry's car plunged down a sheer drop of 150 feet where the engine fell out. The car then bounced off and dropped another 1,000 feet to the canyon bottom. Larry was thrown from the car and landed miraculously on the back seat, that also been thrown out many feet from the impact.

Natal

Larry's natal Ascendant at 0 Virgo 13 is opposition the Sun at 2 Pisces 11 and conjunct the Moon at 1 Virgo 16, as well as several midpoints, suggesting being extremely prone to accidents, being placed in difficult circumstances and intervention in one's destiny, are but a few comments.

Uranus at 16 Aries 50, already in a volatile sign, is connected to many midpoints, and is sesquisquare the Ascendant. One particular midpoint attached to this combination is the Mars/Neptune midpoint at 2 Sagittarius. Ebertin states the that this combination may represent "changing energy levels, states of weakness emerging suddenly, sudden disadvantages caused through lack of energy, a crises in life, an illness or an accident." In light of these energies, note that at the time of the accident Larry had driven at least nine hours and was tired and dozing at the wheel while driving at night through the mountain's very narrow and curvy roads. Larry later confirmed that he had had other personal crises in his life.

Solar Arc

The solar arc for the time of the accident is 22 degrees 40 minutes. First, the solar arc Sun at 24 Pisces 51 and Uranus at 9 Taurus 30 set off all the natal planets mentioned above.

Next, solar arc Neptune at 29 Virgo 24 is semi-square natal Jupiter at 15 Leo 47 retrograde, clearly indicating speculation that the marriage could survive the difficulties at hand.

The solar arc Mars/Saturn midpoint at 6 Pisces 21 opposite natal Neptune at 6 Virgo 44 warns that obstacles and inhibitions may be caused by others, separation, weak vitality, self-torment, a grievous loss, it is also contacting natal Pluto at 20 Cancer 17 and represents the misfortune of having to suffer violent assaults, accidents, the rage or fury of destruction, the intervening of Higher Power.

Solar arc Saturn at 22 Aquarius 27 semi-square natal Venus at 11 Aries 09 points toward the difficulties that were about to begin with his marriage.

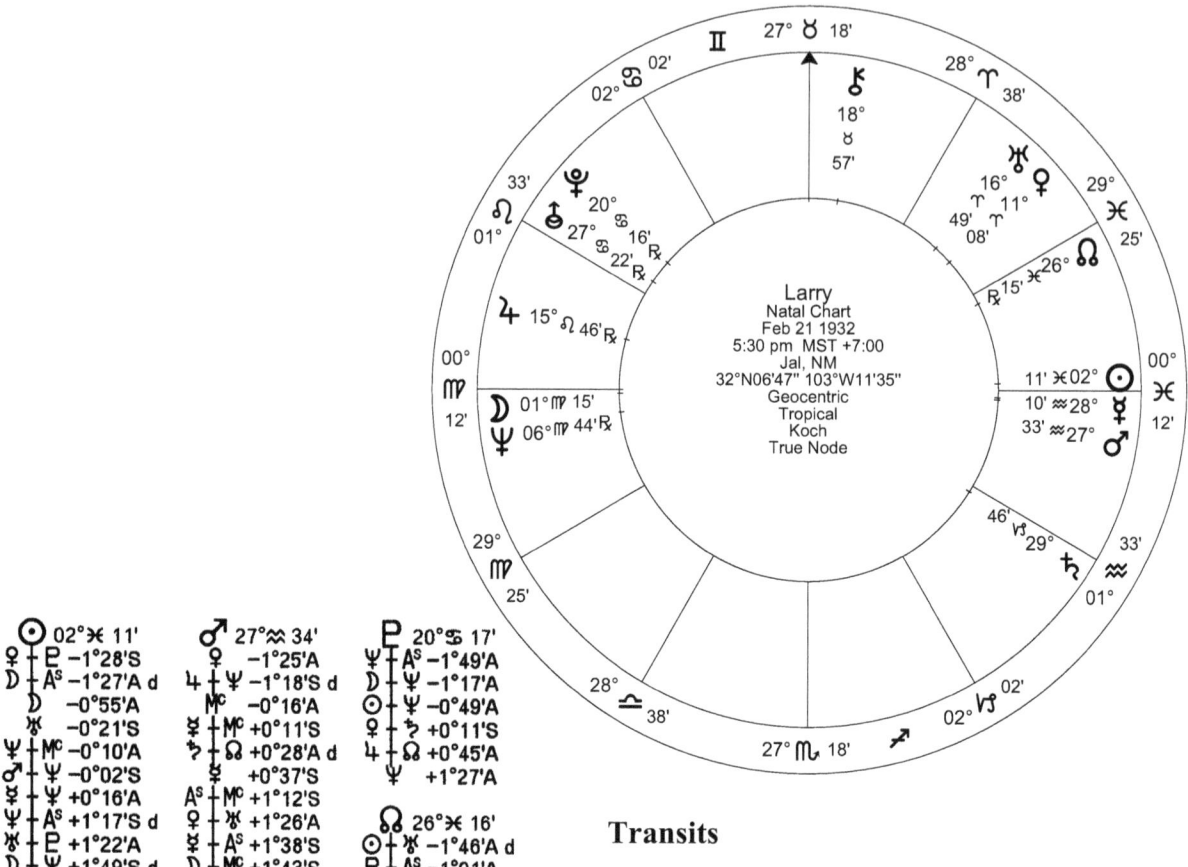

Larry's Midpoints

Transits

Some of the transits decisively reflect the event of this terrifying yet miraculous accident. Transiting Saturn at 8 Scorpio 37 and Mercury at 8 Scorpio 04 are opposite solar arc Uranus at 9 Taurus 30, sesquisquare the Sun at 24 Pisces 51 and semi-square the Moon at 23 Virgo 56 to cause much tension, separations and suffering sudden damage.

The transiting ASC at 25 Virgo 28 and MC at 24 Gemini 54 approaching the above degrees are very much congruent with official reports. The day of any event is generally shown by the transiting Sun. At 12 Libra 42 in this case, it is contacting natal Mars at 27 Aquarius 34 and Mercury at 28 Aquarius 11, causing rashness, quarreling and fault-finding.

The most significant transit is Mars at 20 Capricorn 39 contacting all the personal points of Sun, Moon, Ascendant, MC, plus Mercury and the Part of Fortune, describing all the of the danger and saving grace of this horrific accident.

The midpoint of Mars/Uranus at 24 Libra 00 was semi-square solar arc Jupiter at 8 Virgo 27, offering the delineation of good luck in injuries, accidents and operations.

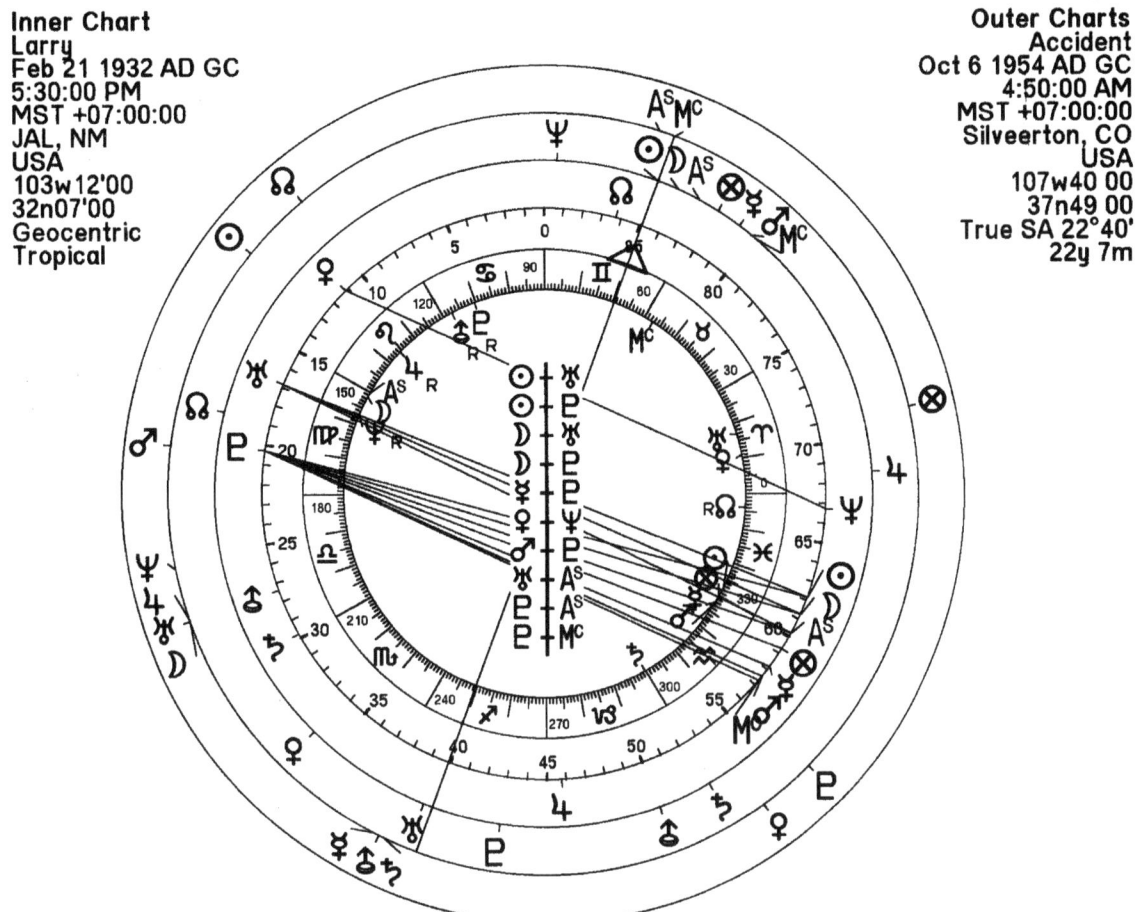

Mercury at 8 Scorpio 04, Saturn at 8 Scorpio 37 and Transpluto at 8 Leo 20 are within orb of the natal Mars/Uranus midpoint at 22 Virgo 22, again indicating the violent destruction and energy concentrated on separation because Larry's military duty was to be transferred.

When any person escapes death the "Thank the Lord" midpoint of Jupiter/Uranus is very prominent. In Larry's close call those two planets were in conjunction within five minutes at 27 Cancer 16 and 27 Cancer 21 and the Moon was opposing the two, bringing about a fortunate turn in life and sudden recognition. Larry was flown by helicopter to the Army Hospital in Denver, Colorado and recuperated from his mild injuries in a few weeks.

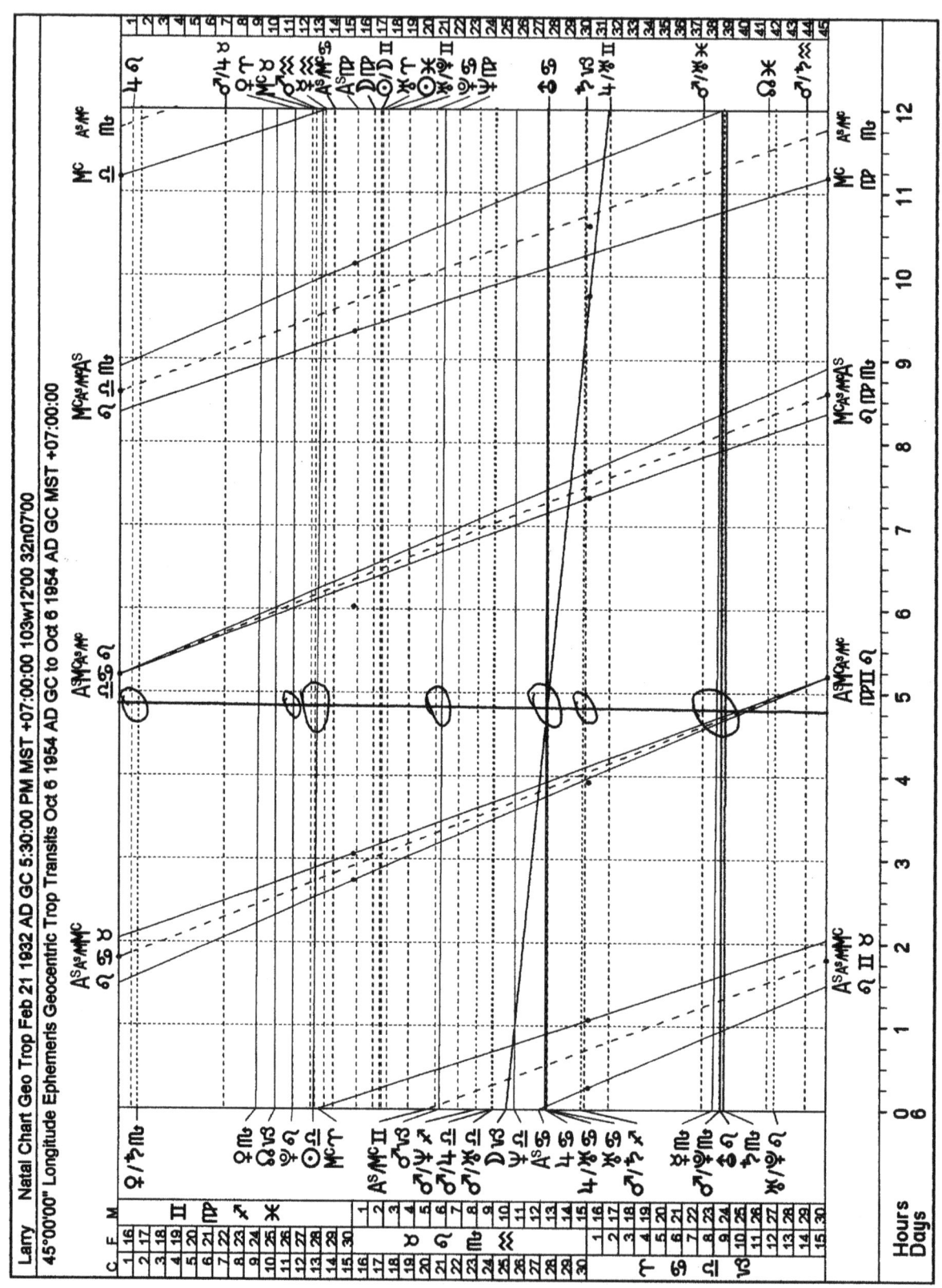

Marilyn Monroe

More than 40 years have passed since the mysterious death of this glamorous, highly visible personality. Many books have been written about Marilyn, and include details about her unfortunate childhood and rise to stardom. But what I find most fascinating is her mysterious death; much information has come to light since that fateful event to assist the astrological explanation.

In August 1982, 20 years after her death, the case was again investigated. Unfortunately, as in previous years, the truth seems obscured in mystery and perhaps the truth will never be known. However, the events of the early morning hours of August 4, 1962, are well known and described. Yet no one who was interviewed or connected with Marilyn mentioned anything happening from 9:00 p.m. on August 4 until about 3:30 a.m. August 5, except that her housekeeper saw light in Marilyn's bedroom. In analyzing any birth chart, astrologers, when evaluating sudden death, establish whether there is a potential for accidents, suicide or murder, or the possibility of being exposed to this kind of activity at some time during life.

Natal

Marilyn Monroe's humble beginnings, shortcomings and fame are prominently displayed through the structure patterns of her natal chart, including the fame that followed her beyond her grave.

A brief outline on her personal points reflects in the Sun at 10 Gemini 27, especially her vivaciousness, restlessness and adaptability, but also her superficiality. She was always eager to please and to try new approaches to situations. The Sun located in the midpoint of Mars/Jupiter would point to a healthy sex life, happy attachments, a desie for marriage and children. Along with the Pluto/MC midpoint, this certainly indicates the fame she enjoyed through the years, as well as the power and authority which is generally attached.

Tension and confusion can be assigned to the Saturn/Uranus and Uranus/Neptune midpoints, and the Moon/Uranus influence emphasizes the unstable emotional life. The Node/MC midpoint reflects the assocciations and friends she enjoyed.

The Moon at 19 Aquarius 00 is always full of ideas and a deep concern for others who are in difficulties. While she was dependent upon others, Marilyn also wanted her independence. The Moon's close square to Saturn and opposition to Neptune and Ascendant point toward depression and suicidal tendencies and enhance the numerous midpoints to further reflect the complicated emotional individual she was.

The natal structure of Mars at 20 Pisces 44 at the midpoint of Sun/Uranus at 4 Scorpio 44 carries a vitality of accident-prone energy. The prominent Ascendant at 13 Leo 05 and Uranus at 29 Pisces 00 create a 135-degree angle, with the personal point of the MC at 6 Taurus 01 contributing another strong combination attracting violence.

Marilyn's natal Saturn at 21 Scorpio 26 retrograde creates many important and curious patterns. Beginning with contacting the midpoint of Moon/Jupiter at 22 Aquarius 58, the combination refers to indifference, negligence, her constant tardiness, inner conflicts, social disadvantages, success through or with older people, diseases of the liver and gallbladder (her gallbladder was removed). The next midpoint connected to Saturn is Sun/MC at 23 Taurus

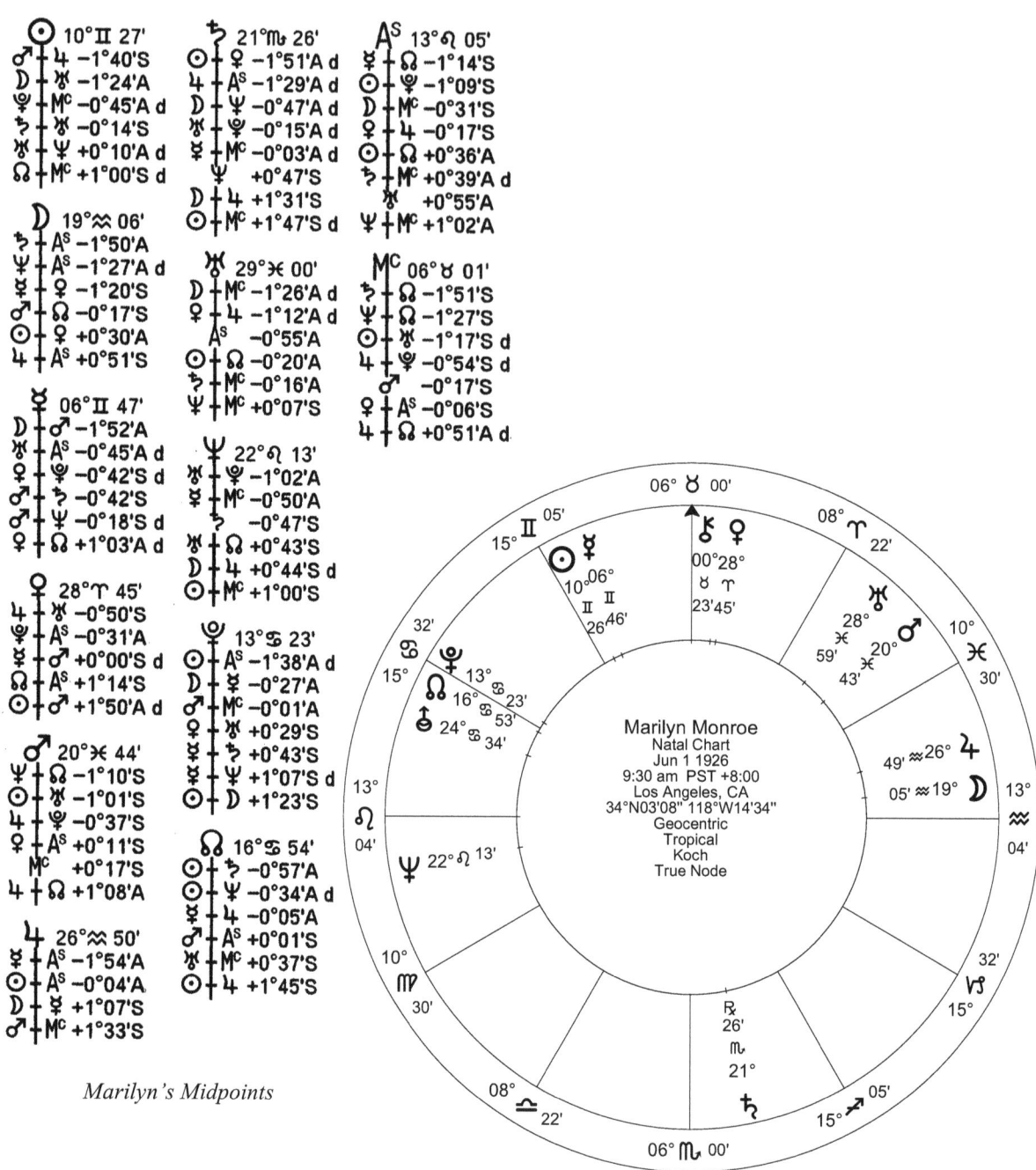

Marilyn's Midpoints

14, producing a negative outlook on life, inhibitions, the tendency to withdraw or to retire, the mood of sadness and the necessity to make grave or difficult decisions. The Mars/Transpluto midpoint at 22 Scorpio 39 with this auspicious Saturn indicates patience and persistence in work requiring determination and tasks that are hard and cruel. Adding the Uranus/Pluto midpoint at 21 Scorpio 02 illustrates exposure to extremely great pressure by others, and separation caused through force majeure. The close square of Saturn to Neptune at 22 Leo 13 demonstrates suffering, renunciation, painful emotional inhibitions, the methodical execution of plans, the slow attainment of success through intense activity and painstaking effort, all of which can be applied to fit Marilyn Monroe.

The structure of Pluto at 13 Cancer 23 is very prominently positioned also, but not in such a manner as suggesting suicide but rather showing the tre-

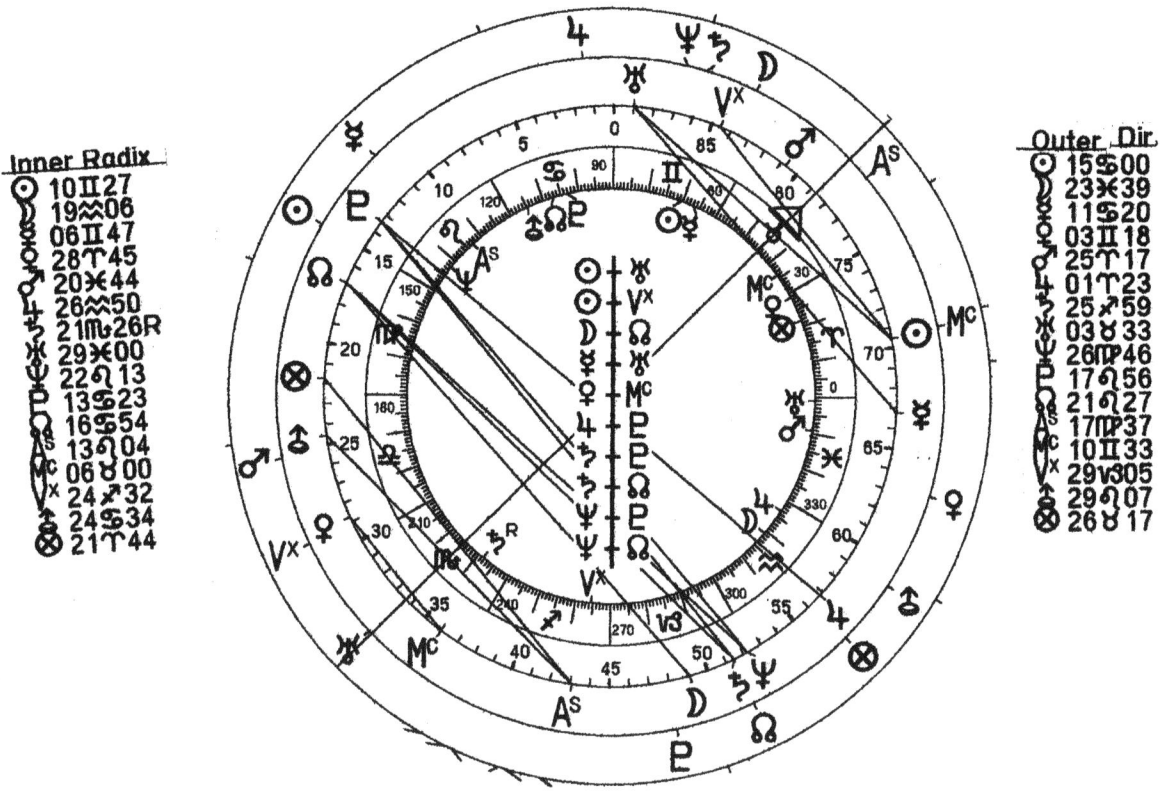

mendous popularity she enjoyed. The Venus/Uranus midpoint at 13 Libra 53 connecting to Pluto indicates the high excitability, blind love and urge toward unconventional attachments. The Mars/MC midpoint at 13 Libra 23 equals extraordinary zeal and great vigor, and the desire to bring great tasks to a successful conclusion. The Moon/Mercury midpoint at 12 Libra 57 brings the necessity to adjust one's thinking to new conditions or circumstances and a reorientation of thinking caused by special events or experiences, coupled with destiny and tragic realization. Marilyn is known to have said to silent-screen star Mary Pickford, "When you next hear about me, I'll be dead." The Sun/Moon midpoint at 14 Libra 47 signifies a soul torn by inner conflict, biased attitude or changed circumstances that can lead to critical phases of development in life or to separations from others. To all these midpoints attached to Pluto, Jupiter at 26 Aquarius 50 at a 135-degree aspect adds the influence of a great amount of information about her unusual success worldwide.

The structure of Mercury at 6 Gemini 47 is a rather serious one. A 135-degree aspect to the midpoint of Mars/Saturn at 21 Aquarius 05 poses hopelessness, thoughtlessness and thoughts on separation, illness, death or the next world, news of mourning and bereavement or murderers. The Mars/Neptune midpoint at 6 Sagittarius 28 would indicate thoughtlessness, nervous weakness (in consequence from drugs or misuse of energy). The Uranus/Asc midpoint at 6 Sagittarius 02 shows the art of criticizing, the tendency to interfere with everything, sudden news, and, in the midpoint of Venus/Pluto at 6 Gemini 04, points to artistic talent, an outsider in the arts and the desire to solve problems of love.

Solar Arc Direction

In order to attract such an untimely end we look to the solar arc direction for the coming year, and indeed it points toward an eventful time ahead. The solar arc was 34 degrees 33 minutes.

The solar arc Sun-Transpluto axis at 14 Cancer 59-29 Leo 06, which Mr. Hawkins describes as charisma and entertainer, moved to the natal midpoint of Pluto/Node at 15 Cancer 09. According to Ebertin

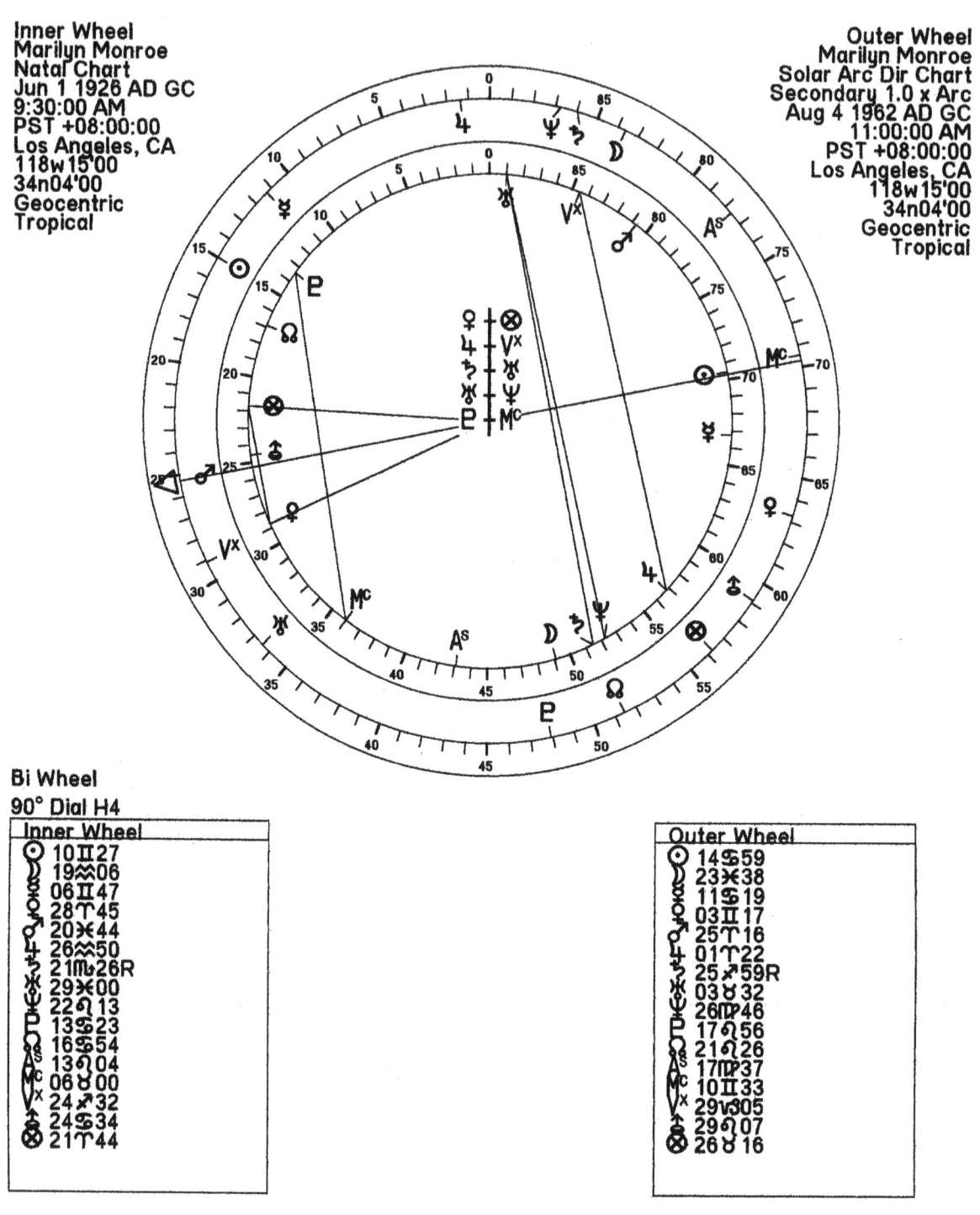

this is defined as the urge to impose one's will upon others with ruthlessness and vice-versa. Hawkins states that this is defined as the urge to persuade large groups of people through charisma, entertaining the masses, violence, brutality and associations that are split. This identifies with Marilyn risking being fired from her studio for going to New York's Madison Square Garden to sing "Happy Birthday" to President Kennedy. It was there that she met Robert Kennedy and subsequently alleged rumors circulated that she fell in love with the younger Kennedy and tried to force him to divorce his wife and marry her. The same axis touched the natal midpoint of Venus/Uranus at 13 Libra 53, revealing deep affection, a peculiar destiny in love, being comical and humorous, enduring love adventures and independence for free-love.

162

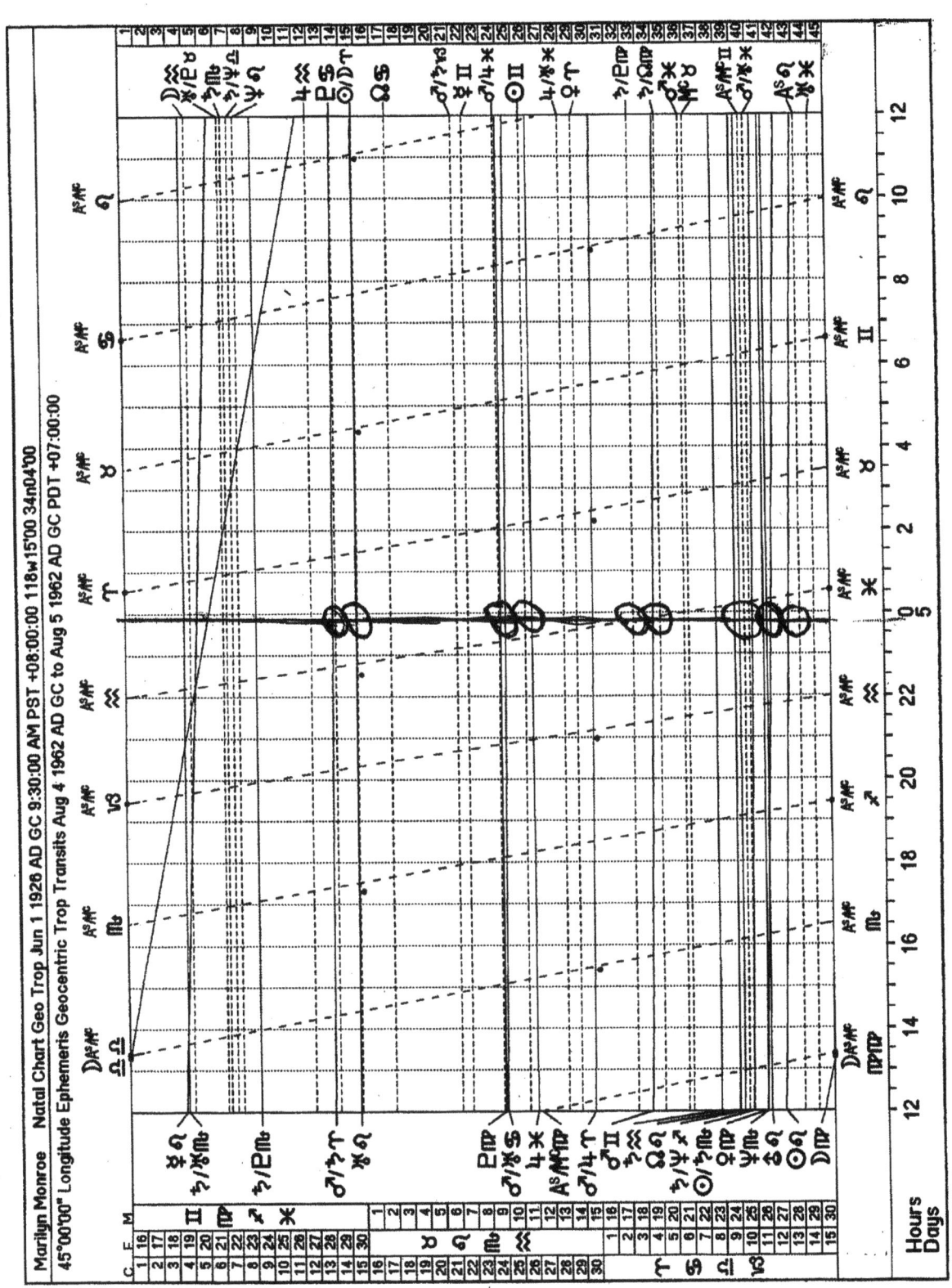

The Moon at 23 Pisces 39 makes aspects to natal Saturn and Neptune/Transpluto midpoints, creating long endurance of emotional suppression and extreme emotional depression. Mercury at 11 Cancer 20 at midpoint of Uranus/Transpluto indicates great mental activity, rebelliousness as well as stubbornness, and at the Sun/Ascendant emphasizes personal interests, relationship with the public and disadvantages through others and separations.

Marilyn's love life was always in the news and in 1962, Venus at 3 Gemini 18 contacts the midpoints Sun/Jupiter, Uranus/MC and Pluto/Transpluto that represent a healthy love-relationship, harmonious sex life, a quick response to the stimulation of the senses, the faculty to arouse physical and sudden desire in others. Promiscuity, powerful intense feelings of love, as well as violent arguments regarding problems of love are equally presented.

The axis of Mars at 25 Aries 17 and MC at 10 Gemini 33 touches off the natal Sun at 10 Gemini 27 and Transpluto at 24 Cancer 34, ushering in rash determination to achieve an aim and financial difficulties. This Mars and MC axis also reach the midpoints Pluto/MC, Moon/Uranus, Saturn/Uranus, Uranus/Neptune and Mars/Jupiter. All this influence breaks forth at once, leading to that fateful event. Some of the manifested energy surfaced as a great striving for the attainment of power, the urge to dominate others and the misfortune to be forced into an unsuited profession or occupation and a crisis in the career, all of which she had at the time. In addition there was excessive ambition, a craving for sensation, a lack of self-control, acting rashly, acts of violence and injury or sudden interference, challenging others and a deprivation of freedom playing a role.

Solar arc Jupiter at 1 Aries 23 sesquisquare Pluto at 17 Leo 57 is evidence of a high political contact and is advancing toward the natal midpoints of Mars/Pluto, Mercury/Transpluto and Moon/Ascendant and can bring the attainment of unusual success, happy and fortunate contacts with females, individual relationships with tragic consequences and an inability to clearly communicate thoughts.

Solar Arc Saturn at 25 Sagittarius 59 and Neptune at 26 Virgo 46 in a vicious square move toward the natal midpoints of Mars/Uranus, Mercury/Pluto, Jupiter/Transpluto and Ascendant, complicating events even more by producing violence, a lack of adaptability, energy concentrated on separation, a heavy injury, even the desire to harm others. In addition, libel, slander and defamation can be experienced as well as depression, separation, mourning, emotional suffering and being surrounded by deceitful people.

Uranus at 3 Taurus 33 and Ascendant at 17 Virgo 37 also show a multitude of contacts that are already described in the above outlines. The solar arc Node at 21 Leo 27 proceeds toward natal Saturn and Neptune and constitutes a depression and suffering combination, which produces mourning and bereavement.

Secondary Progressions

At the time of Marilyn's death the secondary progressed Moon at 21 Gemini 20 was very significant. By turning the Moon back one degree, which would be approximately the beginning of July 1962, it contacted natal Mars at 20 Pisces 44 and MC at 6 Taurus 00 and of course the attached midpoints, which are numerous. Marilyn was bound to make impulsive decisions and prone to premature actions with the desire to impose her willpower.

Transits

In determining the day and hour of an event we have to examine the proper contacts of planets to the directed and natal chart. On August 4, 1962, at 11:00 p.m. the Sun was at 12 Leo 20 conjunct her natal Ascendant at 13 Leo 04 and semi-square the solar arc Neptune at 26 Virgo 46 and sesquisquare Saturn at 25 Sagittarius 59. Venus at 26 Virgo 15 joined this combination causing a lack of energy, suffering in love matters, scenes of jealousy, and separations in love and awaking from emotional infatuation.

Mercury at 19 Leo 32 was semi-square the Moon at 5 Libra 10. This axis moved into orb with solar arc Pluto at 17 Leo 56-Node at 21 Leo 27 imposing the desire to dominate others, the ability to exercise a compelling and magnetically powerful influence upon the community at large, and at the same time contacting natal midpoint of Jupiter/Ascendant at 19 Scorpio 57 referring good news and intense exchange of thoughts concentrating on the concept of love.

Mars at 18 Gemini 41 stimulates solar arc Uranus at 3 Taurus 33, forming an accident axis, but could also indicate a struggle for survival and on the natal midpoint of Neptune/Pluto at 2 Leo 48 creates a lack of energy, the misfortune to be used as a tool for other people's interest, a lack of resistance and stamina and the tendency to succumb to external powers.

Jupiter at 10 Pisces 54 retrograde is at the midpoint of Mars/Uranus, contacting the natal Sun/Transpluto axis at 10 Gemini 27-24 Cancer 34 and the axis of solar arc Mars/MC at 25 Aries 17-10 Gemini 33. This conspicuously positioned Jupiter makes so many contacts that it indicates that whatever happened to Marilyn was successfully completed.

Saturn at 7 Aquarius 44 retrograde at the midpoint of Venus/Mars makes a sesquisquare to the sensitive natal midpoint of Ascendant/MC at 24 Gemini 32 that can be interpreted as a death axis and is also contacting solar arc Mars/Pluto at 21 Gemini 36, which is a murder configuration. In addition it produces weakness, emotional suffering and being hindered and harmed by others.

Uranus at 29 Leo 43 is in the midpoint of Mars/Saturn at 13 Libra 12, semi-square natal Pluto at 13 Cancer 23 and conjunct solar arc Transpluto at 29 Leo 07. All of these planets, known as malefics, are intertwined and indicative of extraordinary and unusual power of resistance. The inclination to apply or receive brute force, a sudden accident, separation or case of death, brutality, the rage or fury of destruction, the intervening of Higher Power, bodily injury or harm or murder.

In any mysterious death where no clarification of final details can be found and especially this case, being less than 40 years old, the planet Neptune must somehow play a prominent role, and in Marilyn Monroe's chart it certainly is the case. Neptune and Transpluto are in a close square at 10 Scorpio 46-11 Leo 00. In a positive connotation this can produce spiritual leaders, abstract aesthetic artists, diplomats, actors and actresses, throat doctors or oilmen. Negatively it suggests impractical dreamers or idealists, weak impressionable people, con men, and/or drug pushers. These two planets are on the axis of solar arc Saturn at 25 Sagittarius 59 and Neptune at 26 Virgo 46, showing the probable manifestations as the methodical execution of plans, the slow attainment of success through intense activity and great painstaking effort, and also painful or tormenting emotional inhibitions and undermining circumstances leading to a state of illness or diseases with causes difficult to ascertain. Transiting Venus at 26 Virgo 15 may represent the setting off all this activity through suffering in love, faintness or feebleness. The transiting Mars/Saturn midpoint at 14 Libra 13 is square natal Pluto at 13 Cancer 23. Ebertin's delineation for this event is brutality, the rage or fury of destruction, the intervening of Higher Power, bodily injury, harm or murder.

In narrowing down an event, the transiting Ascendant and MC and in turn the midpoint between the two, are the most important. The list of transit positions is for 11:45 p.m., August 4, 1962. The Ascendant was at 8 Taurus 44 contacting the solar arc Mars/Pluto midpoint at 21 Gemini 37. The MC at 24 Capricorn 26 and Jupiter at 10 Pisces 54 retrograde arrived at solar arc Mars at 25 Aries 17 and solar arc MC at 10 Gemini 33, as well as natal Sun at 10 Gemini 27.

Since Marilyn was in contact with many people, the Node must also have been prominent at the time of this unfortunate event. The Node at 8 Leo 56 retrograde and is at the natal midpoint of Mars/Uranus at 24 Pisces 52 and Ascendant/MC at 24 Gemini 32 points toward the demonstration of excitement in the presence of others, the experience of sudden events shared with others, the execution of extraordinary and unusual enterprises. It also shows an obliging person and the seeking of contacts with others and new faces in the environment.

This outline is not directed to my own opinion and should not influence you in yours. It should serve a purpose, to realize that the truth in this matter will probably never be known, and I wonder whether it actually matters.If the death was caused by an accidental overdose, it was a tragic end. If it was suicide, Marilyn Monroe was a tortured soul. On the other hand, if her death was caused by murder that is allegedly linked to powerful people, that too is tragic.

Jet Crash

A Mountain Bell jet crashed into a wheat field early Sunday morning, April 3, 1977. The accident occurred shortly after the plane took off from Stapleton Airport. Four people were killed and one miraculously survived.

Pieces of the twin-jet aircraft were strewn over a 350-yard path from the point of impact to where the mangled cockpit came to rest on its side. Radar contact with the aircraft was lost at 4:54 a.m. and no cause for the crash has been determined.

The exact birth data is only available for two of the passengers, who also are lovers.

Andrew

Andrew is an engineering technician who designs equipment and also is a qualified search and rescue pilot, but was not a pilot on this fatal flight. Andrew's natal chart certainly has energetic contacts to attract sudden events. Mars at 12 Pisces 32 contacts the midpoint of Uranus/Ascendant at 27 Cancer 52, representing accidents and intervention in one's environment. This contact also describes the practical cooperation with the technological or industrial sphere. In addition, Pluto at 29 Cancer 16 retrograde within the same midpoints as Mars and Uranus adds the potential for a tragic destiny to the event.

Solar Arc Directions and Transits

Solar arc for Andrew at the time of the accident is 39 degrees 51 minutes. Solar arc Mars at 22 Aries 23 moves to the midpoint of natal Pluto, Transpluto/MC, Sun and Ascendant and represents striving for record achievements, overexertion, a tendency to work to the point of a physical breakdown, exposure to danger, injury and accident.

The above complex was activated by the transiting Moon/Saturn midpoint at 7 Virgo 12, and Moon/Uranus at 22 Libra 36 shows that anxiety, worry about females and adjustments to new circumstances occupied his mind.

Solar arc Pluto at 9 Virgo 07 moved to natal midpoint of Mars/Node at 23 Capricorn 52 showing the performance of joint record achievements and a violent or forced separation, and activated by transiting Node at 24 Libra 19 intensifies the associations he had at the time.

Solar arc Sun at 26 Aquarius 11, Ascendant at 25 Scorpio 49 and MC at 28 Leo 17 are in orb of a semi-square to the natal accident axis of Mars/Uranus at 11 Libra 09 and the transiting Mars/Uranus at 11 Capricorn 02 as well as the transiting death axis of Mars/Saturn at 25 Scorpio 37 supporting this complex energy and suggesting an accident, violence, injury, death of males, obstacles or inhibitions caused by other people, separation, mourning and bereavement.

Beverly

Any person who survives when four others perish must have an extraordinary chart and this is truly the case with Beverly.

The propensity for accidents is prominently shown in the structures of Mars at 10 Libra 22 retrograde, Uranus at 1 Cancer 02 retrograde and MC at 7 Capricorn 09. Mars at the midpoint of Sun/Pluto at 23 Scorpio 00 shows working associations, pursuit of same objectives, and the individual in a state of lameness or paralysis, air travel, spinal bone support-

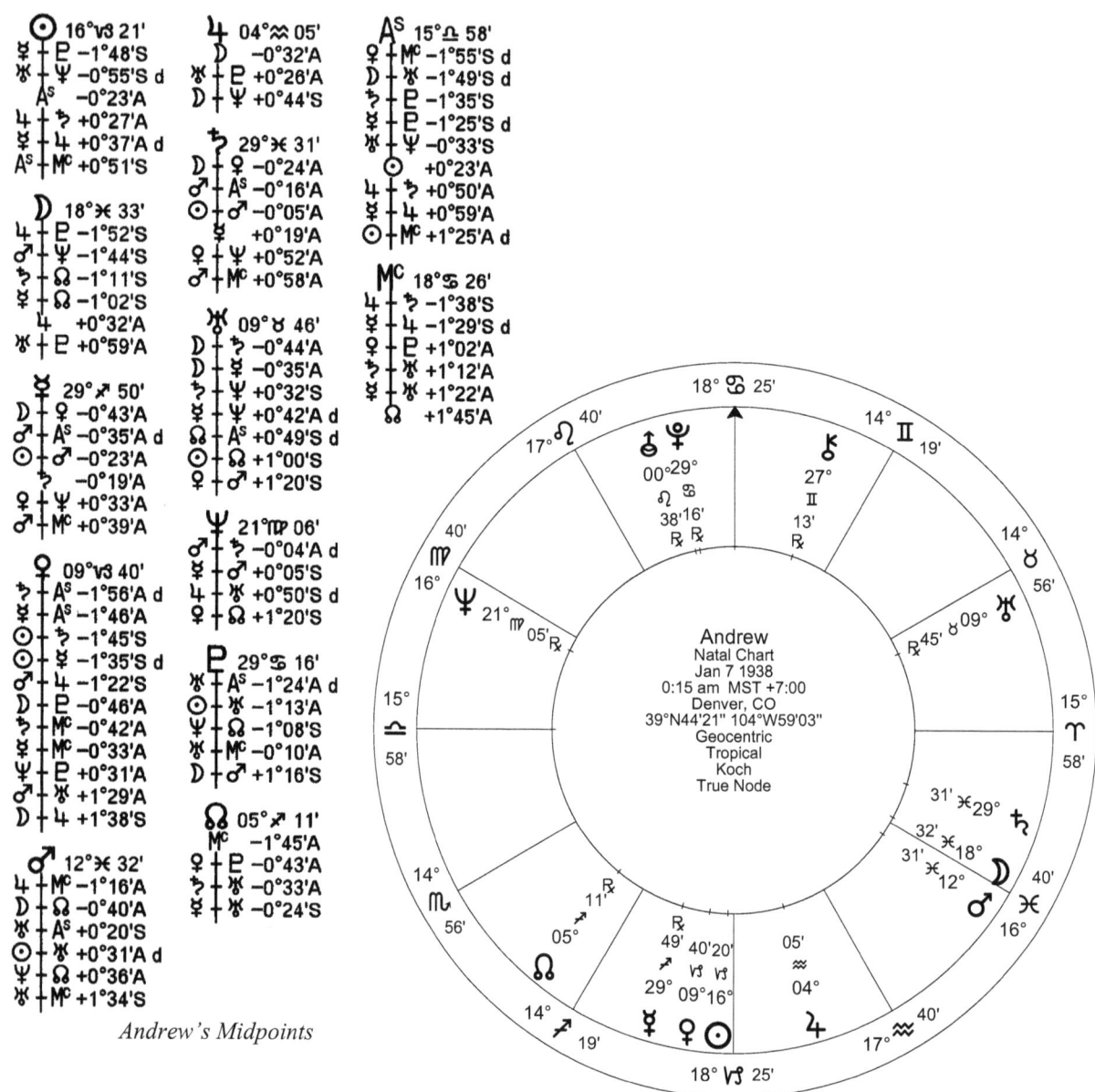

Andrew's Midpoints

ing the neck and record achievements. Mars at the midpoint of ASC/MC at 25 Leo 05 compounds the indications previously mentioned.

Uranus semi-square Pluto at 16 Leo 37 retrograde represents acts of violence, illnesses manifesting suddenly, enforced separations, compulsory confinement or retention, heavy emotional depression, serious illness and transformation. MC at 7 Capricorn is at the midpoint of Mars/Uranus 20 Leo 42 and can lead to drastic and violent accidents, excitement vigorous or active intervention in one's environment and injuries.

Solar Arc Directions and Transits

Beverly's solar arc at the time of the accident was 27 degrees 7 minutes. There are prominent components such as the solar arc accident axis of Mars/Uranus at 17 Virgo 49 and solar arc Jupiter at 16 Pisces in contact with natal Saturn at 17 Virgo 03 retrograde, the Part of Fortune at 15 Gemini 44 and natal Venus at 3 Aquarius 10, reaching a multitude of midpoints to produce heavy injury, violent destruction, sudden adjustments to new circumstances and conditions in life. The correct grasp of a situation coupled with timely action, good luck with injuries and sepa-

Inner Chart
Andrew
Jan 7 1938 AD GC
12:15:00 AM
MST +07:00:00
Denver CO
USA
104w59'00
39n44'00
Geocentric
Tropical

Outer Charts
Accident
Apr 3 1977 AD GC
4:54:00 AM
MST +07:00:00
Denver CO
USA
104w59 00
39n44 00
True SA 39°51'
39y 2m

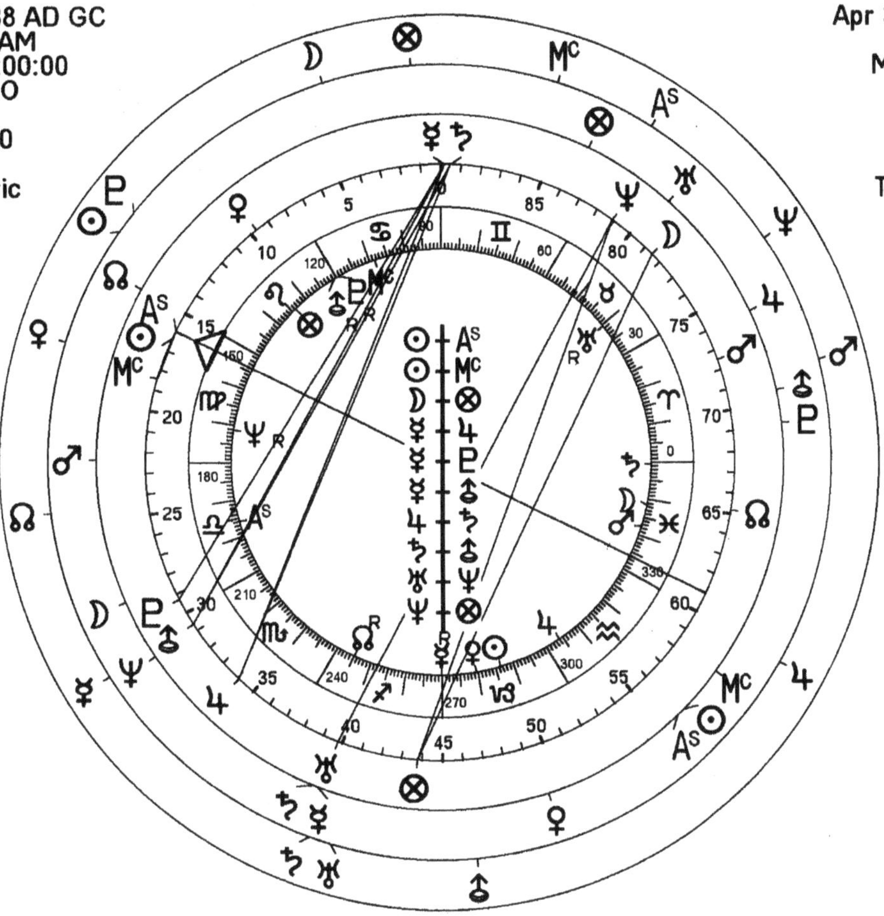

Cosmogram, 90°00' H4 Dial Format

Inner Radix	Middle Directed	Outer Transits
☉ 16♑21	☉ 26♒12	☉ 13♈37
☽ 18♓33	☽ 28♈24	☽ 04♎23
☿ 29♐50R	☿ 09♒41	☿ 00♉37
♀ 09♑40	♀ 19♒31	♀ 18♈05R
♂ 12♓32	♂ 22♈23	♂ 11♓14
♃ 04♒05	♃ 13♓56	♃ 29♉58
♄ 29♓31	♄ 09♉22	♄ 10♌00R
♅ 09♉46R	♅ 19Ⅱ37	♅ 10♏51R
♆ 21♍06R	♆ 00♏57	♆ 16♐05R
♇ 29♋16R	♇ 09♍07	♇ 12♎48R
☊ 05♐11R	☊ 15♑02	☊ 24♎19R
As 15♎58	As 25♏49	As 21♓52
Mc 18♋26	Mc 28♌17	Mc 25♐37
⚷ 00♌38R	⚷ 10♍29	⚷ 16♌17R
⊗ 13♌47	⊗ 23♍38	⊗ 01♎06

169

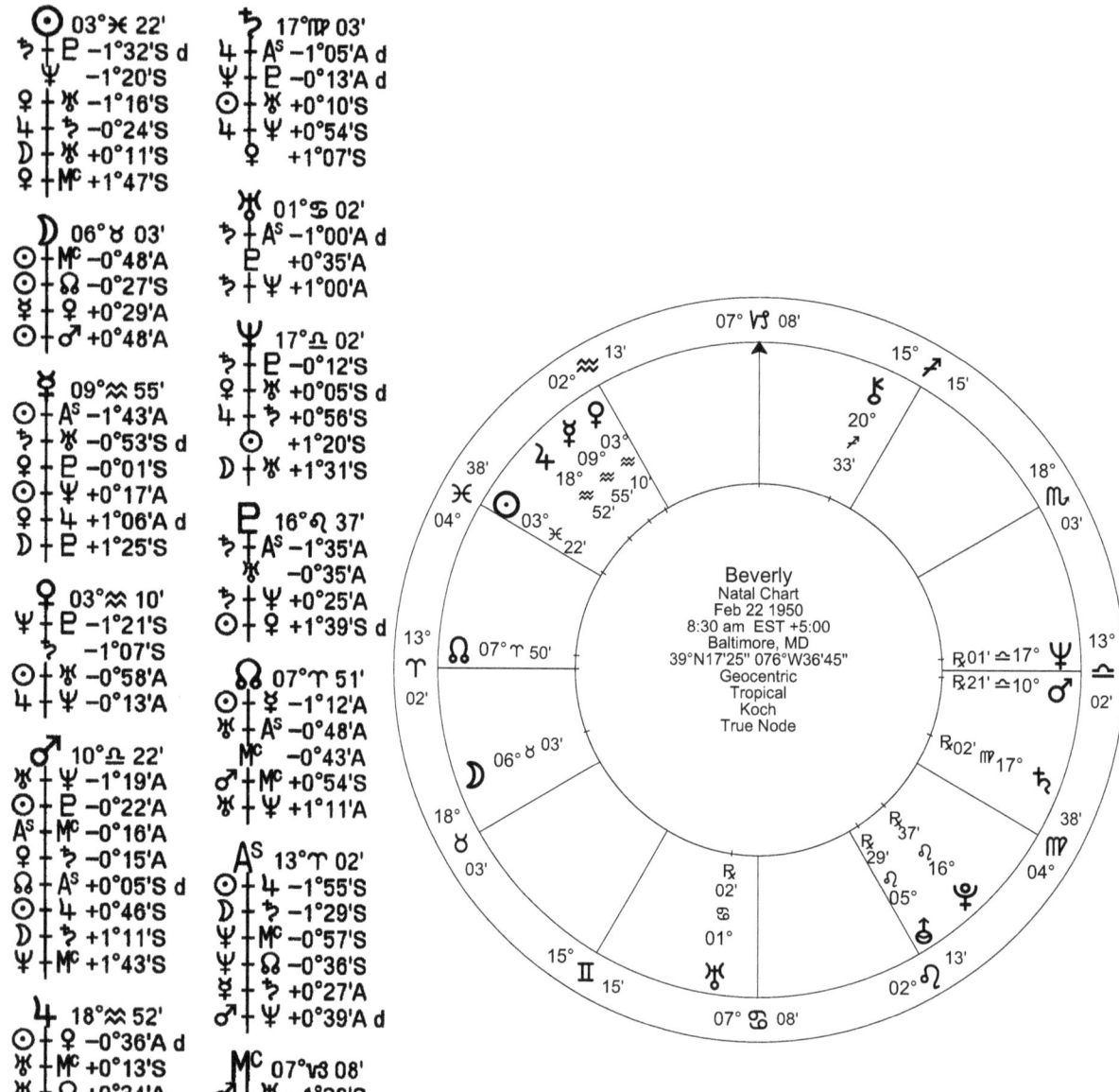

Beverly's Midpoints

rations in love, suffering through love and sudden separation.

This colossal accident portrait is activated by the transiting midpoint of Mars/Ascendant at 16 Pisces 33. Transiting Neptune at 15 Sagittarius retrograde, and the following midpoints: Moon/Jupiter at 2 Leo 10, Saturn/Neptune at 17 Virgo 10, Uranus/Neptune at 2 Scorpio 35.

Solar arc Sun at 0 Aries 29 along with Neptune at 14 Scorpio 09 moves to the midpoint of natal Mars/Saturn midpoint 28 Virgo 42 and natal Uranus at 1 Cancer 02 and indicates unusual powers of resistance, intervention of Higher Power, a sudden accident, separation of case of death, death of the members of the male population.

Transiting midpoint of Mars/Saturn at 25 Scorpio 37 shows the great danger to life, as does Mars/Uranus at 11 Capricorn 02 square natal ASC/MC 25 Leo 25. The transiting Jupiter/Uranus midpoint at 20 Leo 25, on the other hand, is always a saving grace or "Thank the Lord" combination and the transiting Moon at 4 Libra 23 is contacting natal Mars/Uranus midpoint at 20 Leo 42, indeed a life saving combination.

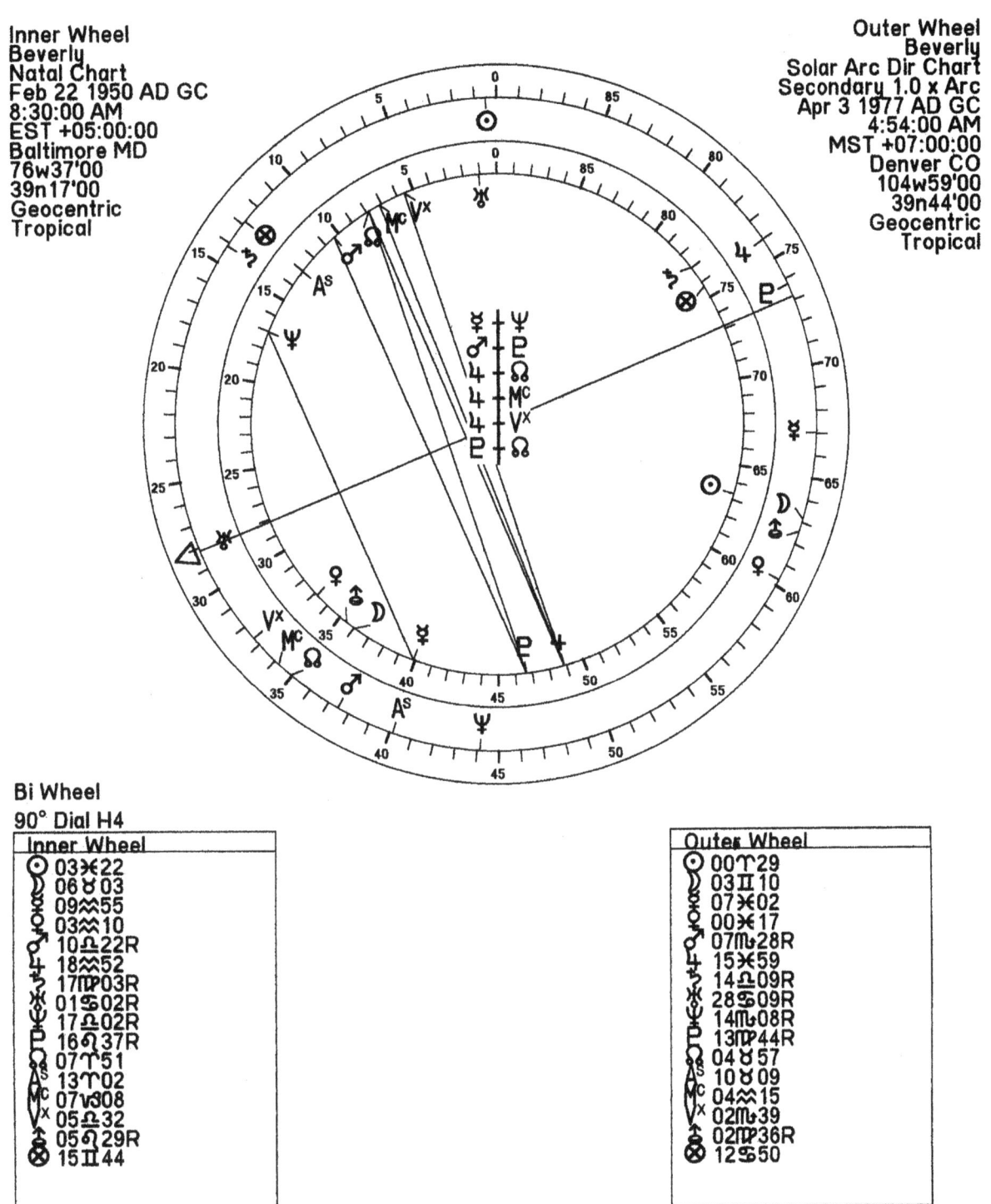

The transiting ASC/MC at 8 Aquarius 55, Saturn at 10 Leo 00 and Uranus at 10 Scorpio 50 contact natal Mercury at 9 Aquarius 56 and solar arc Ascendant at 10 Taurus 09, suggesting separation from others, the fate of standing alone in the world, suffering of difficulties caused by others, mourning and bereavement.

Transiting Transpluto at 16 Leo 17 retrograde and the Venus/Neptune midpoint at 17 Aquarius 06 contact natal Pluto at 16 Leo 37 retrograde, natal Uranus at 1 Cancer 03 and solar arc Sun at 0 Aries 29, showing tragic love, a painful renunciation. According to John Hawkins. This is the most destructive two-planet combination in astrology-cosmobiology.

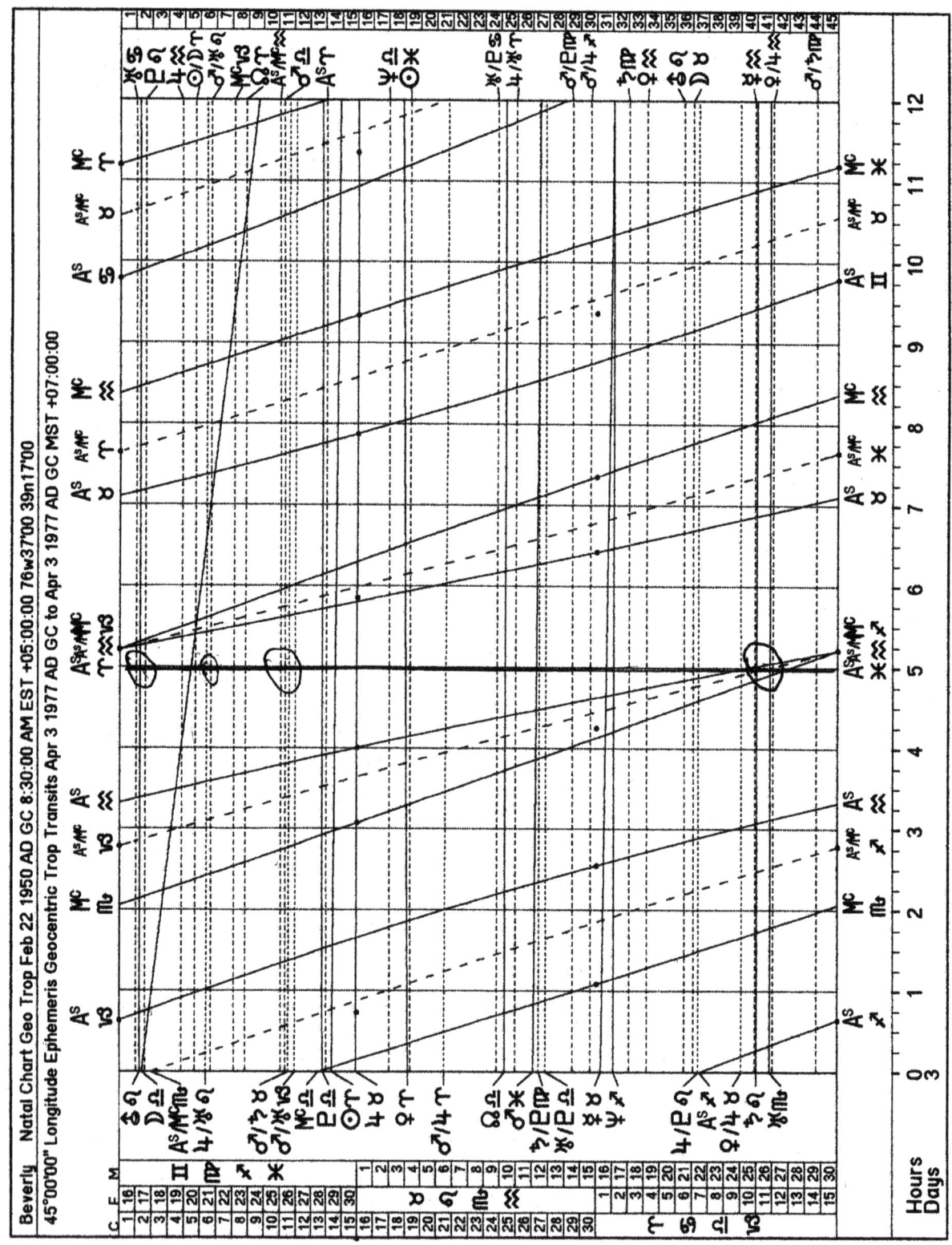

The after-effects create an entirely set of conditions. This combination represents life and death.

Beverly suffered multiple fractures, third degree burns and internal injuries and was paralyzed below the waist. In mid-September of 1977 the company she works for issued a report that Beverly was undergoing physical therapy for back injuries. She was looking forward with great anticipation to getting along without the use of a wheelchair. Her health is good and her attitude is tremendous. The courage of the remarkable young woman is amazing and is depicted by the powerful Sun and Mars in her natal chart.

On August 18, 1979 Beverly married and insisted on walking down the aisle. That year solar arc Venus at 2 Pisces 38 was approaching the natal Sun in 3 Pisces 22, and solar arc Jupiter at 18 Pisces 21 reached natal Venus at 3 Aquarius 10.

Nicole Brown Simpson

Nicole Simpson was found brutally murdered along with her companion Ronald Goldman on June 12, 1994 just before midnight in Brentwood, California. She was married and divorced from one of the most adored and handsome football heroes of his day, O.J. Simpson. The following is a short biography of her life.

Her father was stationed in Germany when Nicole was born to a German mother. Returning to the U.S. after the father's military duty, the family settled in Southern California where Nicole developed an outgoing and beautiful personality and was popular in her high school years.

After graduating she worked for a short time as a waitress in a nightclub where she met O.J. Simpson. Instantly swept off her feet in love and thrust into a life of privilege, surrounded by O.J.'s famous friends and career, her own plans to go on to college and develop a career were stifled.

In 1985 Nicole and Simpson married and settled in Brentwood. A year later their first child was born, a daughter they named Sidney. In 1988 their second child was born, their son, Justin.

Their relationship suffered. Simpson's controlling demands on Nicole, and his physical abuse marred her love for him. This developed into insurmountable difficulties and became unbearable for Nicole to contend with. She filed for a divorce, which was granted in 1992.

Feeling free, she enjoyed the single life style and raising her two children. According to press reports, the evenings were spent going out with girl friends to nightclubs where she enjoyed dancing the night away. She also met Ronald Goldman during that period. During these years she struggled to find herself and was seriously thinking about her future. At times reconciliation with O.J. was attempted, but never became a reality. The fateful day of her horrible murder was June 12, 1994. In the afternoon, Nicole and her family attended a dance recital in which her daughter Sidney participated. Her estranged husband also attended this event, although he was not with the family group. Afterwards the family dined at the Mezzaluna restaurant; O.J. was not invited. Later that night, about 10:30 p.m., as her friend Ronald Goldman was returning a pair of eyeglasses that were left by her mother at the restaurant, someone brutally murdered Nicole and Ronald.

Natal

Analyzing the most personal points of Nicole's birth chart gives the reader a glimpse of Nicole's natal portrait. It is quite interesting in that her natal Sun in Taurus opposite Jupiter, square Pluto and sesquisquare the Node contacting the midpoint of Mars/Saturn produce an individual of great popularity and charm, a person socially active with good health, financial security, but also arrogance and sometimes at odds with her environment.

The square to Pluto interprets as having the craving and attainment for power and realizing new ideas, but also may manifest as physical suffering and danger to her life. The sesquisquare to the Node points to strong family ties, shared experiences and relationship with the public.

The Sun structure pattern adds the Venus influence of beauty and a lovable personality, but the Neptune/MC midpoint show insecurity, pursuit of wrong ideas and being prone to deception. The

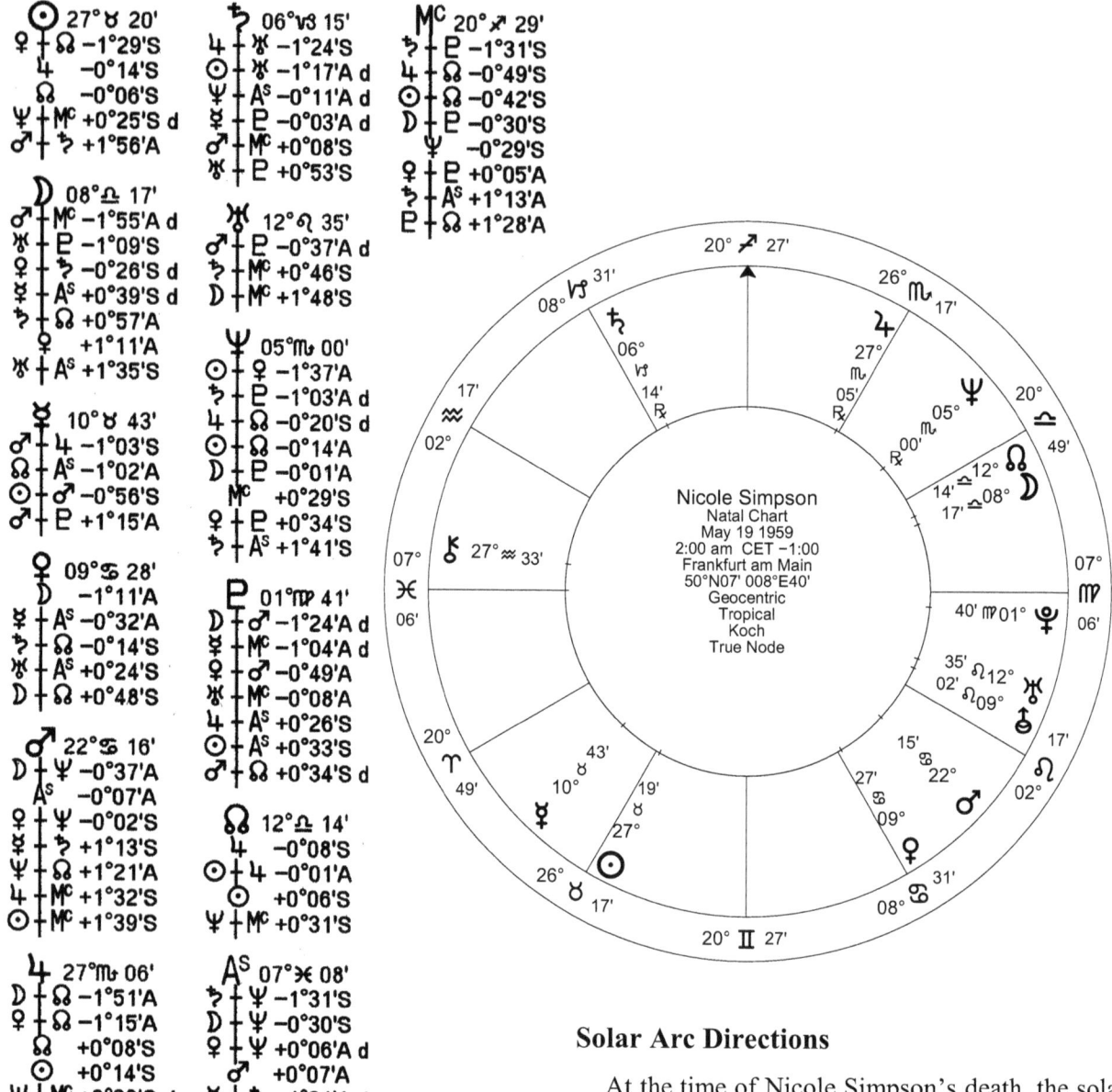

Nicole's Midpoints

Mars/Saturn midpoint always referred to, as the death midpoint is of course potential danger to her vitality and possible subjection to cruelty. The Moon in Libra with a square to Venus supplies devotion to loved-ones, an affectionate nature, and desire for children, but also shows being easily led by others. The square to Saturn can bring about suffering through love, scenes of jealousy and fateful partnerships.

Solar Arc Directions

At the time of Nicole Simpson's death, the solar arc was 33 degrees 34 minutes. Concerning the solar arc contacts, some of them were not at all pleasant. The most striking contacts show her solar arc structure of Sun-Mars/Saturn moving to the natal midpoint of Sun/Neptune at 16 Leo 10. The Neptune influence makes its mark in insufficient power to tackle resistance, losses and a sometimes mysterious death.

The structure of solar arc semi-square of Neptune-Midheaven comes into orb of the natal midpoints of Neptune/Node at 23 Libra 37. This produces emotional suffering and the inability to realize the objective. Furthermore, the Venus/Transpluto midpoint at 24 Cancer 15 indicates the expression of

Inner Chart
Nicole Simpson
May 19 1959 AD GC
2:00:00 AM
CET −01:00:00
Frankfurt/Main
Germany
8e41'00
50n07'00
Geocentric
Tropical

Outer Charts
Murder
Jun 12 1994 AD GC
10:30:00 PM
PDT +07:00:00
Brentwood, CA
USA
118w28 00
34n03 00
True SA 33°35'
35y 0m

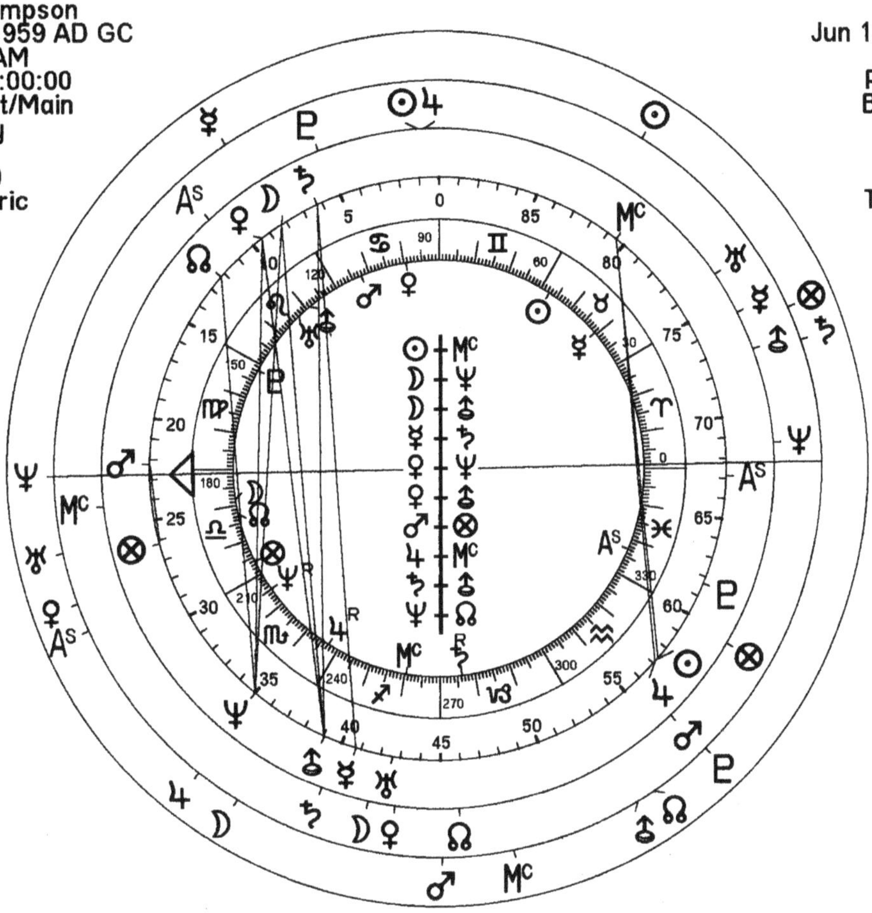

Cosmogram, 90°00' H4 Dial Format

Inner Radix	Middle Directed	Outer Transits
☉ 27♉20	☉ 00♋55	☉ 22♊00
☽ 08♎17	☽ 11♏52	☽ 07♌01
☿ 10♉43	☿ 14♊18	☿ 08♋24R
♀ 09♋28	♀ 13♌03	♀ 27♋33
♂ 22♋16	♂ 25♌51	♂ 15♉03
♃ 27♏06R	♃ 00♑41	♃ 05♏18R
♄ 06♑15R	♄ 09♒50	♄ 12♓19
♅ 12♌35	♅ 16♍10	♅ 25♑37R
♆ 05♏00R	♆ 08♐35	♆ 22♑46R
♇ 01♍41	♇ 05♎16	♇ 25♏59R
☊ 12♎14	☊ 15♏49	☊ 23♏30R
As 07♓08	As 10♈43	As 28♑38
Mc 20♐29	Mc 24♑04	Mc 17♏48
⚷ 09♌02	⚷ 12♍37	⚷ 22♌45
⊗ 26♎11	⊗ 29♏46	⊗ 13♐36

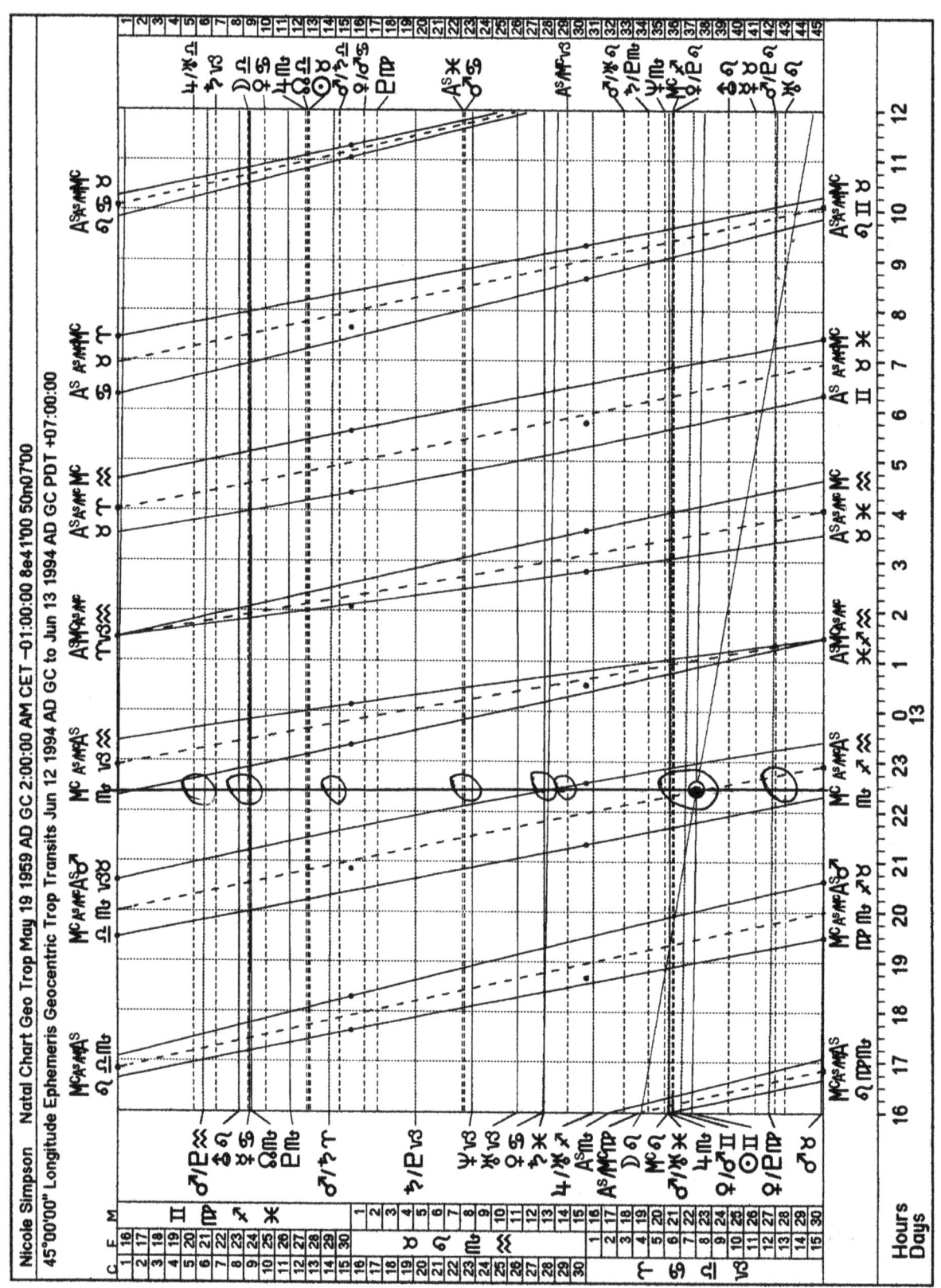

rich feelings and love. The Saturn/Uranus at 24 Libra 25 shows the inability to face emotional stress, falsehood, separation, mourning and bereavement, rebellion and provocation. Moon/Mercury is a symbol for exposure to deceit, deception fabricated by others, but also seeking soul contact plus forming judgment and opinions. Sun/Midheaven often equates the pursuit of wrong objectives and experiencing disappointments.

Pluto at 5 Libra 15 is coming close to natal Saturn at 6 Capricorn 15 and the Mars/Midheaven midpoint at 6 Libra 23 and provides the desire to bring immense tasks to a successful conclusion, but also shows an inability to make decisions or concentrate, suffering harm, damage and separations.

Venus at 13 Leo 03 had just passed an exact conjunction to natal Uranus at 12 Leo 35 (about six months before), causing great excitability in love expressions and romantic love inclinations. Venus approaching the natal Mars/Pluto midpoint at 11 Leo 59 can lead to a passionate disposition. At the midpoint of natal Saturn/MC at 28 Sagittarius 27, (sesquisquare) it causes separation from loved ones, also grief or suffering in love matters.

Mercury at 14 Gemini 18 at the natal midpoint of Mars/Neptune at 13 Virgo 38 can cause nervous weakness of drug misuse and plans without a chance of fulfillment. The Moon at 11 Scorpio 52 is square natal Uranus at 12 Leo 35, causing emotional turmoil, tension, fear and anxiety as well as sudden happenings with women and could include assistance through friends.

The Ascendant at 10 Aries 43 is at the midpoint of Venus/Node at 25 Leo 51 depicts a love affair and a harmonious nature.

Transits

The transits for the estimated time of Nicole Simpson's murder are calculated for 10:30 p.m. on June 12, 1994 at Brentwood, California. The most important planets, especially involving the personal points and some of the applicable midpoints are outlined as follows:

The Sun at 22 Gemini 00 and the Moon at 7 Leo 01 (a quarter Moon) and the Moon/Jupiter midpoint at 21 Virgo 10 contact the natal midpoint of Saturn/Ascendant at 6 Aquarius 42 and reveal the inhibitions Nicole suffered from the environment. She was filled with a keen awareness of her freedom and joy of separation from her ex-husband, but also jaded by feelings of depression.

The Ascendant at 28 Capricorn 38 makes a peculiar contact to the natal midpoint of Mars/Neptune at 13 Virgo 38, as well as the ASC/MC midpoint at 28 Capricorn 49. The Mars/Neptune may manifest through a tendency toward self-destructive forces such as misuse of narcotics. It is rumored that Nicole had dealings with drug pushers. However, prosecutors wanting to convict O.J. Simpson of murdering Nicole Simpson didn't push the issue concerning Nicole's drug use nor did they want to tarnish the reputation. Yet, astrologically, the Ascendant in close contact to the above mentioned midpoints shows the possibility of drug use as a reality. The Midheaven at 17 Scorpio 48 at the midpoint of natal Neptune/Pluto at 3 Libra 21 and Jupiter/Neptune at 16 Scorpio 03 can enhance, self-torment, craving for drugs or alcohol and nicotine and also cause harm or damage through thoughtlessness.

The Node at 23 Scorpio 30 and Mercury at 8 Cancer 24 retrograde, both contacting natal Venus at 9 Cancer 28 and Moon at 8 Libra 17 may support, reflecting on love problems and the urge to be united with a beloved person, love of family and the mother.

The midpoint Mars/Saturn is in opposition to natal Mars/Saturn and emphasizes harmful and destructive energy around her.

Neptune at 22 Capricorn 46 retrograde is opposed to natal Mars at 22 Cancer 16 and is semi-square natal Ascendant at 7 Pisces 08, suggesting a fighting spirit that is weakened and results in becoming ill through the actions of others.

Saturn at 12 Pisces 19 and Venus at 27 Cancer 33, took on prominent positions by contacting the most sensitive midpoint of ASC/MC, which contributes to Nicole's depression, mourning and bereavement.

The midpoint of Venus/Pluto at 26 Virgo 46 is semi-square natal Uranus at 12 Leo 35 and natal Mars/Pluto midpoint at 11 Leo 51, clearly indicating the cruelty and violent brutality she experienced at her death.

The transiting Moon always indicates the hour of

events, and in this case the Moon at 7 Leo 01 came to join the Sun, Jupiter, the Venus/Mars and Mars/Uranus midpoints concentrated at the natal Midheaven (see 45-degree ephemeris), Neptune and natal Venus/Pluto midpoint. In addition, the ASC/MC midpoint at 23 Sagittarius 13 provides the likelihood of intervention of Higher Power that suggests Nicole was destined to experience.

Princess Diana

The details of Princess Diana and Prince Charles, the birth of their two children, their unhappy marriage and their divorce on August 28, 1996 are well known, as are the details of the tragic accident that took the life of Diana and two others.

In July 1997, Diana and her two sons vacationed aboard Mohamed al'Fayed's yacht off St. Tropez and Sardinia and his son Dodi joined them. The elder al'Fayed is an Egyptian billionaire who owns the Ritz Hotel in Paris. In late August Diana vacationed with Dodi al'Fayed in the Mediterranean, causing frantic speculation about marriage throughout the world press. The couple arrived in Paris and had dinner at the Ritz Hotel. After midnight, while driving back in a Mercedes-Benz to Dodi's residence, they crashed in an underpass trying to escape the paparazzi that hounded them every step of the way. Diana, Dodi and driver Henri Paul were killed. Bodyguard Trevor Rees-Jones survived the crash. The newspapers also reported that only the bodyguard had his seatbelt fastened.

The accident occurred August 31, 1997, 12:15 a.m. CED, Paris, and she was pronounced dead at 4:00 a.m.

Natal

The natal chart for Princess Diana is an apt tool to better understand her. We can see the complicated and unique human being Princess Diana was, especially through the personal points of Sun, Moon, Ascendant, MC and the Node. The Cancer Sun makes her the sensitive and nurturing mother she was to her two sons. She showed compassion by visiting hospitals and the underprivileged at home as well as foreign countries.

The structure pattern of the Sun is very powerful reflecting varied midpoints that indicate the gains she had in her life in becoming the Princess of Wales, but also the negative side of restrictions (Saturn), the depressed expression of feelings (Moon, Venus), as well as the self-willed conduct and disputes and rebellion (Uranus).

Her Moon in Aquarius and close trine to the MC perhaps point to the great popularity she had with the common people. Venus square would indicate strong feelings of love and gracefulness. The negative traits of this aspect are perhaps responsible the arguments she had with her husband Prince Charles, about spending too much money for her clothes.

The contacts with Mars point toward rash, abrupt and sudden erratic behavior, much excitement, quarrels, impulsive actions, a fighting spirit and marital differences. The close opposition to Uranus would heighten the former and increase the emotional excitability, stubbornness and states of fear and anxiety. On the more positive side is the assistance from friends and accomplishments. The parallel to Neptune supplies great imagination, a sympathetic understanding for others, self-deception, a feeling of being misunderstood, and sometimes even to be exploited by others.

Since the Sun and Moon are in close sesquisquare the structure is the same except the Moon is also in the midpoint of Jupiter/Ascendant demonstrating happy feelings in regard to the environment, kindness and benevolence.

Her Ascendant in freedom loving Sagittarius did not go over very well at all within the royal household. The aspects to the MC in Libra and Uranus put

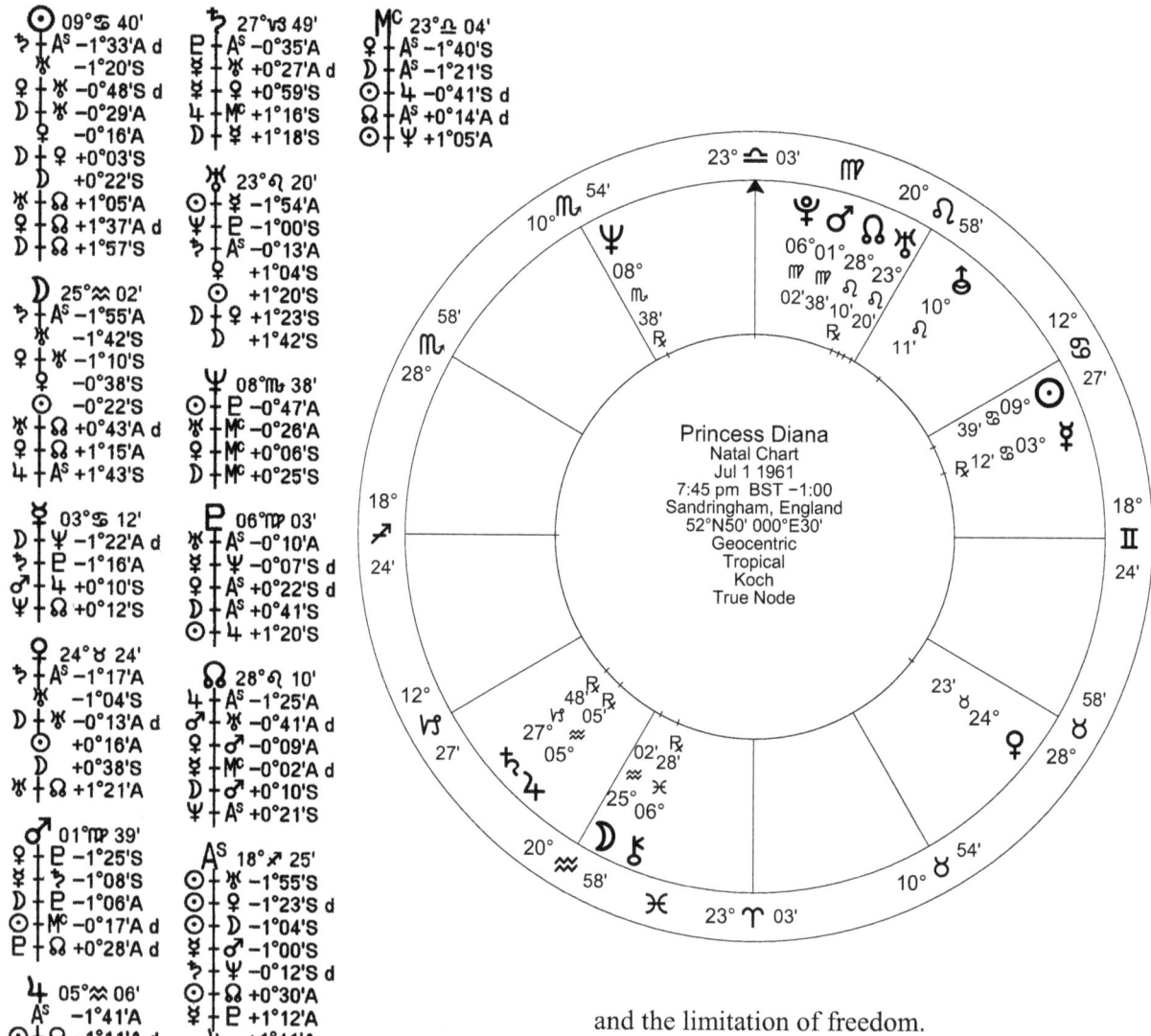

Diana's Midpoints

even more rebellion into her excited and emotional personality.

The structure pattern of the Ascendant is intensely involved with her personality, the revolutionary spirit, the love she was searching for and the strong emotions she was capable of displaying. The Mercury/Mars midpoint describes the often turbulent and stormy proceedings she was involved with, and Pluto's involvement illustrates the heavy verbal assaults from others she endured.

The Saturn/Neptune midpoint with the Ascendant reflects the emotionally depressing environment, oppressing family circumstances, emotional suffering and the limitation of freedom.

The MC in Libra has the signature of advancements through others, cooperation with others, strong material interests and success in life through sociable behavior. The contacts to the Moon, Venus and Ascendant reveal the affectionate and harmonious person she was, while the Sun/Jupiter midpoint elevated her to what she became, and the Sun/Neptune influences the impact of sudden events or emotional upheavals.

The Node in the royal sign of Leo, signifying her connections and blood-relatives is connected to many midpoints. Beginning with the Jupiter/Ascendant showing love of pleasure and social activities. Next, the Mars/Uranus is an indicator for experiencing sudden events. The Venus/Mars midpoint supplies an extreme magnetic personality regarding sexual attractions and Mercury/MC seeks associations with equal interests. Moon/Mars midpoint is very

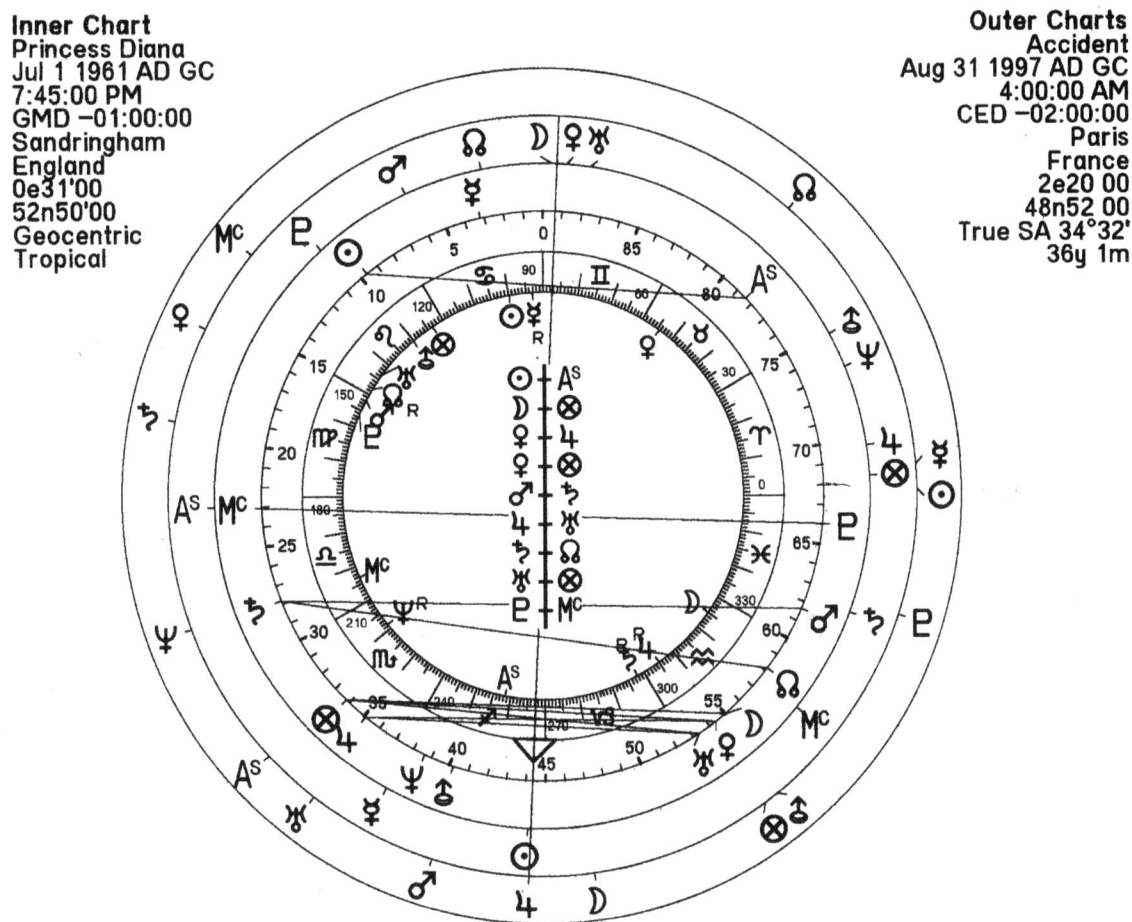

energetic cooperation with others, especially with women. Finally the Neptune/Ascendant relates to being placed in unpleasant family circumstances and inclination to seclusion.

Solar Arc Directions

In 1997 Diana's solar arc was 34 degrees and 32 minutes. Generally speaking, Solar Arc Direction sets the stage for what a person can expect the coming year. Various contacts are disturbing, such as solar arc Pluto square the natal Sun, sesquisquare Moon and Venus, threatening danger to life, separation by Providence, inner shocks, emotional upheavals or extra ordinary stresses in love life.

Solar arc Neptune semi-square natal Saturn can bring suffering and renunciation. In connection with the just mentioned, the suffering would point toward the lover. Solar arc Moon (conjunction) and Venus (square) closing in on the Aries Point suggests the new love the Princess was nurturing. Solar arc Mercury square natal Neptune may be failures through incorrect behavior, also the spiritual and mental relationships between people. The solar arc Node square natal Mercury refers to disturbance of relationships. The solar arc Ascendant had just contacted natal MC (square) and solar arc MC contacted natal Node (square) highlighting her personal relationships.

Transits

The accident occurred at about 12:15 a.m., August 31, 1997. While the Princess struggled to stay alive, 2 hours and 45 minutes passed before the television announced she had passed away at 4:00 a.m. On the graph the circles pinpoint the closest planetary contacts to natal and solar arc positions, including various appropriate midpoints pertaining to the accident and death.

Starting with the slowest planet we notice that Transpluto at 24 Leo 36 contacts natal Moon and Venus displaying warm, enduring feelings of love and

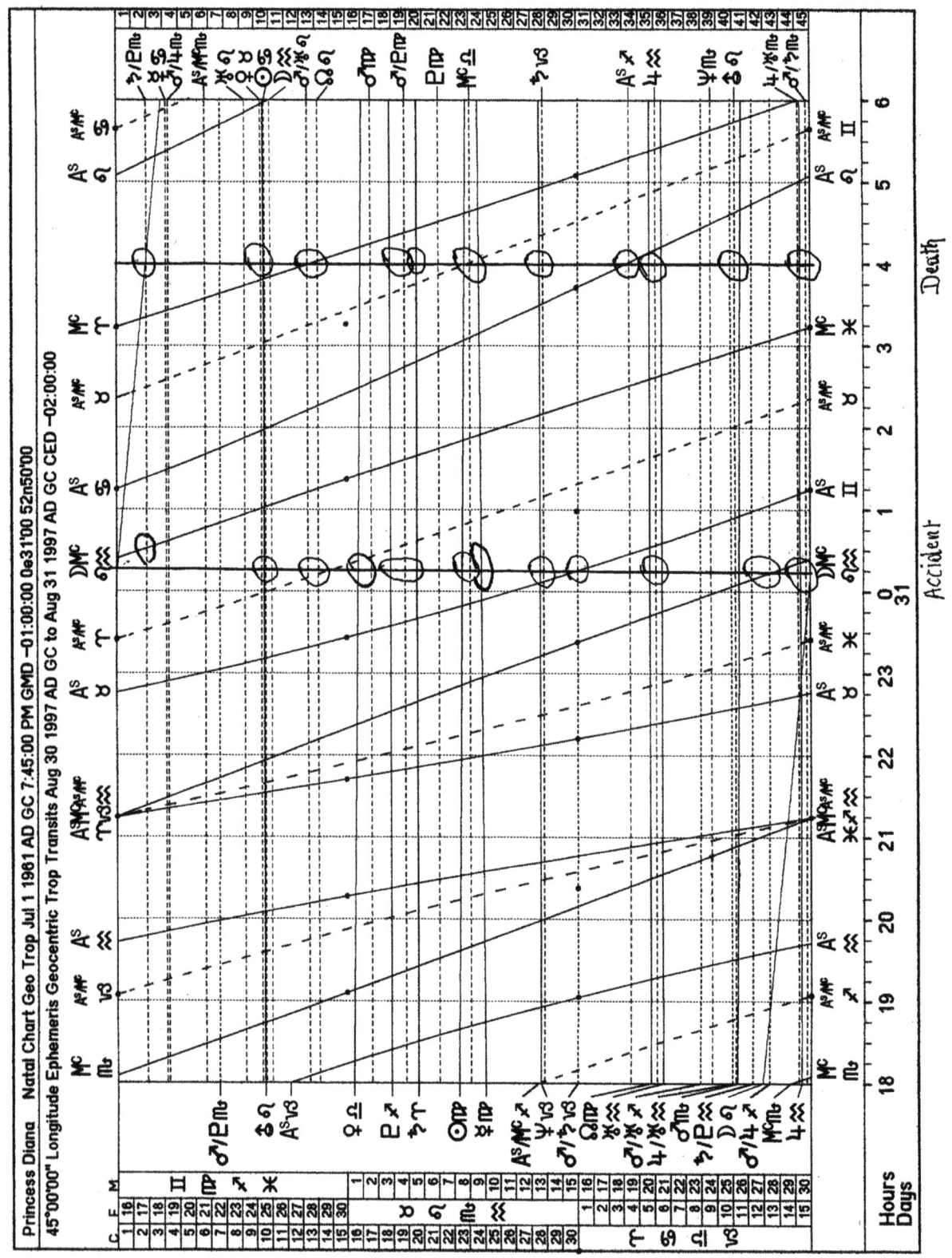

expressing tenderness. Pluto at 2 Sagittarius 55 square solar arc Saturn at 2 Pisces 21 combines with natal midpoint Mars/Pluto, introducing self-destructive energy and the misfortune to suffer violent assaults and injuries.

Neptune at 27 Capricorn 34 retrograde semi-square solar arc Saturn and conjunct natal Saturn offers a dual character, frequent change of moods, insecurity, taking care of others, a struggle between the lower and the higher nature and depression. Uranus at 5 Aquarius 30 retrograde and Node at 19 Virgo 43 retrograde (sesquisquare) on solar arc midpoint of Mars/Saturn at 19 Sagittarius 16 depict the sudden intervention by Higher Power or Providence. On natal Jupiter at 5 Aquarius 06 retrograde, Uranus and Node point to experiences shared with others, the liking of social activities and the sharing of happy experiences with others

Saturn at 19 Aries 39 retrograde in the natal midpoint of natal Mars/Pluto at 1 Virgo 51 bestows the desire to overcome difficulties at all cost, forcibly. Jupiter at 14 Aquarius 21 retrograde opposite solar arc Sun at 14 Leo 12 and natal Mars/Saturn and Jupiter/Uranus midpoints at 14 Scorpio 14 form a T-cross ushers a fortunate separation, a quick dissolution of the body and a very pleasant and easy death. Mars at 10 Scorpio 33 and Saturn/Pluto at 11 Aquarius contacting natal Transpluto at 10 Leo 12 leave the necessity to fight for life.

Venus at 15 Libra 57 semi-square natal Mars at 1 Virgo 39 reflects the love she had for her companion. Mercury at 8 Virgo 38 retrograde sesquisquare solar arc Ascendant at 22 Capricorn 56 and semi-square natal MC at 23 Libra 03 perhaps reflects the critical attitude she had toward the paparazzi at that moment. Sun at 7 Virgo 43 sesquisquare solar arc Ascendant at 22 Capricorn 56 and semi-square natal MC at 23 Libra 03 indicates the relationship between the body and soul. Moon at 17 Leo 38 approaching solar arc Node at 2 Libra 42 and natal Mercury at 3 Cancer 12 retrograde is inclined toward the positive communion of thoughts with others.

The Ascendant at 3 Leo 03 and the Mars/Saturn midpoint at 0 Aquarius 06 joined the natal Ascendant at 18 Sagittarius 24 bringing separation, mourning and bereavement. The MC at 12 Aries 38 sesquisquare solar arc MC at 27 Scorpio 35 and sesquisquare natal Node at 28 Leo 10 retrograde shows a union based on mutual understanding.

Natalie Wood

Natalie Wood was born Natasha Gurdin to Russian immigrant parents. At age four she starred in her first motion picture. From then on she starred in many memorable movies and reaped great success in her roles. She married movie star Robert Wagner, divorced, married Richard Gregson, divorced again and remarried Robert Wagner. She also had two daughters.

On Thanksgiving weekend 1981, she was aboard husband Robert Wagner's boat "Splendor" along with her co-star Chris Walken and fell overboard trying to retrieve a dinghy and drowned.

Natal

There are some disturbing contacts in Natalie Wood's natal chart, especially examining the 90-degree dial. The Sun at 27 Cancer 23 is conjunct Mars at 28 Cancer 37 conjunct Pluto at 29 Cancer 39 and Transpluto at 0 Leo 40 and the Moon at 0 Taurus 59 is square this volatile combination of power. This combination of planetary energy reflects her startling powerhouse nature, dynamo personality and attraction contributing to all the success she experiences in her life, and in 1981 this same complex energy represents and activates a latent self-destructive mechanism.

Solar Arc Direction

In 1981, the solar arc was 41 degrees and 39 minutes. This complex combination just mentioned starts to activate the natal pattern. Moving into the midpoints of Moon, Pluto, Transpluto and Saturn that represents inhibitions, self-control to the point of torment and soul-conflicts.

The solar arc Sun at 9 Virgo 02 at the midpoint of natal Mars/Saturn at 8 Gemini 19 is especially difficult and can result in brutality, ruthlessness and the necessity to fight for existence or life. The solar arc Jupiter at 12 Aries 34 contacts the natal MC at 13 Cancer 20 and Ascendant at 11 Libra 49 and symbolizes the success she enjoyed at the time of her death.

Natalie's love life might not have been the most perfect since solar arc Venus at 19 Libra 13 moves to the natal midpoint of Uranus/Neptune at 18 Cancer 12 and indicates an extremely high sensitivity. The solar arc Neptune at 0 Scorpio 42 is opposite natal Moon and square natal Transpluto at 0 Leo 40m represents a difficult energy for a disappointed woman. Whenever transits contact natal and directed positions, the stage is set to attract situations involving the nature reflecting the planetary combinations.

Transits

Starting with transiting Pluto at 25 Libra 54 forming an axis to the solar arc Moon, Transpluto, Mars and the Sun, all in the vicinity of 9 to 13 degrees of the mutable signs on the 90-degree circle indicates accidents, injury happening to a woman, crises of life and death and unusual courage.

Transiting Uranus at 0 Saggitarius 51 is square natal Jupiter at 0 Pisces 55 retrograde and can be responsible for extreme tension that is suddenly released. Saturn at 19 Libra 05 at the midpoint of natal Neptune/Uranus at 18 Cancer 12 tends toward depression, instability, pessimism, a painful loss, mourning or bereavement.

Jupiter at 0 Scorpio 38 contacts solar arc Neptune at 0 Scorpio 42 and natal midpoint of Moon/Pluto at

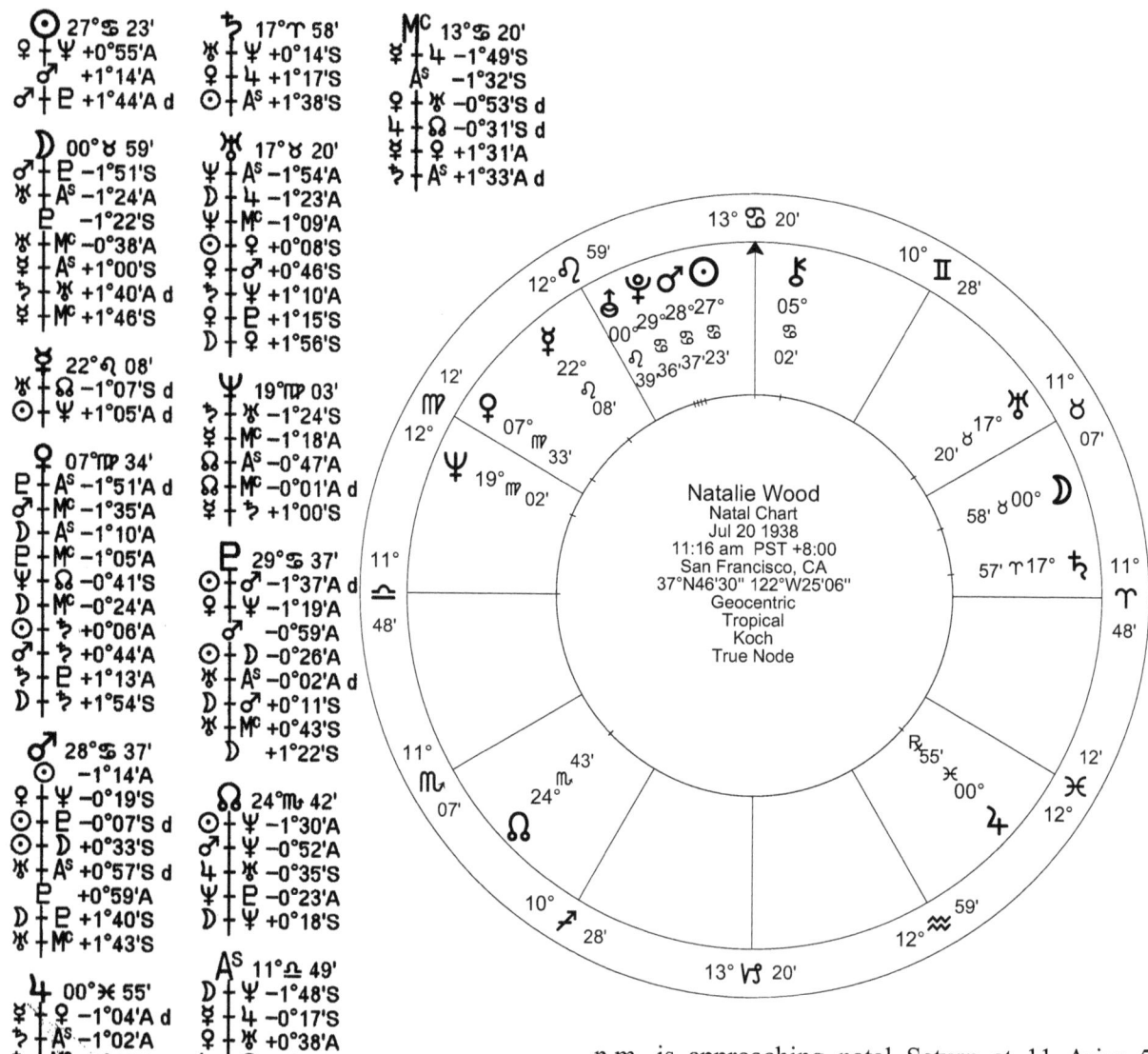

Natalie's Midpoints

15 Gemini 18 and shows a rich and deep emotional life, hypersensitivity, depression and a lack of will power. Unruly Mars at 22 Virgo 17 approaches the natal Mars/Uranus midpoint at 22 Virgo 59, emphasizing the accident-prone configuration

The Sun on November 29, at 7:00 p.m. was at 8 Sagittarius semi-square Venus at 23 Capricorn 20 and the Node at 23 Cancer 09 retrograde, and the natal midpoint of Mars/Saturn at 8 Gemini 17, symbolizing separation in love and marriage, weak vitality and the inability to meet all demands.

Transiting Mercury at 2 Sagittarius 22 at 7:00 p.m. is approaching natal Saturn at 11 Aries 58 (semi-square), signifying that Natalie was doing some serious thinking throughout the entire day with thoughts of estrangement. Presumably the party (her husband, costar and skipper) started ashore for dinner.

Transiting Moon at 15 Capricorn 54 is semi-square natal Jupiter at 0 Pisces 55 retrograde, and may have caused her to feel temporarily more optimistic. However, her moody disposition (Sun in Cancer) and perhaps a secret love (natal Sun in midpoint of Venus/Neptune at 13 Virgo 18) soon experienced a turnabout, and by 9:00 p.m. the Moon at 16 Capricorn 54 was approaching Saturn at 17 Aries 57.

The Mars/Neptune midpoint at 8 Scorpio 17 in the sociological correspondence has an influence over people connected with water and navigation, as well

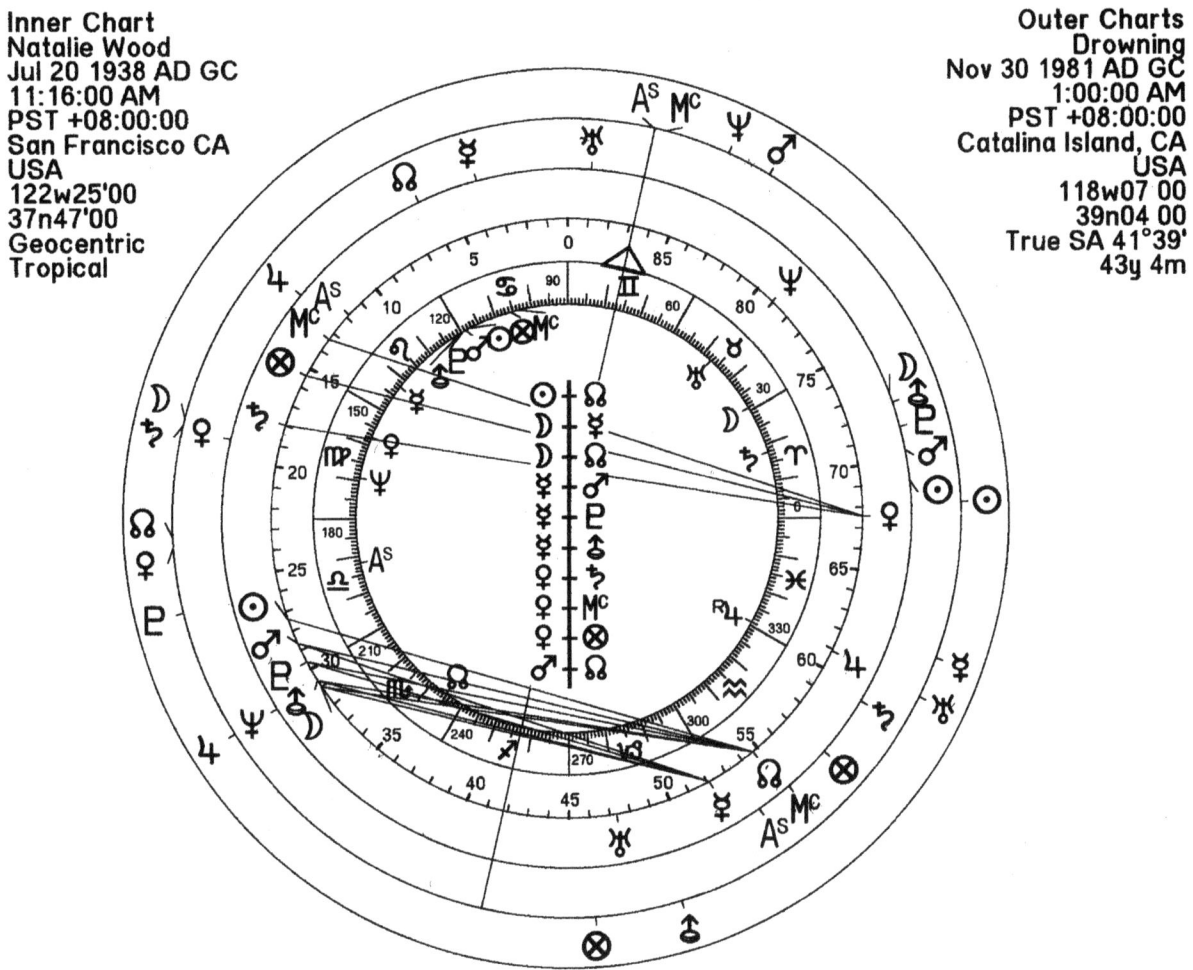

the craving for alcohol, that changes the energy level causing states of weakness, a crisis in life and accidents, set off a multitude of midpoints depicted in the natal chart like Mercury, Node/Sun, Mars, Pluto, Transpluto and the Moon.

The transiting ASC/MC moved from 13 Cancer 50 to 28 Cancer 15 between 11:00 p.m. and 12 midnight, setting off a massive natal structure and midpoints just mentioned, suggesting sadness and weakness. This might have been the height of depression, undermining the vitality and leading to a mysterious death, a grave loss, the ability to bear the suffering of the soul with dignity and without complaint, mourning and bereavement.

According to reports, Natalie went to the stateroom "shortly before midnight." After about 40 minutes the transit ASC/MC midpoint reached 7 Leo 15, contacting those negative midpoints, easing tension and prompting her to do something. She probably fell while boarding the rubber dinghy banging against the boat.

The Moon by that time had reached 18 Capricorn 46 and was almost exactly square transiting Saturn at 19 Libra 06 and solar arc Venus at 19 Libra 13, representing inhibition in love expression, the ability to renounce love, the inclination to stand alone in love or marriage, illegitimate associations and disappointment in love.

Death could have occurred around 1:40 a.m., November 30. The transit MC reached 5 Cancer 30 and the Ascendant at 5 Libra, along with the death axis of Mars/Saturn at 5 Libra 43. These midpoints apply to solar arc Node at 6 Capricorn 21 and the Jupiter/Uranus midpoint at 20 Taurus 46, indicating an easy death. These are only some of the many contacts Natalie experienced at the time of her fated destiny.

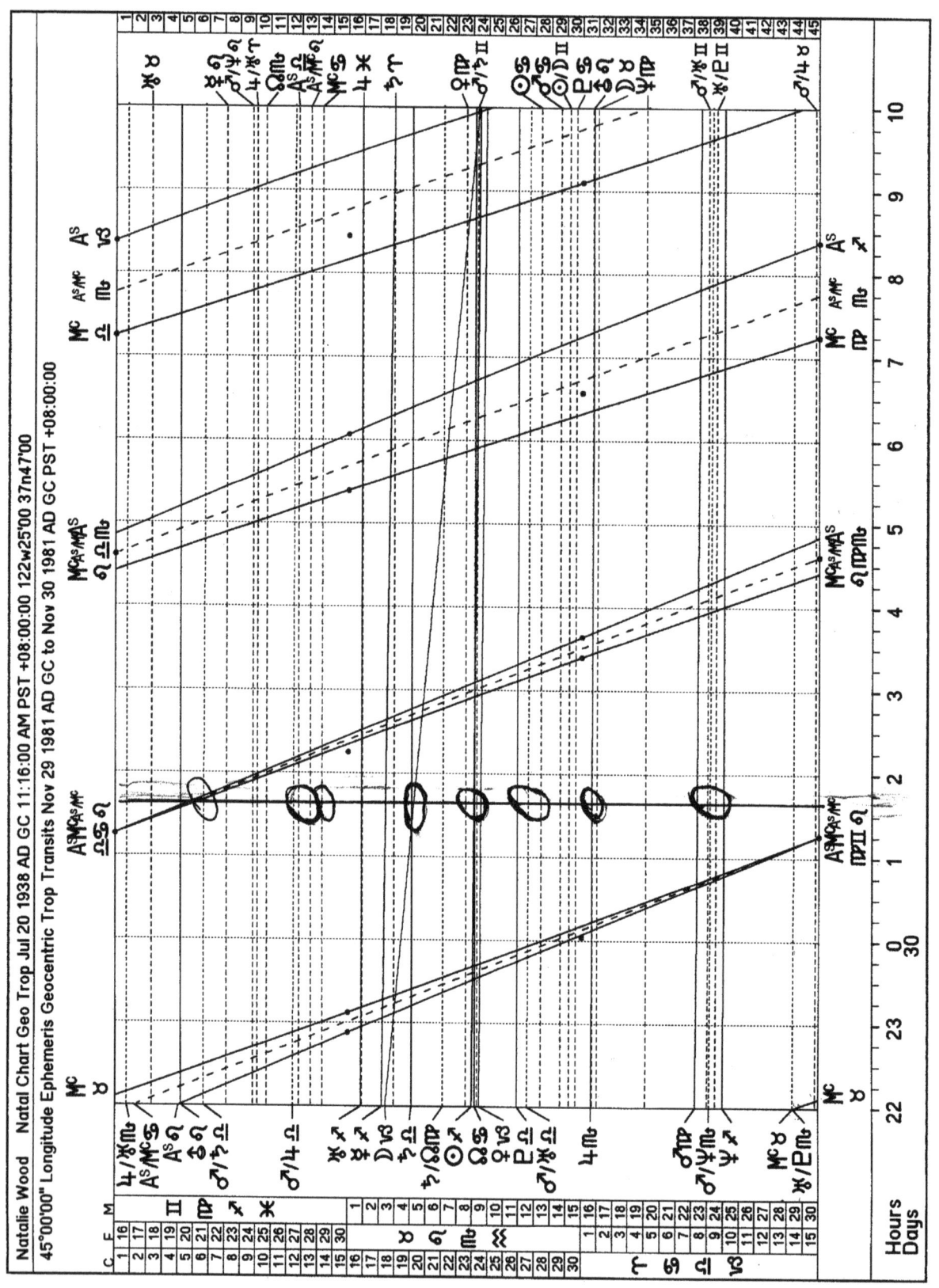

Mario Lanza

Genevieve Wolfson in a June 1983 *American Astrology* article stated it most appropriately: "He became a legend in his life time and the legend remains today. His magnificent tenor voice took her to dazzling heights of fame and success. Mario Lanza the "American Caruso" blazed like a meteor whose light lasts a brief moment in time. He reached the pinnacle of a spectacular career at age thirty, and died a few years later alone and lonely, in a hospital in Rome." Arturo Toscannini dubbed him "the greatest voice of the 20th century."

Mario was the only child of Italian immigrants. His name was Alfredo Arnold Cocozza. Later, as he began his career, he adopted the stage name of Mario Lanza from the masculine form of his mother's maiden name Maria Lanza.

He has an extraordinary chart to say the least. He was born with Pluto in the midpoint of ASC/MC, which Ebertin describes as "An unusual person in unusual surroundings, a fascinating personality, and the power to exercise a strong influence upon the people in one's environment." However, the natal chart has many more aspects to describe his multiple talents, like the many aspects to the Moon that were reflected in his magnificent voice.

At age 15 he started to study to become a professional vocalist, but his career experienced an interruption when he was drafted in the U.S. Army in 1943. The solar arc was 22 degrees and 15 minutes. The solar arc of Uranus was sesquisquare and semi-square natal Neptune and the Sun, bringing sudden upsets or excitement. While in the army he was billed as "The Service Caruso." Mario did not like the discipline of army life and was discharged for medical reasons in 1945. His unhappiness caused him to consume heaps of food and the constant battle with dieting and indulgence haunted him the rest of his life. It was the conflict within him that led to the excess weight problem and consequently to his heart disease and arteriosclerosis.

The difficult aspects of Venus to Mars, Saturn and Neptune are the perpetrators for the above-mentioned conditions. The most noteworthy are the exceptional structures of Mars and Venus. Mars is connected to the entire planetary system except Venus, and the structure of Venus is connected to all the rest except Mars. The opposition to Saturn reveals the lack of stifling of Mars activities and waste of energy by being torn apart. Very interesting is the structure of Saturn. In Virgo it is generally well placed, exercising discipline; however, it is not very strong in connection with the rest of the chart.

His Aries Ascendant provided the sturdy body, and aspects to the Sun, Neptune and Pluto mirrored the complex person he actually was. He liked sports, was a practical joker, was spoiled and had a lack of discipline that haunted him his whole life.

After his return home he married a young pretty woman and they relocated to New York where they lived on a limited income. During their turbulent marriage they produced four children. His wife, however, lacked the understanding and maturity to cope with this very complicated individual.

Mario appeared on radio and in concerts where he performed. He sang from the heart, with tears streaming down his face. It has been written that only Caruso, whom he idolized, had the magic that Lanza possessed.

The Midheaven in Capricorn and in close opposi-

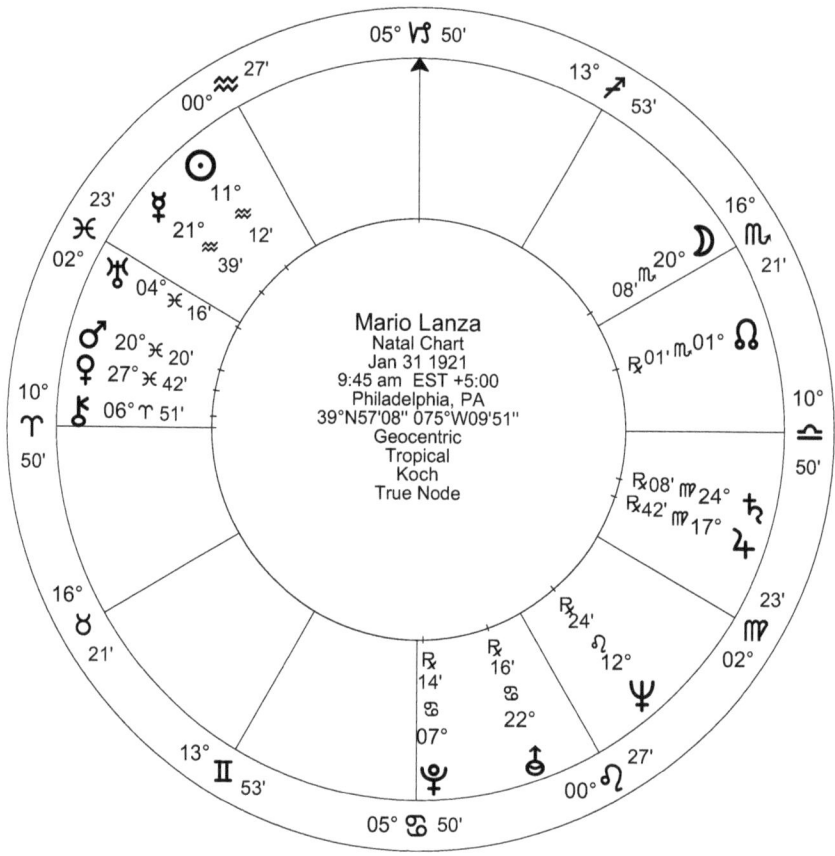

Lanza's Midpoints

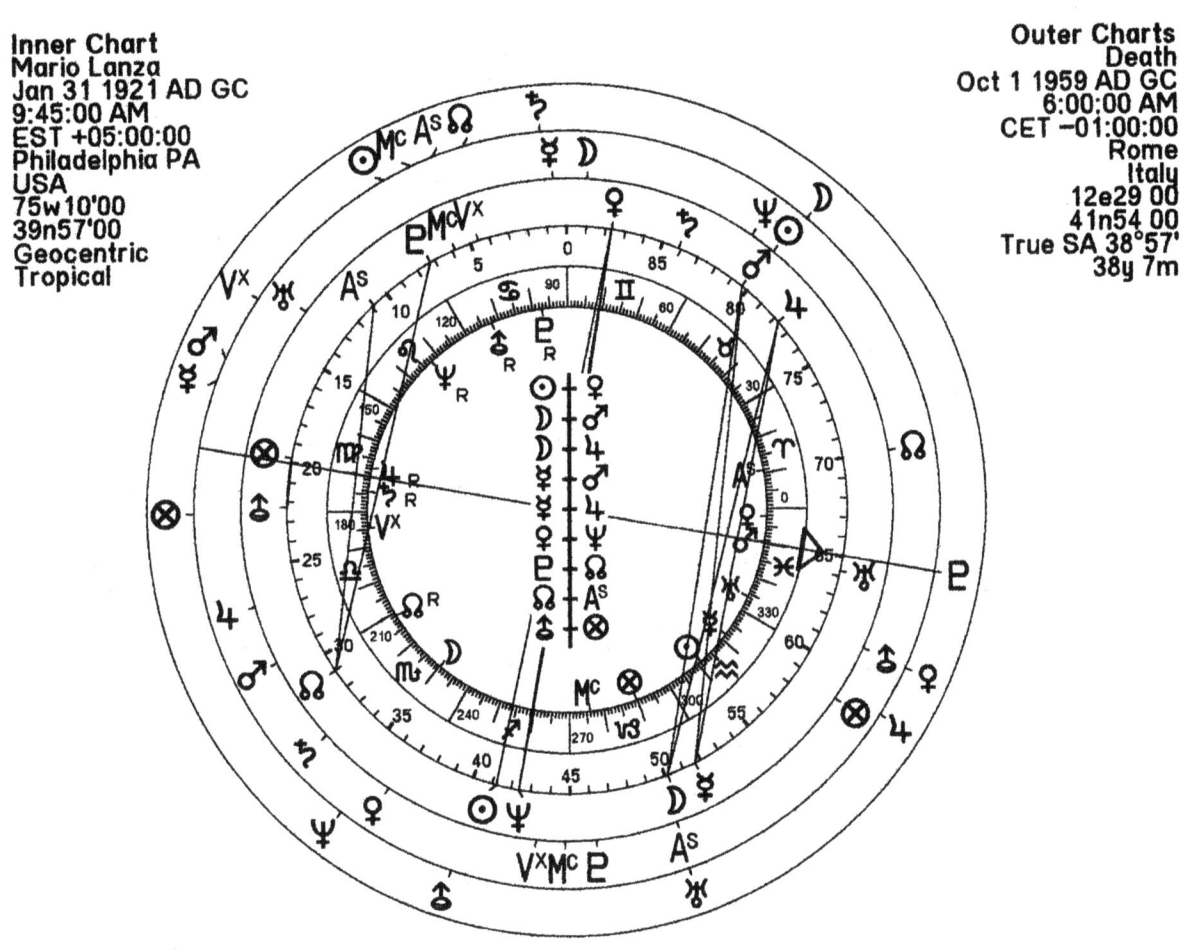

tion to Pluto reflects the ambition, his aim in life and consciousness of objective that shaped his individuality, which was greatly reinforced by Pluto. Positively, those attributes provide success and fulfillment; however, the negative tendency perhaps caused by the square to the Ascendant, reflected all the bad habits which were hard for him to break.

Solar Arc Directions

In 1948 Mario performed on stage at the Hollywood Bowl, singing under the stars like he'd never sang before. MGM chief Louis B. Meyer was so impressed that the next day he signed Mario to a seven-year contract. The solar arc was 27 degrees and 16 minutes. The Midheaven, Pluto, Mercury and Moon reached the natal Mars/Jupiter midpoint and added up to the love of enterprise, great creative powers, a wealth of plans, fortunate arrangements and intuition.

Three years later, in early 1951, when the solar arc reached 30 degrees 17 minutes, he reached the pinnacle of his career. He starred in the motion picture "The Great Caruso." The planetary activity that went on at that time is too much to list here. He became an overnight sensation and a Hollywood star. His record "Be My Love" was his greatest selling. He became the first recording artist to sell two million records. His career skyrocketed, but behind the scenes ominous warning signs were beginning to surface.

His manager, Enrico Rosati, tried to apply a rigid discipline so as to meet Mario's appointments and concert tours, but it all suffered and became physical torture for Mario. Mario started drinking to escape the fears and relieve the tension. In spite of the serious warning signs, his career reached its highest level, but on concert tours between film making there were too many cancellations and Mario's insecurities became increasingly more tortuous. Soon the time came about when drugs and injections had to be applied to control his weight.

Two more films were scheduled and, although Mario considered them unworthy of "Caruso," he reluctantly made one film and after that refused to report for work. Consequently MGM suspended and sued him for breach of contract. There were no further sources of income. However, his excess drinking and eating continued.

In 1957 when the solar arc reached 36 degrees 18 minutes he hoped for a new start by moving his family to Rome. His progressed Moon on his birthday had just passed the conjunction to natal Uranus and was moving toward progressed Sun, and the Midheaven had passed the opposition to his natal Sun and was within minutes of an exact opposition to natal Neptune. Solar arc Saturn was conjunct natal Node within less than 30 minutes. Solar arc Neptune was about 18 months away from an exact opposition to natal Mars. It seemed the bright light of his blazing star was slowly becoming fainter.

In 1958 he starred in "The Seven Hills of Rome" and that same year he toured the U.K. and made a final film, "For the First Time."

Transits

The following are some transits calculated for 6:00 a.m. October 1, 1959. The exact time of death is not known to me, only that he died in the morning. As always the aspects were quite appropriate. The Ascendant was only short of eight minutes from an opposition to natal Ascendant. The Moon was within minutes square natal Jupiter. The transiting Pluto-Mars semi-square was within a degree of natal Uranus. Transiting Uranus was 13 minutes from an exact square to natal Moon. Transiting Midheaven at 11 Cancer 34 was within a degree square natal Ascendant at 10 Aries 50 and both within minutes of a semi-square and sesquisquare respectively to the degree of the heart at 26 Leo. These are but a few of the many contacts.

It is indeed a curious paradox that anyone with such an exquisite voice and acting talent could destroy these God-given abilities. Mario Lanza was known to have said many times he would die young like Caruso. Did his intuition tell him his destiny?

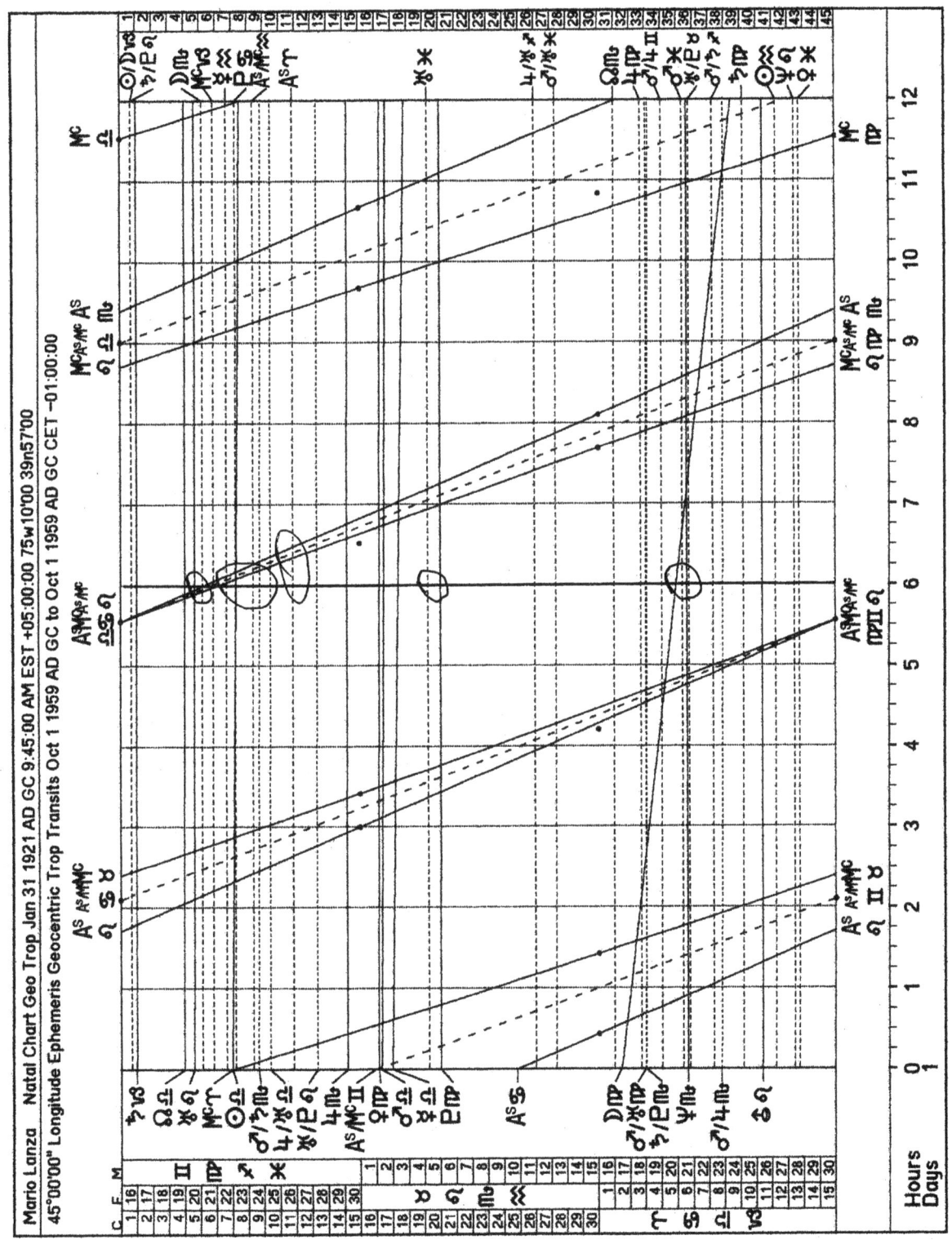

Rachel Joy Scott

On Tuesday April 20, 1999 at 11:21 a.m. stunned students ran for their lives as two gunmen in trench coats sprayed them with relentless firepower. As the gunmen killed classmates at random they giggled and screamed, "Death to the jocks!" These words were the only few spoken words of the killers printed in the Rocky Mountain News of Denver out of all the thousands of words describing the carnage at Columbine High School in Littleton, Colorado.

Rachel Joy Scott, a 17-year-old student, fatefully in the line of fire was shot point blank when the two assassins began the massacre. The perpetrators, Harris and Klebold arrived on the premises of Columbine High School around 11:20 a.m. and the killing spree according to reports lasted about seven and a half minutes and since Rachel was one of the first victims, I am speculating the time of her death to be around 11:25 a.m. This time of death is estimated from the official reports that were published in the papers and Internet.

The following notes are from the book her father wrote and from her own diary. Rachel's parents are quite religious, but they could not resolve the differences that developed during their marriage and consequently divorced a few years before Rachel's death.

Rachel was the middle child of five children and a good student and liked drawing and poetry. She also participated in school plays and enjoyed life to its fullest. Her deep devotion to Jesus Christ came to light after her death from her diary that was discovered in her bullet-riddled backpack. One entry in her diary read, "This is my last year on this earth," and a picture drawn only minutes before her death, a sketch of eyes shedding tears watering a rose. There are thirteen tears in her drawing and by the time the killing ended, there were thirteen victims.

Natal

I was fortunate to obtain Rachel's exact time of birth from her father, Darrel Scott.

The Sun is at 13 Leo 02 and provides self-confidence, a wealth of ideas, organization and leadership. The Sun conjunct Mercury offers circumspection and prudence, and the conjunction to Transpluto adds a rich soul-life and benevolence. The Sun contacting one particular midpoint, Pluto/ASC, requires adjustment to new circumstances, injuries, accidents, even a drastic or radical change of circumstances.

The Moon at 18 Libra 16 shows being sociable, a vivid expression of feelings, the need for love and affection and fateful partnerships. The square to Mars indicates impulsiveness and actions that are directed by the unconscious. The conjunction of Pluto suggests the pursuit of selected objectives with a fanatical zeal. The sextile to Neptune represents subconscious phenomena and a refined sense of feeling and psychometric qualities. The semi-square to the Ascendant may be responsible for hypersensitivity and changes of mood.

Ascendant at 2 Virgo 09 stands basically for the environment, stable conditions, reserve, critical attitude and caution. On the negative side it can also produce pedantry and prejudice. The square to Uranus provides a quick response to the influences of the environment, as well as sudden incidents and accidents.

Midheaven at 27 Taurus 20 represents the

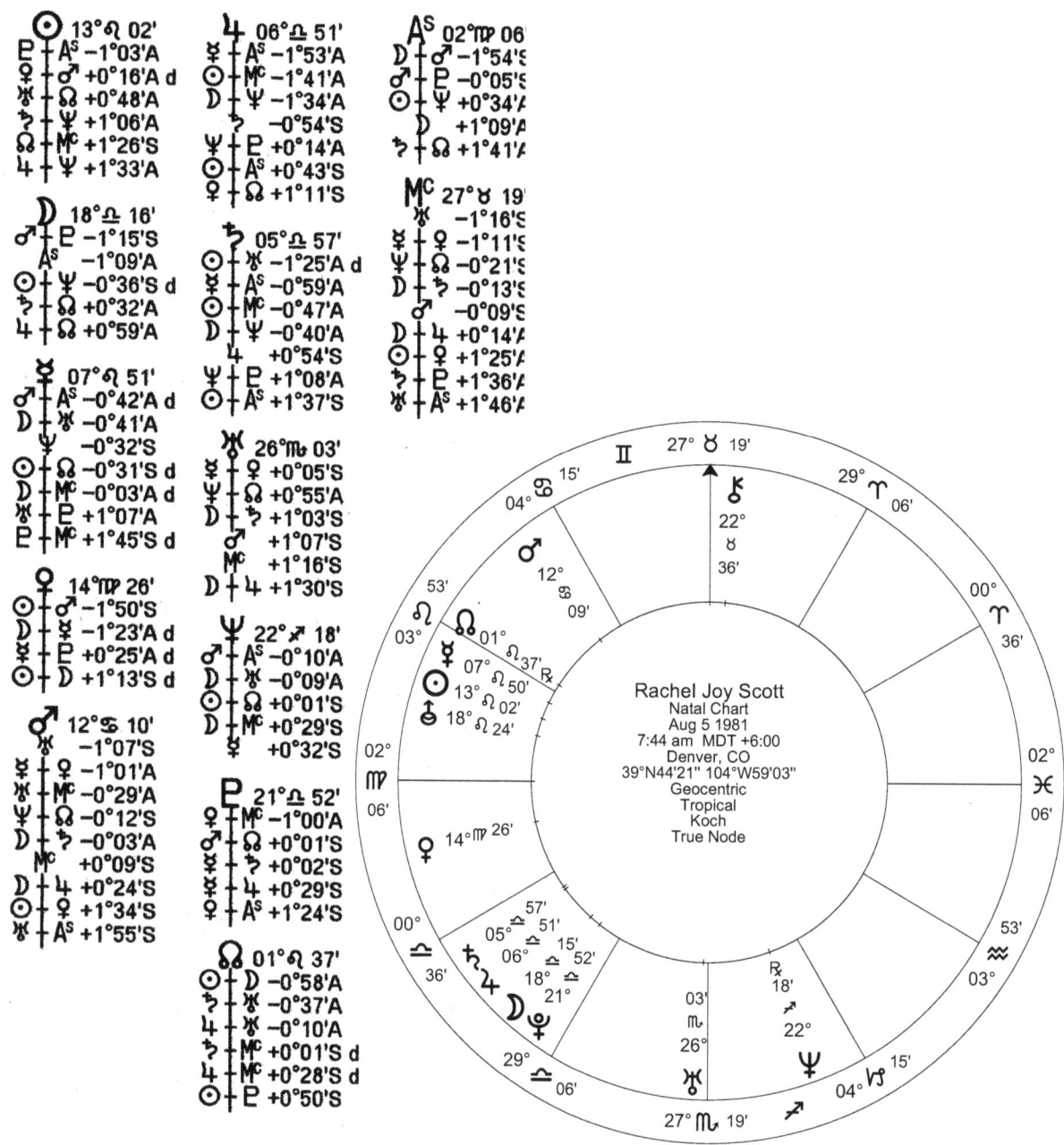

Rachel's Midpoints

ego-consciousness and spiritual awareness. The parallel to Mercury identifies self-knowledge, while the semi-square to Mars a direction with regard to an aim in life. The opposition and parallel to Uranus provides the power of assertion and extraordinary or unusual objectives or aims in life. The Saturn/Pluto midpoint is very interesting, indicating a desire to rise from difficult circumstances through the application of tenacity and endurance. It can also require self-sacrifice.

Solar Arc

At the time of Rachel's death the solar arc was 17 degrees 1 minute.

The Node at 18 Leo 38 in close conjunction to natal Transpluto at 18 Leo 35 shows charisma and personal contacts but it can also mean associations that are forcefully broken apart.

The MC at 14 Gemini 20 is square natal Venus at

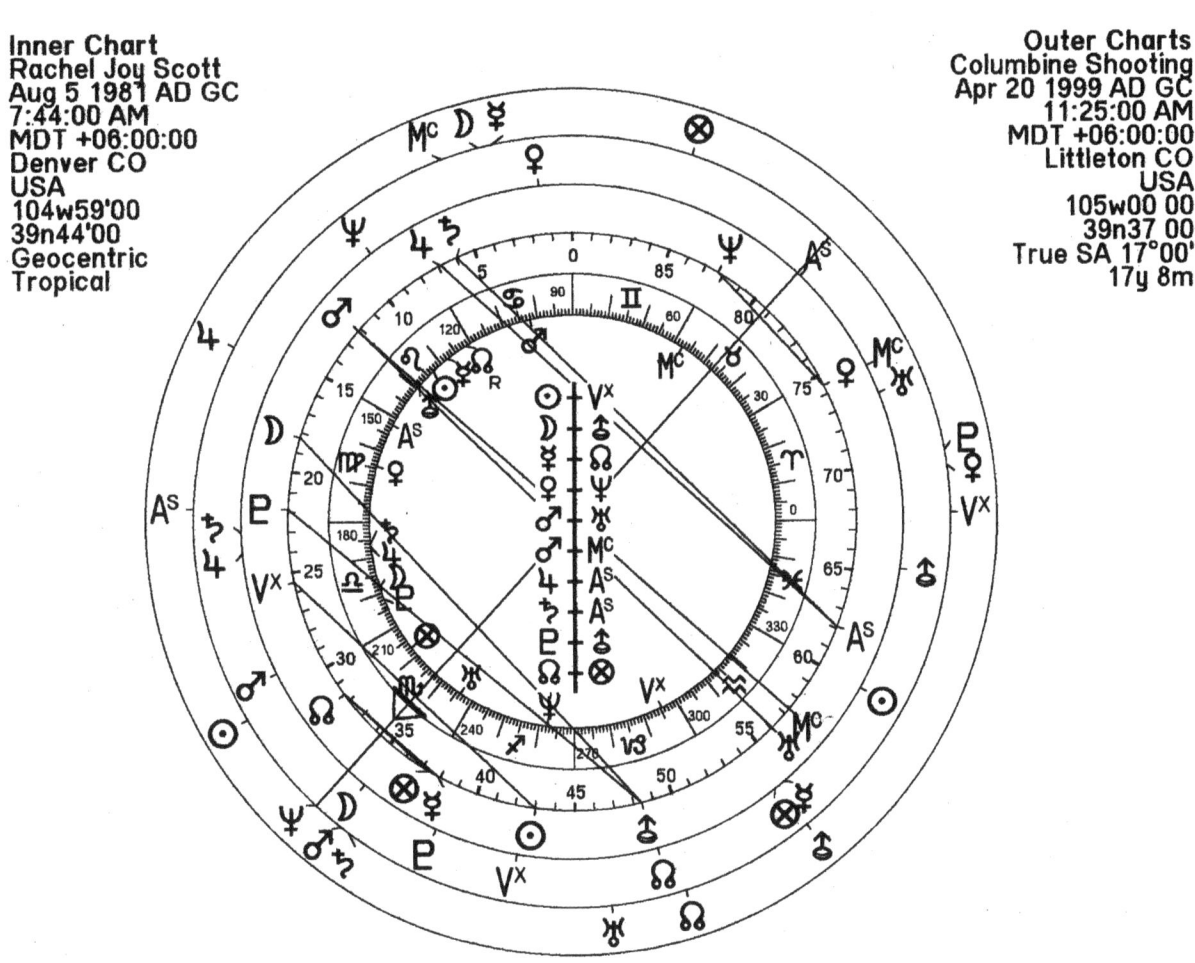

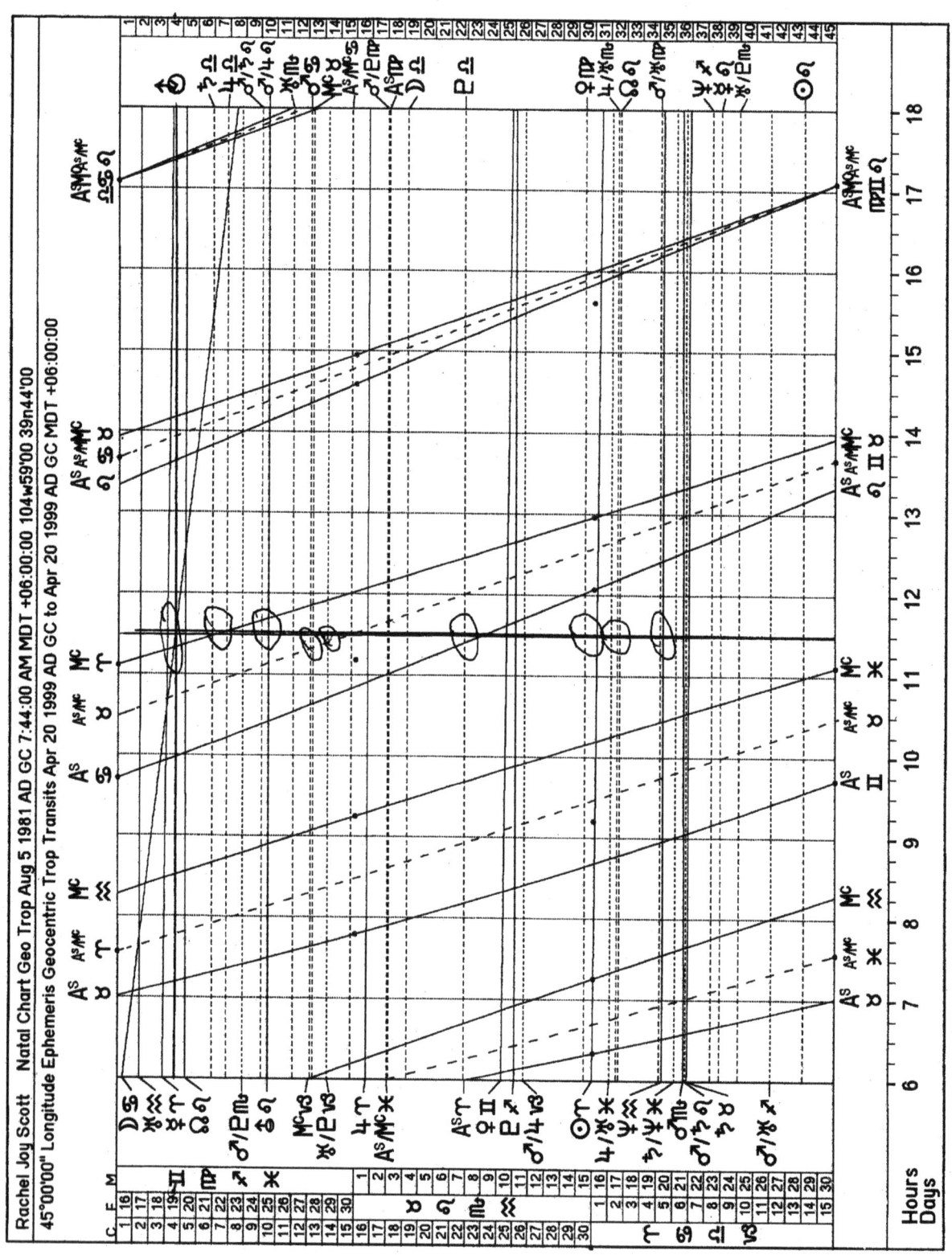

14 Virgo 26 and is a combination that identifies the artist in Rachel and the drawings she made just prior to her death. Mars at 29 Cancer 10 semi-square natal Venus at emphasizing the descriptive talent.

Pluto at 8 Scorpio 53 semi-square Neptune at 27 Sagittarius retrograde could suggest the presentment she had and a progressive spiritual evolution.

The Uranus/Pluto midpoint at 25 Scorpio 59 is in close conjunction with natal Uranus at 26 Scorpio 03, the process of transformation or putting the gun to someone's head, which actually happened.

Transits

Transpluto at 24 Leo 30 retrograde contacts natal Mars/Jupiter and Mars/Saturn midpoints, indicating helpful and constructive events with others, but the Mars/Saturn midpoint shows the ruthless, brutal and cruel approach of her death.

Uranus at 16 Aquarius 24 is two degrees away from an opposition to natal Transpluto at 18 Leo 25 but could have had an impact on the vicious plan of the perpetrators by using the eccentric rebellious bullheadedness.

Neptune at 4 Aquarius 18 is sesquisquare natal midpoint of Mars/Uranus at 19 Virgo 07, showing cunning and deceitfulness and the desire to harm people and a fit of rage.

Saturn at 5 Taurus 54 and Mars at 5 Scorpio 34 retrograde are in opposition and had just passed above the Mars/Uranus midpoint by semi-square, representing violent destruction, heavy injuries, the intervention of Higher Power, separation and cases of death.

Mercury at 3 Aries 06 is sesquisquare natal Transpluto at 18 Leo 25, while Mercury, Node and Moon made aspects to natal Transpluto, identifying the perpetrators as emotionally torn, the common and tragic destiny shared with others and the desire to gain public recognition.

Midheaven at 5 Aries 01 is opposite natal Saturn at 5 Libra 57 and Jupiter at 6 Libra 51, which Ebertin states as the probable manifestation as "It is a great gift of the Gods to find a noble and fine human soul." In my humble opinion that exactly describes Rachel, and the MC-Saturn opposition indicates separation.

Ascendant 22 Cancer 01 is square natal Pluto at 21 Libra 52, indicating a drastic or radical change of circumstances in life.

The Ascendant/MC midpoint at 27 Taurus 19 semi-square natal Mars at 12 Cancer 10 and conjunct natal Midheaven at 27 Taurus 19 suggests the positive attitude toward family and colleagues and successful teamwork.

Bibliography

Ebertin Reinhold, *The Combination of Stellar Influences*, American Federation of Astrologers, Tempe, AZ.

Ebertin Reinhold, *Applied Cosmobiology*, Ebertin Verlag D7080, Aalen Germany 1972.

Ebertin Reinhold, *Directions*, Ebertin Verlag D7080 Aalen, Germany 1976.

Ebertin Reinhold, *Fixed Stars*, Ebertin Verlag D7080 Aalen, Germany.

Gleadow, Rupert, *The Origin of the Zodiac*, Castle Books, New York, 1968.

Kimmel Eleonora, *Pattern of Destiny*, American Federation of Astrologers, Tempe, AZ 1985.

Penfield Marc, *2001: The Penfield Collection*, Vulcan Books, Seattle, WA 1979

Rodden Lois, *The American Book of Charts*, ACS Publications, San Diego, CA 1980.

Charts and graphs by Janus Astrology Software,
Astrology House, 41 New North Road Eden Terrace, Auckland, New Zealand.

Anatomical Degrees

Created by Fritz Brandau; parenthetical notes by C.E.O. Carter;
1986 translation by Mary Vohryzek.

Aries

1. Cerebrum
2. Mid-brain (Mesencaphalon)
3. Cerebellum (Abscess)
4. Pineal Gland (Goiter)
5. Right and left eye (Hair)
6. Orbital cavity (Socket of eye)
7. Ears (Jaundice)
8. Cheekbones
9. Crystalline lens of eye
10. Eyeballs
11. Optic Nerve
12. Tongue (Hair)
13. Cerebral Ventricles, Cranium
14. Frontal Lobes (Brain)
15. Lateral Lobes (Stroke, Suicide)
16. Pons Varoli
17. Spinal cord canal
18. Nerve connections
19. Corpus callosum (cerebri)
20. Hyoid bone
21. Eye muscles
22. Cheek muscles
23. Masticatory muscle
24. Zygomatic muscle
25. Stemocleido mastoid muscle
26. Skull
27. Fornix, frontal (Tuberculosis)
28. Fornix middle and back (Hair)
29. Auditory canal (Bronchitis)
30. Parotid gland

Taurus

1. Throat or Gullet
2. Palate
3. Opening of throat
4. Uvula
5. Throat or larynx space
6. Larynx
7. Vocal Chords
8. Cervical nerves
9. Jugular vein
10. Cervical vein
11. Neck nerves connecting with the spinal cord (Neurasthenia)
12. Neck nerves connecting with the spinal cord
13. Neck nerves connecting with the spinal cord
14. True vocal cords
15. Epiglottis
16. Carotid artery (Abscess)
17. Thyroid gland (Tonsils)
18. Lymph vessels (Appendix, Hair)
19. Maxillary Artery
20. Occipital bone (Goiter)
21. Sinus Artery
22. Hyoid muscle
23. Teeth (Rheumatism)
24. Upper Jaw
25. Lower Jaw (Alcoholism, Tonsils, Glands, Suicide)
26. Nasal Bone
27. Cervical Vertebrae
28. Trigon
29. Trigon (Visual sense)
30. Trapezius

Gemini

1. Trachea
2. Esophagus
3. Upper Right Pulmonary Lobe
4. Lower Right Pulmonary Lobe
5. Upper Left Pulmonary Lobe
6. Lower Left Pulmonary Lobe (Anxiety, Pulmonary Inflammation)
7. Apex of Lungs (Heart)
8. Eyesight (Bronchial Tubes, Bronchial System)
9. Pulmonary Artery, (Rheumatic Fever)
10. Hilus (Lung Root, Typhoid Fever)
11. Thymus Gland
12. Tracheal Mucosa
13. Pulmonary Veins
14. Clavicle (Collarbone)
15. Scapula (Shoulder bone)
16. Pleura
17. First Rib (Bright's Disease, Kidneys)
18. Second Rib (Asthma)
19. Laryngeal muscles
20. Third Rib
21. Arm muscles (Typhoid fever)
22. Upper arm (Appendicitis, Insanity)
23. Trochlea of the humerus (Spine)
24. Olecranon
25. Radius (Gout, Neurasthenia)
26. Wrist bones (Suicide)
27. Phalanges (Fingers)
28. Metacarpal bones (Tuberculosis)
29. Fourth Rib
30. Fifth Rib

Cancer

1. Sixth Rib
2. Seventh Rib
3. Eighth Rib (Sight)
4. Ninth Rib
5. Tenth to twelfth Ribs
6. Diaphragm
7. Thoracic Canal
8. Hiatus (Paralysis)
9. Pylorus
10. Gastric Fundus
11. Gastric Veins (Alcoholism)
12. Large Gastric Curvature
13. Small Gastric Curvature
14. Abdominal Walls
15. Gastric Nerves (Suicide)
16. Pancreas
17. Opening of pancreas into common duct
18. Opening of pancreas into common duct
19. Head of Pancreas, perhaps gall
20. Upper arterial bend
21. Lower arterial bend
22. Gastric Mucosa
23. Gastric Blood Vessels
24. Blood vessels of digestive organs
25. Blood vessels of digestive organs
26. Mammary Glands
27. Nipples
28. Rib cartilage (Hair)
29. Spleen (Bronchitis)
30. Twelfth dorsal vertebra

Leo

1. Left Coronary Artery
2. Aorta
3. Right Coronary Artery
4. Left Carotid Artery
5. Right Carotid Artery
6. Entrance of pulmonary artery (Sight)
7. Left Coronary Vein
8. Lower Vena Cava (Anemia, Sense of Hearing)
9. Upper Vena Cava (Alcoholism)
10. Jugular Vein
11. Clavicular Vein
12. Spinal Column
13. Right Heart Chamber
14. Left Heart Chamber
15. Right Atrium
16. Left Atrium
17. Right Auricle
18. Right cardiac cavity
19. Ventricular system (Spine)
20. Mitral Valve
21. Left Atrium
22. Left Auricle (Appendix)
23. Left Auricle (Rheumatism)
24. Papillary muscle
25. Pericardium (Alcoholism, Abscess)
26. Myocardium
27. Tendons to the heart valve (Goiter)
28. Tendons to the heart valve
29. Cardiac septum (neuritis)
30. Back

Virgo

1. Duodenum
2. Small intestine
3. Cecum (Appendix)
4. Ascending colon (Asthma)
5. Traverse Colon
6. Descending Colon
7. Rectum
8. Abdominal Cavity
9. Right Hepatic lobe (Rheumatic Fever)
10. Left Hepatic Lobe, Gall (Typhoid Fever)
11. Ligament of Trietz and Gall
12. Abdominal Aorta
13. Hepatic Arteries
14. Gall Bladder Artery
15. Bare spot of the liver
16. Hepatic Groove
17. Abdominal muscle
18. Serrate groove
19. Left Hepatic groove
20. Bile Duct
21. Gall-bladder duct (Typhoid Fever)
22. Gall-Bladder
23. Hepatic Cartilage
24. Hepatic Cartilage and tendons of liver
25. Liver (Cancer, Gout, Arthritis)
26. Abdominal Vein (Suicide)
27. Hip Veins (Acute Nephritis)
28. Hepatic Veins (Tuberculosis)
29. Back-lobes of liver
30. Hepatic duct

Libra

1	Kidney Pelvis
2	Renal cortex
3	Adrenals Abscess
4	Kidney surfaces (Goiter)
5	Malpighi's Pyramid
6	Pubis
7	Nervous system (Jaundice)
8	of the kidneys
9	and
10	renal
11	pelvis
12	Left renal system
13	Right renal system
14	Left inguinal gland
15	Right inguinal gland (Suicide, Stroke)
16	Renal arteries
17	Adrenal arteries (Bright's disease)
18	Fatty capsule of the kidneys
19	Great renal calyx
20	Small renal calyx
21	Renal hilus
22	Renal veins
23	Adrenal veins
24	Vascular circulation of the renal cortex
25	Vascular circulation of the renal cortex
26	Vascular system
27	Vascular system of the skin (Tuberculosis)
28	Urinary bladder (Hair)
29	Right Ureter
30	Left Ureter

Scorpio

1	Urethra
2	Urethral meatus
3	Prostate, Uterus
4	Testicles, right side of uterus
5	Testicles, left side of uterus
6	Right epididymis, uterine cavity
7	Left epididymis, right Fallopian tube
8	Scrotum, left Fallopian tube
9	Spermatic duct. Vagina (Alcoholism)
10	Corpus cavernum oseum (Neurasthenia)
11	Penis, Labia majora
12	Seminal Vesicles
13	Glans penis, Labia minora
14	Foreskin, Prepuce
15	Cowper's glands
16	Cochlea, right ovary (Abscess)
17	Testicular lobes, left ovary
18	Efferent ducts. Hymen (Appendix, Hair)
19	Uterine Ligaments, Haller's netz
20	Ligaments of penis, Bartolin's gland (Goiter)
21	Sphenoidal cavity
22	Ethmoid bone and ligaments
23	Nasal bone, Fimbria of Fallopian tubes (Rheumatism)
24	Nasal Septum
25	Coccyx, Ovarian ducts (Tonsils, Alcoholism)
26	Perineum
27	Anus
28	Mucous membranes
29	Vomer
30	Nasal muscles

Sagittarius

1. Pelvic Bone
2. Ilium, (Hipbone)
3. Ischium, (Tail bone)
4. Femur, Thigh
5. Right large femoral artery, (Hair)
6. Left large femoral artery (Anxiety)
7. Right surface femoral artery (Heart)
8. Left surface femoral artery (Sight)
9. Right lymphatic vessels (Rheumatic fever)
10. Left lymphatic vessels (Typhoid Fever)
11. Adductor muscle
12. Large tibial vein
13. Large saphenous vein
14. Surface femoral vein
15. Right hip vein
16. Left hip vein
17. Sciatic nerve
18. Right femur rotator (Asthma)
19. Left femur rotator
20. Head of right femur
21. Head of left femur (Typhoid fever)
22. Right trochanter (Insanity, Appendicitis)
23. Left trochanter (Spine)
24. Hollow of knee. Popliteal fossa cartilage
25. Condyle of right femur (Neurasthenia, Gout)
26. Condyle of left femur (Suicide)
27. Gluteal muscle
28. Right leg muscle
29. Left leg muscle
30. Pear-shaped muscle

Capricorn

1. Right patella
2. Left patella
3. Cutaneous nerves of the upper leg (Eyesight)
4. Cutaneous nerves of tibia
5. Cutaneous nerves of knee
6. Right adductor muscle
7. Left adductor muscle
8. Lymph vessels of knees (Paralysis), Veins of knee
10. Cruciate ligaments right
11. Cruciate ligaments left
12. Right knee joint
13. Left knee joint
14. Right knee cartilage
15. Left knee cartilage (Suicide)
16. Right knotty protuberance
17. Left knotty protuberance
18. Ligaments of right knee
19. Ligaments of left knee
20. Tendons of right knee
21. Tendons of left knee
22. Muscle endings from upper to lower legs
23. Muscle endings from upper to lower legs
24. Muscle endings from upper to lower legs
25. Connections between femur
26. and tibia
27. Deep-lying nerves
28. Artery of right knee)hair)
29. Artery of left knee (Bronchitis)
30. Adductor muscle

Aquarius

1	Right shin bone nerve (Obesity)
2	Left shin bone nerve
3	Right fibula
4	Left fibula
5	Nerve of right fibula
6	Nerve of left fibula
7	Vein of lower right leg
8	Vein of lower left leg (Anemia)
9	Skin of right lower leg (Alcoholism)
10	Skin of left lower leg
11	Right crural band
12	Left crural band
13	Artery of right lower leg, Fibula (Rheumatic fever)
14	Artery of left lower leg (Fibula)
15	Lymph vessel of right lower leg
16	Lymph vessel of left lower leg
17	Nervous system (Bright's disease)
18	of the
19	spinal
20	cord
21	Nervous system of the spinal cord
22	Right gastrocnemius muscle (Appendix, Cecum)
23	Left gastrocnemius muscle (Rheumatism)
24	Right tibial muscle
25	Left tibial muscle (Alcoholism, Abscess)
26	Right fibula (Neurasthenia)
27	Left fibula (Goiter)
28	Right tibia
29	Left tibia (Neuritis)
30	Connections of calf and lower leg

Pisces

1	Right heel bone
2	Left heel bone
3	Nerves of right foot (Appendix)
4	Nerves of left foot (Asthma)
5	Right cuboid bone
6	Left cuboid bone
7	Right ankle bone
8	Left ankle bone
9	Right metatarsus (Rheumatic fever)
10	Left metatarsus (Typhoid fever)
11	Lymph vessels of feet
12	Artery of right foot
13	Artery of left foot
14	Right surface veins
15	Left surface veins
16	Cruciate ligaments of right foot
17	Cruciate ligaments of left foot
18	Right extensor digitorum (Toe extensor)
19	Left extensor digitorum (Toe extensor)
20	Right fibula muscle
21	Left fibula muscle
22	Achilles heel of right foot (Insanity, Appendicitis)
23	Achilles heel of left foot (Spine)
24	Right capsular joint
25	Left capsular joint (Cancer, Gout)
26	Nerves of lower foot (Suicide)
27	Phalanges of right foot (Acute nephritis, Kidneys)
28	Phalanges of left foot (Tuberculosis)
29	Toe-nails of right foot
30	Toe-nails of left foot

www.ingramcontent.com/pod-product-compliance
Ingram Content Group UK Ltd.
Pitfield, Milton Keynes, MK11 3LW, UK
UKHW051117200426
11947UKWH00038B/1824